URBAN AND REGIONAL POLICY AND ITS EFFECTS

VOLUME FOUR

URBAN AND REGIONAL POLICY AND ITS EFFECTS

Building Resilient Regions

MARGARET WEIR

NANCY PINDUS

HOWARD WIAL

HAROLD WOLMAN

editors

BROOKINGS INSTITUTION PRESS
Washington, D.C.

Copyright © 2012
THE BROOKINGS INSTITUTION
1775 Massachusetts Avenue, N.W., Washington, D.C. 20036
www.brookings.edu

Library of Congress Cataloging-in-Publication data
Urban and regional policy and its effects / Margery Austin Turner, Howard Wial, and
Harold Wolman, editors.
   p.   cm.
 Summary: "Brings policymakers, practitioners, and scholars up to speed on the state of
knowledge on urban and regional policy issues. Conceptualizes fresh thinking of different
aspects (economic development, education, land use), presenting main themes and
implications and identifying gaps to fill for successful formulation and implementation of
urban and regional policy"—Provided by publisher.
 Includes bibliographical references and index.
 ISBN 978-0-8157-2284-7 (pbk. : alk. paper)
 1. Urban policy—Congresses. 2. Urban economics—Congresses. 3. Urban renewal—
Congresses. 4. Regional planning—Congresses. 5. City planning—Congresses. I.
Turner, Margery Austin, 1955– II. Wial, Howard. III. Wolman, Harold. IV. Title.
 HT151.U65 2008
 338.973009173'2—dc22   2008016030

9 8 7 6 5 4 3 2 1

Printed on acid-free paper

Typeset in Adobe Garamond

Composition by R. Lynn Rivenbark
Macon, Georgia

Printed by R. R. Donnelley
Harrisonburg, Virginia

Contents

Preface   ix

1   Introduction   1
Margaret Weir, Nancy Pindus, Howard Wial, and Harold Wolman

2   In Search of Regional Resilience   24
Kathryn A. Foster

3   Resilience in the Face of Foreclosures:
How National Actors Shape Local Responses   60
Todd Swanstrom

4   Struggling over Strangers or Receiving with Resilience?
The Metropolitics of Immigrant Integration   100
Manuel Pastor and John Mollenkopf

5   Bringing Equity to Transit-Oriented Development:
Stations, Systems, and Regional Resilience   148
Rolf Pendall, Juliet Gainsborough, Kate Lowe, and Mai Nguyen

6   Economic Shocks and Regional Economic Resilience   193
Edward Hill, Travis St. Clair, Howard Wial, Harold Wolman,
Patricia Atkins, Pamela Blumenthal, Sarah Ficenec, and Alec Friedhoff

7   Building a Resilient Social Safety Net   275
Sarah Reckhow and Margaret Weir

Index   325

BUILDING RESILIENT REGIONS: URBAN AND REGIONAL POLICY AND ITS EFFECTS, VOLUME FOUR, is the fourth in a series of publications that provides scholars, policymakers, and practitioners with accessible summaries of what is known about the effectiveness of selected urban and regional policies. This volume contains edited versions of the papers presented at a conference held at the George Washington University on May 20–21, 2010, and arranged by the editors. The conference and this volume are products of collaboration between the Brookings Institution's Metropolitan Policy Program, the George Washington University's George Washington Institute of Public Policy and Trachtenberg School of Public Policy and Public Administration, the Urban Institute, and the MacArthur Research Network on Building Resilient Regions, based at the University of California, Berkeley. All the papers represent the views of the authors and not necessarily the views of the staff members, officers, or trustees of the Brookings Institution, the George Washington University, the Urban Institute, the John D. and Catherine T. MacArthur Foundation, or the University of California.

Coeditors	Margaret Weir, *University of California, Berkeley*
	Nancy Pindus, *Urban Institute*
	Howard Wial, *Brookings Institution*
	Harold Wolman, *George Washington University*

| Staff | Richard Shearer, *research assistant* |

| Adviser | Alan Berube, *Brookings Institution* |

Contributors	Patricia Atkins, *George Washington University*
	Pamela Blumenthal, *U.S. Department of Housing and Urban Development*
	Sarah Ficenec, *George Washington University*
	Alec Friedhoff, *Brookings Institution*
	Kathryn Foster, *University at Buffalo, State University of New York*
	Juliet Gainsborough, *Bentley University*
	Edward Hill, *Cleveland State University*
	Kate Lowe, *Cornell University*
	John Mollenkopf, *City University of New York*
	Mai Nguyen, *University of North Carolina*
	Manuel Pastor, *University of Southern California*
	Rolf Pendall, *Urban Institute*
	Sarah Reckhow, *Michigan State University*
	Travis St. Clair, *George Washington University*
	Todd Swanstrom, *University of Missouri, St. Louis*
	Margaret Weir, *University of California, Berkeley*
	Howard Wial, *Brookings Institution*
	Harold Wolman, *George Washington University*

Discussants	Scott Allard, *University of Chicago*
	Alan Ehrenhalt, *Pew Center on the States*
	Michael Fix, *Migration Policy Institute*
	Linda Hoffman, *National Governors Association*
	Marie Howland, *University of Maryland*
	Derek Hyra, *Virginia Polytechnic Institute and State University*
	Helen Ingram, *Arizona State University*
	G. Thomas Kingsley, *Urban Institute*
	Jeffrey Lubell, *Center for Housing Policy*
	Robert McDonald, *Nature Conservancy*
	Raymond Sandejas, *U.S. Government Accountability Office*
	Audrey Singer, *Brookings Institution*
	Clarence Stone, *George Washington University*
	Bradley Whitehead, *Fund for Our Economic Future*

Commentators	Raphael Bostic, *U.S. Department of Housing and Urban Development*
	Derek Douglas, *Executive Office of the President*
	Alejandro Mayorkas, *U.S. Citizenship and Immigration Services*
	Erika Poethig, *U.S. Department of Housing and Urban Development*
	Todd Richardson, *U.S. Department of Housing and Urban Development*

Conference Participants	Alan Berube, *Brookings Institution*
	Karina Fortuny, *Urban Institute*
	Emily Garr, *Brookings Institution*
	Diana Hincapie, *George Washington University*
	Heidi Johnson, *Urban Institute*
	Elizabeth Kneebone, *Brookings Institution*
	Robin Koralek, *Urban Institute*
	Robert Lang, *University of Nevada, Las Vegas*
	Jeremy Larrieu, *George Washington University*
	Robert Lerman, *Urban Institute*
	Alice Levy, *George Washington University*
	Amy Liu, *Brookings Institution*
	Jonathan Rothwell, *Brookings Institution*
	Richard Shearer, *Brookings Institution*
	Camille Sola, *George Washington University*
	Brett Theodos, *Urban Institute*
	Adie Tomer, *Brookings Institution*
	Margery Austin Turner, *Urban Institute*

Preface

The *Urban and Regional Policy and Its Effects* series is designed to present evidence about the impacts of urban and regional policies in a format that is accessible to policymakers and practitioners as well as scholars. The series and the conferences on which it is based are the products of a collaboration between the Brookings Institution's Metropolitan Policy Program, the George Washington University's George Washington Institute of Public Policy and Trachtenberg School of Public Policy and Public Administration, and the Urban Institute. For the 2010 conference, these organizations were joined by the Building Resilient Regions Network, an interdisciplinary research network sponsored by the John D. and Catherine T. MacArthur Foundation and housed at the University of California, Berkeley.

This volume and the 2010 Conference on Urban and Regional Policy and Its Effects came about with the support of several people at the sponsoring institutions. At Brookings, Bruce Katz, director of the Metropolitan Policy Program, provided the program's support for this project. At the George Washington University, Joe Cordes of the Trachtenberg School of Public Policy and Public Administration provided useful advice throughout. At the Urban Institute, Robert Reischauer, president, provided institutional support for this project.

A number of other people were instrumental in making the conference and this volume a reality. At the John D. and Catherine T. MacArthur Foundation, Julia Stasch provided support and guidance. We also benefited from the advice of Erika Poethig at the U.S. Department of Housing and Urban Development. Katie Bruder of the George Washington University managed the conference logistics. Jamaine Fletcher of Brookings and Olive Cox and Kim Rycroft of the George Washington Institute of Public Policy provided administrative support for the conference and throughout the publication process. Sarah Ficenec,

Diana Hincapie, Jeremy Larrieu, Alice Levy, and Camille Sola of the George Washington University took notes on the conference sessions. Chad Shearer of Brookings helped prepare the conference papers for publication. Janet Walker of the Brookings Institution Press expertly and gracefully managed the production of the conference volume.

We are grateful to the John D. and Catherine T. MacArthur Foundation, whose support for the Building Resilient Regions Network made possible the research on which this volume is based. We also thank the MacArthur Foundation, the Heinz Endowments, the George Gund Foundation, and the F. B. Heron Foundation for providing general support to the Brookings Metropolitan Policy Program. We acknowledge the Metropolitan Policy Program's Metropolitan Leadership Council, a bipartisan network of individual, corporate, and philanthropic investors who provide financial support to the program but, more important, are true intellectual and strategic partners. We thank the George Washington University for providing funding for the conference through its Selective Excellence Program.

1

Introduction

MARGARET WEIR, NANCY PINDUS, HOWARD WIAL, AND
HAROLD WOLMAN

U rban and regional policy debates are often long on rhetoric but short on
evidence about policy impacts. To redress that imbalance, the Brookings
Institution, the George Washington University Institute of Public Policy and the
Trachtenberg School of Public Policy and Public Administration, and the Urban
Institute held the fourth in a series of annual conferences entitled "Urban and
Regional Policy and Its Effects" at the George Washington University in Washington, D.C., on May 20–21, 2010. They were joined by the Building Resilient
Regions Network, an interdisciplinary research network sponsored by the
John D. and Catherine T. MacArthur Foundation and housed at the University
of California–Berkeley. The conference, whose participants included members
of the network as well as practitioners from the federal government and nonprofit organizations concerned with urban policy, examined the question of how
to build resilient regions. The conference sought to engage authors and discus-
sants in a cross-disciplinary dialogue focused on the central theme of regional
resilience. The chapters in this volume are revised versions of those commissioned papers.

Our examination of regional resilience includes one conceptual chapter
devoted to defining resilience and five chapters that address resilience with
respect to a particular policy challenge that many metropolitan areas and local
communities face. Each chapter, however, uses a different definition of resilience. The chapters cover the following challenges:

The editors would like to thank Kate Foster and Todd Swanstrom for helpful comments on this
introduction.

—*Defining regional resilience,* addressed by "In Search of Regional Resilience," by Kathryn Foster.

—*Home mortgage foreclosures*, addressed by "Resilience in the Face of Foreclosures: How National Actors Shape Local Responses," by Todd Swanstrom.

—*Immigration*, addressed by "Struggling over Strangers or Receiving Them with Resilience: The Metropolitics of Immigrant Integration," by Manuel Pastor and John Mollenkopf.

—*Public transportation*, addressed by "Bringing Equity to Transit-Oriented Development: Stations, Systems, and Regional Resilience," by Rolf Pendall, Juliet Gainsborough, Kate Lowe, and Mai Nguyen.

—*Regional economic development*, addressed by "Economic Shocks and Regional Economic Resilience," by Edward Hill, Travis St. Clair, Howard Wial, Harold Wolman, Patricia Atkins, Pamela Blumenthal, Sarah Ficenec, and Alec Friedhoff.

—*Poverty*, addressed by "Building a Resilient Social Safety Net," by Sarah Reckhow and Margaret Weir.

The goals of this volume are to introduce scholars, policymakers, and practitioners to the concept of regional resilience and to inform them about the state of knowledge on the effectiveness of regional characteristics and public policies in promoting or impeding the resilience of metropolitan areas. Authors were asked to explain the challenge that their chosen policy area poses for regions, define regional resilience with respect to that challenge, present the findings of their own research (qualitative and/or quantitative) on the nature of the challenge for metropolitan areas, and draw policy implications from their research.

Summary of Chapters

Kathryn Foster's chapter, "In Search of Regional Resilience," serves as a useful introduction and background for the other chapters in this volume. Foster begins by noting the range of definitions of resilience that have been used by different disciplines and observes that there is a basic conceptual divide between resilience as an *outcome* (is there a recovery from some stress?) and resilience as a *capacity* (does a person or place have the conditions and attributes that make it more likely to recover from stress?). In setting forth her definition of regional resilience, she incorporates both concepts, defining regional resilience as "the ability of a region to anticipate, prepare for, respond to, and recover from a disturbance." Elaborating, she notes that a region has a pre-stress capacity for resilience and that when it is confronted by a stress, it responds with a "resilience performance." The actual relationship between pre-stress capacity and resilience performance is an empirical question: does pre-stress capacity contribute to resilience performance?

Foster then turns to a conceptual elaboration of each of the three critical terms of the relationship. Capacity relates to a range of resources, characteristics, and attributes that regions possess and are at least hypothetically related to their ability to respond to stress. Stress consists of a negative disturbance and can be either acute or chronic. Stresses may vary in terms of both their duration and magnitude. Regional resilience refers to the actual performance of the region in response to stress: to what extent does the region recover from stress? Resilience can be either absolute (does the region regain its prior state?) or relative to that of other regions. Measuring resilience performance requires specifying exactly what to measure and over what time period, methodological challenges that, Foster notes, hamper comparative resilience assessment.

Foster's primary concern is to develop a "regional resilience index" that can reveal and compare regional resilience capacity and performance for U.S. metropolitan areas. For the regional capacity component, she identifies three subdimensions of the index: regional economic capacity, sociodemographic capacity, and community connection capacity. Regional economic capacity is measured by three variables: regional economic diversity, income, and income distribution. Sociodemographic capacity is measured by education, percentage of population of working age, percentage of population with disabilities, and poverty rate. Community connection capacity is measured by familiarity (percentage of population born in the state), linguistic connection (percentage not linguistically isolated), and age of housing in the region. Foster standardizes these ten variables and uses them to create a regional capacity index for each of the 360 U.S. metropolitan areas.

For the regional performance component, which proves more problematic, Foster examines the responses of gross metropolitan product and regional employment to the economic downturn at the beginning of the twenty-first century. For each of the two measures she develops a measure of stress (for example, increase in unemployment rate during the period) and a measure of recovery (for example, proportion of increase in unemployment rate that was recovered by the end of the period). She calculates a regional performance score for each of the two variables by dividing the measure of recovery by the measure of stress. Finally, she standardizes each of the two measures to create a regional performance index that incorporates both gross metropolitan product and regional employment. The resulting regional capacity and performance indexes enable researchers to relate capacity to performance and can help policymakers better understand their region's capacity for resilience, both in absolute terms and relative to other regions.

As the conference was being held, the nation was in the midst of a weak recovery from its longest recession since World War II. However, mortgage foreclosures, the ongoing result of the collapse of a housing bubble that helped precipitate that recession, continued at record-high levels. In "Resilience in the Face of Foreclosures: How National Actors Shape Local Responses," Todd Swanstrom examines the factors that shape the ability of local and regional actors to prevent foreclosures and mitigate their harmful effects on families, neighborhoods, and local governments.[1] Swanstrom examines the constraints that local housing market conditions, federal and state policies, (un)availability of needed information, and lender incentives place on local and regional responses to the foreclosure crisis. His work is based on institutional analysis and interviews conducted in the St. Louis, Cleveland, Chicago, Atlanta, Riverside, and San Francisco metropolitan areas.

Swanstrom explains the spillover costs that foreclosures create for people other than the foreclosed homeowner. Property values decline and crime increases in the neighborhood where the foreclosure occurs. Declining property values place fiscal stress on local governments, which often curtail public services in response to the decline in their tax base. Involuntary displacement from their home harms children and other family members. These costs are especially severe in weak-market metropolitan areas. Because mortgage lenders do not take these costs into account when making foreclosure decisions, they carry out an excessive number of foreclosures.

In addition to noting general reasons for foreclosures, Swanstrom highlights the role that predatory lending (the making of overly risky loans) played in creating the foreclosure crisis that helped precipitate the Great Recession. He argues that predatory lending, rather than the collapse of the housing bubble, generally weak economic conditions, or federal policies to promote homeownership, was the root cause of the crisis. Federal policies since 1980, including those abolishing state usury laws and allowing lenders to opt for federal rather than more stringent state regulation, helped spur the growth of predatory lending, as did the absence of effective federal regulation of the mortgage market. Federal regulators preempted state attempts to restrict predatory lending and prevent foreclosures. State governments likewise preempted local attempts to do so.

The ideal market response to the problem of too many foreclosures is for lenders to modify mortgages to reduce the amount of principal that defaulting borrowers owe. Swanstrom explains the features of the contemporary mortgage

---

1. Swanstrom's chapter complements Thomas Kingsley's chapter in *Urban and Regional Policy and Its Effects,* vol. 3, which examines local and regional public policies that have been implemented to respond to the foreclosure crisis. Swanstrom focuses instead on the broader economic and political contexts within which those responses have occurred. See Kingsley (2009).

market that give mortgage lenders and servicers an incentive to foreclose rather than to modify loans, even when modification would seem to be in the lender's interest. Chief among them are the pooling and securitization of mortgages, which increase the number of effective "creditors" for each loan and remove local lenders (who presumably understand local market conditions and are in a position to internalize some of the spillover costs of foreclosure) from the foreclosure decision.

On the borrower side of the market, foreclosure counseling can help borrowers avoid foreclosure, find new housing and needed social services, and facilitate short sales as an alternative to foreclosure. However, counseling prevents very few foreclosures, largely because lenders and loan servicers are reluctant to modify mortgages. Likewise, the federal Home Affordable Modification Program, begun in 2009, has helped avert very few foreclosures because it offers relatively small payments to lenders to induce them to modify mortgages and because lender participation in the program is voluntary.

Swanstrom then turns from the prevention of individual foreclosures to the stabilization of neighborhoods in the wake of foreclosures. The goal of neighborhood stabilization policies is to reduce the supply of and/or increase the demand for housing in neighborhoods where housing is underpriced as a result of a large number of foreclosures. Swanstrom notes that the need for such policies varies by metropolitan area and neighborhood. In weak-market metropolitan areas and especially in their typically depressed central city neighborhoods, the negative spillovers and consequent need for neighborhood stabilization policies are especially great. Even in strong-market metropolitan areas, similarly large neighborhood spillovers and needs for stabilization exist in overbuilt outer suburban neighborhoods. In strong-market neighborhoods within strong-market metropolitan areas, however, there is less need for neighborhood stabilization because spillover effects are smaller. Therefore, stabilization policies should be tailored to the market conditions of metropolitan areas and neighborhoods.

Stabilization policies, as well as policies to prevent foreclosures or mitigate their other spillover costs, must be carefully targeted to the right locations at the right times. Swanstrom argues that accurate, real-time, publicly available data on all stages of the lending process prior to, including, and following foreclosure are needed if these policies are to be properly targeted. However, such data are rarely available; instead, available data often are in the hands of private firms, not sensitive to variation in market conditions among neighborhoods, or outdated. In addition to appropriate data, local and regional organizations with the capacity to work together to analyze and act on the data are needed to help stabilize neighborhoods. Such organizations, which include local governments, community development corporations, and real estate brokerages, often lack the needed analytical capacity and rarely collaborate to help stabilize neighborhoods. Swanstrom concludes by recommending that the federal government mandate public disclosure of the necessary data, provide more funding for regional data gathering and analysis, and step up its efforts to promote collaboration among local and regional organizations.

Adding to the challenge of understanding and measuring resilience are changes that may be positive or negative, depending on a region's prior circumstances and response. In "Struggling over Strangers or Receiving Them with Resilience: The Metropolitics of Immigrant Integration," Manuel Pastor and John Mollenkopf conceive of immigration as a "shock" to urban and metropolitan areas that, while providing some immediate and obvious benefits, also may cause significant stress. The stresses may be immediate in terms of public service needs and intergroup tensions caused by competition in labor and housing markets with native-born minority groups. They may also be longer term with respect to the imperative of promoting intergenerational mobility in labor and housing markets.

The authors ask how regions respond to immigration-related shocks. Do regional leaders attempt to generate political support for policies that mitigate the shocks and attempt to incorporate immigrants into the area's social and political systems? Or do they rally public opposition to immigration and focus on enforcement-related measures? The chapter is concerned with factors that lead to positive (resilient) responses to immigration as opposed to negative (rigid) responses.

Pastor and Mollenkopf begin by reviewing national trends and legislation related to immigration. They observe that changes in federal legislation have resulted in a decline in immigration from Europe and an increase in immigration from Latin America and Asia. As a result, the ethnic character of immigrants in the United States has changed from nearly three-quarters non-Hispanic white in 1970 to 80 percent non-white in 2007. The location of new immigrants has also changed to include destinations in states such as Georgia, North Carolina, Arizona, and Nevada along with more traditional destinations in California, Texas, and Illinois. In addition, intra-metropolitan area destinations also have shifted, with immigrants increasingly settling in suburbs rather than in central cities.

The authors conduct case studies to examine the experience of six metropolitan areas: Los Angeles, Chicago, New York, San Jose, Phoenix, and Charlotte. They conclude that some of these areas have exhibited a resilient response while others have not. However, they also note that in nearly all cases the responses varied within the region. Central cities in general provided a more welcoming response than nearby suburbs, partly because cities have more established social service infrastructure, are generally more diverse, and have a larger first- and second-generation immigrant voting base, which can change the calculus for political candidates.

Pastor and Mollenkopf conclude from their case studies that a region's history matters: regions with a long history of immigration (for example, New York and Chicago) exhibit more resilient responses, while resilience is less frequently observed when the shock is newer and larger (Phoenix). They also observe that resilient responses are more likely when immigration is from diverse ethnic groups (as in New York and Los Angeles) or in regions where there are large numbers of "non-racialized" immigrants (Eastern Europeans in Chicago) or higher-skilled immigrants (Asians in San Jose). More rigid responses occur when immigration is "racialized" and seen to be from a single ethnic group (as with Phoenix and migrants from Mexico). Indeed, they observe that race matters in other ways as well. Chicago has traditionally incorporated immigrant groups into the political and social system through its machine politics, and Mexican immigrants have followed in that tradition. Charlotte's regional business elite's desire to present the region as the racially tolerant center of the "new South" has conditioned its response to recent Hispanic immigration. The authors also note that resilient responses are more difficult when political candidates find it advantageous to exploit resentments about the fiscal and social costs associated with immigration. That approach differed across regions but could be seen in at least some jurisdictions in each of the case study regions.

The authors conclude with several observations about possible policy responses to encourage resilience. Since rapid increases in immigration in areas that have not previously experienced substantial immigration flows seem to trigger more rigid responses, they suggest that national immigration policy reform should include special resources and training for such areas. They also argue that the opportunities available to political candidates to engage in anti-immigrant responses can be blunted by encouraging civic engagement and political participation among immigrant groups as well as leadership development and greater naturalization of immigrants, thereby shifting candidates' political cost-benefit calculus. Finally, they note that regional leaders, including those in the business community, can encourage resilient regional responses to immigration. While they already do so in some regions (for example, Charlotte), leaders in other regions should be educated on why doing so is in their interest.

Few policy decisions carry more enduring significance for regions than those related to transportation. Transportation choices establish the region's footprint and shape the lines of its future development. In "Bringing Equity to Transit-Oriented Development: Stations, Systems, and Regional Resilience,"

Rolf Pendall, Juliet Gainsborough, Kate Lowe, and Mai Nguyen examine the intersection of transportation and land use decisions, focusing on transit-oriented development (TOD).

In resilient regions, they argue, transportation policymakers must anticipate future needs when making decisions about building new transit systems, locating transit lines, and siting stations. The authors begin with the proposition that the transportation system and regional form of the last century—based on automobile-centric development—is not well-suited to the challenges of the next half-century, which are being driven by growing demographic diversity and climate change. Transportation infrastructure for the future, in their view, must promote environmental sustainability, broad social inclusiveness, and economic prosperity. Transit-oriented development may work to achieve those goals by locating mixed-use, higher-density neighborhoods with affordable housing near fixed-route mass transportation. Yet the effort to bring equity considerations into transportation decisions may confront significant obstacles.

Three questions guide the chapter. First, what is known from past experience about the challenges involved in creating transit routes and stations that serve low-income communities? Second, what obstacles does transit-oriented development confront and how have local governments sought to ensure that development around stations can take place? Third, is there evidence that a long-term commitment to affordable housing has been incorporated into development surrounding stations? Drawing on interviews, mapping, and census data analysis, they examine these questions in case studies of Denver, Charlotte, Miami, and Boston. Denver and Charlotte have reputations as successful examples of rail development and TOD over the past thirty years while Miami's experience has been more disappointing. In Boston, the authors examine efforts to create a new transit line with TOD around the stations.

The chapter's findings suggest reasons for both caution and optimism about incorporating equity considerations into transit alignments and TOD. On the positive side, the authors find that it is possible to bring equity considerations to light-rail planning in both centralized regions and regions that have many local jurisdictions. Transit development in Charlotte faced the fewest obstacles because it occurred within a single jurisdiction that had well-established relationships among public and private groups. Although Denver had to secure consensus from multiple jurisdictions, a history of building regional ties in the Metro Mayors Caucus facilitated consensus. Furthermore, because many suburban Denver jurisdictions are home to low-income residents, suburban governments were attentive to equity considerations. In Miami, on the other hand, the need to secure agreement from many different jurisdictions with little history of cooperation led to the creation of an ambitious but underfunded plan that ultimately failed by promising too much to everyone.

The authors do not find insurmountable barriers to attracting private developers to TOD sites. Miami and Boston faced the most severe obstacles, but in Boston community-based actors enjoyed public and private support for their development activities. In the Charlotte case, the authors suggest that the participatory processes associated with TOD may actually have built support for denser mixed-income development even outside TOD locations, thereby expanding the vision of possible lifestyles beyond the traditional auto-centered suburban housing development.

The chapter shows that support for mixed-income TOD occurs only when there is a broader commitment to affordable or mixed-income housing in the region. Denver, Boston, and Charlotte, all cities that incorporated affordable housing into TOD, already had significant commitments to housing affordability from regional leaders. The preexisting commitments meant that mixed-income TOD won acceptance as a way to achieve already agreed-on goals. Miami, by contrast, faced two barriers to mixed-income TOD: little history of support for affordable housing among regional leaders and state laws that mandate affordable housing on the basis of historic shares. As a result, the TOD in Miami featured 100 percent–affordable projects in distressed areas.

Pendall and his coauthors conclude by considering several shifts in federal policy that would make it easier to develop transportation systems that serve low-income communities, bring private developers to TOD, and include mixed-income housing. Because equity concerns can be overlooked when it is important to secure suburban support, they suggest that the federal government include additional equity criteria in its assessment of mass transit capital proposals. To ensure that projects with TOD are not disadvantaged by higher upfront land acquisition costs, they recommend changes to the cost-effectiveness criteria in the Federal Transit Administration's New Starts program. Finally, because private developers are unlikely to make housing affordability a priority without incentives to do so, they propose several measures that would greatly strengthen the incentives for affordability.

In the wake of the September 11, 2001, terrorist attacks, Hurricane Katrina, and the precipitous loss of manufacturing jobs in the Midwest after 2000, the resilience of regional economies to economic and non-economic shocks has become an important public policy issue. In "Economic Shocks and Regional Economic Resilience," Edward Hill and his coauthors present a comprehensive consideration of economic resilience—how it is defined and measured as well as the factors that contribute to resilience. Their main concern is why some regional economies that are adversely affected by shocks are able to recover in a relatively short period of time while others are not. They use quantitative analysis at the regional level and case studies of six metropolitan areas to address that question.

The authors define economic resilience as the ability of a regional economy to maintain or return to its previous growth rate after experiencing some type of externally generated shock. Shocks can be of three kinds: shocks caused by downturns in the national economy; shocks caused by downturns in particular industries that constitute an important component of the region's export base; and other external shocks (a natural disaster, closure of a military base, movement of an important firm out of the area, and so forth).

The analysis begins with descriptive statistics on economic shocks; their effects on regional economies; the extent to which regions are resistant to various types of shock; and, if they are not shock resistant, whether they are resilient or nonresilient after suffering the adverse effects of a shock. Regions suffering an employment downturn as a result of a shock were resilient 65 percent of the time. The average length of time from the onset of the downturn to recovery for a region was 2.9 years.

Following the descriptive analysis, the authors specify and estimate four economic models to address the following four questions: What are the characteristics of areas that experience regional economic downturns compared to those of areas that do not? Why are some regions adversely affected when an economic shock occurs while others are not? Why are some areas resilient when experiencing an economic downturn while others are not? What accounts for the length of time that it takes a region that is experiencing an economic downturn to recover?

The quantitative analysis indicates that regional economic structure matters to resilience but that there are no "magic bullets." It appears that some characteristics that make regions less susceptible to downturns also make it more difficult for them to recover. For example, a high percentage of employment in durable manufacturing and a poorly educated population make a region more likely to suffer from an employment downturn but make it easier for the region to recover from the downturn. A high percentage of employment in health care and social assistance has the opposite effects. Labor market flexibility is related to resilience, at least to the extent that right-to-work laws are an indicator of flexibility. Regions with greater income disparities are more likely to experience an employment downturn and take longer to return to their prior growth rate after the downturn. However, income disparities were positively related to resilience in the face of downturns in regional economic output and to the speed with which resilience occurred.

To provide a richer understanding of economic shock and resilience, the authors conducted case studies in six regions: Charlotte, Cleveland, Detroit, Grand Forks, Hartford, and Seattle. Based on their case studies, the authors characterize Detroit and Cleveland as regions that, until the turn of the twenty-first century, simply rode out downturns without changing their economic structure. During the same period, Charlotte was resilient as the result of an economic transformation in which finance and insurance replaced textiles as the primary economic drivers of the regional economy. Seattle's regional economy was successfully transformed twice, first from wood products manufacturing to aircraft manufacturing and then to software. Hartford and Grand Forks, which suffered industry shocks to which they have not been resilient, seem to have established new, lower, long-term rates of employment growth, but Hartford had rapid output growth despite its slow employment growth.

The authors conclude that in virtually all cases, the strategic decisions of individual firms and their leaders as well as decisions by area entrepreneurs were the key actions within a region that affected the region's economy and determined whether it proved resilient. Organizational creation and restructuring were frequent responses to shock. So, in some cases, were increased efforts at collaboration. However, there was no evidence that those activities played a major role in determining whether the region was shock resistant or resilient to downturns caused by shock.

The case studies find little evidence of advance precautionary planning to improve shock resistance or resilience. Rather than criticizing a lack of planning, the authors provide a dose of reality. For example, as some interviewees in Detroit observed, dependence on the auto industry had brought the region prosperity for nearly a century; although it may be paying for that now, a century is a pretty good run for a regional economy. Similarly, Grand Forks offers an example of the contrast between the numbers and local perceptions. Interviewees in Grand Forks stressed how resilient the area was and how successful its recovery was from the industry shock and flood of 1996–97. Yet the data show that the region was nonresilient to that shock and, indeed, seems to have established a new long-term employment growth rate that is considerably lower than the previous one. Regional economic resilience inevitably has a subjective component, and the authors recognize that the definition incorporated in their model cannot reflect the perceptions of leaders in every region.

The chapter concludes with some lessons for policymakers. It is essential to understand the ways in which a particular regional economy is vulnerable to downturns. Changing the regional characteristics that affect shock resistance and resilience is a long-term process that cannot yield immediate results. Although long-term precautionary planning to improve shock resistance or resilience is desirable, it is important to recognize that some of the regions that would most benefit from it are ones in which the economic, demographic, or social structure of the region makes it unlikely that regional leaders will be able to plan effectively. In the absence of such planning, policymakers' efforts to improve existing industries and develop new ones may at least cushion the blow of an economic shock and lay the foundation for the eventual resumption of more rapid economic growth.

During the 1960s, poverty was a major subject of national policy concern. However, the infrastructure for carrying out federally funded antipoverty efforts was largely local, consisting of networks of nonprofit social service providers in the nation's major metropolitan areas. The providers and their clients were located primarily in central cities, where the vast majority of poor people lived at that time. During the last fifteen years, the geography of poverty has become more diverse, with poverty rates growing more rapidly in suburbs than in central cities. Although poverty rates remain higher in central cities, by 2008 most poor people in large metropolitan areas lived in suburbs.[2]

In "Building a Resilient Social Safety Net," Sarah Reckhow and Margaret Weir examine whether antipoverty resources (nonprofit social service organizations and funding to support them) have kept up with the increasing suburbanization of the poor. Reckhow and Weir conceive of this as an issue of regional resilience because they define resilience, in the context of services to the poor, as the ability of a region's institutions to respond to increasing and geographically shifting demands for social services.

The authors base their analysis on case studies of the Atlanta, Chicago, Denver, and Detroit metropolitan areas. Two of the regions, Chicago and Denver, have a history of regional collaboration and institution building, which might be thought to result in more resources for the suburban poor, while the other two regions do not. Likewise, Chicago and Detroit have a longer history of poor suburban jurisdictions, which might also result in more resources for the suburban poor, while in Atlanta and Denver suburban poverty is relatively recent.

In each region, the authors study the distribution of resources by the largest philanthropic organizations and the number and types of nonprofit social service organizations that they fund. Local foundations, they posit, are well situated to address the changing geography of poverty because they know the region well and because their grants can be used for a variety of antipoverty activities in addition to direct service provision (for example, providing information about

2. Kneebone and Garr (2010).

poverty in the region, supporting new organizations and helping existing ones expand, and creating links among organizations). In contrast, government grants are more likely to be restricted to direct service provision.

Reckhow and Weir find that foundation support for social services for the poor generally remains greater in the central cities than in the suburbs of their case study regions. Except in Detroit, foundations provide more funding for worker training, housing, and human service organizations located in central cities than for those located in suburbs. Despite the recent growth of suburban poverty, human service grant funding is concentrated in the central cities of Chicago, Denver, and Atlanta. In all four case study regions, the suburbs with the highest poverty rates have fewer organizations receiving foundation grants than do central cities and richer suburbs. Foundation grants devoted to what the authors call "system change"—grants supporting organizations engaged in networking or capacity building, supporting or convening other organizations, gathering data, or doing research—are much greater and support many more organizations in Chicago than in the other metropolitan areas.

Overall, foundation grants mainly support and connect existing nonprofit organizations, which are located primarily in central cities. Creating new nonprofit organizations and funding suburban organizations are more difficult for foundations. (Notably, however, foundations played an important role in creating a new regional planning organization in the Chicago area.) Foundations have had little success in creating new community foundations in suburbs and have found it difficult to build new organizations and networks in suburbs, especially poorer suburbs. Despite their high level of need for social services, poor suburbs have relatively few nonprofit social service providers because of their political fragmentation (important because local governments have often helped fund social service nonprofits), weak civic sectors, and lack of financial resources. Richer suburbs, with their greater financial resources, have more poverty-oriented nonprofits, although NIMBY ("not in my backyard") politics can block the creation of needed services.

Reckhow and Weir conclude with three policy recommendations designed to spread antipoverty resources to suburbs so that they better reflect the geographic distribution of poor people within metropolitan areas. They call for governments and foundations to strengthen organizations that serve as regional social service intermediaries and coalition builders. They propose that the federal government provide incentives for human services planning to be included within federally supported regional planning efforts. Finally, they recommend that state departments of human services help create regional networks among the social service organizations that they fund.

Building Resilient Regions

Resilience has long figured as a central category of analysis in psychology, engineering, and natural systems; more recently, it has emerged as a way to study social systems.[3] Studies of resilience pose two core questions: do individuals or systems bounce back after experiencing a stress and what determines whether they do or do not? As Swanstrom notes, resilience is not a single theory but an analytic framework for understanding change. In contrast to single measures of "success," the resilience framework directs attention to multiple outcomes and the specific contexts from which they emerge.[4] The large and diverse literature on resilience uses the concept in at least three different ways: the first views resilience as an outcome; the second, as a set of capacities; the third, as part of an adaptive cycle—a developmental process. Aspects of each approach are represented in the chapters of this volume.

As an outcome, resilience assesses whether individuals or systems return to their initial condition after experiencing a serious disturbance. Disaster studies often take this approach: does a city recover its previous level of vitality or resume its earlier growth path after an earthquake or a hurricane?[5] In this volume, Hill and coauthors define resilience as an outcome, asking whether regions return to their earlier growth trajectories after an economic shock. Outcome measures rely on decisions about what aspects of the initial conditions are most salient for resilience. Hill and coauthors, for example, use growth rate rather than level of employment and gross metropolitan product. Outcomes also require decisions about the appropriate time frame for assessing recovery. Shocks that threaten the very basis of an economy may require a much longer recovery period than do shifts that affect only a segment of the local economy.

A second approach sees resilience as a set of capacities that help a system weather shocks. Resilience in this case is a "measure of robustness and buffering capacity of the system to changing conditions."[6] Hill and coauthors' discussion of regional "shock resistance" captures a similar idea: some regions are more robust in mitigating shocks than others. Kathryn Foster's chapter offers an inventory of capacities that have been associated with resilience in the literature on metropolitan areas. Her three categories of capacities—economic, sociodemographic, and community connectivity—reflect the diverse capacities that can serve as buffering mechanisms and highlight the complexity of regional systems. Critical as buffering capacities are, Foster's analysis shows that simply pos-

---

3. See the review of the literature in Pendall, Foster, and Cowell (2010).
4. Swanstrom (2008).
5. See Vale and Campanella (2005).
6. Berkes and Folke, cited in Pendall, Foster and Cowell (2010).

sessing buffering capacities does not ensure resilient outcomes. Capacities associated with resilience must be activated if they are to provide buffers and contribute to recovery.

The third approach sees resilience as part of an "adaptive cycle" in which a system is constantly adjusting to change. As the chapters by Swanstrom and by Reckhow and Weir argue, the most resilient systems display flexibility when confronted with stresses. Flexibility contributes to shock resistance and increases the likelihood of crafting positive adaptations to stress. This approach pays particular attention to the interaction among different levels of a system, positing that resilience at one level is greatly influenced by the levels above and below it;[7] for example, developments in the national economy influence local economies and vice versa. This complexity means that feedback across levels is a critical component of resilience. For example, feedback from stressed elements of a system prompts buffering changes elsewhere in the system. Even so, as systems grow more mature, they are likely to exhibit rigidities that make them less adaptable—and thus more vulnerable—to shocks. Periods of low resilience are critical phases of the adaptive cycle marked by structural vulnerability and destabilization; following some precipitating event, from a match lit in a dry forest to the election of a new leader, the system experiences rapid release and upheaval. In the wake of that release, experimentation flourishes and creates the basis for greater resilience under more uncertain and opportunity-filled conditions.

Institutional Challenges to Adaptation

The notion of resilience as an outcome, a set of capacities, and adaptive cycles provides useful starting points for considering resilience as a trait that regions can actively cultivate. Yet building resilience in metropolitan areas—whether resilience is conceived of as specific capacities, such as a more highly educated population, or as a process, such as experimentation—requires working through existing institutions, altering them, or creating new ones. Not only do individual institutions need to be flexible, but the connections among them may also need rewiring to respond effectively to stress. As Foster notes in her chapter, "Rather than single-capacity variables driving resilience . . . it may be that the interplay and networking of these capacities and their accumulative impact are most salient."

Institutions can, of course, resist changes that would promote resilience. Powerful groups that benefit from the institutional status quo may block reforms that would enhance resilience. Alternatively, entrenched customs and expectations can make it difficult for institutional leaders to envision alternatives

---

7. Walker and others (2004).

to existing practices.[8] Barriers that prevent cross-organizational connections can further weaken resilience. Within regions, local political boundaries can serve to buffer parts of the region, leaving other parts with fewer resources for robust adaption to stress. The challenges involved in making regional institutions flexible are compounded by the way in which regions fit into the federal system. In resilience theory, cross-scale relations (called "panarchy") constitute an essential component of resilience: actors operating at one scale can support or undermine resilience at a different scale.[9] The chapters by Swanstrom and Pastor and Mollenkopf underscore the important influence that decisions made by states or the federal government have on regional resilience. These chapters demonstrate that federal and state policies can both create the stressors that confront regions and, at the same time, shape the set of responses that regional leaders can muster. For metropolitan regions to cultivate resilience, then, both the horizontal and the vertical connections among institutions must be geared to buffer against stress.

Consideration of how institutions and the connections among them can influence resilience suggests four types of institutional rigidities that may undermine resilience. The first is the inability to register a shock or to understand the nature of the shock. Natural disasters, such as earthquakes or floods, swiftly command attention and the mobilization of resources to meet the challenge. Other shocks may be much less obvious. Pendall, Foster, and Cowell distinguish between acute and chronic, "slow burn," shocks.[10] In the case of slow burns, such as deindustrialization or climate change, regional actors may take a long time to recognize the challenge that they face because such shocks are spread across multiple administrations in time and place, making it difficult to develop a coordinated understanding of and response to the issue. Even when actors discern the shock, they may mistake its magnitude or nature. For example, Hill and coauthors suggest that in regions that are centers of durable manufacturing, "residents and businesses may come to believe that their regional economies will always bounce back from shocks even when those shocks are due more to fundamental, long-term changes in the regional economy (such as the decline of the auto industry) than to the ordinary ups and downs of the business cycle."

A second type of rigidity occurs when feedback mechanisms fail to buffer against a shock and instead transmit the impact of a stressor throughout the sys-

---

8. For different approaches to understanding institutions, see Hall and Taylor (1996). See Lang (2011) for a consideration of resilience and new institutionalism.

9. According to Folke and others, "The ability for reorganization and renewal of a desired ecosystem state after disturbance and change will strongly depend on the influences from states and dynamics at scales above and below. . . . Such cross-scale aspects of resilience are captured in the notion of a panarchy, a set of dynamic systems nested across scales." Folke and others (2010, p. 558).

10. Pendall, Foster, and Cowell (2010).

tem. Feedback mechanisms are a critical component of resilience in interconnected systems. They send information about a shock throughout the system so that protective adaptations can occur. Feedback processes can also have the opposite effect when unbuffered stresses cascade throughout the system. For metropolitan regions, scale is central in assessing whether feedback processes are buffering shocks or transmitting stressors. Higher levels of government may enact laws that make regions more or less vulnerable to a stress. They may also enact laws that limit or empower local actors to take creative actions to cope with stresses.

In the case of foreclosures, Swanstrom shows that higher levels of government undermined the resilience of local areas in multiple ways. The federal government's decision to relax mortgage underwriting standards exposed localities to new stressors. By sanctioning predatory lending, the federal government made it more likely that the number of foreclosures would increase. Federal regulators undermined local resilience even further by using their power of preemption to prevent localities from banning predatory lending once localities began to register the shock of foreclosures. In the language of adaptive cycles, the federal government's failure to register the harms that foreclosures were causing represented a failure in system feedback. In a more resilient system, feedback from localities to higher levels of government would prompt new restrictions on predatory lending.

The failure of adaptation in this case highlights some of the differences between natural systems and social worlds. In the U.S. federal system, there is no guarantee that information about a local stressor will prompt action at higher levels of government. The interests of different groups and their relative power in different parts of the system will deeply influence buffering capabilities. Powerful groups will deliberately target their efforts where they are more likely to be effective. Swanstrom highlights the ability of the mortgage lending industry to "venue shop," ensuring that it could block responses by higher levels of government to the stresses that foreclosures were causing at the local level. The consequence has been a negative spiral in which spillovers from foreclosures—declining property values, social disorder and crime, and fiscal stress—create multiple new stressors for localities.

A third type of institutional rigidity restricts experimentation and innovation, both of which are essential for resilience. In resilience theory, experimentation, especially at smaller scales, allows systems to try out different ways to respond to challenges. When they can be connected to cross-scale learning, small-scale experiments can renew an entire system.[11] This process of experimental learning

---

11. Folke and others (2010). See also Ansell (2011).

allows systems to shake off the institutional rigidities that inevitably build up over time.

One aspect of experimentation is the "repurposing" and "recombining" of institutions to attack problems in novel ways. Swanstrom shows that nonprofit housing organizations engaged in that kind of experimentation when they switched from focusing on housing rehabilitation to foreclosure counseling. Studies of innovation highlight the significance of leaders who move from one organization to another, bringing with them new ideas about how to use organizational resources and new approaches to the organization's mission. For example, Walter W. Powell's work examining why the biotechnology industry flourished in Cambridge (Massachusetts), San Diego, and San Francisco but not in other cities that possessed many similar strengths shows how the fluid movement of people across organizations and the diversity of organizational ties supported innovation.[12]

Although the capacity for innovation and experimentation remains one of the celebrated virtues of the U.S. federal system, higher levels of government routinely block regional and local innovation.[13] As noted above in the discussion of foreclosures, the federal government and states regularly use their powers of preemption to restrict the scope for innovation at lower levels of government. Another barrier to experimentation is institutional "lock-in," a process that occurs over time as institutions become sclerotic and resistant to change. Among regional economic geographers, the idea of "lock-in" has been used to explain the failure of older economies to respond effectively to competitive challenges. External shocks such as new competition or new technologies fail to spark experimentation and instead set off "a spiral of negative 'lock-in' effects whereby the region's firms react in terms of defensive cost-cutting and quality reduction rather than by innovative investment or moving into new productive fields."[14]

Similarly, entrenched interests may stymie changes that threaten their hold over existing institutional arrangements. Over time, groups that win significant benefits from institutions can coalesce to defend their stake in the status quo. As Pastor and Mollenkopf show, opposition to immigrants is often animated by fear that resources will be diverted from the native-born residents to immigrants. Alternatively, groups that have been harmed by public initiatives in the past may use what little power they have to block new initiatives that they perceive as threatening. Pendall and coauthors show that fear of displacement, based on

12. Powell, Packalen, and Whittington (2010).
13. Frug and Barron (2008).
14. Martin and Sunley (2006, p. 417).

decades of hard experience, made the African American residents of Miami's Overtown district wary of new proposals for transit-oriented development.

Reckhow and Weir's chapter highlights another type of institutional rigidity that limits experimentation. Their analysis shows that poverty-oriented non-profit organizations, which got their start decades ago in cities, have found it difficult to respond to growing levels of suburban poverty, in part because of "sunk costs." These organizations have long-established connections to resources and information in their current urban setting, and most do not have the knowledge or resources to expand their activities to new contexts in which they have few ties. Powell's work on biotechnology highlights the important role of "anchor tenants," organizations that launch innovative cycles and stay involved in diverse roles. Such organizations are important because they serve as "organizations that create organizations."[15] Reckhow and Weir's chapter shows that although some local philanthropic organizations have sought to fill this role, they have far to go before they can be considered "anchor tenants."

The final type of institutional rigidity that can undermine resilience stems from the jurisdictional boundaries that divide metropolitan America into a patchwork of political jurisdictions. Despite nearly a century of efforts to promote metropolitan consolidation, local boundaries, once in place, have been notoriously resistant to change.[16] The difficulty of altering local boundaries has not put an end to experiments in regional governance, but it has significantly restricted their scope. For example, experiments that entail redistribution, such as tax-base sharing and "fair share housing" (which distributes affordable housing throughout the region), are especially difficult to launch. Moreover, jurisdictional boundaries facilitate the strategy of "selective buffering," in which parts of the region shield themselves from shocks, effectively leaving other parts to bear the brunt of a challenge with reduced resources. In their chapter, Pastor and Mollenkopf note that many suburbs with significant immigrant populations do not provide services themselves, relying instead on cities to provide services to immigrants living in suburbs as well as in cities.

Developing Flexible Institutions and Adaptive Governance

Although institutions can undermine regional resilience, deliberate efforts to establish early warning signals for stressors, open feedback channels, promote

15. Powell, Packalen, and Whittington define "anchor tenants" as organizations that "occupy positions that provide them with access to diverse participants and the legitimacy to engage with and catalyze others in ways that facilitate the extension of collective resources." Powell, Packalen, and Whittington (2010, p. 13).

16 . Weir (2000); Foster (1997); Orfield (2002).

experimentation, and build new regional connections can work against institutional rigidities. The literature on regional innovation and the chapters in this volume suggest three approaches to fostering the flexibility that is the hallmark of adaptive governance.

The first is to ensure that influential groups in the region adopt a forward-looking perspective and that timely information about shocks is available. Inadequate information may make it impossible to detect shocks or to launch efforts to buffer against them. Swanstrom argues that detailed, timely information about foreclosures would allow local actors to take more effective steps to stem their spillover effects. As he notes, "Without sophisticated data systems, local actors often grope forward based on inconsistent and out-of-date data."

Networks and cross-organizational collaboration offer a second strategy for promoting regional resilience. The call for collaboration is hardly a novel idea. Disillusion with government has made collaboration a panacea for all sorts of challenges. However, we need a better understanding of how to build collaborations and more data about the conditions under which collaborations are effective. Studies of regional innovation suggest that some types of networks may be more effective than others. For example, Powell's analysis of the emergence of the biotechnology industry shows that regions with strong horizontal ties among diverse organizations within a region succeeded far more than did regions where local organizations built fewer ties inside the region and more ties to external organizations. This finding resonates with those of AnnaLee Saxenian, who argues that Silicon Valley's success can be traced to strong horizontal connections among firms. By contrast, the initial development of Route 128, Boston's high-technology corridor, was hindered by the predominance of vertical ties that discouraged cross-fertilization among firms.[17] Sean Safford's analysis of the divergent fates of Youngstown, Ohio, and Allentown, Pennsylvania, in the face of deindustrialization also emphasizes the importance of specific types of network ties. Safford argues that the single, tightly knit civic and business network that connected Youngstown's elites made the region unreceptive to new ideas and shrank the space for innovation. Allentown's distinctive but overlapping civic and business networks, by contrast, created a conduit for novel ideas and promoted experimentation that made the region more resilient.[18]

Much of the literature on networks and collaboration emphasizes the roles of business and civic elites. Yet effective collaborations that include organizations representing low-income communities are likely to require a different approach.[19] Many of these organizations operate close to the margin and lack

17. Powell, Packalen, and Whittington (2010); Saxenian (1996).
18. Safford (2009).
19. Pastor, Benner, and Matsuoka (2009).

the time and money to initiate collaborations. Moreover, because many of them work at the neighborhood level, they may lack the knowledge needed to initiate broader collaborations. As a result, collaborations that address the concerns of low-income residents require more external assistance to gain momentum. They are also likely to need ongoing financial support in order to stay active. In Reckhow and Weir's chapter, foundations provided ongoing support for collaboration among Chicago's poor southern suburbs when they applied for federal stimulus grants. Swanstrom's chapter also highlights the important role that philanthropic organizations are playing in building collaborative efforts among housing nonprofits, although assistance from philanthropic organizations alone may not be sufficient to sustain collaboration. As Reckhow and Weir argue, nonprofit organizations that serve the poor may also require active assistance from state governments in order to build regional networks.

A final strategy for promoting institutional flexibility relies on initiatives from higher levels of government. As the chapters of this book make clear, the options for regional action are strongly shaped by higher levels of government. In many cases, state and federal regulations restrict the scope for local experimentation. Removing restrictions is often the most effective strategy for promoting regional resilience. But states and the federal government can also use their power to help disrupt mounting institutional rigidities in regions. Higher levels of government possess a wide variety of tools to alter the operation of local institutions and the terms of interaction among them. Federal requirements for community participation or multi-jurisdictional joint funding applications are no magic wand, but they can enlarge the cast of stakeholders and, over time, expand agendas. The chapter by Pendall and coauthors shows how broad participation on transit in Charlotte not only built support for the light-rail line but also helped to disseminate a new vision of more compact, walkable neighborhoods for suburbs as well as cities. The federal government can also create new decisionmaking venues, as it did when it assigned new responsibilities for transportation planning to metropolitan planning organizations. As studies of regional transportation policies show, even though these organizations have fallen far short of transforming transportation, they have allowed for more experimentation with a wider range of transportation alternatives than in the past.[20]

Although higher levels of government possess the tools to encourage regional experimentation, they often fail to use them because entrenched interests in Washington or in the states block initiatives that threaten them. In some cases, nonprofit policy groups, such as the Center for Transit-Oriented Development discussed in the chapter by Pendall and coauthors, can help fill the gap. Groups

20. Weir, Rongerude, and Ansell (2009); Swanstrom (2007).

that wish to expand the scope of regional action may need to weigh in at the national level in order to open up the federal policy agenda. Depending on the support that they can muster, such groups may pursue modest initiatives, such as inserting provisions in federal laws that allow for more local experimentation, or they may seek more sweeping changes. The Transportation Equity Network, for example, has won provisions to encourage more local hiring from minority communities on federal transportation projects, and it continues to mobilize for changes in federal law that would enable greater local experimentation.[21]

Strains and stresses, whether from economic, demographic, or natural sources, will inevitably pose challenges to regions. Responses to those challenges come not from a single entity called "the region" but from the myriad institutions that populate the region—firms, school systems, and transportation agencies, to name just a few. Regions will be only as resilient as those institutions are flexible and innovative. Strategies for enhancing resilience ultimately alter perceptions and carve out new pathways for action. Interactions among diverse institutions— across sectors and across levels of government—are the critical backdrop for the feedback and experimentation that supports adaptive governance. The many walls that now segment metropolitan regions—across political jurisdictions and across institutions—must come down and the gaps that separate federal laws from regional realities must be bridged if regions are to cultivate resilience.

References

Ansell, Christopher K. 2011. *Pragmatist Democracy: Evolutionary Learning as Public Philosophy.* Oxford University Press.

Folke, C., and others. 2010. "Resilience Thinking: Integrating Resilience, Adaptability, and Transformability." *Ecology and Society* 15, no. 4: 20 (www.ecologyandsociety.org/vol15/iss4/art20).

Foster, Kathryn A. 1997. "Regional Impulses." *Journal of Urban Affairs* 19, no. 4: 375–403.

Frug, Gerald E., and David J. Barron. 2008. *City Bound: How States Stifle Urban Innovation.* Cornell University Press.

Hall, Peter A., and Rosemary C. R. Taylor. 1996. "Political Science and the Three New Institutionalisms." *Political Studies* 44, no. 5: 936–57.

Kingsley, G. Thomas. 2009. "Policies to Cope with Foreclosures and Their Effects on Neighborhoods." In *Urban and Regional Policy and Its Effects,* vol. 3, edited by Nancy Pindus, Howard Wial, and Harold Wolman, pp. 22–63. Brookings.

Kneebone, Elizabeth, and Emily Garr. 2010. "The Suburbanization of Poverty: Trends in Metropolitan America, 2000 to 2008." Brookings.

Lang, Thilo. 2011. "Urban Resilience and New Institutional Theory: A Happy Couple for Urban and Regional Studies?" In *German Annual of Spatial Research and Policy 2010,* edited by Bernhard Müller, pp. 15–24. Heidelberg, Germany: Springer-Verlag.

---

21. Swanstrom and Banks (2009).

Martin, Ron, and Peter Sunley. 2006. "Path Dependence and Regional Economic Evolution." *Journal of Economic Geography* 6: 395–437.

Orfield, Myron. 2002. *American Metropolitics: The New Suburban Reality*. Brookings.

Pastor, Manuel, Jr., Chris Benner, and Martha Matsuoka. 2009. *This Could Be the Start of Something Big: How Social Movements for Regional Equity Are Reshaping Metropolitan America*. Cornell University Press.

Pendall, Rolf, Kathryn Foster, and Margaret Cowell. 2010. "Resilience and Regions: Building Understanding of the Metaphor." *Cambridge Journal of Regions, Economy and Society* 3, no. 1: 71–84.

Powell, Walter W., Kelley Packalen, and Kjersten Whittington. 2010. "Organizational and Institutional Genesis: The Emergence of High-Tech Clusters in the Life Sciences." In *The Emergence of Organizations and Markets*, edited by John Padgett and Walter W. Powell (www.stanford.edu/group/song/papers/Chapter_13.pdf).

Safford, Sean. 2009. *Why the Garden Club Couldn't Save Youngstown: The Transformation of the Rust Belt*. Harvard University Press.

Saxenian, AnnaLee. 1996. *Regional Advantage: Culture and Competition in Silicon Valley and Route 128*. Harvard University Press.

Swanstrom, Todd. 2007. "Regional Network Governance and Resilience: The Case of Transportation." Paper prepared for the Annual Meeting of the American Political Science Association, Chicago.

———. 2008. "Regional Resilience: A Critical Examination of the Ecological Framework." Paper prepared for the Annual Meeting of the Urban Affairs Association, Baltimore.

Swanstrom, Todd, and Brian Banks. 2009. "Going Regional: Community-Based Regionalism, Transportation, and Local Hiring Agreements." *Journal of Planning Education and Research* 28, no. 3: 355–67.

Vale, Lawrence J., and Thomas J. Campanella. 2005. *The Resilient City: How Modern Cities Recover from Disaster*. Oxford University Press.

Walker, Brian, and others. 2004. "Resilience, Adaptability and Transformability in Social–Ecological Systems." *Ecology and Society* 9, no. 2: 5 (www.ecologyandsociety.org/vol9/iss2/art5).

Weir, Margaret. 2000. "Coalition Building for Regionalism." In *Reflections on Regionalism*, edited by Bruce Katz, pp. 127–53. Brookings.

Weir, Margaret, Jane Rongerude, and Christopher K. Ansell. 2009. "Collaboration Is Not Enough: Virtuous Cycles of Reform in Transportation Policy." *Urban Affairs Review* 44, no. 4: 455–89.

2

In Search of Regional Resilience

KATHRYN A. FOSTER

A thought experiment: Imagine you are walking down the street one fine spring afternoon. Another stroller happens by and you nod pleasantly, whereupon the stroller hauls off and punches you in the gut. As you lay sprawled on the ground getting your bearings, you wonder, "How resilient am I?"

We might conclude there is evidence of total resilience—define it as bounce-back from a stress—if you hop up, dust yourself off, smile at the strangeness of the world, and head on your way, never to suffer a lingering side effect, such as forever weakened stomach muscles or perpetual fear of spring walks and spring walkers.

Shy of that outcome, however, your degree of resilience likely depends on a number of factors. How hard were you hit? Was it a glancing, ultimately benign blow or a particularly intense one? Where did the blow fall? Did it hit the strongest, thickest part of your midsection or did it zero in on an especially sensitive or vulnerable spot?

Factors one or two levels removed from the immediate stress may also play a role in your post-blow resilience. How experienced are you in receiving and recovering from hits to the stomach? How have you fared in the past recovering from physical and mental stresses? Jaunty walk on a spring day aside, how generally stressed are you these days? What is the state of your health and well-being? How strong is your support network from friends, family, and the broader community to assist you in a time of duress? How accessible and affordable is the nearest hospital, health clinic, or mental health facility for addressing your symptoms, both immediate and lingering, of the gut punch?

And what of spiraling effects? Did the time it took for you to regain your post-punch bearings cause you to miss your bus connection and hence your appointment for a job interview? Did that further cause you to miss out on a

24

good employment opportunity after months of unemployment such that you turn morose and bitter, lash out at those in your orbit, suffer your partner leaving you, and plunge into a deep, miserable existence? And, if so, how resilient are you to that?

Given the many conditions and factors that may affect outcomes—"for want of a nail, the war was lost"—defining and measuring resilience in the face of a challenge itself require a strong stomach. As the thought experiment attests, determining resilience is tricky enough for a single individual case. For a complex region facing a daily barrage of stresses, multiple influences, hundreds of thousands of actors and changing conditions, assessing regional resilience and identifying and isolating factors affecting it are conceptually and methodologically tough.

I have worked with others in the MacArthur Foundation Research Network on Building Resilient Regions and with a team of colleagues at the University at Buffalo Regional Institute to investigate the potential for a generalized regional resilience index. The goal is to develop for broad use an online measurement tool enabling regional leaders to gauge their region's resilience to specific challenges, where resilience encompasses not only post-stress recovery but also pre-stress readiness. By measuring resilience capacities and performance for a range of metropolitan regions, scholars and practitioners may compare regions by their resilience and gain insight on why one region may have fared better than another in the face of a stress. Perhaps more important, users will learn which factors associated with resilience are less well developed in their regions and, thus, which policy and program choices might best improve levels of resilience capacity. While this method by definition, using a large number of observations, lacks the nuance and depth of single-stress case studies—the approach taken in most contributions to this volume—it offers the breadth and potential of comparative analysis for multiple regions and stresses.

As this chapter reveals, even the seemingly simple parts of the resilience index exercise complicate quickly and measurement challenges abound. Conceptual and methodological reconnaissance has prompted the resilience index team to focus initially on measuring resilience capacity, emphasizing the factors that prime a region for strong response in anticipation of future unknown disturbances. As methods enable and realities allow—the latter demanding a sufficient number of regions experiencing similar types of stress at roughly similar time periods—the team will pursue a generalized index measure for resilience performance.

To illuminate these practical conclusions, the chapter steps sequentially through defining, conceiving, and measuring resilience, the last offering a sample test based on resilience data from national sources.

Defining Resilience

Resilience is widely understood by most who hear the word. A subject, say an individual, household, school, neighborhood, facility, region, or larger system endowed with certain capacities for resilience, exists at some pre-stress state. The subject suffers a stress, such as loss of a job, divorce, riot, drought, fiscal crisis, or political coup. The subject draws on its capacity to respond to the stress and bounce back to its pre-stress norm.

Although simple in concept, this norm-stress-response formulation is complex in practice, engendering numerous definitions and methodological approaches. Disciplines as varied as psychology, ecology, and management have adopted resilience as a useful idea and construct for field development. While there is considerable consensus around the basic notions of norm, stress, and response, a primary conceptual divide is whether resilience is demonstrated by an *outcome*, that is, a person or place is resilient to the degree it recovers from a stress, or whether resilience is a *capacity*, that is, a person or place is resilient to the degree it has the conditions and attributes to potentially recover from a stress.[1] Review of the resilience literature finds the term used widely to convey both capacity and performance, with that choice based typically on the purpose of the research.

Resilience has long interested psychologists seeking to understand coping mechanisms and why some people fare better than others in dealing with difficult circumstances and major life events.[2] While faculties of an individual differ from those of a multifaceted region, two concepts from psychology stand out as useful to understanding regional resilience. First is that resilience is an *ordinary* rather than *extraordinary* way of being.[3] Although they will choose different means—exercise, prayer, journal writing, barking at the moon, and so forth—people suffering trauma generally have the capacity and inclination to bounce back over time. Second, resilience is not simply an inherent personal trait but also represents capacities, behaviors, and resources one can develop to deal with difficult challenges.[4] Resilience can be acquired and fostered through internal steps, such as strengthening one's friendship networks and taking physical and

---

1. Covering more bases are Norris and others (2008), who discuss resilience as an abstraction, a metaphor, a theory, a set of capacities, and a strategy. Pendall, Foster, and Cowell (2010) also review alternative conceptions of resilience.

2. Bonanno and Mancini (2008) offer a useful review.

3. According to Norris and others (2008, p. 146), "There is something to be said for viewing [resilience] as an inevitable, inherent, universal quality of the human spirit." See also American Psychological Association, "Resilience: After a Hurricane" (www.apa.org/helpcenter/hurricane-resilience.aspx).

4. Winfield (1994); Bonanno and Mancini (2008).

mental care of oneself, and through society's external interventions, such as social structures like good schools, health clinics, and services networks.

Ecologists likewise formulate resilience as a process and attribute, in their case to understand natural phenomena such as how forests regenerate after a fire or lakes recover from pollutants. Ecologists define resilience as a measure of vulnerability to surprise and shocks, rather than as a response to such stresses.[5] High resilience is associated with low vulnerability, as occurs when a system is in a high state of reorganization and regeneration, such as shown by a forest following a devastating fire. The system is then most responsive to and interactive with external forces, making surprises unlikely. In contrast to studies of individual resilience, the ecological resilience literature links resilience to natural, rather than human-driven, responses to disturbance, and puts more stock in the ability of an ecological system to withstand, rather than adapt to, change motivated by human action.[6]

Capacities and human behaviors likewise garner interest from engineers and planners who point to resilience as a core capacity of disaster response.[7] As the much-studied case of New Orleans after Hurricane Katrina suggests, people with high vulnerability and regions with low resilience cope poorly with disturbance, faltering in the face of environmental, political, and economic blows.[8] People and regions with high resilience more readily absorb such disturbance, either because they better anticipate and prepare for impending crises or because they are better endowed or structured—with such assets as sound infrastructure, ample human capital, functional communications systems, and strong external relations—to react effectively to a disaster.

Management researchers enter the resilience conversation through interest in why some enterprises perform better than others in the face of business disruptions. As firms embraced "just-in-time" delivery systems and increased their dependence on global supply chains, the risk assessment and preparation aspects of resilience assumed special importance. Yossi Sheffi has examined natural disasters (for example, Toyota supply chains disrupted by fires, Unilever plants shut down by a hurricane) and non-natural disasters (for example, U.S. Pacific ports shut down by strategically timed labor strikes, McDonald's suffering as a target

5. Holling and Gunderson (2002). A more popular account of this perspective is Maywa Montenegro, "Urban Resilience," SeedMagazine.com (http://seedmagazine.com/content/article/urban_resilience/). See also materials available from the Resilience Alliance (www.resalliance.org).

6. See, for example, Walker and Salt (2006).

7. See, for example, Godschalk (2003); Berke and Campanella (2006); Vale and Campanella (2005). Godschalk (2003) summarizes this planning perspective. See also Godschalk (2010, p. 48).

8. See, for example, Olshansky and Johnson (2010); Campanella (2006); Birch and Wachter (2006); Colton, Kates and Laska (2008); Liu and Plyer (2010); Cutter and others (2006).

of anti-American protests) to distill factors making one business more resilient than another.[9] Sheffi identifies redundancy and flexibility as the two key resilience factors enabling a firm to mitigate and bounce back from a disruption. Companies achieve redundancy through strategically positioned back-up systems (technology, parts, labor, and suppliers), standardized parts and processes, and deep collaborative relations with each link in the supply chain. They achieve flexibility through decentralized and crosstrained leadership and decisionmaking systems, effective communications to distribute useful knowledge, and adaptable parts and contracts able to change on short notice.

Despite safeguards and good intentions, however, some societies perform better than others at assessing situations, preparing for the future, stewarding community assets, and thriving economically, environmentally, and politically. From his recent analysis of societal and environmental collapse in ancient and modern settings as varied as Easter Island, Mayan civilization, Rwanda, and Montana, Jared Diamond distills five factors often or always present in situations of social failure.[10] The first four, which vary across the cases in their significance and may be uncontrollable or inadvertent, are environmental damage, climate change, hostile neighbors, and friendly trade partners. The fifth factor, which always proved significant to the collapse, is society's response to its environmental problems. In Diamond's analysis, resilience depends not only on properties of the environment—the fragility of an ecosystem or ecological cycles, for example—but also on properties of people, such as prudence, the nature of external relations, and habits of conservation.[11]

This scan of alternative concepts reinforces that resilience is used to convey two different though connected notions, namely resilience as capacities and resilience as performance. This twin formulation implies that resilience performance can be developed through resilience capacity—or "built" in the language of the Building Resilient Regions Research Network—through intentional actions to strengthen the means and ends of resilience.

Because both of these conceptions are of interest to regional leaders and policymakers—capacity, because it offers insights on which areas of intervention offer the greatest potential for increasing regional resilience, and performance, because it reveals the degree to which a community has effectively activated its capacity to achieve resilient outcomes—both this chapter and the resilience index effort under way use a definition of resilience incorporating both capacity and performance. In particular, we define regional resilience as

---

9. Sheffi (2005).
10. Diamond (2005).
11. Diamond (2005, pp. 11–15).

the "ability of a region to anticipate, prepare for, respond to, and recover from a disturbance."[12]

Conceiving Resilience

For many regional leaders, interest in resilience generally and a regional index in particular stems from several place-based questions: "How resilient is my region compared to others?" "Why is Region X more resilient than we are?" "If we increase our resilience capacity, will that translate to better resilience performance?" Before contemplating such questions and elaborating on concepts of resilience capacity and performance, I first link these facets of resilience.

A useful working formulation is to presume a process in which a region has a certain pre-stress capacity for resilience, is confronted by a stress, and responds to that stress with resilience performance. A relevant hypothesis would be that a region's resilience performance, that is, its recovery from stress, is a function in part of its resilience capacity, that is, pre-stress conditions and resources, as in:

$$\text{resilience performance} = f(\text{resilience capacity, attributes of the stress,}$$
$$\text{non-capacity factors})$$

The logic is straightforward. Just as walkers are better positioned to recover from midsection blows if they are physically strong, have health insurance, and harbor a good attitude, so may regions better position themselves with a combination of endowments, resources, forethought, preparation, and adaptations to mitigate or recover from challenges. Other factors, including the nature and severity of the stress, and non-capacity factors, including luck, may also shape resilience performance.[13]

This relationship between resilience capacity and resilience performance can be visualized as a continuous cycle as shown in figure 2-1. To realize capacity, regional actors may anticipate various types of stresses and prepare for their arrival. Preparation comes in many forms, including developing and testing

12. This definition echoes that of Plodinec (2009), who concludes for the Community and Regional Resilience Institute (CARRI) that resilience is "the capability to anticipate risk, limit impact, and bounce back rapidly through survival, adaptability, evolution, and growth in the face of turbulent change." Plodinec identifies forty-five definitions of resilience from literatures addressing ecological, physical, social, community, and individual resilience. His definition reflects CARRI's interest in assisting communities to adapt both in advance of (to anticipate and prepare) and following (to respond and recover from) a disturbance.

13. At first glance, the severity of a stress appears independent of resilience capacity, given its insusceptibility to policy intervention. On further consideration, however, characteristics of the stress may link to resilience capacity, given the potential for regional leaders to anticipate, plan and prepare for, and therefore mitigate the intensity of a particular future stress.

Figure 2-1. *Cycle of Resilience Capacity and Performance*

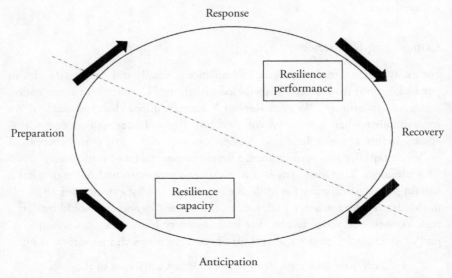

Source: Author.

emergency management systems, shoring up bridges and hospital systems, and providing a strong social safety net for a region's most vulnerable. To realize performance, regional actors respond to the stress and take action to recover from it, either returning to a pre-stress norm or transforming to a "new normal" for the region. Strong performance itself feeds back into resilience capacity, increasing the region's stock of experience and confidence, which in turn may help prepare for and respond to the next regional stress.

A more particular formulation posits regions following any of four capacity-to-performance pathways starting before and continuing after a stress. In the pre-stress period a region has either above-average or below-average-capacity for resilience to withstand a disturbance. For example, as illustrated in figure 2-2, regions A and B have above-average pre-stress capacity, while regions C and D have below-average capacity. Following the stress, regions exhibit either above-average or below-average resilience performance. Depending on this outcome and considering their starting place, labels can be applied to each regional resilience trajectory, say as "thriving" (high capacity, high performance), "faltering" (high capacity, low performance), "transforming" (low capacity, high performance), or "failing" (low capacity, low performance). In this example, regions A and D are thriving and failing, respectively, region C has transformed itself, overachieving based on its below-average pre-stress capacity, and region B has

Figure 2-2. *Alternative Resilience Pathways*

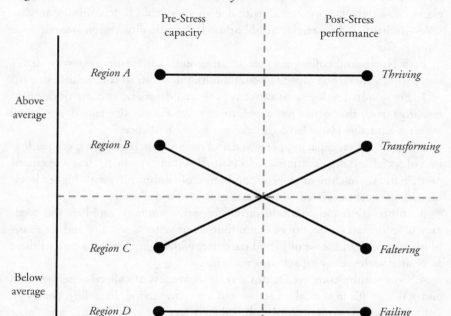

Source: Author.

faltered, underperforming expectations based on its above-average, pre-stress capacity. Earlier work corroborates such patterns, finding that some regions "rise to the occasion," exceeding expectations in performance based on pre-stress capacity and, alternatively, that other regions underperform based on pre-stress capacity levels and expectations.[14]

Conceiving Capacities

The literature on resilience capacity identifies a range of resources, attributes, and actions enabling individuals, households, and broader communities to effectively respond to a stress. There are three conceptual tasks for understanding pre-stress capacities as an element of regional resilience: (1) theorizing what

14. Foster (2000).

factors constitute general or specific capacity in the face of a stress; (2) contemplating how these factors interact with one another; and (3) determining at what scale—individual, household, neighborhood, municipality, region—to measure capacity factors.

Fran Norris and colleagues turn to an extensive literature review to distill four sets of generalized capacities communities draw on to cope with a stress:[15]

1. Economic development capacity: volume, diversity, and distribution of resources, such that better resourced, more economically diversified, and more resource-equitable places have greater capacity for resilience.

2. Social capital capacity: perceived and received social support, embeddedness of social and organizational links (formal and informal ties), levels of citizen participation, attachment to place, and sense of community, with higher levels on each of these associated with greater capacity for resilience.

3. Information and communications capacity: amount, rapidity, and accuracy of information, quality of communications systems, quality and responsibility of media, and sense of shared narrative, with higher levels on each of these associated with greater capacity for resilience.

4. Community competence capacity: effectiveness of collective deliberation and action, skills in critical reflection and problem solving, flexibility, creativity, collective empowerment, and political partnerships, with higher and more strategic levels of each of these associated with greater capacity for resilience.

Additional factors likely matter for specific types of stress, such as natural or economic disasters. In their study of regional readiness for a flood, earthquake, hurricane, or other natural disaster, for example, Susan Cutter and colleagues identify over thirty capacity indicators germane to resilience in the face of a natural disturbance.[16] These fall into five categories, namely social resilience (indicators of demographics, mobility, and health), economic resilience (indicators of employment and income, industrial character, and property ownership), institutional resilience (indicators of planning, mitigation, and organizational readiness specifically for a natural disaster), infrastructure resilience (indicators of shelter, medical, educational, and other emergency facilities), and community capital resilience (indicators of place attachment, civic engagement, and social connectivity). Research by Edward Hill and colleagues in this volume identifies capacity indicators such as the level of durable goods manufacturing and the number of export-based sectors as relevant to resilience in the face of a regional economic stress.[17]

15. Norris and others. (2008).
16. Cutter, Burton, and Emrich (2010, p. 5).
17. See chapter 6 in this volume by Hill and others.

A third challenge in assessing resilience capacity is the question of scope. A region is a complex construct, at once a geographic, social, economic, and political system of interacting individuals, households, businesses, structures, organizations, and processes. At any time some but not all of these individuals, households, businesses, and so forth may be prepared for stresses to come—that is, have capacity to respond effectively and recover well from disturbances—but others will not. On the logic that a region is resilient only to the level of its least-resilient link, one way to conceive resilience capacity is to measure it at the individual level. Emerging work by Rolf Pendall and colleagues points to the vulnerability of individuals (from disability or poverty, for example), the precariousness of their conditions (living in substandard housing, for instance), and the turbulence of their broader environments (situated in drought- or earthquake-prone places, for example) as elements of a region's resilience capacity.[18] Regional actors can thus increase regional resilience by addressing any of the conditions—individual vulnerability, housing precariousness, or environmental turbulence.

Findings from case study research suggest that the link between pre-stress capacity and post-stress resilience performance is more complex than simple trend lines suggest. Rather than single capacity variables driving resilience, for example, it may be that the interplay and networking of these capacities and their accumulative impact are most salient. Building community resilience requires a combination of steps to, in the words of one research team, "reduce risk and resource inequities, engage local people in mitigation, create organizational linkages, boost and protect social supports, and plan for not having a plan, which requires flexibility, decision-making skills, and trusted sources of information that function in the face of unknowns."[19] Such findings, combined with limitations of national datasets, imply that both methodologically and in practice, understanding and building community resilience is complicated, requiring considerable technical, cultural, and governance resources and coordination.

Three conclusions emerge from the assessment of resilience capacity. First, for an online multiregion assessment tool, general rather than specific indicators of resilience capacity are of greatest use. Second, a multi-stress, multiregion resilience index is not conducive to untangling capacity factor interactions, although it will be possible, as this chapter later demonstrates, to assess the relative strength of a region's capacity factors. Finally, notwithstanding the potential to change regional resilience at the individual or housing unit level, to the

18. Pendall, Theodos, and Franks (2010).

19. Norris and others (2008, article abstract). The authors also conclude that resilience is an abstraction "whose value lies not in whether it can be easily captured and quantified but in whether it leads to novel hypotheses about the characteristics of—and relations between—stressors, various adaptive capacities, and wellness over time" (Norris and others 2008, p. 146).

degree that resilience performance metrics are measured at the regional scale, it makes methodological sense to measure resilience capacity at that scale also.

Conceiving Stress

The study of resilience presumes a stress. While typically portrayed as a negative disturbance to a person or region—an urban riot, flood, or recession, for example—positive disturbances, such as metropolitan growth, winning the lottery, or hosting the Olympic Games, are conceptually similar. Both types of stress strain a region or person and both imply the need for recovery.

More significant for conceptual purposes is a second kind of distinction between stress types. The walker vignette offers a prime example of an "acute shock," the type of stress occurring at a single moment over a short period, even if the recovery period lingers. Acute shocks are the basis for disaster studies, which focus on preparation for and recovery from blizzards, terrorist attacks, and other point-in-time natural or man-made disasters. Distinct from these are "chronic stresses," slow burn challenges such as prolonged economic decline, the suburbanization of poverty, or the aging of society that play out over comparatively long time periods from months to decades.[20]

It is technically easier to measure before and after conditions for an acute, one-time shock than for a chronic stress. Chronic stresses tend to have a fuzzy beginning, middle, and end and may exhibit a "two steps forward, one step back" pattern of change. Also making chronic stresses harder to evaluate is the difficulty of isolating their impacts from those of many other stresses and events occurring over any extended time period. One possible approach is to conceive of chronic stresses as a series of acute stresses occurring over time. Sound measurement of pre-stress capacity and post-stress performance, however, would be impossible given the timing of data releases and the burden of isolating variables.

Further complicating measurement and understanding of pre-stress capacity and post-stress performance are notions of time. While some chronic stresses, such as a national economic recession, may hit every region at roughly the same time, other chronic and most acute stresses only rarely affect places simultaneously. Consider, for example, the stress on physical systems and economic activities of building a major mass transit system. While many regions have built transit systems over the past century, the fact that urban size, density, transit governance, fiscal and policy conditions, and technologies have changed so appreciably over time makes it impossible without detailed case studies to com-

---

20. Rae (2004) and Diamond (2005) focus on responses to chronic stresses, with the former examining long waves of urban change and the latter slow-moving environmental trends.

pare resilience experiences fairly across regions. Even for a selection of metropolitan regions opening a system from the mid-1970s to mid-1990s—San Francisco BART in 1972, Washington, D.C., Metro in 1976, Miami Metrorail in 1984, and Los Angeles Metro in 1993, for example—the varied size, breadth, funding arrangements, and community characteristics of these transit efforts varied sufficiently to complicate resilience measurement and interpretation.

Many challenges, moreover, are unique. New York City's recovery from the 2001 terrorist attack or the 2010 mudslides in southern Mexico offer no sound comparison over time and place, even though these and other regions have experienced similar shocks. Fair comparisons require researchers to identify sufficiently similar stresses occurring at roughly the same time. This restriction necessarily decreases the number of observations for analyses, rendering some resilience performance comparisons impossible.

A final consideration in conceiving stress is magnitude. It makes sense intuitively that the harder a person or place is hit, the greater the resilience challenge. Consider the case of snowstorms. Most would agree that regions with the most inches of snowfall in a storm—twenty-four inches compared to twelve inches, say—are most stressed, given the need for more or heavier plows, road salt, and emergency personnel to cope with the storm. But consider additionally the *commonality* of the stress. If a familiar stress is less debilitating than a rare or one-time shock, then twelve inches of snow dumped on Baltimore or Washington, D.C., would constitute a greater strain than twelve inches of snow in Buffalo or Minneapolis, places relatively accustomed to managing winter precipitation. Most observers might expect snow-tested regions to show superior resilience capacity and performance not only for the same magnitude of snow stress but for even greater magnitude of snow given the frequency of snow storms, experience with snow removal, greater investment in and trained labor to manage heavy plows, cultural familiarity with snowstorm practices, and more ample piles of road salt. Is it fair to judge the Baltimore or Washington regions' resilience to the "Snowmageddon of 2010" by the standards of Minneapolis or Buffalo? By that same token, should Minneapolis or Buffalo need a greater stress or a greater recovery to meet resilience expectations in a snowstorm? Is it fair or reasonable to evaluate resilience differently for a highly conditioned and athletic, all-season walker with hard-as-rock abs versus an occasional seasonal stroller?

Conceiving Performance

Resilience performance is, as its name implies, a concept of actuality rather than potential. Evidenced only after the stress, performance measures not whether the region has the capacity to respond effectively to and recover from a stress, but rather whether it does. Assessing such performance raises three key conceptual questions: (1) absolute or relative resilience performance? (2) measured by what performance factors? and (3) recovering over what time period?

Question 1: Absolute or Relative Resilience?

Resilience can be thought of as an absolute or relative concept. Relative conceptions are easiest for assessment, given the lighter data requirements and ease of interpreting interregional comparisons. But absolute concepts have a purer standing in theory and perhaps reflect better the intent of the resilience paradigm. Consider the case of three metropolitan regions, A, B, and C, each suffering an economic stress, as illustrated by the stress "hit" in figure 2-3. The dotted lines illustrate the recovery responses of each region, with Region A more than offsetting its stress loss, Region B recovering some of its stress loss, and Region C recovering none of its stress loss and in fact continuing to decline in performance.

Conceiving of resilience in absolute terms requires determination of a threshold performance recovery associated with the label of "resilient." For example, any region recovering at least 50 percent of its stress loss might be deemed resilient. Regions that do not achieve this recovery threshold are not resilient. In this instance, regions A and B fall into the resilient category while region C is labeled not resilient. Much like the U.S. poverty threshold based on a fixed income level—below the threshold a person lives in poverty, above the level the person does not—the threshold level itself controls the number of regions falling into the resilient or not resilient categories. Changing the threshold, say, to require the region to fully recover 100 percent or more of its pre-stress performance to earn the label "resilient," would accordingly change the number of resilient regions. Just as policy analysts create additional categories for poverty—income below 50 percent of the poverty line is "severe poverty," for example—researchers or policymakers using an absolute definition of resilience could more fully differentiate regions by creating categories of "non-resilience," "low resilience," "medium resilience," or "high resilience" based on the percentage of stress impact the region recovers.

In contrast, resilience performance could be conceived in relative rather than absolute terms. By this approach, Region A is more resilient than Region B, which is in turn more resilient than Region C, regardless of their absolute performance in recovering from the stress. A resilience index ranking metropolitan regions from highest to lowest or dividing them into quintiles, as the Brookings *MetroMonitor* does in assessing performance of metropolitan regions in coping with the current economic recession, employs such a relative definition of resilience.[21]

21. Wial and Shearer (2011).

Figure 2-3. *Assessing Absolute or Relative Resilience*

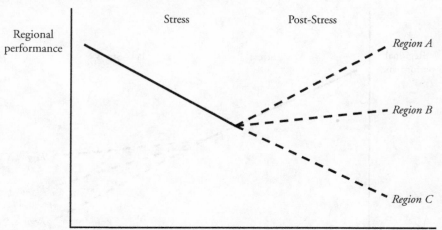

Source: Author.

Although easy to interpret and widely appreciated by regional leaders seeking to know how their resilience levels compare to that of other regions, a relative conception of resilience can yield curious results. Consider, for example, regional resilience for metropolitan regions X, Y and Z, as shown in figure 2-4. None of the regions has recovered any of its stress impact, with each declining in the post-stress period. A relative conception of resilience nonetheless ranks Region X as most resilient, even while it was not, in an absolute sense, resilient. A similar dilemma of interpretation arises if all regions in a group recover fully, thus achieving the classification of "resilient" on an absolute scale, but necessarily deeming one-fifth of the group as "lowest 20 percent" in rank.

One challenge to both the absolute and relative conceptions of resilience is that they ignore the pre-stress state of a region in considering its recovery from a stress. If pre-stress conditions come into account, resilience classifications, rankings, and interpretations warrant adjustment. Consider again the case of Region C, which is not resilient either in absolute terms or relative to other regions. But suppose that Region C was faltering in advance of the economic stress as shown in figure 2-5. The stress accelerated its decline. Because Region C did not recover any percentage of this stress loss, it can be labeled non-resilient. Note, though, that Region C's post-stress recovery performance is superior to its pre-stress performance, that is, its declines have lessened, as might be true for an economy in which job loss continues but at a slower pace. Taking into account pre-stress performance could imply that Region C, while not

Figure 2-4. *Assessing Absolute or Relative Resilience*

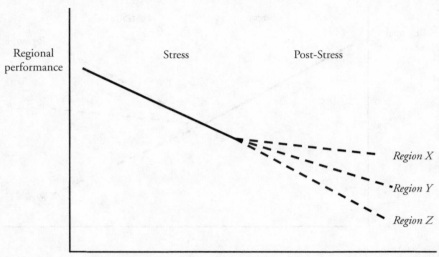

Source: Author.

resilient absolutely or relative to its peers, nonetheless exhibited impressive resilience performance relative to its history.

Although there is no right or wrong version of resilience, there is a burden on researchers, policymakers, and developers of resilience indexes to specify which approach applies. Both because research establishing absolute regional resilience levels does not exist and because regional comparisons are a central purpose of the analysis, the resilience index project uses relative resilience performance to convey its results.

Question 2: Resilience of What?

A second resilience performance question asks what variables constitute good indicators of resilience performance. Resilience performance of the individual walker, for example, could be measured by the amount and pace of physical recovery of stomach muscles, the rapidity with which the walker returns to walking, the degree to which trust of other walkers returns to pre-punch levels, or by system variables such as emergency vehicle response times or the quality of hospital care.

Michel Bruneau and his colleagues identify four categories for place-based resilience performance, each with numerous possible indicators.[22] These are:

22. Bruneau and others (2003). The authors' primary interest is in resilience in the face of acute disasters such as earthquakes or hurricanes.

Figure 2-5. *Interpreting Pre- and Post-Stress Performance*

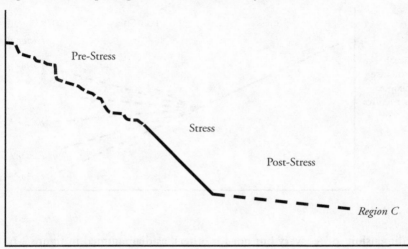

Source: Author.

1. Technical, encompassing measures of natural and physical systems and infrastructure;

2. Organizational, including assessment of governance systems and service delivery;

3. Economic, measuring fiscal capacity and market functioning; and

4. Social, bridging both community relations and individual recovery measures.

A community's resilience to an earthquake, for instance, might be evaluated by the viability of its bridges, levees, and power supplies (technical performance), the number and coverage of disaster assistance centers set up after the disaster (organizational performance), the percentage of grocery stores and businesses that stay open and retain jobs (economic performance), and the morale of affected individuals in the wake of the crisis (social performance). Brookings's New Orleans Index, which tracks rebuilding progress in the wake of Hurricane Katrina, takes such an approach.[23]

This scheme implies that researchers and policymakers must consider a daunting number of indicators to assess resilience performance, measured potentially at multiple points following the stress. Complicating an already complex condition is the likelihood that a place or person may be resilient for

23. Liu and Plyer (2010).

Figure 2-6. *Varied Performance of Resilience Factors*

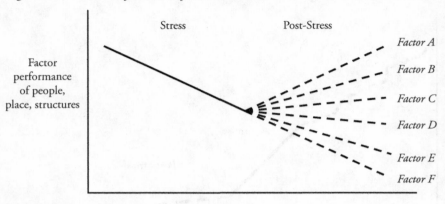

Source: Author.

some dimensions of recovery but not for others, as diagrammed in figure 2-6. Mass transit capacity and hospital systems in an earthquake-challenged region may show remarkable resilience, for example, thanks to forethought and investments that reduced earthquake vulnerability prior to the disaster. But other regional dimensions, such as consumer spending, job recovery, or governance capacity, may prove non-resilient to the earthquake, faltering in the wake of the disaster and perhaps never again achieving pre-stress levels. Similarly, in response to an economic stress a region might achieve fiscal resilience—measured perhaps by debt levels, revenue increases, or reduction in expenditures—by laying off workers and raising taxes and fees. Such fiscal resilience could well come at the expense of social resilience, however, if layoffs and higher fees exacerbate conditions of poverty and income inequality.[24] A cohesive story line is thus difficult for regions exhibiting mixed performance across different resilience factors. One performance factor, say, job growth, may return to its pre-stress level, while another, such as income growth, may stagnate or decline. Without value judgments—which matters more, job growth or income growth?—there is no simple statement about resilience performance.

One resolution in practice is to disaggregate resilience performance into its individual factors, drawing conclusions about the resilience of a particular group, system, or facility, but not about resilience of the region as a whole.

24. Of course, the diagram has already simplified a more complex reality. The pre-stress performance for these factors (not shown) likely varied, with some factors on the ascendance and others in decline. Each factor would also exhibit a different stress experience; some factors might be unaffected by the stress while others feel the stress to different degrees. In the chapter by Hill and others in this volume, the authors recognize this reality in considering stress resistance before measuring stress performance.

Because any single stress could generate dozens of individual resilience scores, one for each technical, organizational, economic, or social attribute of interest, summary reports would yield findings in a form such as this: "The region was resilient on eighteen of thirty-three indicators and not resilient on the other fifteen of thirty-three." Not surprisingly, many purveyors of multiple-measure concepts, such as *Places Rated Almanac* and college rankings from *U.S. News and World Report*, seek to simplify their results by computing an aggregate multifactor index value and simultaneously report underlying values for individual factor performance.

Similarly, there are trade-offs in resilience performance. By downsizing its operations and offshoring three-quarters of its workforce, for example, a firm may make itself resilient to global fiscal and economic strains. Yet these actions may diminish resilience performance not only for the firm's workers but also for the firm's local suppliers (who lose business), for municipal, county, and state governments (whose tax revenues fall), and for the region more generally (by loss of a major employer). Likewise, actions or policies to increase the resilience of low-wage workers to economic stress—living wage policies, extended unemployment benefits, and social supports, for instance—can diminish the resilience performance of business owners, state and federal government, and other people or organizations made less well off by the benefits provided to low-wage workers. Such tradeoffs, which are inherent in policy questions, imply underlying value choices by decisionmakers to benefit one group, issue, or time period—say long-term over short-term—in assessing impacts.

A final conceptual dilemma is that individual factor performance will fluctuate before and after—and perhaps regardless—of a stress. Consider a performance indicator, say, "health benefits of walking," which exhibits a positive trajectory before a stomach punch, a negative "hit" during the stress period, and renewed positive performance shortly after the stomach blow. A logical interpretation would be that a decline in health benefits during the stress period stems from the stress itself, that is, the punch was a setback to what is otherwise a steady trend of increasing walking benefits, bump aside. Consider, though, the behavior of three measures exhibiting different before-, during-, and after-stress patterns. One measure, the walker's income, continues a steady upward trajectory starting before and continuing during and after the stress. A second, the walker's bowling scores, does the opposite, continuing a steady downward trend before and after the stress. A third measure, the walker's frequency of text messages to friends, holds steady. While each factor exhibits a different trend, one conclusion might be that none is affected by the stomach stress. Yet although these indicators appear to be stress-resistant or insusceptible to the stress, it's impossible to say. Perhaps the walker was resolving during the stroll to slow down the pace of text messages to friends, but the stress of the surprise assault delayed putting that resolution into action. Or perhaps the walker's steadily rising income was about to level off, but a sympathetic boss kept the raises coming on hearing about the traumatic walking incident.

The point is that performance indicators measured before and after a stress will likely register some change. Whether or not that change is attributable to a certain stress, however, is hard to say. Regional analysts are challenged to determine how much variation in, say, gross metropolitan product, housing affordability, or social service cases stems from a specific stress and not from other internal or external factors or events, such as business cycles, new laws, or poor management. This situation especially affects chronic stresses, which play out in complex regions with multiple actors, events, and policies. Measurement to support a resilience index, therefore, necessarily inclines researchers toward assessing resilience performance for acute stresses, such as stomach blows, and away from chronic forces such as economic transformation.

Question 3: Recovery over What Time?

Finally, how long shall we give our sucker-punched stroller to recover from the blow? What is a reasonable time period for demonstrating resilience to this or any other stress? Does faster recovery signal greater resilience? Is a person or place deemed resilient only after recovery from all aspects of the stress? Or might resilience emerge gradually as different elements recover from stress? Such questions raise conceptual (and, as we shall see in the next section, methodological) issues.

Different aspects of a person or place have different periodicities for recovery. It might take a generation or more to repair an ecosystem or social indicator knocked back by a stress, but less than a year for an economic or infrastructure indicator. One approach to determining recovery times is to calculate norms and averages from the universe of regions or people encountering such a stress. This approach is common with people and structures: physicians, for example, provide pre-, during- and post-stress norms for surgery recovery; teachers calculate averages for exam performance; and engineers generate stress-recovery data for bridges and tunnels. Although identifying norms for regions is conceptually similar, the database for calculating such norms is notably less rich than that for medical, educational, and infrastructural performance.

It is clear, nonetheless, that time plays a central role in recovery from distress. In tracking post-traumatic stress disorder in individuals following the 2010 floods and mudslides in Mexico and the September 11 terrorist attacks in New York City, Norris and colleagues formulated six possible stress responses—one labeled "resilience" in a more particular sense than used in the Building Resilient

Figure 2-7. *Resilience Trajectories*

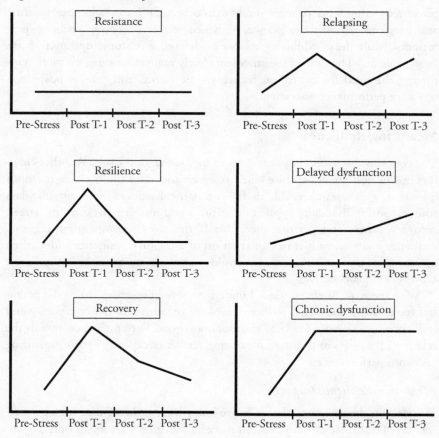

Source: Norris, Tracey and Galea (2009).

Regions research—each distinguished by a specific trajectory over time.[25] As diagrammed in figure 2-7, in which the y-axis tracks levels of stress, these are (1) resistance (signifying no appreciable symptoms of disaster-prompted stress); (2) resilience (relatively rapid and complete bounce-back after significant stress); (3) recovery (gradual return of function after significant stress); (4) relapsing (short-term recovery followed by return to stress condition); (5) delayed dysfunction (apparent resistance followed after a period by disaster-related stress; and (6) chronic dysfunction (persistence of the initial stress reaction).

25. Norris, Tracey, and Galea (2009).

Regions exhibit similar types of resilience performance trajectories, with some places recovering faster or more surely than others. Differences in nomenclature aside, regions exhibiting resistance, resilience, and recovery are "resilient" performers, while those exhibiting relapse or delayed or chronic dysfunction are "non-resilient." The time of measurement clearly matters for categorization, reinforcing the need for clarity on recovery time norms and care in post-stress resilience performance assessment.

Measuring Resilience

The concepts discussion implies a host of methodological issues. As other chapters in this volume attest, case study research addresses the trickiest methods questions, with researchers able to draw on particularities of place, singular data sources, and individually applied definitions and measures of capacity, stress, recovery times, and performance. But if the aim is comparative regional resilience analysis, as it is in construction of a regional resilience index, then assumptions and conventions, as employed below, are necessary to generate cross-region insights.

With these qualifiers in mind, I undertook several exercises to test the potential for creating a regional resilience tool for revealing resilience capacity and resilience performance for U.S. metropolitan areas. The application reveals the relative advantages and ease of measuring resilience capacity versus measuring resilience performance.

Measuring Resilience Capacity

Drawing on the literature, the resilience index team gathered data for a generalized set of resilience capacity indicators useful to regional actors regardless of the type of stress encountered.[26] As in other empirical research, data availability restricted the variables tested, with indicators gauging adaptability, flexibility, anticipation, trust, and preparation especially troublesome for quantitative analyses.[27]

26. Especially helpful are Cutter, Burton, and Emrich (2010) and Sherrieb, Norris, and Galea (2010). Evolution of resilience capacity variables is evident in the Resilience Capacity Index, now online at http://brr.berkeley.edu/rci.

27. In their study of community resilience, Sherrieb, Norris, and Galea (2010) whittled a "wish list" of eighty-eight variables of economic development and social capital to seventeen that were sufficiently available, accurate, distinctive, and reliable. The researchers gave up on measuring information and communications and on community competence on grounds they "were characterized more by processes (for example, communication network formation, decisionmaking, and consensus building) that are possible to measure but not with archival secondary data" (Sherrieb, Norris, and Galea 2010, p. 2).

Table 2-1. *Variables by Dimension, 2009*

Category	Variable	Definition	Data source
Regional economic capacity	Economic diversity	Inverse of sum of absolute deviations of metropolitan area from all-metropolitan area average for goods-producing, service-producing, and government jobs	Bureau of Labor Statistics, Quarterly Census of Employment and Wages
	Income	Median household income in last twelve months, inflation-adjusted	American Community Survey, table B19013
	Income distribution	Inverse of Gini coefficient of income inequality	American Community Survey, table B19083
Sociodemographic capacity	Education	Ratio of population aged 25+ with bachelor's degree/ without high school diploma	American Community Survey, calculated from tables 15003–21 15003–21
	Working age	Percent population aged 18–64	American Community Survey, table B01001
	Ability	Percent population without a disability	American Community Survey, table B18101
	Poverty	Percent population above the poverty line	American Community Survey, table B17001
Community connection capacity	Familiarity	Percent population born in state	American Community Survey, table B05002
	Linguistic connection	Percent population not linguistically isolated	American Community Survey, table B16002
	Housing	Percent housing built before 1970	American Community Survey, table B25034

The variables selected for this exercise fall into three groups, as shown in table 2-1.[28] Regional economic capacity variables capture aspects of the region's industrial structure and the economic wherewithal of its population. Employment diversity gauges how far the distribution of employment in a metropolitan

28. The ten variables are a subset of a broader group of general resilience indicators prepared for the resilience capacity index. Note that resilience capacity studies for a specific type of stress, such as a natural disaster, would also include particular indicators of capacity, such as hospital accessibility, percent of population covered by a recent hazard mitigation plan, or water quantity and pressure for fire suppression. Studies including particular measures include Cutter, Burton, and Emrich (2010), Lansford and others (2010), and Zahren and others (2008). For present purposes, the ten indicators offer a sufficient group to test methods and suggest findings.

region is from that of all U.S. metropolitan areas combined; I assume that high diversity represents greater capacity for resilience. Just as a financial portfolio with all its eggs in one stock basket leaves the investor vulnerable to market shocks, so does an industrial portfolio that specializes in one or a limited few industries leave a region open to economic vulnerabilities in times of sector downturn. In addition, the level of median household income measures regional economic resources. Because more resources permit more options for combating and responding to a disturbance, higher median income signals the presence of a regional cushion for the unexpected and the potential for post-stress responses of greater magnitude. Income inequality, measured by the metropolitan-level Gini coefficient, conveys intraregional disparity across income groups. Because social cohesion is important in times of disaster, I assume that regions with wider income disparities would have lower capacity for resilience.[29]

Four variables capture elements of sociodemographic resilience. Education levels, measured in this instance by the ratio of the population aged twenty-five years and over with a bachelor's degree to those without a high school diploma, reflect the notion that persons with higher education are more flexible and options-rich in the face of a regional stress.[30] Similar reasoning pertains for variables measuring the percentage of the population in working age cohorts, those without physical or mental disabilities, and those living above the poverty line. In all instances, I assume that these characteristics are associated with greater capacity to effectively respond to a crisis mentally, physically, or materially.

The three community connection variables measure how familiar with and loyal to a regional community its members are. The share of the region's residents born in the state implies a general understanding of and potential commitment to place, a capacity factor useful in responding to regional stress. Lin-

29. In their metropolitan-level analysis of economic resilience, Hill and others find no statistically significant relationship between a Herfindahl index of industrial diversity and economic resilience measured by bounceback in either employment or GMP (see tables 6-7 and 6-8 in chapter 6 of this volume). Notably, metropolitan areas with a higher percentage of employment in either durable manufacturing or tourism-related industries—a potential measure of industrial specialization—have higher economic resilience measured by employment (this does not hold for GMP), a finding explained for durable manufacturing by the cyclical nature of these industries. Because the logic of diversification is not to maximize high performance, but to reduce risk of low performance, the lack of a link between industrial diversity and economic resilience is understandable. Diversification tempers extremes—holders of a diversified portfolio should expect less severe losses and less impressive gains than would be expected from a more specialized industrial portfolio. Hill and others' findings on income inequality support the hypothesis that greater income inequality reduces economic resilience, but only when measured by employment rather than GMP.

30. Findings by Hill and others (see tables 6-7 and 6-8 in chapter six of this volume) do not support this hypothesis, although the different measures used to gauge educational attainment make verification impossible. They found that the higher the proportion of the population with a high school degree or less, the more economically resilient the region when measured by employment (no effect for GMP).

guistic connection, measured by the percentage of households that have at least one adult member who speaks English "very well," offers a capacity for comprehension in the time of crisis, including the potential to give and receive emergency communications by newspaper, radio, or TV.[31] Like place stability, the share of the region's housing built before 1970 represents community stability, a contrast to the unfamiliarity with place associated with a large proportion of newly built housing stock and subdivisions.[32]

The resilience scores shown in table 2-2 result from a process of data rescaling and aggregation for the universe of 360 U.S. metropolitan areas as defined by the U.S. Office of Management and Budget and reported in data from the American Community Survey and other sources. Variables were defined and measured to ensure that a high value would correspond to greater resilience capacity. For example, data measure the population above, rather than below, the poverty line given that non-poverty, rather than poverty, is associated with higher resilience capacity. A similar convention required using the inverse of the Gini coefficient to ensure that higher levels of income inequality signal lower resilience capacity. To create a comparable and comprehensible assessment scheme across wide-ranging variable types, values on each variable were translated into z-scores. The z-score for any region represents the number of standard deviations the region falls above (positive values) or below (negative values) the all-region mean. The "total resilience capacity score" is the simple average of z-scores for all ten capacity variables equally weighted. The resilience capacity score for each dimension is the average of the z-score values for each variable underlying that dimension, three for regional economic resilience, four for sociodemographic resilience, and three for community connection resilience.

Findings shown in table 2-2 reveal patterns of resilience and support this methodology as a basis for a resilience capacity index. In this test, Rochester, MN, emerges as the highest-ranked metropolitan area, with an average of .91 standard deviations above the regional mean for the ten capacity factors. Rounding out the top five are Ames, IA; Madison, WI; Minneapolis-St. Paul-Bloomington, MN-WI; and Burlington-South Burlington, VT. Each achieves a high rank on the strength of its sociodemographic capacity, which tends to be high in college towns

31. From data on the language spoken at home and the level of English proficiency, the U.S. Census Bureau constructs a linguistic isolation variable at the household level. A linguistically isolated household is one in which all members age fourteen years and over speak a non-English language and also speak English less than "very well." Linguistic connection in the current study is measured as the inverse of linguistic isolation, that is, "not linguistically isolated."

32. A counterargument holds that places with more new housing have experienced recent growth, a sign of regional vitality and thus regional capacity. From the perspective of infrastructural resilience, Cutter, Burton, and Emrich (2010, p. 9) see the proportion of housing built before 1970 or after 1994 as having a negative effect on resilience capacity, judging these stocks to be more vulnerable in a disaster.

Table 2-2. *Metropolitan Areas with Most and Least Capacity for Resilience*

Rank	Metropolitan area	Total resilience capacity score[a]	Regional economic capacity[b]	Socio-demographic capacity[c]	Community connection capacity[d]
Most resilience capacity					
1	Rochester, MN	0.91	0.96	1.46	0.14
2	Ames, IA	0.88	−0.83	2.59	0.31
3	Madison, WI	0.85	0.41	1.64	0.24
4	Minneapolis-St. Paul-Bloomington, MN-WI	0.84	1.01	1.26	0.12
5	Burlington-South Burlington, VT	0.83	0.95	1.27	0.11
6	Sioux Falls, SD	0.81	1.11	0.47	0.96
7	Washington-Arlington-Alexandria, DC-VA-MD-WV	0.80	1.64	1.42	−0.87
8	Appleton, WI	0.79	0.55	1.01	0.73
9	Bloomington-Normal, IL	0.78	0.49	1.28	0.41
10	Cedar Rapids, IA	0.78	0.73	0.83	0.77
Least resilience capacity					
1	McAllen-Edinburg-Mission, TX	−1.98	−1.26	−2.09	−2.54
2	Brownsville-Harlingen, TX	−1.66	−1.40	−1.93	−1.57
3	El Centro, CA	−1.64	−1.82	−1.22	−2.01
4	Elmira, NY	−1.57	−1.90	−1.03	−1.96
5	Merced, CA	−1.33	−1.38	−1.34	−1.27
6	Yuma, AZ	−1.31	−0.62	−1.28	−2.02
7	Dalton, GA	−1.14	−1.37	−1.15	−0.91
8	Las Cruces, NM	−1.13	−0.83	−0.93	−1.71
9	Visalia-Porterville, CA	−1.07	−1.42	−0.92	−0.93
10	Laredo, TX	−1.02	−0.34	−1.77	−0.53

Source: Author's calculations from data identified in table 2-1.
a. Average z-score for all capacity variables (10).
b. Average z-score for regional economic capacity variables (3).
c. Average z-score for sociodemographic capacity variables (4).
d. Average z-score for community connection variables (3).

such as these and offsets relatively lower resilience capacity in the regional economic and community connection dimensions. Metropolitan areas with low resilience capacity—led by McAllen-Edinburg-Allen, TX, with an average z-score of nearly two standard deviations below the mean for the ten capacity variables—are uniformly lacking across each of the three dimensions. Notably, the magnitude of negative capacity scores is nearly double that of the magnitude of positive scores for the high-ranking metropolitan areas, which is to say that the lows are lower than the highs are high in this test of resilience capacity.

The data in tables 2-3 and 2-4 offer additional insights. Overall, findings reinforce the utility and versatility of the resilience index methodology, while underlining the significance and ambiguity of variable interpretation. Table 2-3 identifies the top and bottom five regions by resilience capacity by dimension, demonstrating that regions may have high levels of one but not necessarily other types of resilience capacity. There are no repeat regions among the top five regions across the three dimensions and only one repeat, McAllen-Edinburg-Allen, TX, among the lowest five regions in each dimension. The regional economic variables reveal the potential for within-state economic variation, given that New York, California, and, to a slightly lesser degree, West Virginia, each has metropolitan areas in the highest and lowest ranks of regional economic resilience capacity. The sociodemographic variables in this model favor college towns, reinforcing the resilience capacity of communities with dominant higher education institutions.[33] The community connection variables favor older, slow-growing regions over faster-growing ones with high levels of newcomers and linguistically isolated residents. This implies that communities with more non-English-speaking residents are less resilient, a finding reflecting recent work by Robert Putnam showing a reduction in social solidarity, at least in the short term, as places diversify racially and ethnically.[34] An alternative view connecting resilience to regional accommodations for new immigrant communities is represented in this volume's chapter by Manuel Pastor and John Mollenkopf.

The data in table 2-4, which show resilience capacity scores for the ten most populous metropolitan regions, reveal another feature of resilience capacity analysis. At least for these ten indicators of capacity, population size is not associated with high or low resilience capacity. Resilience capacity rankings for large metropolitan areas with populations above 1 million vary from Washington-Arlington-Alexandria, DC-MD-VA-WV (average z-score of 0.80 and rank of 7 for all metropolitan areas), to Miami-Fort Lauderdale-Pompano Beach, FL (average z-score of -0.83 and rank of 342). Here, too, the underlying subdimension scores provide nuance. The Washington metropolitan area achieves its relatively high resilience despite a community connection capacity score below the metropolitan average, a predictable outcome for a national capital city with high transience. Similarly, the New York-Northern New Jersey, Long Island, NY-NJ-PA, metropolitan area achieves a midlevel rank on the strength of its above-average sociodemographic capacity, which offsets below-average regional economic and community connection capacity.

33. Each of the top five metropolitan areas hosts a large public university.
34. Putnam (2007).

Table 2-3. *Metropolitan Areas with Most and Least Resilience Capacity, by Dimension*

	Regional economic		Sociodemographic		Community connection	
Rank	Metropolitan area	Score[a]	Metropolitan area	Score[a]	Metropolitan area	Score[a]
Most resilient						
1	Anchorage, AK	1.69	Ames, IA	2.59	Johnstown, PA	1.92
2	Washington-Arlington-Alexandria, DC-VA-MD-WV	1.64	Lawrence, KS	2.51	Bay City, MI	1.72
3	Poughkeepsie-Newburgh-Middleton, NY	1.36	Boulder, CO	2.23	Altoona, PA	1.71
4	Vallejo-Porterville, CA	1.33	Corvallis, OR	1.95	Elkhart-Goshen, IN	1.63
5	Fairbanks, AK	1.26	Iowa City, IA	1.85	Danville, IL	1.63
Least resilient						
1	College Station, TX	-2.24	McAllen-Edinburg-Mission, TX	-2.09	McAllen-Edinburg-Mission, TX	-2.54
2	Elmira, NY	-1.90	Brownsville-Harlingen, TX	-1.93	Las Vegas-Paradise, NV	-2.17
3	El Centro, CA	-1.82	Laredo, TX	-1.77	Naples-Marco Island, FL	-2.16
4	Gainesville, FL	-1.72	Merced, CA	-1.34	Miami-Fort Lauderdale-Pompano Beach, FL	-2.11
5	Morgantown, WV	-1.58	Pine Bluff, AR	-1.32	Yuma, AZ	-2.02

Source: Author's calculations from data identified in table 2-1.

a. Values are average z-scores for all variables in dimension category.

Table 2-4. *Resilience Capacity Scores for Ten Most Populous Metropolitan Areas, by Resilience Rank*

| Metropolitan area | Resilience capacity score | Rank (of 360 metropolitan areas) | Capacity scores, by dimension[a] | | |
			Regional economic	Sociodemographic	Community connection
Washington-Arlington-Alexandria, DC-VA-MD-WV	0.80	7	1.64	1.42	-0.87
Boston-Cambridge-Quincy, MA-NH	0.72	15	0.60	1.13	0.29
Philadelphia-Camden-Wilmington, PA-NJ-DE-MD	0.40	78	0.31	0.39	0.51
Chicago-Naperville-Joliet, IL-IN-WI	0.35	90	0.40	0.53	0.05
New York-Northern NJ-Long Island, NY-NJ-PA	0.13	151	-0.05	0.50	-0.19
Atlanta-Sandy-Springs-Marietta, GA	0.10	156	0.36	0.62	-0.84
Dallas-Fort Worth, TX	-0.06	208	0.32	0.32	-0.95
Los Angeles-Long Beach-Santa Ana, CA	-0.07	213	0.30	0.33	-0.97
Houston-Sugar Land-Baytown, TX	-0.26	263	-0.02	0.22	-1.16
Miami-Fort Lauderdale-Pompano Beach, FL	-0.83	342	-0.61	-0.04	-2.11

Source: Author's calculations from data identified in table 2-1.

a. Values are average z-scores for all variables in dimension category.

The resilience capacity exercise discloses the importance of careful indicator selection and interpretation. Sensitivity tests by indicator suggest findings are susceptible to variable selection, a concern addressed in part by adding capacity variables to the analysis. The index formulation also reinforces the problem of data availability. Data for several often-purported elements of capacity, including the nature of internal and external relationships, the quality and cross-border compatibility of a region's communications infrastructure, and how well regional actors anticipate coming stresses, are simply not available in national databases, and the usefulness of substitute variables used here and in other studies is uncertain.

Measuring Resilience Performance

Recalling our spring walker, the ultimate question of resilience performance is not solely how able or prepared the walker is to withstand the blow, but how well the walker bounces back to recover from it. To test the degree of resilience performance requires three measurement tasks: identifying stress and recovery indicators (the set of metrics gauging stress and response), calculating a resilience performance score (measuring the degree to which the region recovered from stress on each indicator), and calculating a total resilience performance index (aggregating individual resilience scores into a single regional resilience performance measure).

Unlike resilience capacity, which permits snapshot assessments in advance of an unknown future stress, measuring resilience performance requires researchers to be precise about the timing and nature of both stress and recovery. Given the need for comparable cases marked by a similar stress facing multiple regions at a similar time, not all stresses faced by regions lend themselves to comparable regional analysis. A hurricane hitting the Atlantic Coast in 2006, for example, may not affect to any appreciable degree conditions in, say, Boise or Honolulu, making it meaningless for these regions to measure recovery from the hurricane stress. Measuring resilience performance also introduces a time constraint: the stress must have occurred long enough in the past that there is sufficient time to monitor and report regional recovery indicators. It is not possible to measure resilience to the current economic recession, for example, until sufficient time has passed to give regions the opportunity to demonstrate recovery and report post-stress data. Unfortunately, recovery time norms are not yet established in resilience analysis to the degree they are in fields such as medicine, in which massive amounts of data and analysis validate normal recovery ranges for knee operations to the common cold. There is no consensus on how long regions should have to demonstrate their resilience.

Such constraints prompt the resilience index team to focus on resilience capacity, rather than performance, in the first iteration of the online resilience tool under development. Simply as an illustrative exercise to assess the viability of resilience performance methods for future index iterations, however, the team tested a resilience performance methodology using as a sample shock the national economic recession of the early 2000s. As this volume's chapter by Edward Hill and others details, even "national" recessions hit regions variably, some experiencing no shock and others significantly affected. Because the measurement of resilience performance for a comparative index nonetheless requires presumptions about timing and coverage of a shock, items outlined below, the importance of the following exercise rests not in its findings, but in the reinforcement it offers on the challenges of resilience performance measurement.

Animating the comparative exercise required the research team to presume impact across all metropolitan areas and fixed time periods for the stress and recovery periods.[35] While the early 2000s recession, known also as the "dotcom" recession, has no single agreed-upon time period nor evidence of equal impact, it has the advantage of affecting all parts of the nation and exhibiting common effects on economic indicators.

An additional complexity is the selection of stress and recovery indicators. Standard economic indicators such as GMP, employment growth, wages, and unemployment rates each illuminate some aspect of how well a region bounced back from economic stress. Ideally researchers will also measure resilience performance—and stress, as well—not only by economic indicators, but also by non-economic indicators. Useful indicators for an economic stress include social and governance measures of poverty, income inequality, and local government revenue levels often strained by an economic downturn. Complicating the measurement task, of course, are different recovery time period norms for these variables. This is further complicated by the tendency of some variables to be leading indicators and others lagging indicators.

Bearing these issues in mind, the research team drew on trends in GDP growth and unemployment to date the recession stress period as 2000 to 2003.[36]

---

35. Many stresses, such as rapid growth or the influx of immigrants, do not affect all regions and thus do not meet this criterion for comparative analysis. A separate analysis of immigrant influx, for example, identified only thirty-nine of the 100 largest metros as "stressed" by immigration—where stressed was defined as above the all-metro average based on a metric calculated as the share of the 1990 population represented by immigrants arriving in the 1990s.

36. According to the Bureau of Labor Statistics (stats.bls.gov), overall unemployment rates hit a thirty-year low of 4.0 percent in 2000, after which rates climbed to 6 percent in 2003 before falling again through 2007. Data from the Bureau of Economic Analysis and presented at TradingEconomics.com indicate that year-over-year annual GDP growth rate fell steadily from a peak in March 2000 to a trough

We further selected two basic measures of economic stress and recovery, GMP and unemployment. The recovery period was determined to be 2003 to 2006.[37]

Following these research choices, the first step in calculating a resilience score is to measure the degree of stress and degree of recovery for each of the recovery indicators, as shown in table 2-5 for an alphabetic sample of metropolitan regions.

The sample data exhibit the range of regional resilience performance experiences, with regions showing varying degrees of unemployment stress and recovery. Boston, a dot-com powerhouse, experienced more than a doubling of unemployment over the stress period from 2.6 to 5.7, a 119.2 percent increase, while unemployment in Baltimore increased by only 1 percentage point, from 3.8 to 4.8, or 26.3 percent, through the dot-com recession. By the end of the recovery period in 2006, five of the six sample metropolitan areas recovered from at least some of their unemployment stress, led by Boise, which saw unemployment rates drop by 85.1 percent from the 2003 peak. The exception was Augusta, in which the unemployment rate continued upward from 5.0 to 5.8 through the dot-com recovery period.

From these raw values we calculated a resilience performance score (second to last column of table 2-5), measured as the ratio of the recovery to the stress, and a resilience performance z-score (final column) based on the average and standard deviation for the 97 most populous metropolitan regions in the analysis.[38] A resilience performance ratio of 1.0 would signal complete recovery from the

---

in January 2002, after which it remained tepid at levels under 2 percent until March 2003 before climbing to over 4 percent in March 2004. Note that other indicators, including stock averages and NASDAQ data, imply different start and stop periods for the recession. Using data including real GDP, employment, and real income, the National Bureau of Economic Research determined that the U.S. economy was in recession for only eight months, from March 2001 to November 2001, a determination the National Bureau of Economic Research subjected to adjustment but ultimately affirmed (www.nber. org/cycles/general_statement.html). For a review of the politics of recession dating, see Nell Henderson, "Economists Say Recession Started in 2000," *Washington Post*, January 22, 2004.

37. A significant challenge in stress and recovery performance analysis is evident in the selection of the date by which a crisis ends. A test analysis for unemployment rate resilience using 2007 rather than 2006 as the endpoint for the dot-com recovery altered regional outcomes and rankings. Eleven regions dropped over twenty places in the resilience rankings, the result of unemployment rate increases from 2006 to 2007. Notably, with the exception of Minneapolis, all these regions (Tampa, Stockton, Palm Bay, Sacramento, Bradenton, Cape Coral, San Diego, Riverside, Oxnard, and Lakeland) were in Florida or California, suggesting that 2007 was the start of the housing-based recession rather than the end of recovery for the dot-com recession. Such volatility based on the selection of recovery time periods reveals the perils in constructing a comparative resilience performance index.

38. The z-score calculation is: (regional value – total metropolitan average value)/total metropolitan standard deviation.

stress, returning the region to its pre-stress unemployment rate. The combination of Baltimore's 26.3 percent increase in unemployment over the stress period and 20 percent recovery during the recovery period yields a resilience score of 0.76, signifying that the region bounced back to recover 76 percent of the magnitude of its unemployment stress. The resilience performance scores in this set range from –0.44 percent for Augusta—denoting that not only did this region offset none of its unemployment gains during the stress period, it continued to spiral downward, ending with higher unemployment after the recovery period than before—to 242 percent for Boise, which more than offset its unemployment gains by dropping to 2.7 unemployment, even lower than the region's 3.7 pre-stress unemployment rate.

To facilitate overall rather than individual-indicator resilience performance comparisons, a last step in resilience analysis is to combine individual recovery scores into a single resilience index. There are multiple approaches to index formulation, including treating all indicators as equally important to the overall resilience performance index or attaching different weights to specific recovery indicators to signal the greater importance of some over others. Following Cutter and colleagues, we equally weight the two variables in our analysis with the aggregate resilience index calculated as a simple average of individual z-scores for each resilience performance indicator.[39]

The data in table 2-6 summarize the results for the sample of six metropolitan regions. Of these six, Boise, which had resilience performance z-scores of 1.71 and 2.78 for GMP and unemployment, was the most resilient to the challenge of dot-com recession. (Boise was second only to Hartford, not shown in the sample, in the full ranking of regional resilience performance.) With an overall resilience performance index of –1.19, Augusta exhibited the least resilience to the dot-com challenge, not only for this sample set, but for all ninety-seven metropolitan regions in the analysis.

Variations on this analysis could yield additional insights. Incorporating other dot-com resilience indicators, such as poverty rates, government revenues, and income inequality, would permit cross-region comparisons by different dimensions of recovery. Within a region, cross-indicator comparisons would help regional leaders identify strong and weak aspects of their resilience performance and how it relates to the degree of stress experienced. Analysts could also map results to reveal geographic patterns of resilience performance or group regions by size or economic structure to build typologies of metropolitan resilience.

39. Cutter and others (2010).

Table 2-5. Analysis Excerpt, Resilience Performance for Unemployment Rate

| Metropolitan area | Unemployment rate | | | Performance assessment | | | |
	2000	2003	2006	Stress: percent change, 2000–03	Recovery: percent change, 2003–06[a]	Resilience performance: recovery/stress	Resilience performance z-score[b]
Augusta	3.8	5.0	5.8	31.6	-13.8	-0.44	-1.67
Baltimore	3.8	4.8	4.0	26.3	20.0	0.76	0.19
Baton Rouge	4.7	6.2	3.9	31.9	59.0	1.85	1.89
Birmingham	3.4	4.7	3.2	38.2	46.9	1.23	0.92
Boise	3.7	5.0	2.7	35.1	85.1	2.42	2.78
Boston	2.6	5.7	4.4	119.2	29.6	0.25	-0.60

Source: Author's calculations from Bureau of Labor Statistics data.

a. Calculated so that greater unemployment declines signify greater recovery.

b. Based on universe of ninety-seven largest metropolitan areas in analysis.

Table 2-6. *Analysis Excerpt, Resilience Performance Summary, 2000–06*

Metropolitan area	GMP resilience z-score	Unemployment resilience z-score	Resilience performance index (average of GMP and unemployment z-scores)	Resilience rank (of 97 largest metropolitan areas)
Augusta	−0.71	−1.67	−1.19	97
Baltimore	−0.33	0.19	−0.07	42
Baton Rouge	−0.19	1.89	0.85	11
Birmingham	0.04	0.92	0.48	21
Boise	1.71	2.78	2.25	2
Boston	0.68	−0.60	0.04	35

Sources: Author's calculations from Bureau of Labor Statistics (unemployment data) and Bureau of Economic Analysis (GMP data).

Where This Leaves Us

In 1964 U.S. Supreme Court Justice Potter Stewart famously remarked that although it was difficult to define hard-core pornography, "I know it when I see it." For many students and observers of metropolitan regions, this gut-level understanding may be true also of resilience. Many have a keen sense that New York City was resilient to the September 11 terrorist attacks of 2001, while New Orleans was not in the near-term aftermath of Hurricane Katrina and subsequent flooding. Yet to back up that understanding with facts and numbers and compare a region's response to stress with those of other regions experiencing similar circumstances, the art of regional resilience analysis encounters considerable challenges—not so much to determine pre-stress capacity as to document post-stress performance. Not least among the challenges are identifying comparative cases—those with sufficiently similar starting points and stress impacts to qualify an analysis as a test of resilience rather than of other external and internal factors—and comparative performance variables, ones with similar recovery norms.

Researchers thus necessarily remain in search of regional resilience. Within this volume alone are alternative definitions, measures, and interpretations of resilience. Across the disciplines are yet more perspectives and uses. Agreeing on a single concept or metaphor of resilience is both unlikely and unnecessary, however. A more pertinent goal, toward which this chapter and a regional resilience index strive, is to find a way for the concept of resilience—resting in part on the ideas of adaptation and flexibility—to be sufficiently malleable and specifically defined to bring useful insights to scholars and policymakers alike.

References

Berke, Philip R., and Thomas J. Campanella. 2006. "Planning for Postdisaster Resiliency." *The Annals of the American Academy of Political and Social Science* 604, no. 1 (March): 192–207.

Birch, Eugenie L., and Susan M. Wachter, eds. 2006. *Rebuilding Urban Places after Disaster: Lessons from Hurricane Katrina.* University of Pennsylvania Press.

Bonanno, George A., and Anthony D. Mancini. 2008. "The Human Capacity to Thrive in the Face of Potential Trauma." *Pediatrics* 121, no. 2 (February): 369–75.

Bruneau, Michel, and others. 2003. "A Framework to Quantitatively Assess and Enhance the Seismic Resilience of Communities." *Earthquake Spectra* 19, no. 4 (November): 737–38.

Campanella, Thomas J. 2006. "Urban Resilience and the Recovery of New Orleans." *Journal of the American Planning Association* 72, no. 2 (June): 141–46.

Colton, Craig E., Robert Kates, and Shirley Laska. 2008. *Community Resilience: Lessons from New Orleans and Hurricane Katrina.* Oak Ridge, Tenn.: Community and Regional Resilience Initiative.

Cutter, Susan L., Christopher G. Burton, and Christopher T. Emrich. 2010. "Disaster Resilience Indicators for Benchmarking Baseline Conditions." *Journal of Homeland Security and Emergency Management* 7: 1–22.

Cutter, Susan L., and others. 2006. "The Long Road Home: Race, Class, and Recovery from Hurricane Katrina." *Environment* 48, no. 2 (March): 8–20.

Diamond, Jared. 2005. *Collapse: How Societies Choose to Fail or Succeed.* New York: Viking Penguin.

Foster, Kathryn A. 2000. "Regional Capital." In *Urban-Suburban Interdependencies*, edited by Rosalind Greenstein and Wim Wiewel, pp. 83–118. Cambridge, Mass.: Lincoln Institute of Land Policy.

Godschalk, David. 2003. "Urban Hazard Mitigation: Creating Resilient Cities." *Natural Hazards Review* 4, no. 3 (August): 136–43.

———. 2010. "Pick Yourself Up, Dust Yourself Off . . ." *Planning* (July).

Holling, C. S., and Lance H. Gunderson. 2002. "Resilience and Adaptive Cycles." In *Panarchy: Understanding Transformations in Human and Natural Systems*, edited by Lance H. Gunderson and C. S. Holling, pp. 27–33. Washington: Island Press.

Lansford, Tom, and others. 2010. *Fostering Community Resilience: Homeland Security and Hurricane Katrina.* Surrey, UK: Ashgate.

Liu, Amy, and Allison Plyer. 2010. "An Overview of Greater New Orleans: From Recovery to Transformation." In *The New Orleans Index at Five.* Brookings and Greater New Orleans Data Center.

Norris, Fran H., and others. 2008. "Community Resilience as a Metaphor, Theory, Set of Capacities, and Strategy for Disaster Readiness." *American Journal of Community Psychology* 41, nos. 1-2: 127–50.

Norris, Fran H., Melissa Tracey, and Sandro Galea. 2009. "Looking for Resilience: Understanding the Long-Term Trajectories of Responses to Stress." *Social Science and Medicine* 68, no. 12 (June): 2190–98.

Olshansky, Robert B., and Laurie A. Johnson. 2010. *Clear as Mud: Planning for the Rebuilding of New Orleans*. Chicago: APA Planners Press.

Pendall, Rolf, Brett Theodos, and Kaitlin Franks. 2010. "Vulnerable People, Precarious Housing, and Regional Resilience: An Exploratory Analysis." Paper presented at the 51st Annual Conference of the Association of Collegiate Schools of Planning. Minneapolis, October 7.

Pendall, Rolf J., Kathryn A. Foster, and Margaret M. Cowell. 2010. "Resilience and Regions: Building Understanding of the Metaphor." *Cambridge Journal of Regions, Economy and Society* 3, no. 1: 71–84.

Plodinec, M. John. 2009. "Definitions of Resilience: An Analysis." Oak Ridge, Tenn.: Community and Regional Resilience Institute.

Putnam, Robert D. 2007. "E Pluribus Unum: Diversity and Community in the 21st Century. The 2006 Johan Skytte Prize Lecture." *Scandinavian Political Studies* 30, no. 2: 137–74.

Rae, Douglas. 2005. *City*. Yale University Press.

Sheffi, Yossi. 2005. *The Resilient Enterprise: Overcoming Vulnerability for Competitive Advantage*. MIT Press.

Sherrieb, Kathleen, Fran H. Norris, and Sandro Galea. 2010. "Measuring Capacities for Community Resilience." *Social Indicators Research* 99, no. 2: 227–47.

Vale, Lawrence J., and Thomas J. Campanella. 2005. *The Resilient City: How Modern Cities Recover from Disaster*. Oxford University Press.

Walker, Brian, and David Salt. 2006. *Resilience Thinking: Sustaining Ecosystems and People in a Changing World*. Washington: Island Press.

Wial, Howard, and Richard Shearer. 2011. "MetroMonitor: Tracking Economic Recession and Recovery in America's 100 Largest Metropolitan Areas." Metropolitan Policy Program, Brookings.

Winfield, Linda F. 1994. *Developing Resilience in Urban Youth. Urban Monograph Series*. Chicago: North Central Regional Educational Laboratory.

Zahren, Sammy, and others. 2008. "Risk, Stress, and Capacity: Explaining Metropolitan Commitment to Climate Protection." *Urban Affairs Review* 43, no. 4 (March): 447–74.

3

Resilience in the Face of Foreclosures: How National Actors Shape Local Responses

TODD SWANSTROM

Since 2008 the United States has witnessed mortgage foreclosure rates not seen since the Great Depression. According to one estimate, between 10 and 13 million American homes will face foreclosure by 2014.[1] Because foreclosures were endemic to the financial collapse of 2007–08, most of the national conversation has been about their macroeconomic effects and impacts on broader financial markets. But foreclosures also have local effects, leaving behind disrupted families, devastated communities, distressed municipalities, and damaged regions. My focus here is on efforts to deal with the local *place* effects of foreclosures; I say little about the impact of foreclosures on the national economy and deal with the effects on individuals and families only indirectly.

I examine foreclosure responses through the lens of "resilience." Resilience is essentially the ability of a subject to bounce back from a stress or challenge and return to pre-stress functioning.[2] At this point, resilience is more than a metaphor but less than a theory. As a conceptual framework, however, it suggests a hypothesis worth testing. The central hypothesis explored here is the tension between efficiency and resilience.[3] A region may maximize wealth accumulation by concentrating resources on one or more industries that give it a comparative advantage. But such specialization can make the region less resilient when consumer demand changes, competition from technical innovation arises, or globalization challenges the status quo. Other things being equal,

---

1. Hatzius and Marschoun (2009), p. 16; as reported in Weed and Garrison (2010).
2. See chapter 2 by Foster in this volume. Resilience is gaining increasing prominence in the social sciences. Between 1997 and 2007 the annual references to the term "resilience" in the *Social Science Citation Index* increased by more than 400 percent (Swanstrom 2008).
3. Swanstrom (2008).

as reported in Hill and others in this volume, a regional economy with diverse industries will be more resilient than one that relies on only a few industries. Similarly, large-scale production with extensive specialization of labor may make an organization more efficient, but it also may make it less flexible and less able to alter organizational routines in response to an external challenge. Using these insights of resilience theory, I explore here the central question of whether national actors have enhanced or detracted from local resilience in the face of foreclosures.

Before proceeding, an observation on the scale of resilient processes is in order. This volume is organized around *regional* resilience, the idea that effective responses require action at the scale of regions or metropolitan areas.[4] With housing policy in the United States administered primarily at the county and municipal levels, systematic regional responses to foreclosures have been rare. In addition, most of the effects of foreclosures are highly local, negatively influencing surrounding property values, according to researchers, within about one-eighth of a mile. Regions have many housing submarkets, and with many privileged parts of metropolitan areas relatively untouched by foreclosures, there is little political will to attack the problem of foreclosures regionally. The majority of responses have been organized at the neighborhood and municipal levels. Although a good case can be made that coordinated regional responses would have been more effective, at this point resilience in the face of foreclosures has been mostly local and not regional in scale.[5]

Local resilience is constrained by what I call the "opportunity space," the economic, legal, and institutional conditions that either expand or constrict opportunities for effective local responses (figure 3-1).[6] The opportunity space within metropolitan areas is shaped by state and national actors. A good example is the length of the foreclosure process, which is largely determined by state law. States with nonjudicial foreclosure processes (not overseen by the courts) reduce the time from first foreclosure notice to sheriff's sale, giving the borrower and foreclosure counselors less time to raise funds or modify the mortgage.[7] Of course, local actors may have ample opportunity space, but they may not take advantage of it. In other writing I have focused on why some regions and local actors have

4. See Pastor, Lester, and Scoggins (2009).

5. There are important exceptions to this generalization, such as the Regional Homeownership Preservation Initiative (RHOPI) in Chicago and regional collaborations such as the Atlanta Neighborhood Development Partnership. See Swanstrom, Chapple, and Immergluck (2009).

6. Swanstrom, Chapple, and Immergluck (2009, pp. 4–5).

7. Foreclosure processes that are too long can also be problematic. Long foreclosure processes discourage families from seeking loan reinstatement, because they have an incentive to stay in the home rent free during the long legal process. Cutts and Merrill (2008) argue that there is a "sweet spot" in the length of the foreclosure process around the state average of 120 days.

Figure 3-1. *Resilience Model*

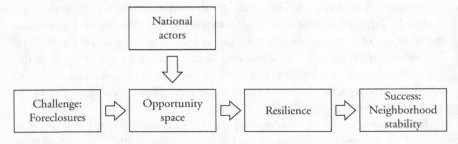

Source: Author.

been more resilient in the face of foreclosures than others.[8] Here, I focus on how national actors, private as well as public, shape the opportunity space at the local level. I conclude with recommendations on how national policies can enhance local resilience.

The data to support my argument come from the rapidly growing literature on foreclosures and on case studies of local responses that I, along with colleagues from around the country, have conducted. As part of the Building Resilient Regions project funded by the MacArthur Foundation, I conducted a series of interviews in St. Louis and Cleveland and my collaborators did likewise in Chicago, Atlanta, Riverside–San Bernardino, and the East Bay area.[9] I have also been fortunate to attend two gatherings organized by the National League of Cities at which local practitioners discussed their responses to foreclosures, and I participated in a forum in Washington, D.C., on foreclosures organized by the Brookings Institution.[10] I also draw on the growing literature and websites on local best practices by organizations such as the National Housing Conference and Living Cities.

The evidence for my argument is largely qualitative and based on case studies. To my knowledge, no one has devised a quantitative measure of local resilience to foreclosures, nor have any rigorous national studies been conducted, with controls, to determine what local actions lead to successful outcomes. My focus is on what local actors have done—on the process of resilience,

8. See Swanstrom, Chapple, and Immergluck (2009, 2011).

9. See Swanstrom, Chapple, and Immergluck (2009).

10. For the second NLC gathering, in April 2010, I wrote a memo on the St. Louis response to foreclosures, and five other scholars wrote similar memos on their metropolitan areas (Michael Rich, Atlanta; Geoff Smith, Chicago; Liz Strom, Tampa–St. Petersburg; Claudia Coulton, Michael Schramm, and April Hirsh, Cleveland; and Gary Painter, Riverside–San Bernardino). I draw freely on these memos, which are available from the authors. For a synthesis of the findings from the NLC meetings, see Swanstrom and Brooks (2010).

not on the successful outcomes. Using Foster's terms in this volume, I study resilience *capacity*, not resilience *outcomes*. I have little hard evidence on whether these local actions contributed to successful outcomes. Indeed, as Tom Kingsley has noted, "There is a lack of solid research literature on such [local foreclosure] policies and their results."[11] With a few exceptions, we simply do not know what local actions make a difference.[12] Nevertheless, it stands to reason that local actors who are able to shift organizational routines, redeploy assets, and strategically target foreclosure prevention and mitigation efforts on key neighborhoods will achieve more successful outcomes—which I define below as creating a stable balance of supply and demand for housing in communities.

Nature of the Foreclosure Challenge for Places

Every foreclosure is a challenge, or stressor, for the individual or family involved. By forcing people out of their homes, foreclosures disrupt social networks and school performance. By damaging credit scores, foreclosures weaken people's ability to access credit, or even rent an apartment or get a job. The ability of people to bounce back from a foreclosure depends on the strength of their social networks, their financial resources, and their psychological resilience.

Similarly, foreclosures are challenges or stressors for *places*. In the case of individuals, resilience could be defined as the ability to places to return to the normal state of functioning before the disturbance or foreclosure occurred. But what would resilience look like in the case of places? For a neighborhood suffering before foreclosures, returning to the status quo would probably not represent resilience. The ecological concept of resilience differs from the engineering concept of resilience in that it accommodates the possibility of multiple equilibria.[13] Resilience can mean that an ecosystem adapts to a drought, for example, with a new ecosystem composed of drought-resistant flora and fauna. Similarly, in the face of foreclosures resilient neighborhoods need not return to their prior state but in many cases will need to reinvent themselves in order to achieve successful outcomes.

It is not enough to say, however, that resilience can mean many different outcomes. How would we know successful place-based resilience to foreclosures if we saw it? The essence of the foreclosure challenge for places, I argue, is an imbalance between housing demand and supply. For example, a period in which demand far outstrips supply and housing prices soar is followed by a vicious

11. Kingsley (2010); Kingsley, Smith, and Price (2009).

12. An important exception is the Urban Institute evaluation of the National Foreclosure Mitigation Program's foreclosure counseling program, which it concludes had positive outcomes. Although the program is federally funded, it is usually implemented by local NeighborWorks organizations. See Mayer and others (2009, 2010).

13. Swanstrom (2008).

cycle of foreclosures and plummeting housing prices that leaves a swath of social destruction in its wake. Basically, a successful neighborhood would be one that was able to avoid huge swings in housing prices and establish a healthy balance between the supply of and demand for housing.

According to economic theory, free markets automatically produce a balance of supply and demand. Negative feedback acts like a thermostat guiding the system toward equilibrium: as demand for housing increases, for example, the supply of housing expands to meet the new demand, moderating price increases and bringing supply and demand back into balance.

The foreclosure crisis, however, contradicts market theory. It cannot be understood by linear processes or by self-correcting feedback loops. Foreclosures must be understood in terms of system dynamics: reinforcing loops of positive feedback that produce oscillating imbalances of supply and demand that can lock people and places into destructive cycles of boom and bust.[14] The main outlines of the process are clear: based on a flood of credit and lax underwriting standards, demand for housing soared from the late 1990s to 2007. The supply of housing, however, being quite inelastic, failed to keep pace with rapidly rising demand and housing prices climbed rapidly, especially in metropolitan areas with artificial constraints on supply, such as restrictive zoning.[15] Nearly everywhere, house prices increased more rapidly than economic essentials, such as growth in productive capacity and household incomes. Monthly housing costs grew as a proportion of income—a trend which is unsustainable in the long run.[16] Normally, if households take out loans that are unsustainable, they will default and quickly go into foreclosure.[17] Rapid price appreciation, however, covered over the unsustainability of the loans: if borrowers were unable to meet monthly payments, they could simply refinance or sell the home to pay off the loan. The market should have also self-corrected as investors refused to buy bad loans, thus cutting off the supply of mortgage capital. The story of the voracious appetite of investors for subprime mortgages, obscured by complex securitization practices and corrupt ratings agencies, is too familiar to be told here.[18] Suffice it to say that the market was not self correcting and a reinforcing cycle of easy credit, rising demand, and soaring home prices was set in motion.

14. For an introduction to system dynamics thinking, see Richardson (1999).
15. Glaeser, Gottlieb, and Gyourko (2010).
16. U.S. Department of Housing and Urban Development (2010, p. 38).
17. Of course, another market mechanism that should have prevented the crisis was the unwillingness of investors to invest in risky mortgages destined to fail on the secondary market, thus choking off mortgage credit and moderating demand. Federal Reserve Board Chairman Alan Greenspan clearly believed, at the time, that market mechanisms would correct any imbalances and the benefits of increased homeownership were worth the risk of foreclosures (Greenspan 2007). He later admitted he was wrong.
18. For an insightful account, see Immergluck (2009a).

Figure 3-2. *Vicious Cycle of Foreclosures*

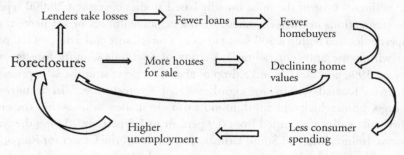

Soure: Author.

The housing bubble in which demand far outstripped supply was unsustainable and was inevitably followed beginning in 2006 by a vicious cycle in the opposite direction: foreclosures suddenly flooded the market with a supply of homes driving down prices, which left more people vulnerable to foreclosure, further driving down prices (figure 3-2). In addition, burned by foreclosures, lenders tightened their underwriting standards, further depressing effective demand for homes, reinforcing the cycle of falling prices and rising foreclosures. And as home prices plummeted, consumer spending fell, increasing unemployment and tipping more households into foreclosure. With bad mortgages leveraged 20 and 25 times through financial devices like credit default swaps, mortgage foreclosures pulled a huge amount of available capital out of the economy, dragging down the national and even the global economy.

Besides market failures at the national level, foreclosures also involve market failures at the local level that impose significant costs on places. The literature identifies three main local spillovers of foreclosures (negative effects on households and people who are themselves not involved in a foreclosure): declining property values, crime and social disorder, and local government fiscal stress and deteriorating services.[19] This is not the place to discuss the full range of local spillovers, but a quick survey will demonstrate that they are significant indeed.

Declining Property Values

Scholarly research has consistently found a negative impact of foreclosures on the market value of homes located within approximately one-eighth mile (660 feet) of a foreclosure. The Center for Responsible Lending estimates that by 2012,

---

19. This categorization is taken from Kingsley, Smith, and Price (2009), a valuable synthesis of the research on the local spillover effects of foreclosures.

92 million households will have suffered declines in property values totaling $1.2 trillion.[20] One of the most broadly based studies covering 628,000 repeat sales transactions in thirteen states found a negative impact of 1.3 percent on properties located within a 300-foot radius of a foreclosure and a drop of 0.6 percent within the 660-foot radius.[21] A study of St. Louis County foreclosures between 1998 and 2007 found a drop of about 1.0 percent in the sales prices of properties located within one-eighth mile of a foreclosure.[22] In a study of Chicago, Immergluck and Smith found a drop in market value within the one-eighth-mile radius that varied from 0.9 percent to 1.8 percent.[23] Using the conservative Immergluck and Smith estimate (0.9 percent), the Center for Responsible Lending (CRL) calculated that on average nearby homeowners will lose about $5,000 in value per foreclosure.[24]

Social Disorder and Crime

Involuntary displacements caused by foreclosures disrupt social connections and deplete social capital. Children are in many ways the most disturbing innocent victims of foreclosure. When they are pulled out of one school and put in another their learning is disrupted. According to one estimate, 1.952 million children were impacted by foreclosures as a result of subprime loans made in 2005–06.[25] This imposes huge costs on families, communities, and schools. Frequent residential moves can increase violent behavior in high school by 20 percent and reduce the odds of graduating from high school by more than 50 percent.[26] Foreclosures can also damage the health of children, negatively affecting diet and healthy body weight. Involuntary displacement puts stress on families, leading to higher rates of divorce, child abuse, and addictive behaviors.[27]

Foreclosures are also associated with crime. According to the "broken windows" theory, signs of disorder in a neighborhood, as small as a broken window that is not fixed, encourage crime. Foreclosures, especially when the home lies vacant and not properly maintained (such as tall grass or trash out front), can create a sense of disorder in a neighborhood and encourage crime. Research has

20. Weed and Garrison (2010).
21. Harding, Rosenblatt, and Yao (2008).
22. Rogers and Winter (2009).
23. Immergluck and Smith (2006a)
24. Center for Responsible Lending (2008).
25. Lovell and Isaacs (2008).
26. Rumberger (2003).
27. The literature on the costs of involuntary displacement is large. For a recent synthesis, see Fullilove (2004). See also Craig E. Pollack and Julia F. Lynch, "Foreclosures Are Killing Us," *New York Times*, October 3, 2011.

confirmed this connection. A study of Chicago found that for each 1 percentage point increase in the foreclosure rate, the number of violent crimes in a census tract increased by 2.33 percent.[28] A study by the Charlotte-Mecklenburg Police Department found that both violent and property crime rates were higher in the high-foreclosures neighborhoods compared to neighborhoods that had not yet experienced high rates of foreclosure.[29]

Local Government Fiscal Stress and Deteriorating Services

The impact of foreclosures on local governments is double-edged—both on the revenue and expenditure side. On the revenue side, foreclosures shrink revenues. The impact of foreclosures on property taxes is especially significant. Once assessments catch up with declining property values, governments will be forced to increase property tax rates to maintain revenues. Additionally, local governments will have to deal with increased tax delinquencies and failure to pay utilities.

At the same time that revenues are declining, local governments face increased costs as employees miss work, productivity declines, and families seek additional social services. These indirect costs are difficult to estimate but researchers have measured the direct costs of foreclosures on local governments. The best scholarly study on the cost of foreclosures to municipalities examined Chicago, quantifying costs of foreclosure based on five scenarios.[30] If a property goes into foreclosure and is quickly put back on the market, the researchers estimate it will cost the local municipality only $430. At the other end, if the foreclosure leads to vacancy and abandonment, ultimately requiring demolition, the cost to the local municipality can soar to as high as $34,199.

In sum, foreclosures have significant spillover effects on surrounding property owners, households, and local governments. Market theory is correct: rational actors will not take into account the spillover effects of foreclosures and therefore local actors will need to intervene to protect the public. Foreclosures become especially challenging when the spillover effects begin to reinforce one another in positive feedback loops. As the study cited above on the impact on local governments suggests, the costs of foreclosure vary significantly from place to place. The negative impact of foreclosures on places depends on foreclosure density and the strength of the local housing market. Dispersed foreclosures in strong housing markets have minimal effects. Concentrated foreclosures in weak housing markets

28. See Kelling and Coles (1996) on the broken windows theory, and on Chicago, Immergluck and Smith (2006b).
29. Bess (2008).
30. Apgar and Duda (2005).

Figure 3-3. *Foreclosures and Reinforcing Process of Neighborhood Decline*

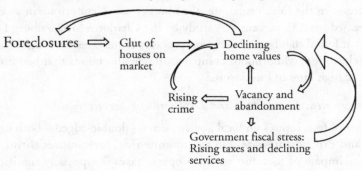

Source: Author.

can have devastating effects on neighborhoods. In strong markets, robust demand ensures that the relatively small number of foreclosed properties will quickly be purchased and re-occupied. Other than an unusually large number of "For Sale" signs, a casual observer driving through the neighborhood may see little change.[31] On the other hand, concentrated foreclosures in weak markets generate reinforcing processes of neighborhood decline (figure 3-3) marked by obvious signs of distress, such as vacant and boarded-up houses.

Reinforcing processes of neighborhood decline are rooted in the fact that real estate markets are highly social or interactive. The self-correcting equilibrium of market economics is based on rational actors making *independent* decisions. If the housing prices fall below the inherent characteristics of the neighborhood (condition of stock, amenities, location relative to jobs, and so forth), then presumably buyers, seeing an opportunity, will jump in and bring prices back up to equilibrium. But as the growing literature on behavioral economics has taught us, market actors do not always act rationally or independently.[32] Economic decisionmakers are prone to social contagion in which they follow the herd rather than make cold-hearted rational decisions based on the merits of each case. This is especially true in the case of real estate markets where the value of each property depends so much on what happens to neighboring properties. Admittedly, market fundamentals will always reassert themselves in the long

31. But the costs to individuals and families can still be considerable. Indeed, in metropolitan areas with strong markets, foreclosures may be harder on families because affordable replacement housing is more difficult to obtain than in weak markets. For a review of the relatively thin scientific research on the effects of foreclosures on families and individuals, see Kingsley, Smith, and Price (2009).

32. For an insightful application of behavioral economics to the foreclosure issue, see Barr, Mullainathan, and Shafir (2008).

run. But as Keynes once remarked, "In the long run we're all dead." It is like having a thermostat that brings your home back to 70 degrees, but only after forcing you to swelter in 100 degree heat for weeks.

Foreclosures are not randomly distributed within metropolitan areas. Subprime and predatory lending, which is highly correlated with foreclosures, was concentrated. Foreclosures are correlated with each other in space. Predatory loans, the root cause of the crisis, were not sold; they were aggressively marketed—especially in minority neighborhoods. They were not marketed to the poorest areas but primarily to moderate- and middle-income minority neighborhoods. Prior to the wave of foreclosures, many of these neighborhoods had enjoyed revitalization, often due to the hard work of community development corporations (CDCs). Ironically, this hard work in pushing up market values may have attracted subprime lenders.[33]

Concentrated foreclosures can set in motion a cycle of decline that destroys place-based assets: financial capital, physical capital, and social capital.[34] Foreclosures wipe out home equity, depriving families of the capital to pay for education or start a business. When vandals ransack foreclosed homes, breaking windows and ripping out the copper wiring, the physical capital of the neighborhood is devalued. And households that are forced to move lose many social connections. Social capital is destroyed.

In sum, the fundamental challenge for communities is that foreclosures can generate significant spillovers, reinforcing cycles of decline and destroying the financial, physical, and social capital accumulated in places. Neighborhoods then become "stuck," unable to renew themselves or serve as springboards for individuals and families to succeed. Instead of springboards, they act more like quicksand.[35] The severity of the foreclosure challenge varies significantly across and within metropolitan areas. The greatest challenge is in weak market areas with concentrated foreclosures. Inoculating places against the contagion of subprime and predatory lending would have been the most effective response. But as we will demonstrate in the following section, local actors, who are responsible for dealing with the damage caused by foreclosures, have little power over the drivers of foreclosures.

33. For example, Slavic Village, the epicenter of the foreclosure crisis in Cleveland, had one of the most active and successful CDCs in the area.

34. Home equity represents 60 percent of the total wealth of middle-class households. Before the recent wave of foreclosures, African American household wealth was less than one-tenth of white households (Shapiro 2004, pp. 47 and 107). There is every reason to believe that the recent wave of foreclosures wiped out proportionally more home equity among African American households than among whites. See Kochar and Gonzalez-Barrera (2009) and McCue (2009).

35. For an analysis of the idea of "stuck" neighborhoods, see Ashton and Schnell (2010).

The Fundamental Cause of Foreclosures: Predatory Lending

The foreclosure challenge is different in one important way from the challenges addressed by resilience studies in other fields. In the field of ecology, for instance, the stressor or challenge, such as a hurricane or drought, is viewed as external, or exogenous. The challenge is taken as given; the only question is how the ecosystem reacts to the challenge and reestablishes equilibrium. Foreclosures, however, are not an act of nature; they are a product of human action. By far the most effective action by local actors would have been to prevent foreclosures from happening in the first place. In order to determine whether local actors have this option, what could be called preemptive resilience, we need to know the underlying cause of the foreclosure epidemic.

There has been a great deal of debate in the literature on the underlying cause of the foreclosure crisis. Some argue that it is a classical housing bubble: when it burst, it left borrowers underwater (or owing more than their houses were worth) and then, according to option-based theory, borrowers ceded their property to the lender in a so-called ruthless default. Others point to rising unemployment and other triggering events as the primary causes of foreclosures. And still others assert that the Community Reinvestment Act (CRA) pushed lenders into making loans to borrowers who lacked the economic resources to sustain homeownership.[36]

A Department of Housing and Urban Development (HUD) study—"Report to Congress on the Root Causes of the Foreclosure Crisis"—debunks all three of these explanations. Although declining prices are strongly correlated with foreclosures, they are not the root cause of the foreclosure crisis. Falling home prices simply eliminated one way for borrowers with unsustainable loans to avoid foreclosure (refinancing or selling their home to pay off the loan). Past foreclosure waves were often caused by economic weakness, but the recent wave of foreclosures, the HUD report observes, occurred *before* unemployment began to rise.[37] In fact, it is more correct to say that foreclosures caused economic weakness, rather than that economic weakness caused foreclosures. (Now, of course, we are facing a second wave of foreclosures, often of prime loans, driven increasingly by rising unemployment and underemployment.)[38] And government regulations, such as those implemented under CRA, were not a significant cause of the foreclosure crisis, the HUD report concludes, because the vast majority of loans that went into foreclosure were originated by lenders who were not regulated by the federal government.

---

36. U.S. Department of Housing and Urban Development (2010); Howard Husock, "Housing Goals We Can't Afford," *New York Times*, December 11, 2008, p. A49.

37. U.S. Department of Housing and Urban Development (2010, pp. 1, 21).

38. Edmiston (2009).

Rejecting the bursting housing bubble, the faltering economy, and misguided federal regulations as primary causes, the HUD report to Congress concludes that "highly risky loans . . . were the root cause of the current crisis." In short, the recent foreclosure crisis was driven by a huge increase in risky subprime loans that were doomed to fail, or predatory loans.[39] The market share of risky loans (subprime, Alt-A, and home equity loans) increased from 16 percent in 2003 to 48 percent in 2006.[40] Collapsing housing prices suddenly left people vulnerable to foreclosure, but lower housing prices were not the driver of the crisis. In fact, the authors of the HUD report stress, rising prices had come about because of the flood of easy credit caused by loose underwriting standards.[41] When enough borrowers defaulted on their loans and went into foreclosure, the whole house of cards collapsed into a vicious cycle in which supply exceeded demand and plummeting house prices and rising unemployment exposed more households to foreclosure (see figure 3-2).

Predatory lending was enabled by state and federal policies, what Ned Gramlich called "a gigantic hole in the supervisory safety net."[42] And such lending was further enabled by Wall Street investors who bought up subprime loans without properly evaluating the risks. Local governments and nonprofits have had responsibility for cleaning up the mess from the spillovers of foreclosures, but, as we will see, they have had little authority over the primary cause of foreclosures—predatory lending.

Foreclosure Prevention: Controlling Predatory Lending

The most effective way local actors could have prevented the foreclosure crisis would have been to limit predatory lending within their borders. When cities acted to regulate predatory lending, however, courts ruled that they lacked home rule powers for that purpose or that state laws preempted local laws.[43] Similarly, when states stepped in to regulate risky lending, they were preempted by federal laws. Finally, competing federal regulators engaged in a "race to the bottom" that gutted regulation of predatory lending. Successful venue shopping by the

39. All predatory loans are subprime but many subprime loans are not predatory. Predatory loans involve "onerous lending practices, which are often targeted at vulnerable populations and result in devastating personal losses, including bankruptcy, foreclosure and loss of borrowers' homes" (Engel and McCoy 2001, p. 6). Subprime loans are simply high-interest loans whose higher interest rates may have been justified by the additional risk and therefore were not onerous or exploitative.

40. U.S. Department of Housing and Urban Development (2010, p. 25). For a list of the five characteristics of predatory loans, see Engel and McCoy (2001, p. 7).

41. Glaeser, Gottlieb, and Gyourko (2010) argue that low interest rates and high approval rates did not play a major role in the housing bubble.

42. Gramlich (2007, p. 21).

43. Frug and Barron (2008, p. 196).

mortgage lending industry within the federal government and across federal, state, and local governments undercut efforts to regulate subprime lending.[44]

The origins of the recent wave of predatory lending go back to a 1980 federal law that phased in the abolition of state usury limits on first mortgages by depository institutions.[45] Part of the rationale then was that allowing higher interest rates would increase access to credit by higher risk households, giving them a chance to become homeowners. In 1982 another federal law allowed mortgage companies that originate loans and sell them to investors to choose to be governed by federal regulations rather than those of the state in which they were located.[46] This enabled mortgage companies to get out from under more stringent state regulations.

In 1994 the federal government enacted the Home Ownership and Equity Protection Act (HOEPA), which prohibited certain loan terms and practices on high-cost loans that were considered onerous, such as prepayment penalties extending more than five years from loan origination. The definition of "high cost," however, was so high (generally 8 percent above the rate on comparable Treasury securities) that it applied to very few loans. In 2006, for example, less than 0.1 percent of refinancing and home improvement loans fell under the law.[47]

In 1996 the Office of Thrift Supervision (OTS) issued a sweeping regulation preempting all state laws regulating mortgage lending for federal savings institutions. The Office of the Comptroller of the Currency (OCC), under pressure from its members, in 2004 issued a similarly sweeping preemption regulation for all national banks. Both agencies exempted mortgage banking operating subsidiaries, which were heavily involved in subprime lending, from state regulation as well.[48]

By the 1990s greenlining (marketing bad loans to vulnerable populations) replaced redlining (refusing to lend to minorities) as the main lending issue for local housing activists. In 1999 North Carolina became the first state to enact comprehensive anti-predatory lending legislation. The law was modeled on HOEPA but set the threshold much lower so that it applied to a larger segment of subprime loans. Other states followed suit so that by 2007 only seven states had no mini-HOEPA statutes on their books to regulate predatory lending.

44. The story of the failed efforts of local, state, and federal regulators to limit subprime lending is told in U.S. Department of Housing and Urban Development (2010) and more completely in Immergluck (2009a). I draw freely from these accounts. For the concept of "venue shopping," see Baumgartner and Jones (1993).

45. Depository Institutions Deregulation and Monetary Control Act.

46. Alternative Mortgage Transaction Parity Act (1982).

47. Avery, Brevoort, and Canner (2007), as reported in U.S. Department of Housing and Urban Development (2010, p. 34).

48. In 2007 the U.S. Supreme Court upheld this extension of preemption powers.

These laws were generally ineffective, however, partly because they were pre-empted by federal regulators who competed for members (mortgage lenders), which paid fees to the regulating institutions.[49] As noted, financial institutions have some freedom to choose which regulator they will fall under and they shopped around for the best deal.

As is often the case in our federal system, when the federal and state governments withdrew from effective regulation of subprime lending, local governments moved in to fill the void. A 2005 study identified eighteen local anti-predatory lending laws.[50] For example, Chicago and Cook County enacted anti-predatory lending laws in 2000 and 2001, respectively, which sought to withdraw municipal business and deposits from firms that engaged in predatory lending. However, most local laws were preempted by state legislation or state courts ruled that they lacked authority to regulate financial institutions. An excerpt from a dissenting opinion in a California Supreme Court case, which invalidated Oakland's pioneering anti-predatory lending law, justifies local authority over predatory lending by citing the local spillover effects of foreclosures:

> Oakland's particular interest in regulating subprime loans goes beyond merely protecting its particularly vulnerable citizens. . . . Predatory home mortgage lending has enormous impacts on targeted neighborhoods. . . . "Foreclosures, especially in low- and moderate-income neighborhoods turn what might be typically viewed as a consumer protection problem . . . into a community development problem, in which increased foreclosures lead to property abandonment and blight."[51]

In short, efforts to regulate subprime lending, the root cause of the foreclosure crisis, were gutted by state preemption of local laws, federal preemption of state laws, and a race to the bottom by federal regulators. In our terms, the actions of state and federal governments shrank the opportunity space for local actors to prevent foreclosures. Most subprime loans were originated by mortgage brokers who were lightly regulated by the states and the federal government. After foreclosures led to huge losses by investors in pools of mortgages containing subprime loans, subprime lending largely came to a halt because investors refused to buy them any longer. By that time, however, subprime loans were going into default all over the nation. Preventing the massive spillovers of foreclosures on local communities is much more difficult after subprime loans have been originated than

49. Bostic and others (2007), as reported in U.S. Department of Housing and Urban Development (2010). Passage of these laws was actually associated with an *increase* in subprime lending, as noted by Bostic and others (2007).

50. Ho and Pennington-Cross (2006).

51. Immergluck and Smith (2004, p. i), quoted in Frug and Barron (2008, p. 197).

before. But how effective could local actors have been if given the opportunity? After all, they benefit from housing price increases that boost property tax revenues.[52] In any case, they were not given the authority to regulate subprime and predatory lending and found themselves in the situation of having to respond after bad loans had already been made.

Foreclosure Prevention in the Wake of Predatory Lending: Loan Modifications

At the local level, foreclosure "prevention" is a misnomer because, as we have seen, local actors have little authority over the primary cause of foreclosures—predatory loans. Foreclosure prevention at the local level means mostly helping homeowners already in the foreclosure process to stay in their homes by reducing monthly payments through a loan modification. Supported by federal grants, local actors, particularly housing nonprofits, have been quite resilient in responding to the need for loan modifications by creating housing counseling networks with broad public outreach. However, the rate of loan modifications has been disappointingly low. Once again, the local opportunity space for resilience has been shrunk by the actions of national actors, in this case largely by the policies of remote mortgage servicers.

Strong arguments can be made for loan modifications, not only because they protect the public but also because they protect the interests of private investors in mortgages. As we have seen, the public has a strong incentive to prevent foreclosures, given their large spillover effects, especially for weak market areas with concentrated foreclosures. Taking into account the transaction costs and loss in home values following foreclosures, investors in mortgage-backed securities would be better off in many cases with loan modifications that enabled borrowers to stay in their homes and continue making lower monthly payments. Loan modifications can be win-win for the lender and the borrower. Despite the powerful public and private interests in favor of loan modifications, the rate of loan modifications has been low. Vertical disintegration of the mortgage financing market has pulled key decisions about loan modifications out of the hands of local lenders and put them into the hands of remote servicers. Constrained by "hyperrigid" mortgage pools, lacking adequately trained employees, and with a

52. I thank Howard Wial for this point. Clearly, federal action to limit predatory lending practices would have been the best protection against foreclosures. The Bureau of Consumer Financial Protection, which was authorized in July 2010 as part of the Dodd-Frank financial reform legislation backed by President Obama, will regulate mortgage lending. As a consumer agency under the Federal Reserve but not dependent on fees from regulated institutions, the new bureau may avoid the venue shopping by banks that undermined past federal regulatory efforts.

business model biased in favor of foreclosures, loan servicers have often acted against the interests of investors and refused to modify loans.[53] Taking into account the public interest, or the spillovers of foreclosures, the rate of loan modifications falls even further below the social ideal.

Investors in mortgages lose a great deal when a mortgage goes through foreclosure. Estimating these losses is difficult because they vary so much in different parts of the country and under different scenarios. Clearly, however, the losses are high. Loss severities have been estimated at about 50 percent for prime mortgages and 70 percent for subprime mortgages. According to one study of subprime loans going through foreclosure, about 42 percent of the loss was due to legal fees, sales commissions, maintenance expenses, and missed mortgage payments. About 44 percent of the loss was a deadweight loss—a decline in the value of the home for which there is no compensating gain by anyone else. Part of the loss is due to the general decline in prices. Part is due to vandalism and stripping. And a significant part is due to the stigma that a foreclosure sale puts on a property—which is estimated at about 28 percent below equivalent standard sales.[54] A study of 900 subprime loans estimated the cost to investors of foreclosure at over 50 percent. With an average principal balance of $190,000, that means a loss of about $95,000 on each foreclosure. That leaves a great deal of room for the lender and borrower to negotiate a win-win loan modification.

The deadweight loss to private investors is much more severe in weak market metropolitan areas. In the city of Cleveland, for example, most properties that go through foreclosure—so-called real-estate owned properties (REOs)—are taken over by the bank. In 2007 properties sold by banks in Cleveland fetched only 13 percent of their estimated market value before foreclosure filing. In 2008, 80 percent of REO properties in Cleveland's East Side sold at extremely distressed prices of less than $10,000.[55] In the Cleveland area property losses on foreclosed properties now exceed a billion dollars. In such situations investors should be highly motivated to cut their losses by modifying loans for borrowers who still can make monthly payments.[56]

The public sector has an additional motive to prevent foreclosures because of the massive negative spillovers discussed earlier. It would especially make public

---

53. "Hyperrigid" is not my term but is taken from Gelpern and Levitin (2009).

54. Cordell and others (2009, pp. 7, 12, 8).

55. Coulton, Schramm, and Hirsch (2010).

56. If the re-default rate on loan modifications is high, it will not be in the interest of investors to modify loans. The default rate on HAMP modifications, which reduce monthly payments to 31 percent of income, is only 11 percent after nine months. See "Making Home Affordable Servicer Performance Report through September 2010" (www.financialstability.gov/docs/Sept%20MHA%20Public%202010.pdf). Re-default rates would be even lower if the principal of loans were reduced to bring them more in line with housing values.

policy sense to prevent foreclosures in transitional areas where risky loans are concentrated and foreclosures could set in motion reinforcing cycles of decay.[57] Some of these spillovers are quantifiable, such as losses by nearby property owners, but many are difficult to quantify. Nonmonetary benefits of stable homeownership are indicated by the fact that homeowners put a value on staying in their homes even when it does not make economic sense. Studies have shown that only a small minority of homeowners who are underwater walk away from their homes in a so-called strategic default.[58] This suggests that homes are not just a financial investment but have substantial "use values" that are nonfungible and nonportable, such as community identity, accumulated social capital, and a satisfying daily routine.[59] Parents, with good reason, are reluctant to pull their children out of local schools in order to achieve a financial benefit. In short, the economic *and* non-economic spillovers make a powerful argument for public intervention to prevent foreclosures.

The main argument against public support for loan modifications to prevent foreclosures is the risk of creating a moral hazard: helping homeowners who took on risky debt could encourage more risky behavior in the future. This is a valid concern. It is difficult to estimate the effect of loan modifications on future household behavior, but the substantial private and public benefits of loan modifications, I argue, outweigh concerns about moral hazard. First, the explosion of risky mortgages was less related to risky consumer behavior and more tied to deceptive lending practices by mortgage brokers. Sudden risky behavior by borrowers does not explain the timing of the crisis; the emergence of risky, exotic mortgage products does. Many borrowers did not know what they were agreeing to when they signed a mortgage. Education of borrowers about the risks of subprime lending is helpful but, given the complexity of mortgage instruments, the best way to limit future risky lending is to regulate risky and unsustainable lending practices, such as negative amortization, yield-spread premiums, no-doc loans, and exploding ARMs. Given the serious spillover effects of foreclosures, especially concentrated foreclosures in weak markets, it makes sense to act quickly to minimize the damage. A firefighter does not first ask whether the homeowner was smoking in bed before putting out the fire.

---

57. For a definition and empirical identification of transitional areas, see Mallach (2008) and Goldstein (2008).

58. A study of all homeowners in Massachusetts, for example, found that in the early 1990s only 6.4 percent of borrowers who were underwater ended up in foreclosure. Cited in U.S. Department of Housing and Urban Development (2010, pp. 15–16). The HUD report cites a number of other studies to support this finding.

59. For an explication of the concept of use values, see Logan and Molotch (1987).

Resilience can be defined as the ability to respond to a challenge by
—redeploying assets or expanding organizational repertoires;
—collaborating within and across public, private, and nonprofit sectors;
—mobilizing or capturing resources from external sources.[60]

Using this three-part definition, local actors, especially housing nonprofits, have been quite resilient. They have shifted employees from housing rehabilitation and other activities to foreclosure counseling—an effort greatly aided by the National Foreclosure Mitigation Counseling (NFMC) program funded by the federal government and administered through NeighborWorks America. Counselors become HUD-certified by receiving training in the intricacies of home financing, usually funded by scholarships. NFMC counseling agencies provide free counseling to homeowners who are in trouble, not only helping them to avoid foreclosure but also advising them in the event of a foreclosure on how to find replacement housing and access social services. Up to December 2009, $475 million had been appropriated, mostly for grants to local counseling agencies that receive between $150 and $350 per client depending on the extent of the counseling.[61] On August 12, 2010, NeighborWorks America announced that more than 1 million homeowners facing foreclosure had received counseling.

A good example of resilient local efforts to prevent foreclosures is the Homeownership Preservation Initiative (HOPI) in Chicago. Begun in 2003, HOPI included Neighborhood Housing Services (NHS) of Chicago, many local CDCs, nonprofit counseling organizations, legal services providers, the city of Chicago, and local foundations. It used Chicago's 311 non-emergency hotline to link homeowners to counselors. By May 2008 HOPI reported it had prevented 1,700 foreclosures.

Foreclosure prevention has been vigorous in other metropolitan areas as well. In 2005 Cuyahoga County launched a foreclosure initiative that included nine housing nonprofits, numerous municipalities, and a number of lenders. Funds from Temporary Assistance to Needy Families (TANF) and fees from tax delinquent properties were shifted to foreclosure counseling. The county invested almost $2.5 million in the program up to 2008 and raised about another half a million dollars from local foundations and banks. Between March 2006 and February 2007 the program reported preventing 1,497 foreclosures.[62] The city of St. Louis has now invested more than $1 million in foreclosure prevention,

60. Swanstrom, Chapple, and Immergluck (2009, p. 4).
61. For helping with applications for the Home Affordable Modification Program, an Obama initiative, counseling agencies can now receive up to a maximum of about $500. Congress appropriated additional funds for the NFMC program in 2010 ($59.5 million) and 2011 ($67.7 million). Another $45 million for housing counseling assistance is in the FY2012 HUD budget.
62. Swanstrom, Chapple, and Immergluck (2009).

including the creation of a foreclosure rescue fund that can make small payments to help homeowners secure a loan modification.[63] Foreclosure counseling agencies in St. Louis partnered with the local public television station (KETC) to create programs and a local website to encourage people to seek help. The KETC initiative was later duplicated in twenty-five cities around the country with the help of grants from the Corporation for Public Broadcasting.[64]

The capacity of local actors to engage in foreclosure prevention varies significantly. CDCs have been "first responders" in the wake of the foreclosure epidemic. Unfortunately, many suburban areas hard hit by foreclosures lack robust networks of CDCs. Chicago responded to this gap by creating a regional HOPI, called RHOPI, which was led by NHS, Chicago Community Trust, and the Federal Reserve Bank of Chicago. The RHOPI foreclosure counseling task force developed a report mapping gaps in access to housing counseling agencies, which was used to better target counseling resources. Significant foundation and government funding for counseling in the Chicago area has filled many gaps. But this is not true in other metropolitan areas.[65]

In 2010 the Urban Institute published preliminary findings of its evaluation of the NFMC counseling program.[66] The study uses rigorous methods to isolate the effects of counseling, comparing approximately 180,000 households that received foreclosure counseling with a control group of 155,000 similar households that did not receive counseling. The researchers found counseled homeowners were 70 percent more likely to "cure" a foreclosure than those who had not received counseling. Counseling also produced a 45 percent increase in the likelihood that a modification would be sustained. Additionally, the Urban Institute study concluded that loan modifications received by homeowners through the NFMC program resulted in significantly reduced monthly mortgage payments after a loan modification (–$267 on average, thereby further decreasing the likelihood of re-defaults and foreclosures).

Research supports the conclusion that the benefits of foreclosure counseling exceed the costs. The Urban Institute study calculated that 32,000 NFMC clients "cured" their foreclosure who would otherwise have defaulted if they had not received counseling. Using the HUD estimate—that each foreclosure generates costs of about $37,000—the foreclosures prevented by NFMC counseling produced benefits of about $1.2 billion. And as I discuss above, the benefits of

63. In November 2009 St. Louis received a Silver Award for Municipal Excellence from the National League of Cities (giving $1,000 to the charity of its choice).

64. Swanstrom (2010).

65. See Swanstrom, Chapple, and Immergluck (2009). The authors also provide GIS maps of the location of housing nonprofits in metropolitan areas, showing their central city concentration.

66. Mayer (2010).

foreclosure prevention are considerably higher if the nonmonetary costs to households and places are counted. It should also be noted that even if they are not able to keep clients in their homes, counselors provide benefits by facilitating a short sale and referring them to appropriate agencies to find a new place to live or access social services. In any case, at a cost of $475 million, it is clear that the NFMC counseling program had a positive benefit-cost ratio.

Most people do not enjoy the benefits of taxpayer-funded counseling. One study found that about half of households that went through foreclosure never even communicated with their servicer. Early communication increases the likelihood of staying in your home and foreclosure counseling increases this. The authors conclude that "the availability of the service [foreclosure counseling] is low relative to the need."[67] Given the huge social costs generated by foreclosures, it seems clear that the federal government should have invested much more in foreclosure counseling. Local actors who have invested their own resources in foreclosure counseling have probably reaped significant social and economic benefits beyond the costs.

The problem with foreclosure counseling is that it does not get close to addressing the magnitude of the problem. While 32,000 foreclosures were prevented by NFMC counseling, this represents a drop in the bucket when foreclosures are running at over 1 million a year. The resilience of the foreclosure counseling system is low in absolute terms—that is, relative to the need to prevent foreclosures in order to stabilize the supply and demand for housing in local communities.

The main reason for the low rate of foreclosure prevention is that servicers are reluctant to modify loans. In order to address this problem, the Obama administration in March 2009 launched the Making Home Affordable program designed to help 7 to 9 million households. Over 85 percent of all mortgages are covered by the program.[68] Intended to strengthen the ability of homeowners and local counselors to negotiate sustainable mortgage modifications, the program has two main components—a Home Affordable Refinance Program (HARP), for homeowners whose loans are held by the government-sponsored entities, and a $75 billion Home Affordable Modification Program (HAMP), designed to produce sustainable loan modifications for loans held by conventional lenders. Of the two, HAMP had the greatest potential to reduce foreclosures, and it also has been the most disappointing. The main components of the program are incentives to servicers to modify loans and requirements to bring monthly payments down to 31 percent of household income.[69] Despite the

67. Cutts and Merrill (2008, pp. 211, 252).

68. Cordell and others (2009).

69. The program offers three payments to servicers paid at different stages of the modification process totaling $3,000, as well as payments to subsidize the mortgage to bring monthly costs of the loan down to 31 percent of the borrower's income.

Figure 3-4. *Permanent Modifications under the U.S. Treasury's Home Affordable Modification Program, 2009–11*

Number of modifications

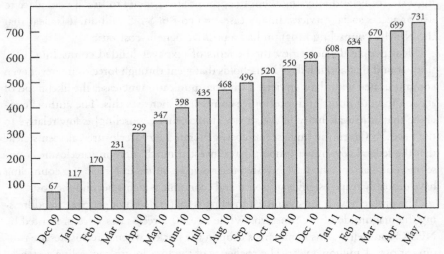

Source: "Making Home Affordable Servicer Performance Report through May 2011" (www.treasury.gov/initiatives/financial-stability/results/MHA-Reports/Documents/May%202011%20 MHA%20Report %20FINAL.PDF).

almost 3 million eligible delinquent loans through May 2011, as figure 3-4 shows, only 731,000 permanent modifications had been started.

For those who do receive a modification under HAMP, the savings can be significant. The median monthly savings for borrowers in permanent modifications is $520.68, or 36 percent of their monthly payment before modification.[70] Although HAMP has reduced monthly payments, it has done little to reduce principal owed. In fact, it is common to increase overall mortgage debt by capitalizing unpaid interest and payments in arrears into the overall loan amount due in a balloon payment at the end of the loan. Borrowers are made more resilient in the short term, but in the long term they may be less resilient as they still face crushing debt and often a home that is worth less than the mortgage. By this method, HAMP has been structured so that it has little if any negative effect on lenders' balance sheets. Instead of co-responsibility for lending excesses, final responsibility rests almost entirely on the shoulders of the homeowners.[71]

70. "Making Home Affordable Program: Servicer Performance Report through September 2010" (www.treasury.gov/initiatives/financial-stability/results/MHA-Reports/Pages/default.aspx [November 2010]).
71. Ashton (2010).

The main reason for the dismally slow pace of loan modifications is that the incentives offered by HAMP are not great enough to overcome servicer incentives to delay or proceed to foreclosure. Resilience theory helps to explain this result. According to resilience theory, as noted earlier, specialization and increased scale can increase efficiency at the expense of resiliency. Local housing nonprofits are small and did not have a highly developed internal division of labor. They were able to quickly shift employees and alter organizational routines to focus on foreclosure counseling. Highly specialized and remote loan servicers, on the other hand, were rigid instead of resilient. Over time, the servicers had become large, specialized organizations highly efficient at collecting and distributing mortgage payments. "As a result of the consolidation in the industry, servicers have realized large economies of scale in payment processing and collections, so that the costs of servicing have trended down over time."[72] Loss mitigation, or loan modification, however, is less subject to economies of scale and does not fit the servicers' business model. Loan modification is labor intensive and requires detailed knowledge of local housing markets to determine whether a loan modification is in the interest of the investors. It was as if employees at McDonald's were suddenly asked to prepare haute cuisine.

The robo-signing scandal that erupted in the fall of 2010 gave further proof of the inadequacies of the loan servicing industry. As foreclosure volume increased, loan servicers outsourced the paperwork to specialized law firms. Called "foreclosure mills" by critics, these law firms were paid modest fees, for example, $1,200 per foreclosure, but with high volume and low-level employees doing most of the work, supervised by a few lawyers, they could be quite profitable. Foreclosure mills were known to have hired teenagers and hair stylists to document complex paperwork. Robo-signers signed affidavits testifying to the validity of 10,000 or more documents in a month. Clearly, they had no chance to read them, let alone determine their legal validity.[73]

Loan modifications have also been constrained by the pooling and servicing agreements (PSAs) that govern pools of mortgages. Over 90 percent of mortgages initiated in recent years have been securitized. Gelpern and Levitin call the PSAs "Frankenstein contracts"—brilliant human creations that come back to haunt us because we have no way of stopping the destruction they wreak. "The continuing foreclosure epidemic holds an important lesson for the future: even where rigidity makes perfect sense for the contracting parties, widespread barriers to modification can unleash catastrophic social consequences." While contracts should be

72. Cordell and others (2008, p. 15).
73. Yves Smith, "How the Banks Put the Economy Underwater," *New York Times*, October 31, 2010, p. WK9; Gretchen Morgenson, "Banks' Flawed Paperwork Throws Some Foreclosures into Chaos," *New York Times*, October 4, 2010, p. A1.

difficult to break, the authors stress, "private contracts must not be read to interfere with legitimate public policymaking."[74] They cite numerous instances, including corporate bonds and policies initiated in response to the foreclosure crisis of the Great Depression, where contracts were renegotiated in order to protect the parties involved and the broader society.[75] As the HUD report to Congress concluded, "There is growing consensus that the rules governing securitization can and do limit the flexibility of servicers to pursue modifications, even in situations where an aggressive modification would benefit both the borrowers and the investors."[76]

Finally, the servicers' incentives, written into their contracts, motivate them to proceed to foreclosure or stretch out the process rather than modify a loan.[77] Servicers are paid a fee based on the unpaid principal balance of the loans in the pool and, therefore, do not want to refinance loans or reduce the principal owed. In addition, they make money on loans in default through late fees and "process management fees." If a loan goes through foreclosure, servicers recover all their expenses before any of the investors get paid, but get paid nothing for the loss mitigation work they perform.

To sum up, the policies and practices of national decisionmakers, private as well as public, have constricted the opportunity space for local actors to modify loans, prevent foreclosures, and stabilize local housing markets. Decisions about loan modification have been pulled out of the hands of knowledgeable local actors and placed in the hands of national servicers who lack the expertise and the local knowledge to act effectively. In addition, servicers have conflicts of interest with the mortgage investors, for whom they supposedly work, and with the public.

Congress and the Obama administration chose foreclosure prevention and loan modification policies that were all carrots and no sticks. Relying almost entirely on carrots, or incentives, to change behavior, the HAMP program has been remarkably ineffective. A good example is the net present value (NPV) calculation, which participating servicers are required to conduct and which is designed to determine if the owners of the mortgage would be better off modifying the loan or proceeding to foreclosure. Large servicers, whose servicing

74. Gelpern and Levitin (2009, pp. 1081, 1080, 1134).

75. The rigidities of PSAs come in many different forms. PSAs sometimes simply limit the number of mortgages that can be modified. Another problem is that the mortgage pools are owned by thousands of investors from all over the world and in many cases modifying loans requires the consent of each investor to modify its right to receive principal and interest payments. Modifying a particular loan can affect different investors differently because they invest in different "tranches" or slices of the overall pool. The result can be so-called tranche warfare.

76. U.S. Department of Housing and Urban Development (2010, p. 48).

77. My discussion of servicer incentives relies on Thompson (2009).

book value exceeds $40 billion, may use their own default and redefault rates without having to publicly defend them. Even smaller servicers have the right to adjust the standard discount rate set by the federal government, up to 2.5 percentage points, which can have a huge effect on whether the NPV calculation supports a loan modification.[78] As noted earlier, in many instances loan modifications would be in the best interest of the investors, primarily because of the large drop in value following a foreclosure. Servicers, however, can easily manipulate the NPV calculation to justify foreclosure over loan modification.

As Lester Salamon has observed, policy tools that are noncoercive often are more politically popular but less effective in achieving policy goals.[79] The Making Home Affordable program is more effective at protecting the balance sheets of the banks than keeping people in their homes or protecting neighborhoods. It would appear that incentives to servicers would have to be very generous to significantly raise the loan modification rate. More coercive policies would be more effective at less cost. Including mortgages in bankruptcy proceedings, so-called cram-down legislation, would put pressure on servicers to modify loans because judges otherwise could force them to accept much less than the face value of the mortgage from bankrupt homeowners.[80] The federal government could have performed the NPV calculations itself, or required that they meet certain standards, and then *required* loan modifications where the NPV calculation supported such action.[81] Such "sticks" would have greatly increased the opportunity space for local foreclosure counselors to modify loans, keep families in their homes, and stabilize neighborhoods.

Neighborhood Stabilization in the Wake of Foreclosures

Largely lacking the power to prevent foreclosures, local actors find themselves in the unenviable position of trying to minimize the damage from foreclosures after they occur. As discussed earlier, foreclosures generate significant spillover effects that are quite localized and can quickly generate reinforcing feedback cycles that can lead to neighborhood decline (figure 3-3). Effective post-foreclosure resilience requires intervening early in so-called transitional areas where concentrated foreclosures could trigger market decline or even contagious

78. Cordell and others (2009, p. 28).

79. Salamon (2002, p. 26).

80. In the first year of the Obama administration, cram-down legislation passed in the House but was defeated in the Senate.

81. That said, it is worth noting that an objective NPV calculation only takes into account private interests in loan modifications. A social NPV calculation that took into account the huge negative spillover effects of foreclosures would mandate many more loan modifications as being in the public interest.

abandonment. Successful resilience will be measured not by how many families were helped or how many homes were put back on the market but by the ability to stabilize the supply and demand for housing in marginal neighborhoods. In short, place-based resilience must involve a market recovery strategy.[82]

Market recovery strategies must be adapted to the conditions of regional housing markets and submarkets. The foreclosure challenge varies—both among metropolitan areas and within them. The recent wave of foreclosures flooded across a metropolitan landscape that varied in market strength. Some metropolitan areas, driven by robust job growth and high levels of immigration, have a perpetual housing shortage relative to demand. As a result, the so-called sand states, such as Florida, Arizona, and California, experienced huge run-ups of housing prices in the boom, followed by precipitous price declines. Because of the underlying strong market, however, they have experienced relatively low levels of vacancy and abandonment due to foreclosures. In such states local actors may only need to enforce housing codes strictly and make sure that temporarily empty homes do not end up blighting the neighborhoods. As noted earlier, place-based resilience in the wake of foreclosures is more difficult in weak market metropolitan areas.

Market conditions also vary *within* metropolitan areas. Overbuilding on the suburban fringe can cause geographical booms and busts that destabilize housing submarkets in outer ring suburbs as well as central cities. Many central cities in the northern manufacturing belt have suffered from weak demand for housing and resulting vacancies and abandonment for decades. Inner-city decline is not primarily the result of a weak regional economy but of imbalances of supply and demand within regions that result in vacancy and abandonment at the end of the filtering chain. In many metropolitan areas, more houses are built on the suburban fringe than are needed to meet demand. In the 1990s, for example, the city of Buffalo produced 3.89 more units of housing for every new household formed in the region.[83] The inevitable result of such overbuilding is vacant and abandoned housing. One of the tragedies of the recent foreclosure tsunami is that it inundated communities that had pulled themselves up with focused community development efforts over many years. Concentrated foreclosures wiped out decades of hard work. As little as 3 to 5 percent abandoned properties can lead to contagious abandonment.[84]

And while foreclosure rates may be high in inner cities, in most metropolitan areas they are higher in one or more suburban counties.[85] Exurban areas with so-

82. Ashton and Schnell (2010).
83. Bier and Post (2006).
84. Mallach (2006, p. 9).
85. Lucy (2010).

called "drive 'til you qualify" mortgages have suffered from a buildup of REOs (bank-owned properties).[86] A study of 40,000 mortgages in Chicago, Jacksonville, and San Francisco found a statistically significant correlation, after controlling for income, between the likelihood of mortgage foreclosure and neighborhood vehicle ownership rates.[87] This is not surprising because working families making from $20,000 to $50,000 a year spend a higher proportion of their incomes on transportation (29 percent) than on housing (28 percent) and the farther they live from work, the higher the transportation burden.[88]

The resilience literature suggests what types of neighborhoods will be more resilient to the foreclosure challenge. Areas with a diverse portfolio of housing types, transportation choices, and better access to jobs and amenities will be more resilient. According to William Lucy, neighborhoods built before 1940 have retained their housing values better than areas built between 1945 and 1970 when developers tended to separate uses and build large numbers of similar, often quite small, homes. "Pre-1940 neighborhoods (certainly not all of them, but many) were widely varied in their housing types and quality, nearly always were more accessible, sometimes were in prime areas, including close to downtown jobs, and became attractive places to remodel or to demolish and rebuild."[89]

Housing policy is generally focused on affordability and production. In weak market areas beset by foreclosures, however, a focus on producing affordable units will not address the problem of reinforcing cycles of decline. Indeed, fixing up and marketing abandoned homes may only lead to abandonment in some other part of the city. A market recovery strategy requires shifting focus from properties to places. If there is an oversupply of housing, a demolition strategy in the worst-off areas can help bring supply and demand into better balance in the stronger areas.[90]

Besides limiting supply, market recovery programs in weak market areas must boost demand.[91] Success requires becoming a community of choice where people want to live in sufficient numbers to replace the normal population turnover. Healthy demand for housing in an area depends not just on the quality of the housing stock, but on an array of other factors, including low crime

86. Immergluck (2009b).

87. Reported in National Resources Defense Council (2010).

88. Lipman (2006).

89. Lucy (2010, p. 64).

90. This has come to be known as "right sizing." City governments, such as those of Detroit and Youngstown, have come to believe that they need to depopulate parts of the city in order to support renewal in other parts of the city.

91. For an early seminal statement on the need for a market recovery strategy in weak market areas, see Brophy and Burnett (2003).

and access to good schools, jobs, and quality public spaces. An effective market recovery strategy requires what is called "cross-silo" planning. Ultimately, what matters is market confidence.[92] Are homeowners confident enough about an area to invest in their homes? Housing investment is like a game of prisoner's dilemma: if everyone invests then all can be confident they will get a good return on their investment; but if one person invests alone, he or she will almost certainly not get back the investment on sale of the home. The importance of market confidence suggests the need to act quickly to address signs of disorder, like high grass around or broken windows in a foreclosed home. Market stability is not only possible in wealthy neighborhoods; working class neighborhoods can be stable if there is a high level of market confidence.

The Fog of Foreclosures: Data and Local Empowerment

If the foregoing analysis of the foreclosure challenge is correct, interventions need to be precisely targeted across time and space. Local actors need to intervene early in the process—before foreclosures have set in motion reinforcing processes of decline. Second, local actors need to identify areas where interventions could make a difference. This means transitional communities that had healthy demand but where concentrated foreclosures could tip the area into contagious abandonment and decline. For these reasons, real-time, fine-grained data on the foreclosures are necessary for effective local interventions. Without sophisticated data systems, local actors often grope forward based on inconsistent and out-of-date data.[93] One of the major reasons why local actors often operate in a "fog of foreclosures" is because mortgages and foreclosures are essentially a private transaction and public access to accurate data is limited.

The foundation of an effective market recovery strategy is identifying transitional neighborhoods. This is not an easy task. The Reinvestment Fund in Philadelphia has pioneered using cluster analysis to identify such neighborhoods.[94] This requires collecting a wide range of housing data at the block group or neighborhood level. A statistical technique is then applied (cluster analysis) to identify which neighborhoods are performing similarly. Neighborhoods can be arrayed from the strongest to the weakest, with transitional areas in the middle.

92. Buki and Schilling (2010).
93. Good data are also crucial for putting the foreclosure issue on the public's agenda. As Deborah Stone (1998, p. 187) has observed, "The process of counting something makes people notice it more. . . ." In metro area after metro area, visually arresting GIS maps showing the growth and spread of foreclosures across a region have been crucial in garnering public attention. For a discussion of local agenda setting, see Swanstrom, Chapple, and Immergluck (2009).
94. Goldstein and Closkey (2006).

Cluster analysis requires a wide array of parcel-based data and a skilled analyst. The technique is not automatic. It requires knowledge of local markets in order to identify the number of clusters, and final results must be evaluated in the context of developments not captured by the data, such as where a new school or grocery store is being built.

The foreclosure challenge is a complex process. There are at least seven stages that are important to track: (1) loan origination, (2) delinquency, (3) foreclosure notice, (4) sheriff's sale, (5) disposition of bank-owned (REO) properties, (6) vacant units, and (7) abandoned properties. After a REO sale by the bank, for example, local actors need to know whether the property was bought by an owner-occupier, a local housing nonprofit, a local investor, or a national speculator. The foreclosure challenge is constantly changing, so responders need up-to-date data to adjust their policy responses. If local actors know the location and timing of different kinds of loans, they can anticipate foreclosure trends. Many subprime loans began to reset to higher interest rates in two years, but Alt-A loans often have resets after about five years. To anticipate when neighborhoods will be hit with more delinquencies and foreclosures, local actors need to know how many Alt-A loans were originated and when they will reset. They also need to be able to disaggregate the data to small geographies. Housing markets are local and processes of contagious abandonment are very local. Research has shown that foreclosures damage property values in a circle with a radius of about one-eighth mile, or 660 feet (see earlier discussion of spillover effects on surrounding homeowners). To track the spillover effects of foreclosures we need data at the census tract level and smaller—even down to the block or parcel level.

Simply counting foreclosures is difficult because of data inadequacies. National data on subprime lending were not collected until 2004 when reporting required by the Home Mortgage Disclosure Act was expanded to include information on high-cost loans. In retrospect, these data were crucial in putting the issue before the public and making the connection between subprime loans and foreclosures. But they do not include ARMs and do not tell who originated the loans—among other flaws. Data on completed foreclosures are even weaker. Because the foreclosure process is regulated by the states, the process varies and the data recorded are often not comparable. To obtain meaningful data, labor-intensive cleaning and compiling of data are necessary. In addition, without a national data depository on foreclosures, private sector firms, such as Realty-Trac, have stepped in. While RealtyTrac is often relied on for foreclosure counts, its data are notoriously uneven and unreliable. Local actors frequently use it anyway because it is free. McDash Analytics, now CoreLogic, has compiled more accurate data but access to the data is expensive.

Good data are also needed about loan performance in order to prevent people from going into foreclosure and being forced from their homes. Research has shown that contacting homeowners early in the process facilitates better outcomes. Probably because of the stigma of foreclosure, people often do not take action to avoid foreclosure by talking to their servicer or seeking counseling. As a result, it is important to reach out to those facing foreclosure. In order to do this, counseling agencies need data on where loan delinquencies are concentrated. Thus, for example, it would be useful to have data on loan delinquencies as a precursor to a foreclosure notice. The Mortgage Bankers Association conducts a survey of mortgage delinquencies, but it is not disaggregated to pinpoint specific areas and, therefore, cannot guide outreach efforts.

Data are equally important in the post-foreclosure process. Here, once again, the fog can be thick. Data on the number and duration of REO properties are an excellent indicator of market recovery. The accumulation of REO properties in specific areas indicates a weak market and possible contagious abandonment. Dan Immergluck states the problem bluntly: "Data on foreclosures and post-foreclosure properties, such as REO, are not compiled on a regular, uniform basis by any public agency at a multistate level."[95] Forced to use a private national database, Immergluck found that REO properties are not just accumulating in central cities in weak market metropolitan areas but also in distant "drive-'til-you-qualify" suburbs in strong market metros. After a property is sold out of REO, local governments often do not even know who owns it, and, therefore, they cannot hold the owner accountable for cost of maintenance—such as grass cutting or boarding up vacant properties. Vacancy data would also be useful in determining which neighborhoods are vulnerable to contagious processes of abandonment and decay. The United States Postal Service has data on vacancies but with many flaws.

Despite the obstacles, some regions have developed sophisticated regional data utilities that expand the opportunity space for local actors. Under the leadership of the Northeast Ohio Community and Neighborhood Data for Organizing (NEO-CANDO), established in 1992 at Case Western Reserve University, the Cleveland metropolitan area has developed one of the best data collection and analysis systems in the nation. NEO-CANDO gathers neighborhood data for seventeen counties in Northeast Ohio and makes them available to the public on its website. It has strong support from area foundations and has played a key role in the rethinking of community development in Cleveland from a bricks-and-mortar orientation to one focused strategically on fortifying markets in a handful of transitional neighborhoods.

95. Immergluck (2009b, p. 3).

The sophisticated regional data system in Cleveland is more the exception than the rule, because under present rules developing such a system is expensive, labor-intensive, and politically challenging. The first problem is that the private nature of foreclosure data and the fragmented collection of parcel-level data at the state and county level mean that every metropolitan area must reinvent the wheel, cleaning and organizing the data in an expensive and time-consuming process. Creating a regional data utility requires significant public or foundation funding. Moreover, much of the parcel-level data are controlled by county assessors who are concerned about tax rates and assessment practices, not public policy. Many are underfunded and the data are not digitized, requiring laborious hand entry. Some counties sell the data. Acquiring access to these data at a reasonable cost and on a regular basis requires negotiating political deals with each county.[96]

The solution to the problems of data on foreclosures is a policy of "targeted transparency." Targeted transparency policies have five essential characteristics or "parts":

—Mandated public disclosure

—By corporations or other private or public organizations

—Of standardized, comparable, and disaggregated information

—Regarding specific products or practices

—To further a defined public purpose

When problems are widely dispersed across the nation or locally variable—two characteristics of the foreclosure challenge—a policy of targeted transparency makes the most sense. Governments act as "stewards of transparency policy by compelling disclosure of needed information when participants cannot obtain it, fostering common definitions and accurate metrics, and providing feedback and analysis to encourage transparency improvement."[97]

A good example of targeted transparency is the 1975 Home Mortgage Disclosure Act (HMDA). Motivated by fears of redlining and discrimination in lending, HMDA required federally regulated lenders to report on the loans they made by census tract; later, they were required to report on the race of applicants and loan recipients. The 1977 Community Reinvestment Act (CRA) required regulated lenders to "meet the credit needs of their communities." Community-based organizations have used HMDA data to challenge the banks, and during the formal period of the challenge the lending institution is prohibited from merging with another bank or opening new branches. In order to avoid negative publicity and stop the challenge, banks often have negotiated community lending agreements in which they agree to lend to low-income and minority neighborhoods.

96. Newman (2010).
97. See pp. 6 and 17 of Fung, Graham, and Weil (2007), plus the discussion on targeted transparency in general.

According to the National Community Reinvestment Coalition, between 1992 and 2000 the value of CRA agreements totaled $1.09 trillion.[98] A study by the Federal Reserve Board concluded that CRA opened up new profitable business opportunities for banks and CRA loans generally performed as well as non-CRA loans.[99]

HMDA, originally designed to address the problem of redlining, could be reformed and expanded to address the problem of greenlining. First, HMDA needs to be extended from federally regulated institutions to all mortgage lending. Data should be reported in a common format and standardized way to track mortgage lending from loan origination to REO sales so that they can be more targeted, preferably to census tracts or smaller. In addition, data should be reported as close to real time as possible so that actors can keep pace with fast-changing trends. The Internet enables data to be shared almost instantaneously with users. In addition, HUD should encourage county assessors to share parcel-level data in a standardized and digitized form. There is no reason why each county should record and store parcel-based data in a different way. HUD could condition grants on developing statewide standardized property reporting requirements. In order to facilitate digitizing data, HUD should consider competitive grants to states or county assessors.[100]

Once the necessary data are made available in a common format and on a timely basis, the problem remains of regional actors developing the analytical capacity to manipulate the data in meaningful ways. Regional data clearinghouses, like NEO-CANDO, have developed in metropolitan areas across the country, usually by university-led groups. Community foundations have played key roles in developing regional data clearinghouses. However, many regions lack strong community foundations. National organizations like the National Vacant Property Campaign, the National Neighborhood Indicators Project, and Living Cities have played the role of national intermediaries in promoting regional data capacity, but this varies tremendously across regions. HUD should consider start-up grants for regional data clearinghouses. Modest amounts of funding could leverage meaningful increases in data gathering and analytical capacity.

98. National Community Reinvestment Coalition (2001), as cited in Fung, Graham, and Weil (2007, p. 251).

99. Board of Governors of the Federal Reserve System (2000), as cited in Fung, Graham, and Weil (2007, p. 252).

100. HUD will also need a sophisticated regional data system to evaluate National Stabilization Program (NSP) grants. This will require an understanding of the NSP interventions and an analysis of housing market dynamics that will enable researchers to isolate policy effects from normal neighborhood trajectories. See Kingsley, Smith, and Price (2009, p. 43).

Federal Policy and Neighborhood Stabilization in the Wake of Foreclosures

The primary federal policy to help areas rebound from foreclosures is the aptly named Neighborhood Stabilization Program (NSP). Originally funded at $3.92 billion under a formula grant (NSP1), the program received an additional $1.92 billion in competitive grants (NSP2) in 2009, and in 2010 another $1 billion was authorized for formula grants. Most of the money has been used to buy foreclosed properties, fix them up, and put them back on the market. The program is small relative to the need. Under NSP1, for example, St. Louis County, Missouri, received $16.5 million ($9.3 million as a direct allocation from the federal government and $6.2 million from the state). At $100,000 per home, this is enough to buy, improve, and sell about 165 properties. In a county where 4,516 foreclosures were completed in 2010, this means the funds could treat only 3.7 percent of the foreclosed properties.[101]

Given the low level of NSP funding relative to the need, it is clear that funds must be strategically targeted to make a difference.[102] Spreading the funds around—the so-called peanut-butter approach—risks wasting taxpayers' money when market dynamics overwhelm rehabilitated homes. Instead, investments must be concentrated on transitional neighborhoods where foreclosures could tip a previously stable area into decline.[103] NSP funds can produce the biggest bang for the buck in these promising neighborhoods where the negative spillovers of foreclosure could multiply.

NSP rules, however, made neighborhood stabilization more difficult by impeding the ability of local actors to tailor the program to local conditions. Under NSP1, for example, recipients were required to spend the funds only on foreclosed properties. But if the goal of the program is neighborhood stabilization, local actors should have the freedom to help other properties if they are essential to market recovery. Under NSP1 at least 25 percent of the funds were obligated to house families whose incomes did not exceed 50 percent of the area median income. Such a requirement, however, will shrink the opportunity space if a community needs to concentrate on attracting working class and middle-income households in order to stabilize housing demand. NSP required that the funds be allocated within eighteen months, even though neighborhood stabilization requires a much longer time frame. This is not the place to go into a

101. Of course, if the properties are sold the NSP funds can be recycled so that more properties can be helped over the long run.

102. For evidence on the need to target expenditures to achieve market recovery, see Galster, Tatian, and Accordino (2006).

103. See Goldstein (2008) and Mallach (2008).

full-scale critique of the NSP program except to say that giving recipients more freedom to pursue a market recovery strategy would make sense. At the same time, requiring recipients to concentrate resources in neighborhood strategy areas would also help, partly by helping communities to overcome political pressures to spread the money around, or what Anthony Downs called the "law of political dispersion."[104]

The sophistication required to develop and implement an effective market recovery strategy raises the issue of local capacity. There are two general kinds of capacity. One could be called "administrative capacity," which refers to the ability of local NSP recipients to spend the money in a timely fashion while still meeting all regulations. Implementation of NSP requires a daunting array of competencies: identifying foreclosed properties and contacting the new owners, negotiating a purchase price that meets the federal requirement to pay below appraised value, assessing the need for rehabilitation and evaluating whether the combined costs of purchase and rehab will keep the house affordable, assessing the demand to purchase or rent rehabbed homes, finding homebuyers or renters who meet the guidelines, clearing the title, and meeting environmental regulations, such as those on lead or brownfields.

Many recipients of NSP funds, especially suburban governments, have little or no experience buying and rehabbing properties. Just getting the money out the door in a timely fashion is a challenge. In May 2010 HUD estimated that as much as $1 billion of the $3.92 billion would be unobligated by the deadline and would be reallocated.[105] To HUD's credit, it has revised the rules to speed up implementation and worked with local recipients to increase their administrative capacity.

The second type of capacity, what I call "strategic collaborative capacity," is in even shorter supply. Strategic collaborative capacity refers to the ability of an NSP recipient not just to spend the money in a timely fashion but to develop and implement a targeted market recovery strategy. Strategic collaborative capacity requires collaborating across policy functions, sectors (public, private, nonprofit), and governments.

Cross-functional collaboration is required because sustaining housing demand depends on not just housing but on other policy functions, including schools, transit, police, and parks.

Cross-sectoral collaboration is required because local governments lack the knowledge to implement neighborhood stabilization programs effectively. An

---

104. Downs (1980).

105. The final amount of unobligated funds appears to be much lower, on the order of 5 percent. See *Community Development Digest* (www.housinganddevelopment.com/cdd/index.php?mod=spub&str=2153).

effective market recovery strategy requires identifying blocks where a few lower-quality homes or foreclosures are pulling down the values of a significant number of higher quality homes.[106] Nonprofit community development corporations (CDCs) possess the political legitimacy and block-by-block knowledge of housing markets needed for effective market recovery. The cooperation of real estate agents and lenders is also necessary to sustain market confidence.

Cross-governmental collaboration is needed because small suburban governments lack the scale and expertise to implement effective market recovery strategies and because transitional neighborhoods need to be connected to regional job opportunities. Moreover, smart growth policies that limit suburban development facilitate the success of neighborhood recovery in weak market regions.

Strategic collaborative capacity varies tremendously, both across and within metropolitan areas. Collaborative capacity is based on trust, which, in turn, depends on a history of collaboration. As Robert Putnam has observed, unlike financial capital, which is depleted with use, social capital is enhanced with use; the more you use it, the more you have.[107] Every time two actors collaborate to achieve a mutually beneficial outcome, it becomes easier to trust that the parties will live up to their obligations the next time. Some regions have robust networks of housing nonprofits and long histories of collaboration across the public, private, and nonprofit sectors. Community foundations have played key roles in developing this capacity in metropolitan areas such as Chicago, Minneapolis, and Cleveland.

In 2008 Living Cities, a partnership of leading national foundations, initiated a $5.25 million, ten-city pilot program to support promising initiatives to mitigate the effects of concentrated foreclosures on urban neighborhoods.[108] For the most part, this was a capacity-building program. Living Cities supported Neighborhood Progress, Inc. (NPI) in Cleveland to develop its Strategic Investment Initiative (SII), one of the most promising market recovery projects in the nation.[109] NPI identified six neighborhoods (expanded to nine in 2010) where NSP and other funds will be concentrated. The neighborhoods were picked because they are transitional and possess strengths such as new schools or retail centers as well as strong CDCs able to coordinate a sophisticated market recovery strategy. The goal is to demolish 100 homes, redevelop 121 vacant homes, and prevent 100 homeowners from losing their homes through foreclosures. With thousands of foreclosures dumped on an already weak housing market,

---

106. Buki and Schilling (2010).
107. Putnam (2000).
108. For an evaluation of the Living Cities initiative, see Mayer and Temkin (2009).
109. SII is supported by the city of Cleveland and the Cleveland and Gund foundations.

success is not guaranteed.[110] But without a targeted strategy, the chances of success would be practically nil.

In short, uneven strategic collaborative capacity is a huge barrier to effective local resilience in the wake of foreclosures. Federal policy should pay much more attention to developing regional collaborative capacity.[111] HUD faces a dilemma: on the one hand, formula grants such as NSP1 risk funding jurisdictions that lack administrative and collaborative capacity; on the other hand, competitive grants such as NSP2 risk rewarding the "gazelles," those regions that already have strong capacity. More funds should be committed to capacity building.[112] To its credit, HUD has begun to address the capacity issue through its Sustainable Communities Planning grant program, which sets aside part of the funding for regions for collaborative processes of sustainable community planning. Originally financed at only about $100 million annually, the Sustainable Community Planning grants do not come close to meeting the need for capacity building.

Conclusion: Federal Policy and Local Resilience

According to a recent Pew Research Center Survey, "Americans are more skeptical of Washington than ever."[113] Even in the wake of widespread predatory lending and the abuses by Wall Street, public opinion has shifted toward wanting smaller government with fewer services. The victories of the Tea Party candidates in the 2010 off-year election were more evidence of mounting distrust of the federal government. While only 38 percent of respondents to a 2010 national survey viewed the impact of the federal government on their lives as positive, a majority (51 percent) reported a positive view of local government.[114] The foregoing analysis suggests a way to encourage a more local approach to federal programs that could cross the partisan divide. Strong federal policies do not necessarily undermine local self-reliance; they can expand the opportunity space for local actors to respond effectively to local challenges such as foreclosures.

Although the emphasis here has been on local resilience, basic regulation of mortgage lending belongs with the federal government. The greatest contribution the government could have made to local resilience would have been to limit the subprime and predatory lending that unleashed the foreclosure crisis in

110. NPI has negotiated an agreement with servicers to freeze the foreclosure process for ninety days to prevent vacant properties from flooding their target areas in an untimely fashion.

111. NSP2 did include $50 million for capacity building.

112. For recommendations along these lines, see Brophy and Godsil (2009, ch. 4).

113. Anthony Kohut, "Americans Are More Skeptical of Washington than Ever," *Wall Street Journal*, April 19, 2010.

114. Pew Research Center Survey (http://pewresearch.org/pubs/1569/trust-in-government-distrust-discontent-anger-partisan-rancor).

the first place. It is unrealistic to expect local or even state governments to regulate mortgage lending effectively because they have a stake in a prosperous real estate sector and rising property values and, therefore, will be biased toward loose credit standards. So long as federal regulators are freed from competing for fees from regulated entities, they should be able to represent the interests of consumers and work to support sustainable lending policies.[115]

The question now is how to cope with the waves of foreclosures that will continue for years into the future. We need resilient local actors, both to keep as many people in their homes as possible and to minimize the damage from completed foreclosures. There is much the federal government can do to expand their opportunity space. The federal government can put in place a system of carrots *and sticks* to motivate servicers to work with local foreclosure counselors to modify loans and keep families in their homes. Only the federal government has the resources to fund post-foreclosure neighborhood stabilization policies at a level commensurate with the need. Locally devised market recovery strategies involving collaboration across governments, functions, and sectors are the keys to neighborhood stabilization. Above all, the federal government needs to address the uneven administrative and collaborative capacity of local actors to devise and implement sophisticated market recovery strategies.

Finally, resilience theory suggests what kinds of places will be most resilient to future challenges such as foreclosures. According to the theory, diversity and flexibility are correlated with resilience. Places with a diverse housing stock that can accommodate households at different income ranges and different life stages will be more resilient than neighborhoods with only one type of housing. Neighborhoods with a wide range of transportation choices (auto, transit, biking, and pedestrian) will be more resilient than completely auto-dependent areas. And communities with flexible local organizations that are able to track real estate trends in real time, shift resources quickly, and collaborate across sectors will be more resilient than communities without such organizations. National policies can help build such resilient places.

References

Apgar, Willam C., and Mark Duda. 2005. "Collateral Damage: The Municipal Impact of Today's Mortgage Foreclosure Boom." Prepared for the Homeownership Preservation Foundation, Minneapolis (May).

Ashton, Philip. 2010. "The Financial State of Emergency and the Reconfiguration of Credit Risk." Manuscript, University of Illinois Chicago, Department of Urban Planning and Policy.

115. See Frug and Barron (2008, p. 197).

Ashton, Philip, and Susanne Schnell. 2010. "'Stuck' Neighborhoods: Concentrated Subprime Lending and the Challenges of Neighborhood Recovery." Manuscript, University of Illinois Chicago, Department of Urban Planning and Policy.

Avery, Robert B., Kenneth P. Brevoort, and Glenn B. Canner. 2007. "The 2006 HMDA Data." *Federal Reserve Bulletin* 93 (December).

Barr, Michael S., Sendhil Mullainathan, and Eldar Shafir. 2008. "Behaviorally Informed Home Mortgage Credit Regulation." In *Borrowing to Live: Consumer and Mortgage Credit Revisited*, edited by Nicolas P. Retsinas and Eric S. Belsky, pp. 170–203. Brookings.

Baumgartner, Frank R., and Bryan D. Jones. 1993. *Agendas and Instability in American Politics*. University of Chicago Press.

Bess, Michael. 2008. "Assessing the Impact of Home Foreclosures in Charlotte Neighborhoods." *Geography and Public Safety* 1, no. 3: 2–4.

Bier, Thomas, and Charlie Post. 2006. "Vacating the City: An Analysis of New Home Construction and Household Growth." In *Redefining Urban and Suburban America: Evidence from Census 2000*, edited by Alan Berube, Bruce Katz, and Robert E. Lang. Brookings.

Board of Governors of the Federal Reserve System. 2000. "The Performance and Profitability of CRA-Related Lending." Washington.

Bostic, Raphael W., and others. 2007. "State and Local Anti-Predatory Lending Laws: The Effect of Legal Enforcement Mechanisms." *Journal of Economics and Business* 60, nos. 1-2: 47–66.

Brophy, Paul, and Kim Burnett. 2003. *Building a New Framework for Community Development in Weak Market Cities*. Denver: Community Development Partnership Network.

Brophy, Paul C., and Rachel D. Godsil. 2009. *Retooling HUD for a Catalytic Federal Government: A Report to Secretary Shaun Donovan*. Philadelphia: Penn Institute for Urban Research.

Buki, Charles, and Elizabeth Humphrey Schilling, 2010. "The Right Interventions to Restore Confidence in Weak Markets." Planetizen, February 4.

Center for Responsible Lending. 2008. *Subprime Spillover: Foreclosures Cost Neighbors $202 Billion; 40.6 Million Homes Lose $5,000 on Average*. Durham, N.C.

Cordell, Larry, and others. 2008. "The Incentives of Mortgage Servicers: Myths and Realities." Finance and Economics Discussion Series. Washington: Board of Governors of the Federal Reserve System.

———. 2009. "Designing Loan Modifications to Address the Mortgage Crisis and the Making Home Affordable Program." Finance and Economics Discussion Series. Washington: Board of Governors of the Federal Reserve System.

Coulton, Claudia, Michael Schramm, and April Hirsch. 2010. "Foreclosure Crisis and Response in Cleveland and Cuyahoga County." Internal memo prepared for Metropolitan Response to the Foreclosure Crisis: A Dialogue between Researchers and Practitioners. Cleveland: Center on Urban Poverty and Community Development, Mandel School of Applied Social Sciences, Case Western Reserve University.

Cutts, Amy Crews, and William A. Merrill. 2008. "Interventions in Mortgage Default: Policies and Practices to Prevent Home Loss and Lower Costs." Working Paper 08-01. McLean, Va.: Freddie Mac.

Downs, Anthony. 1980. "Using the Lessons of Experience to Allocate Resources in the Community Development Program." In *Housing Urban America*, edited by Jon Pynoos, Robert Schafer, and Chester W. Hartman, pp. 522–535. 2nd ed. New York: Aldine Publishing.

Edmiston, Kelly. 2009. "Characteristics of High-Foreclosure Neighborhoods in the Tenth District." *Economic Review*: 51–75. Federal Reserve Bank of Kansas City, Second Quarter.

Engel, Kathleen C., and Patrick McCoy. 2001. "A Tale of Three Markets: The Law and Economics of Predatory Lending." *Texas Law Review* 80, no. 6: 1255–367.

Frug, Gerald E., and David J. Barron. 2008. *City Bound: How States Stifle Urban Innovation.* Cornell University Press.

Fullilove, Mindy. 2004. *Root Shock: How Tearing Up City Neighborhoods Hurts America, and What We Can Do about It.* New York: Random House.

Fung, Archon, Mary Graham, and David Weil. 2007. *Full Disclosure: The Perils and Promise of Transparency.* Cambridge University Press.

Galster, George, Peter Tatian, and John Accordino. 2006. "Targeting Investments for Neighborhood Revitalization." *Journal of the American Planning Association* 72, no. 4: 457–74.

Gelpern, Anna, and Adam J. Levitin. 2009. "Rewriting Frankenstein Contracts: Workout Prohibitions in Residential Mortgage-Backed Securities." *Southern California Law Review* 82: 1075–152.

Glaeser, Edward L., Joshua Gottlieb, and Joseph Gyourko. 2010. "Did Credit Market Policies Cause the Housing Bubble?" Policy Brief. Rappaport Institute/Taubman Center, Harvard University.

Goldstein, I. 2008. "Targeting Neighborhood Reinvestment Strategies: Using TRF's Market Value Analysis to Strategically Target the Acquisition of Vacant and Foreclosed Properties." Presentation to St. Louis Federal Reserve Strengthening Neighborhoods in Weak Markets Conference. St. Louis (September).

Goldstein, Ira, and C. Sean Closkey. 2006. "Market Value Analysis: Understanding Where and How to Invest Resources." *Bridges* (Summer): 1–2.

Gramlich, Edward M. 2007. *Subprime Mortgages: America's Latest Boom and Bust.* Washington: Urban Institute.

Greenspan, Alan. 2007. *The Age of Turbulence: Adventures in a New World.* New York: Penguin.

Harding, John P., Eric Rosenblatt, and Vincent W. Yao. 2008. "The Contagion Effect of Foreclosed Properties." *Journal of Urban Economics* 66, no. 3: 164–178.

Hatzius, Jan, and Michael A. Marschoun. 2009. "Home Prices and Credit Losses: Projections and Policy Options." Global Economics Paper 177. New York: Goldman Sachs.

Ho, Ghiang, and Anthony Pennington-Cross. 2006. *The Impact of Local Predatory Laws on the Flow of Subprime Credit: North Carolina and Beyond.* Federal Reserve Bank of St. Louis.

Immergluck, Dan. 2009a. *Foreclosed: High-Risk Lending, Deregulation, and the Undermining of America's Mortgage Market.* Cornell University Press.

————. 2009b. "Intrametropolitan Patterns of Foreclosed Homes: ZIP-Code-Level Distributions of Real-Estate-Owned (REO) Properties during the U.S. Mortgage Crisis." Discussion Paper 01-09. Federal Reserve Bank of Atlanta.

Immergluck, Dan, and Geoff Smith. 2004. *Risky Business—An Econometric Analysis of the Relationship between Subprime Lending and Neighborhood Foreclosures.* Chicago: Woodstock Institute, March.

————. 2006a. "The External Costs of Foreclosure: The Impact of Single-Family Mortgage Foreclosures on Property Values." *Housing Policy Debate* 17, no. 6: 57–79.

————. 2006b. "The Impact of Single-Family Mortgage Foreclosures on Neighborhood Crime." *Housing Studies* 21, no. 6: 851–866.

Kelling, George, and Catherine Coles. 1996. *Fixing Broken Windows: Restoring Order and Reducing Crime in Our Communities.* New York: Free Press.

Kingsley, G. Thomas. 2010. "Policies to Cope with Foreclosures and Their Effects on Neighborhoods." In *Urban and Regional Policy and Its Effects*, vol. 3, edited by Nancy Pindus, Howard Wial, and Hal Wolman, pp. 22–63. Brookings.

Kingsley, G. Thomas, Robin Smith, and David Price. 2009. "The Impacts of Foreclosures on Families and Communities." Report prepared for the Open Society Institute. Washington: Urban Institute.

Kochar, Rakesh, and Ana Gonzalez-Barrera. 2009. *Through Boom and Bust: Minorities, Immigrants and Homeownership.* Washington: Pew Research Center.

Lipman, Barbara J. 2006. *A Heavy Load: The Combined Housing and Transportation Burdens of Working Families.* Washington: Center for Housing Policy.

Logan, John R., and Harvey Molotch. 1987. *Urban Fortunes: The Political Economy of Place.* University of California Press.

Lovell, Phillip, and Julia Isaacs. 2008. "The Impact of the Mortgage Crisis on Children." *First Focus* (May): 1–5.

Lucy, William H. 2010. *Foreclosing the Dream: How America's Housing Crisis Is Reshaping Our Cities and Suburbs.* Chicago: American Planning Association.

Mallach, Alan. 2006. *Bringing Buildings Back: From Abandoned Properties to Community Assets.* Montclair, N.J.: National Housing Institute.

———. 2008. *How to Spend $3.2 Billion: Stabilizing Neighborhoods by Addressing Foreclosed and Abandoned Properties.* Federal Reserve Bank of Philadelphia.

Mayer, Neil, and Kenneth Temkin. 2009. *Evaluation of the Living Cities Foreclosure Mitigation Initiative, Final Interim Report.* Washington: Urban Institute.

Mayer, Neil. 2010. *National Foreclosure Mitigation Counseling Program Evaluation: Preliminary Analysis of Program Effects* (September Update). Washington: Urban Institute.

McCue, Daniel. 2009. "The Painful Impact of the Housing Downturn on Low Income and Minority Families." *Shelterforce* (Fall): 26-29.

National Community Reinvestment Coalition. 2001. "CRA Commitments." Washington: National Community Reinvestment Coalition.

National Resources Defense Council. 2010. "Reducing Foreclosures and Environmental Impacts through Location-Efficient Neighborhood Design" (January).

Newman, Kathe. 2010. "Using Publicly Available Data to Understand the Foreclosure Crisis." *Journal of the American Planning Association* 76, no. 2: 1–12.

Pastor, Manuel, T. William Lester, and Justin Scoggins. 2009. "Why Regions? Why Now? Who Cares?" *Journal of Urban Affairs* 31, no. 3: 269–96.

Putnam, Robert D. 2000. *Bowling Alone: The Collapse and Revival of American Community.* New York: Simon and Schuster.

Richardson, George P. 1999. *Feedback Thought in Social Science and Systems Theory.* Waltham, Mass.: Pegasus Communications.

Rogers, William, and Will Winter. 2009. "The Impact of Foreclosures on Neighboring Housing Sales." *Journal of Real Estate Research* 31, no. 4: 455–80.

Rumberger, Russell. 2003. "The Causes and Consequences of Student Mobility." *Journal of Negro Education* 72 no. 1: 6–21.

Salamon, Lester M. 2002. "The New Governance and the Tools of Public Action: An Introduction." In *The Tools of Government: A Guide to the New Governance*, edited by Lester M. Salamon, pp. 1–47. Oxford University Press.

Shapiro, Thomas M. 2004. *The Hidden Cost of Being African American: How Wealth Perpetuates Inequality.* Oxford University Press.

Stone, Deborah. 1998. *Policy Paradox: The Art of Political Decision Making.* New York: W. W. Norton.

Swanstrom, Todd. 2008. "Regional Resilience: A Critical Examination of the Ecological Framework, Building Resilient Regions." Working Paper 2008-07. University of California (April).

——. 2010. "Foreclosure Challenge and Response: St. Louis City and County." Memo prepared for Metropolitan Response to the Foreclosure Crisis: A Dialogue between Researchers and Practitioners (February). Washington: National League of Cities.

Swanstrom, Todd, and James A. Brooks. 2010. *Resilience in the Face of Foreclosures: Lessons from Local and Regional Practice.* Research Report. Washington: National League of Cities.

Swanstrom, Todd, Karen Chapple, and Dan Immergluck. 2009. "Regional Resilience in the Face of Foreclosures: Evidence from Six Metropolitan Areas." Working Paper 2009-05. University of California (May).

——. 2011. "Regional Resilience in the Face of Foreclosures: The Role of Federal and State Policies," in *Forging a New Housing Policy: Opportunity in the Wake of Crisis,* edited by Christopher Niedt and Marc Silver. Hempstead, N.Y.: National Center for Suburban Studies.

Thompson, Diane E. 2009. "Why Servicers Foreclose When They Should Modify and Other Puzzles of Servicer Behavior: Servicer Compensation and Its Consequences" (October). Boston: National Consumer Law Center.

U.S. Department of Housing and Urban Development. 2010. *Report to Congress on the Root Causes of the Foreclosure Crisis.* Washington: U.S. Department of Housing and Urban Development.

Weed, Sara, and Sonia Garrison. 2010. *Foreclosure as a Last Resort.* Policy Brief (October). Durham, N.C.: Center for Responsible Lending.

4

Struggling over Strangers or Receiving with Resilience? The Metropolitics of Immigrant Integration

MANUEL PASTOR AND JOHN MOLLENKOPF

I n April 2010 the Arizona legislature passed a law (Senate Bill 1070) that required law enforcement and public agency officials to determine the immigration status of individuals when they had "reasonable suspicion" that they might be undocumented immigrants. A maelstrom of national debate ensued, with advocates of the legislation arguing that the state was right to protect itself against a surge of "illegals," while opponents suggested that Arizona would soon fall into racial profiling and scare away hard-working legal residents. The only thing that both sides seemed to agree on was that local authorities were taking a long-established federal responsibility into their own hands. This localization of immigration enforcement was soon paralleled by a similar local or regional character in response to Arizona's action. While immigrant advocates all over the country were angry about SB 1070, the largest protest took place on May 1, 2010, in Los Angeles, with the city's mayor and its Catholic archbishop welcoming thousands of marchers at the demonstration's terminus.

The geographic diversity in attitudes toward immigrants hints at a key point: while the federal government has the formal responsibility for determining how

We thank the Building Resilient Regions Research Network of the MacArthur Foundation for supporting this work. Special thanks to Audrey Singer, Michael Fix, Hal Wolman, Margaret Weir, Howard Wial, and Ali Mayorkas for their comments on an earlier draft. Thanks as well to our colleagues on this project who conducted much of the field research on which we report: Michael Jones-Correa, Els deGraauw, Juan David de Lara, Jaime Dominguez, Paul Lewis, Rhonda Ortiz, Marta Pichardo, Marie Provine, Rachel Rosner, and Jennifer Tran. Finally, thanks to Justin Scoggins, Jennifer Tran, and Mirabai Auer for creating and updating the database used in the regional profiles and to Vannesa Carter for editorial assistance.

many immigrants come into the country and for barring those who lack permission to come, local and regional jurisdictions frame the living experience of immigrants as well as who welcomes or resists their presence. In the context of a stalemate over revising federal immigration law, states and localities are taking quite different approaches, with actions ranging from granting undocumented residents municipal ID cards in New Haven, Connecticut, and promoting immigrant integration in the state of Illinois, on the positive side, to Phoenix sheriff Joe Arpaio's tightened enforcement and Hazelton, Pennsylvania's attempt to prevent landlords from renting to unauthorized residents on the negative side.[1]

What determines the nature of a region's response to the presence of immigrants? One useful approach to answering that question involves thinking of international migration as a sort of "shock" for urban and metropolitan areas. As with any shock, there may be upsides—immigrants often add to the labor force, contribute more in taxes, and start new businesses. However, cities, regions, and states generally have more concerns when the immigrant "shock" is large scale, represents a significant increase from the base of foreign-born residents, and consists primarily of low-income and poorly educated individuals, particularly those without authorization. In this case, there can be significant fiscal stress for local jurisdictions stemming from the need to provide the most immediate public services (such as law enforcement and ensuring public health standards) to new and different groups who may not speak English and to meet basic public service mandates (like education and health care), as well as the longer-term imperative of promoting intergenerational upward mobility in the labor and housing markets. Rapid recent immigration can also have disconcerting effects on the mainstream population's sense of cultural integrity and erode social solidarity.[2] Finally, immigrant workers may compete with vulnerable native-born minority groups in labor markets and neighborhood housing markets, creating various racial and other tensions.[3]

In prior decades, new immigrants and their attendant negative (and positive) impacts were concentrated primarily in the large central cities that have traditionally served as the main receptors for immigrants—places like New York, Miami, Chicago, Los Angeles, and San Francisco. The long history of immigration to many of these cities helped them to develop a wide range of institutional mechanisms to ease their arrival and transition. However, in the last decade and a half, immigration has diffused away from these traditional destinations toward both the suburbs within these metropolitan areas and entirely new metropolitan

1. Varsanyi (2010).
2. Putnam (2007).
3. Catanzarite (2004); Pastor and Marcelli (2004).

areas like Charlotte, North Carolina, or Phoenix, Arizona. Lacking past experience with immigrants, many of these places were not equipped with institutional shock absorbers.

Two broad trajectories can be distinguished for managing the impact of rapid recent immigration. On the one hand, local civic and political leaders may rally public opinion to recognize the emergence of immigration shocks and generate political support for public policies and programs that mitigate these shocks and make the most of immigrant upside potential. On the other, civic and political leaders may rally public opposition to immigration, particularly unauthorized immigration, and adopt enforcement-oriented measures that chill the reception of new immigrants and underutilize or even reject their talents. The politically fragmented nature of most metropolitan areas complicates the picture because central cities may react differently from their suburbs, especially when the former have a history of receiving immigrants while the latter do not.

Immigration is but one of many shocks or shifts a metropolitan region can experience. Relying on work by our colleagues, most notably Katherine Foster, we argue that "regional resilience" is the capacity of a metropolitan area to absorb a shock and return to a sustainable path of development.[4] With regard to immigration, a "resilient" region is one that can turn the rising immigrant presence to its advantage, diminish the negative effects, contain conflicts generated by the arrival of new migrants, and promote immigrant educational and labor market attainments. In a fully resilient region, informal or formal collaboration between an experienced central city and the exurban parts of the region might help the latter resolve the inevitable problems arising from the influx of immigrants. A partially resilient region might evidence positive responses in the urban core but negative ones in the suburban periphery with no regional collaboration. And a non-resilient region would show negative responses to new immigration across the board, resulting in political squabbles that may damage regional prospects in other arenas (for example, by becoming less attractive to talent needed to revitalize the metropolitan economy or creating a fragmented and fractious polity).

It is important to stress what we are *not* saying in this definition of resilience with regard to immigration: while we ourselves believe that positive responses to new immigrants will generate the best long-term results for regions in terms of stronger economic growth, less political conflict, and greater eventual social cohesion, we are not trying to substantiate that argument in this chapter. After all, it is hard to prove that case one way or the other; while there is a strong correlation between immigration and metropolitan economic growth (think Houston versus Cleveland), it is also the case that growing locations attract immi-

---

4. See chapter two by Foster in this volume.

grants and so it is hard to disentangle and demonstrate directions of causality.[5] Instead, we simply suggest that regions that adopt the most negative reactions and measures to most strongly deflect new immigrants to other destinations are generally working against some natural population pressures; we therefore classify them as demonstrating rigidity rather than resilience.

This chapter thus focuses on the factors and forces that lead to positive or negative responses to rapid recent immigration within and across metropolitan areas. We measure positive urban and regional receptivity or "resilience" primarily in terms of the adoption of new programs to promote immigrant integration, the redesign of existing programs to take account of new immigrant client groups, the enforcement approach taken by local governments toward undocumented immigrants, and the degree of cooperation between local governments, nonprofit service delivery organizations, and immigrant advocacy groups. We measure negative receptivity or "rigidity" in terms of the presence of anti-immigrant mobilization, the adoption of strong enforcement measures, and the failure to adopt measures like the provision of translation services in everyday transactions with local government. We further investigate the degree to which suburban and central city areas show a similar or different response to the shocks of rapid recent immigration.

We look specifically at six metropolitan areas: Los Angeles, Chicago, New York, San Jose, Phoenix, and Charlotte. Our basic logic is to compare responses to the arrival of new immigrants both *across* older and newer receiving destinations and *within* them—looking both at the central cities where immigrants initially concentrate but also the suburban and exurban areas where they are a newer phenomenon. We conclude that (1) resilience is harder when the shock is newer and larger—that is, in areas that are receiving a large influx in the context of little past experience with immigrant populations; (2) resilience is harder when immigrants are racialized and less-skilled—that is, when they are perceived as outside the mainstream and when their economic contribution is less obvious; (3) resilience and receptivity are more likely when earlier waves of immigrants have "mainstreamed" and become a constituency base for a more positive attitude; and (4) resilience and receptivity are more challenging when political entrepreneurs find it advantageous to exploit resentments about the fiscal costs and social stress associated with newcomers. Finally, we suggest as a further hypothesis that resilience and receptivity may be more likely when regional actors—for example, a regional business leadership group—believe it to be in their interest to promote a sense of welcome and thus act as a counterweight to anti-immigrant political entrepreneurs.

5. Fiscal Policy Institute (2009).

To develop this set of arguments, we begin with a broad look at the changing presence of immigrants in America's metropolitan areas and consider the main existing explanations for metropolitan variance in the reaction to immigrants. We then explain why we chose these particular cases to explore these explanations and provide some quantitative measures of the nature of the immigrant populations across these regions. That sets the stage for detailed discussions of the dynamics of immigrant receptivity and integration in each case, based on qualitative work gathered through both historical analysis and interviews in the regions. We then return to the high-level conclusions highlighted above and draw some preliminary policy lessons for both local actors and the federal government.

Immigration and Reception

The contemporary wave of immigration—and the immigration "shock" it has posed for the country and its metropolitan regions—can be traced to the Hart-Celler Act of 1965.[6] Prior to this, restrictionist laws passed back in 1924 and 1927 had capped overall immigration and limited admissions from any particular county with quotas based on the presence of immigrants from these countries in the United States in 1890. This meant that most immigrants came from western Europe and, due to restrictions, immigration generally steadily declined over time (figure 4-1). While native white Protestants looked down on the ethnoreligious heritages of the European immigrants, falling levels of immigration and the upward mobility of their children after World War II reduced differences between immigrant ethnic groups and native-born whites and swelled the number of second- and third-generation Americans. This process, along with postwar economic support for suburbanization, enabled the children of central and southern European immigrants to assimilate and achieve a norm of "whiteness."[7]

The Hart-Celler Act in 1965 raised the overall limits on immigration and changed the country quotas by instituting a first-come, first-served system for distributing a pool of visas for the Eastern and Western Hemispheres.[8] Along with a shift to promoting family reunification (and not counting arriving family members under the quota system), this launched a new dynamic in terms both

6. This section draws on Pastor (2011).
7. See Alba and Nee (1997, pp. 845–46); Katznelson (2005); Singer (2010).
8. Keely (1971). The 1965 law capped visas to no more than 20,000 from any single nation in the Eastern Hemisphere but did not apply a country limit in the Western Hemisphere. Prior to the shift, visas from traditional western European countries—the United Kingdom, Ireland, and Germany—were going unused even as there were backlogs for eastern and southern European countries.

Figure 4-1. *Percent of U.S. Population Foreign-Born, 1850–2009*[a]

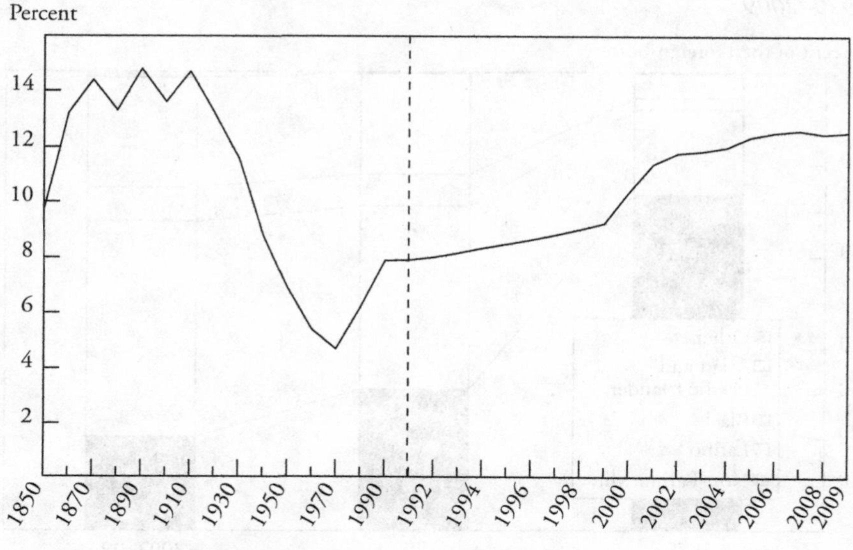

Percent

a. Data by decade 1850–1990, then by year through 2009.

of the overall flow of immigrants and their geographic origins. As a result, more immigrants hailed from Latin America and Asia, and they changed the ethnic character of the foreign-born from nearly three-quarters non-Hispanic white in 1970 (the first year for which we have reliable date on ethnicity) to 80 percent non-white in 2007–09 (figure 4-2).[9]

It was not just Hart-Celler, of course. By providing amnesty to nearly three million undocumented residents, mostly from Mexico, the Immigration Reform and Control Act (IRCA) of 1986 hastened this ethnic shift, particularly as the newly legalized then brought family members to the United States. Since 1990 efforts to reinforce border controls at major gateways from Mexico, especially Tijuana–San Diego and El Paso, led Mexican and Central American immigrants to enter through Arizona and also to move toward nontraditional metropolitan areas and rural areas with more demand for unskilled labor than Southern California.[10] As a result, Mexican migrants made Georgia, North Carolina, Arizona,

9. The 1970 Census is an appropriate base because it provides much more specific race and origin information than did the 1960 Census. Iceland (2009, p. 36) estimates that about 86 percent of legal immigrants between 1900 and 1920 were European, while 87 percent of legal immigrants in the 1980–2000 period were non-European; including undocumented residents would tip the balance further in the direction of non-European immigrants.

10. Massey (2008, pp. 333–35); Light (2006).

Figure 4-2. *Changing Racial Composition of Foreign-Born in the United States, 1970–2009*

Percent of total foreign-born

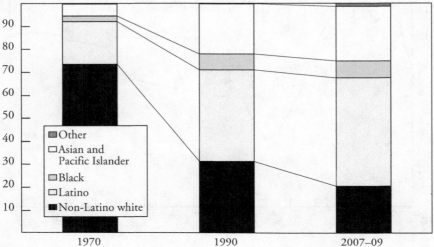

and Nevada into major destinations alongside California, Texas, and Illinois.[11] Home to 35 percent of the nation's immigrants in the late 1980s, California attracted only 19 percent of all new arrivals from 2004 to 2007.[12]

Immigrant destinations have also shifted *within* metropolitan regions. The traditional view, best expressed by Massey, equated upward socioeconomic mobility with outward residential mobility; as immigrants gained an economic foothold, they would pull themselves out of economically disadvantaged inner-city neighborhoods and head to the suburbs.[13] Although this narrative fit traditional gateways like New York and Chicago, and seemed to capture overall trends for many decades, new analyses have challenged this notion of spatial assimilation.[14] On the one hand, existing patterns of racial and class segregation constrained non-white immigrants to live side by side with blacks.[15] Meanwhile, wealthier immigrants established suburban enclaves and relatively poor immigrants moved to inner-ring suburbs being abandoned by the native lower middle class (like Maywood in Los Angeles, a case to which we return below).[16] Immigrants even

11. Zúñiga and Hernández-León (2005, p. xiv).
12. Bohn (2009).
13. Massey (1985).
14. Iceland and Scopilliti (2008).
15. Clark and Blue (2004); Blackwell, Kwoh, and Pastor (2010).
16. On the wealthier immigrant enclaves, see Zhou (1999).

moved to exurban areas in need of low-skilled service workers.[17] All this means that some places within metropolitan areas were experiencing an immigrant presence for the first time, with many ill-equipped for the consequences.

In appraising these trends, Audrey Singer has developed a new typology of receiving areas.[18] She suggests that "spatial assimilation" by movement to the suburbs only fits "continual gateways" like New York and Chicago, where the foreign-born share has historically exceeded the national average and where the built environment (a crowded central city adjoined by clearly distinct suburbs) suits the process.[19] In many metropolitan areas that emerged after World War II, the foreign-born percent exceeded the national average only after 1950; while these sprawling regions—places like Los Angeles and Miami—are also considered traditional (but more recent) gateways, the usual socioeconomic distinctions between city and suburb are less sharp and many immigrants in these metropolitan areas have headed directly for the suburbs.[20] Finally, Singer also identifies newly emerging immigrant receiving regions in which traditionally low foreign-born shares surged rapidly after 1980; as with the postwar cities that more recently arrived at their designation as traditional gateways, immigrants in these emerging areas have often "leapfrogged" directly into suburbs.

What does all this imply for understanding how receptivity varies within and across regions? Scholars who have examined this question in the United States and western Europe have often focused on individual attitudes (which when aggregated presumably drive local political responses) and how local political opportunity structures and other contextual factors shape those individual responses.[21] Some scholars have suggested that when the overall political atmosphere is heated, public agencies may practice receptivity by flying "under the radar" to assist immigrants, especially the undocumented, in ways that local public opinion might not accept were these practices to become visible.[22] The presence and the degree of organization among earlier immigrant groups, particularly as reflected in the extent and shape of local immigrant-serving and immigrant advocacy organizations, also has an impact.[23]

In general, previous research suggests that local demographic context does count. A recent rapid rise in immigration is certainly a strong predisposing factor

17. Marcelli (2004).

18. Singer (2007). Singer gives little attention to immigrant movements into traditional black neighborhoods, which is also a singularly important phenomenon. See Pastor (2012); Pastor and Carter (2009).

19. Singer (2004, p. 10).

20. Orfield (2002); Pastor (2001).

21. Hopkins (2010); Ramakrishnan and Wong (2010); Hochschild and Mollenkopf (2009).

22. Jones-Correa (2008).

23. DeGraauw, Gleeson, and Bloemraad (2010).

toward anti-immigrant responses; a long history of large immigrant populations, elected officials who are Democrats, and urban density all tend to insulate against such responses. Systematic analysis of larger datasets as well as accumulated case studies suggest, however, that actual outcomes are also highly sensitive both to the tenor of national debate about immigration and to the ways in which local and national political actors seek to frame or politicize (or even racialize) the issue.[24]

Local political entrepreneurs, for example, may wish to mobilize anti-immigrant sentiment as a way to shift the political balance in their favor, with considerable anecdotal evidence suggesting that conservative grassroots activists and Republican political strategists believe that taking positions against providing services to immigrants and in favor of national and local enforcement can stir up a base for other broader issues and electoral campaigns. On the other hand, there may also be political entrepreneurs who will take pro-immigrant positions, either because of the presence of an immigrant (or immigrant-sympathetic) voting bloc or because it may serve other interests (such as presenting the image of a more diverse and tolerant region in order to attract business).

Selecting and Previewing the Cases

Although our focus is on the variation that metropolitan areas demonstrated in response to an immigrant "shock," our study is but one of many that the Building Resilient Regions (BRR) network is conducting into the nature of shocks to and the resilience (or lack thereof) displayed by various metropolitan areas of the United States. To maximize our ability to compare results across shocks (such as economic decline, rapid growth, or the suburbanization of poverty, all issues described elsewhere in this volume), the network has agreed to focus on a broad set of twenty metropolitan areas.

Working from this list of twenty, we chose the New York and Los Angeles regions as the two biggest traditional gateways (with the former "continual" and the latter more recent). Each of these metropolitan areas has a highly diverse set of new and "mature" immigrant communities (with three in ten immigrants in the United States living in one or the other, along with slightly more of their children, according to the March 2009 Current Population Survey). They provide a matched pair with complicated mixes of immigrants and natives but also have core cities with well-developed infrastructures for immigrant organizing, advocacy, and service that sometimes work outside the central cities but may also not fully stretch across the entire metropolitan area. Both have recently

24. For example, high-impact events such as the September 11, 2001, attack on the World Trade Center and the subsequent volatility of public opinion about Muslim immigrants have altered the context of local political mobilization against immigrants.

been the subject of major studies on the trajectories of second-generation youth.[25] Finally, immigrants are moving straight into the suburbs of both regions, blurring the historical patterns of initial arrival in the central city followed by spillover into adjacent suburbs and allowing us to examine variation in response *within* a particular metropolitan area.

We chose Chicago and San Jose not only because they both have large and diverse immigrant populations but also because both have adopted successful immigrant integration policies. Chicago, a traditional gateway, has experienced new migration from Mexico and Eastern Europe. San Jose, the capital of Silicon Valley, a relatively new immigrant destination, has attracted both Asian immigrants to its sprawling primary city and its northern suburbs (some of which are now counted as principal cities) as well as Mexican immigrants to its southern and eastern agricultural areas.[26] Both regions also have nationally notable immigrant integration programs; learning why and how these programs evolved can provide a better understanding of what explains resilience as well as pointing to useful policy lessons for the future.

Charlotte and Phoenix are new destinations that seem to have offered contrasting welcomes. While not without tensions and gaps in service delivery, Charlotte has been relatively welcoming, partly because its business and civic leadership wants to present the city as a model for the "New South." Phoenix has offered a decidedly cooler reception, with its county sheriff providing a celebrated instance in which local law enforcement has taken up the enforcement of immigration law.

Figure 4-3, showing the relative sizes of the overall and foreign-born populations of the six metropolitan areas, indicates that Los Angeles and New York have much larger shares of immigrants as well as much larger populations.[27] Though Chicago is a traditional gateway with a large immigrant population, its foreign-born share is smaller than that in San Jose. Charlotte and Phoenix both have smaller overall populations and Phoenix has a larger foreign-born share.

The six regions have distinct immigrant population growth patterns. Figure 4-4 compares the traditional metropolitan areas (Los Angeles, New York, and Chicago) with the emerging ones (San Jose, Charlotte, and Phoenix); subsequent figures are ordered in similar fashion to contrast the type of experience. As noted, we think of

25. Kasinitz, Mollenkopf, and Waters (2004); Telles and Ortiz (2008).

26. This may surprise some who think of San Jose as having long had a Mexican presence, but this presence was from U.S.-born Mexican Americans, not new immigrants.

27. Taken from a database assembled for the BRR network that contains economic, civic, social, housing, geographic, and demographic measures for several decades for all 934 Core-Based Statistical Areas (CBSAs) in the United States. CBSA boundaries have been made consistent to compare measures across the 1970, 1980, 1990, and 2000 Censuses and the 2009 American Community Survey (ACS). Most measures concerning immigrants were specially tabulated from the Public Use Microdata samples.

Figure 4-3. *Total Population by CBSA, 2009*

Millions

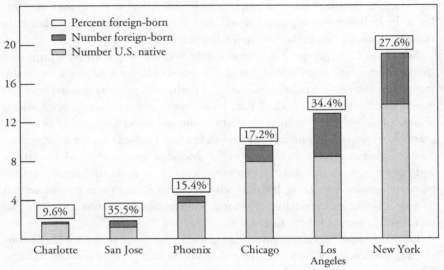

the first two as large and long-established immigrant gateways, the second two as highly diverse and successfully integrating gateways, and the last two as new gateways with contrasting degrees of receptivity.

Los Angeles and New York clearly had the highest foreign-born shares in 1980, and this share rose in both locales during the 1990s. Los Angeles was affected by a wave of Central American migrants and family members that IRCA allowed newly legal residents to bring in. In the most recent period, however, the immigrant population has begun to level off; indeed, the foreign-born share has actually declined slightly in the Los Angeles CBSA (or Core-Based Statistical Area), something that runs contrary to the usual popular image of immigrants continuing to stream to Los Angeles.[28]

Chicago shows a similar tapering in growth, although it has lower immigrant shares than the two other big gateways. San Jose has shown the most rapid share increases for the foreign-born; while this also seems to be leveling off, San Jose has a higher share than either Los Angeles or New York.[29] Charlotte and Phoenix

28. Myers, Pitkin, and Ramirez (2010) show that California's population has become increasingly "home-grown"—that is, more likely to be born in California than to have migrated from abroad or other states—although a significant portion of that California-born population are the children of immigrants.

29. San Jose had a higher percentage of foreign-born than Chicago in our base year of 1980 (13.6 versus 9.8). Singer and others see San Jose as an emerging gateway because it lacked the older European

Figure 4-4. *Percent Foreign-Born Population by CBSA, 1980–2009*

Percent

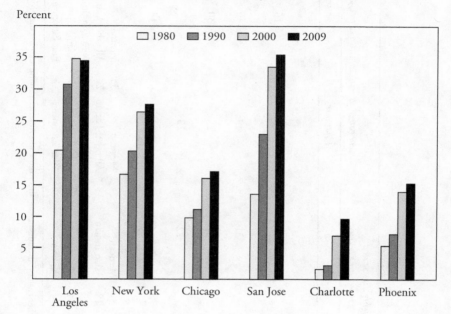

both had few immigrants in the 1980s and 1990s, but high growth during the 1990s—the Latino population grew 394 percent in Charlotte over that period— though the final immigrant share in both locales was still well below the other four regions.

Table 4-1 breaks out the foreign-born population by recency of arrival, with the top line indicating the share of immigrants in the population and the next four lines indicating the composition of those immigrants in terms of year of arrival. New York and Los Angeles have the lowest shares of recent arrivals among their foreign-born, reflecting their status as mature gateways. The figures for Chicago and San Jose of the foreign-born who arrived in the most recent decade or the one before that are similar to those for New York and Los Angeles. Note, however, that immigrants make up a higher share of the overall population in San Jose than in Chicago, making the former city's comparatively grace-ful acceptance of immigrants of special interest. Charlotte and Phoenix have the highest shares of recent arrivals, with Charlotte's immigrant population even

ethnic groups and because its foreign-born share was only 8.0 percent in 1960, while it was 9.7 percent in the Chicago metropolitan area. See www.census.gov/population/www/documentation/twps0029/twps 0029.html and www.bayareacensus.ca.gov/.

Table 4-1. *Selected Statistics on Immigrants, by CBSA, 2007–09*

Percent

	Major established immigrant gateways		Highly diverse and successfully integrating gateways		New gateways with contrasting reception	
Migration	Los Angeles	New York	Chicago	San Jose	Charlotte	Phoenix
Recency of migration (2007–09)						
Percent of population foreign-born	34	18	16	37	10	16
Of that:						
Migrated last 10 years	25	30	30	31	49	40
Migrated 11 to 20 years ago	28	29	30	31	28	30
Migrated 21 to 30 years ago	26	20	18	22	13	17
Migrated over 30 years ago	22	21	22	16	9	14
Nativity of immigrants who migrated in last 10 years (2007–09), ordered by group size						
1st	Mexican 35	All other Latino 27	Mexican 37	Mexican 24	Mexican 35	Mexican 60
2nd	All other Latino 18	West Indian 18	East European 18	Asian Indian 19	All other Latino 24	All other Latino 9
3rd	Filipino 7	Mexican 9	Asian Indian 9	Chinese 11	Asian Indian 9	West European 5
4th	Chinese 6	Asian Indian 8	All other Latino 7	Vietnamese 7	African 7	Asian Indian 5
5th	Korean 6	East European 6	Chinese 7	Filipino 4	West European 6	East European 4

Source: Authors' calculations from a pooled sample of the 2007–09 ACS. The category "other Latinos" includes immigrants from Latin American countries other than Mexico.

more recent than that of Phoenix (although Phoenix's overall share of immigrants in the population is higher).

The sources of recent immigrants, indicated in the second panel of table 4-1, may also influence the politics of reception. For the Los Angeles metropolitan area (which includes Orange County), 35 percent of recent arrivals are Mexican-origin, followed by other Latin Americans (including the major Central American groups) and then Asian groups. In New York, non-Mexican Latin Americans make up the recent flow, with Dominicans being most prevalent among a diversity of other national origin groups. Following them are those from the West Indies, a fast-rising Mexican population, and then Asian Indians and Eastern Europeans.[30]

Mexicans are an even larger share of recent arrivals in Chicago than in Los Angeles, but their share of the overall population is about half of that of Los Angeles, simply because immigrants in general make up a smaller share of Chicago's population. Chicago's second largest group of recent immigrants is eastern European, a fact that may help to "de-racialize" immigration by reminding current residents of populations that assimilated in the past (and from which they descended). In San Jose, Mexican immigrants are slightly under a quarter of all recent arrivals, with Asian populations—particularly from India, China, and Vietnam—making up the next largest groups. This creates another sort of "de-racialization"—in the San Jose context, the word "immigrant" does not conjure up only images of lower-skilled Mexican laborers, but also higher-income and highly educated Asian immigrants (although many Asian immigrants are also poorly educated and not faring well).

Over 35 percent of Charlotte's recent immigrants are Mexican, followed by a group of diverse national origins. Meanwhile, 60 percent of Phoenix's recent immigrants are Mexican-origin, the highest measure for any of our six regions. As we explore below, this vast preponderance of Mexicans, many undocumented, has made "racialization" of immigrants especially easy.

It is challenging to estimate the undocumented. After all, those without legal status are seeking not to be noticed, let alone counted. Table 4-2 gives the most reliable estimates, which are at the state level. However, it is reasonable to put undocumented populations at nearly 200,000 in San Jose, even more for Chicago, nearly 700,000 in New York, and around one million in Los Angeles County.[31] In

30. We pool all Latin Americans because no single national origin group is large enough to exceed the fifth largest recent migrant group. The group that comes closest to deserving a break-out is Dominicans in New York, but they still fall below New York's fifth-place group, eastern Europeans.

31. A Silicon Valley Community Foundation report uses Kidsdata.org for the Silicon Valley number. The Chicago number comes from Mehta and others (2002) and squares with Ready and Brown-Gort (2005). The New York number comes from a Pew Research Report on undocumented immigrants

Table 4-2. *Estimated Unauthorized Immigrant Population and Range of Estimates by State, 2008*

State	Estimate[a]	Range
California	2,700,000	2,500,000–2,850,000
New York	925,000	800,000–1,050,000
Arizona	500,000	475,000–550,000
Illinois	450,000	375,000–525,000
North Carolina	350,000	300,000–400,000

Source: Pew Hispanic Center, "A Portrait of Unauthorized Immigrants in the United States," 2009 (http://pewhispanic.org/files/reports/107.pdf).

a. Estimates based on augmented March CPS for 2006–08.

Los Angeles County, the undocumented immigrants may constitute 10 percent of the total population.[32] Although we have no specific number for Phoenix, its undocumented population probably constitutes more than half of Arizona's 900,000 foreign-born residents, another reason why immigration has attracted so much negative attention in that state.

How have these trends played out within these metropolitan areas? A first cut at answering that question is provided by breaking out the foreign-born share in every metropolitan area's principal cities and suburbs from 1980 to 2009.[33] As can be seen in figure 4-5, the foreign-born shares have increased steadily in both the principal cities and suburbs of Los Angeles. The divergence between the two is not significant and appears to be lower than in any of the other metropolitan areas. This is partly due to the rise of relatively well-off immigrant suburbs such as Monterey Park and also reflects the movement of immigrants into older inner-ring suburbs, such as the industrial suburbs along the Alameda Corridor known as the Hub Cities, including Huntington Park, Bell, Bell Gardens, and South Gate.[34]

The principal cities in the New York metropolitan area have long had large shares of immigrants, while the suburbs have not. But their recent growth in the suburbs has been sharp, perhaps contributing to the turmoil in Long Island about day laborers. The gap between city and suburb is lower in Chicago, but its suburbs

reported in www.gothamgazette.com/article/demographics/20060406/5/1809. See Pastor and Ortiz (2009) for the Los Angeles number.

32. The share is most likely lower for the Los Angeles metropolitan area (or CBSA) since it includes Orange County.

33. The database breaks data out among principal cities and suburbs within the CBSAs. However, many older suburbs are defined as principal cities and the various types of suburbs are not distinguished. Metropolitan regions vary greatly in how suburbs and inner cities relate to one another. For this reason, we offer only one chart on the city-suburb distinction and conduct most of our analysis of central city–suburban dynamics in the qualitative case studies.

34. Pumak (2004); Pastor (2011).

have also seen a sharp rise. The principal cities of Charlotte and Phoenix show the sharpest rises of any of the metropolitan regions, though the pattern was steadier in Phoenix and more recent in Charlotte. Charlotte and Phoenix also seem to show immigrant movement directly to the suburbs.

San Jose appears to have experienced the fastest principal city growth in percent foreign-born with a rising gap compared to its suburbs. This may be partly an artifact of the census describing some of its older suburbs as principal cities. As Singer notes, more than a third of immigrants in larger metropolitan areas live in high-density suburbs adjoining the central city—and the census counts some of these as "principal cities."[35] Still, it appears from mapping exercises by census tract level done for the larger project of which this is a part that immigrants are indeed concentrated in the urban centers of the San Jose metropolitan area.

How do immigrant incomes stack up in these various metropolitan areas? Figure 4-6 compares median household incomes for U.S.-born whites, U.S.-born blacks, U.S.-born and immigrant Latinos, and U.S.-born and immigrant Asians. In general, U.S.-born blacks have the lowest incomes while U.S.-born whites and Asians have the highest, although U.S.-born blacks, U.S.-born Latinos, and immigrant Latinos all have equally low incomes in New York. In Los Angeles, U.S.-born Latinos fare better than blacks, who are rivaled by immigrant Latinos. Immigrant Latinos outpace blacks in Chicago but fare worse in Phoenix. Immigrant Asians fare worse than native-born Asians in Los Angeles, New York, and Charlotte but better elsewhere. Asians, however, are small shares of the population in Charlotte and Phoenix and largest as a share in San Jose—where their income actually exceeds that of U.S.-born whites. As previously noted, if Asian immigrants are perceived to have high incomes, this can create a different and more positive reaction to all immigrants that may rub off for those who are less skilled and even undocumented.

One measure of immigrant progress is English acquisition over time. Figure 4-7 indicates English ability by year of arrival for the foreign-born in each metropolitan area. Note that English acquisition is the flattest for the first two decades in San Jose, suggesting that its high share of foreign-born may be slowing the initial acquisition of English. Charlotte is the stellar performer, perhaps reflecting that older immigrants were less populous and hence in a "sink or swim" situation. Los Angeles has consistently lower numbers than Chicago or New York but the slopes are quite similar. Phoenix is squarely in the middle, with plenty of English proficiency with time in the country. The problem, of course, is that Phoenix is frontloaded with recent immigrants, creating what Dowell Myers calls a "Peter Pan" fallacy—the notion that the population will never "grow up."[36]

35. Singer (2010, p. 65).
36. Myers (2007).

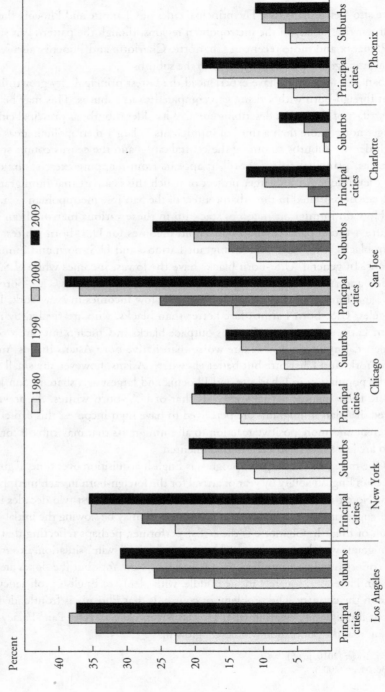

Figure 4-5. *Percent Foreign-Born Population Living in Principal Cities and Suburbs, by CBSA, 1980–2009*

Percent

Legend: 1980, 1990, 2000, 2009

Los Angeles: Principal cities, Suburbs
New York: Principal cities, Suburbs
Chicago: Principal cities, Suburbs
San Jose: Principal cities, Suburbs
Charlotte: Principal cities, Suburbs
Phoenix: Principal cities, Suburbs

Figure 4-6. *Median Household Income, by CBSA, 2007–09*

Dollars

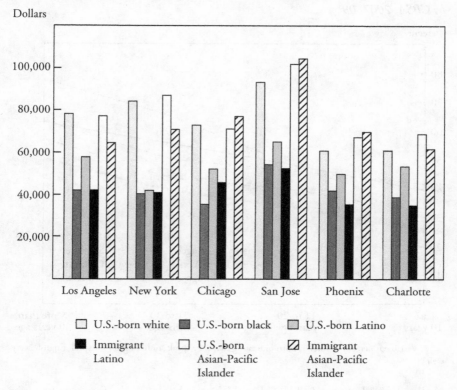

Los Angeles   New York   Chicago   San Jose   Phoenix   Charlotte

☐ U.S.-born white   ■ U.S.-born black   ☐ U.S.-born Latino

■ Immigrant   ☐ U.S.-born   ▨ Immigrant
  Latino   Asian-Pacific   Asian-Pacific
                       Islander   Islander

Another potential source of conflict has to do with the different age distributions of immigrants (and their children) and the native-born.[37] Where the former predominate among the young people and the latter among their elders, a "demographic divergence" can result.[38] Older voters may not have much sympathy for young people who are quite unlike them, creating what William Frey calls a "cultural generation gap."[39] Frey notes that such a gap can mean that "setting public priorities and fostering social cohesion . . . may take on added

37. Several of the regions boast a very high percent of those below the age of 18 who have at least one immigrant parent: while Charlotte brings up the bottom with only 18 percent of its youth with immigrant parents, Chicago and Phoenix have 30 percent and 32 percent, respectively, the New York metropolitan area has 42 percent, and Los Angeles and San Jose each have just under 60 percent of young people with at least one immigrant parent. All calculations derived using a three-year pooled sample of the American Community Survey.

38. Pastor and Reed (2005).

39. Frey (2010, pp. 84–85).

Figure 4-7. *English Language Skills, by Date of Arrival in the United States, by CBSA, 2007–09*[a]

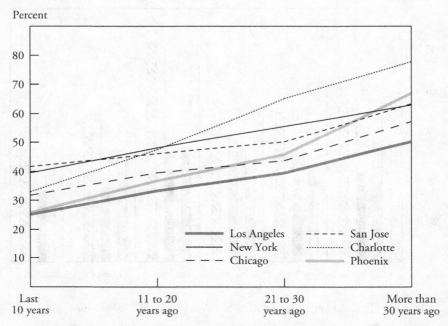

Percent

Last
10 years

11 to 20
years ago

21 to 30
years ago

More than
30 years ago

a. Variable is percent of foreign-born indicating that they speak "only English" or speak English "very well."

challenges."[40] Figure 4-8 shows that this gap is largest in the fractious Phoenix metropolitan area and actually also quite large in Los Angeles.

Another relevant background dimension has to do with educational attainment. Figure 4-9 shows educational attainment for the native-born and immigrants (above the age of twenty-five and, therefore, likely to be available for the labor force). As might be expected, immigrants have less education than the native-born, with the interesting exception of San Jose, where immigrants are both slightly more likely to be college educated *and* to lack a high school diploma. Phoenix has the least-educated immigrants, who show a particularly large gap with natives in the share failing to complete high school.

Finally, to give a picture of the relative influence of immigrant-origin voters in the electorate, table 4-3 examines the votes cast by immigrants, the children of immigrants, and native-stock citizens in the November 2008 presidential election. (The item "2.5 generation" refers to voters who have only one immi-

40. Frey (2010, p. 85).

Figure 4-8. *Demographic Divergence of the Young and Old, by CBSA, 2007–09*

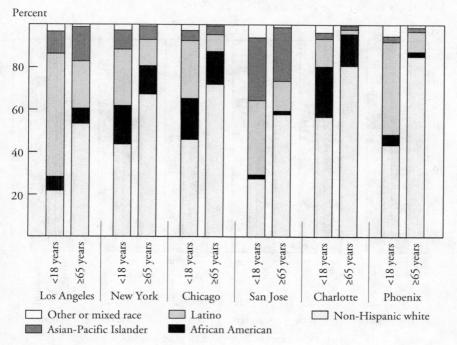

Percent

Los Angeles | New York | Chicago | San Jose | Charlotte | Phoenix

☐ Other or mixed race   ☐ Latino   ☐ Non-Hispanic white

■ Asian-Pacific Islander   ■ African American

grant parent, while second generation voters have two immigrant parents.) We again break up the regions into principal cities and suburbs. Immigrants and their children make up substantial shares of the active electorate not only in the central cities of Los Angeles, New York, and San Jose, but also a surprisingly large share of their surrounding suburbs. On the other hand, native-stock voters make up the predominant share of the voters in Chicago, Phoenix, and Charlotte. This, of course, creates different terrains for political entrepreneurs seeking to make electoral mileage from tensions around new populations.

The demographic patterns described here take us part way toward understanding differences in regional receptivity to immigrants and the progress immigrants themselves are making. Recency of arrival can make a difference and differences in immigrant nationality, education, and income can shape the ways in which they can be "racialized" by the native-born. Differences in the presence of undocumented immigrants and the spatial location of immigrants within metropolitan areas may influence native responses as well. And differences in the backgrounds and affiliations of voters can set the terrain for whether anti-immigrant sentiment can be utilized (and created) for political gains. But to

Figure 4-9. *Educational Attainment of U.S.-Born and Immigrant Population Older than Twenty-Five Years, by CBSA, 2007–09*

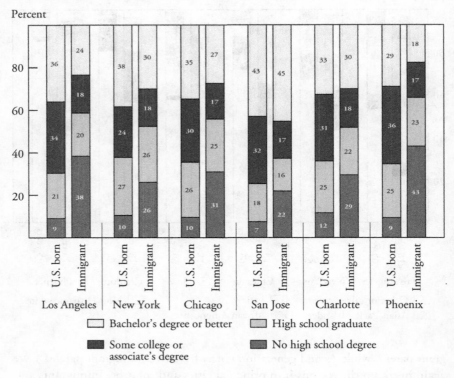

Percent

☐ Bachelor's degree or better   ☐ High school graduate

■ Some college or associate's degree   ■ No high school degree

fully understand *why* immigrants might be welcomed and their fortunes advanced in some areas more than in others, we must turn to a closer examination of the institutions and attitudes in each region.

Receptivity and Resilience across Six Metropolitan Areas

To provide a more nuanced understanding of receptivity and resilience in our six metropolitan areas, we convened a team of researchers to conduct historical background research and interview a mix of regional actors, using a standard interview protocol and a common set of questions.[41] Interviews were generally

41. John Mollenkopf, Els de Graauw, and Marta Pichardo covered New York, while Jaime Dominguez examined Chicago, Michael Jones-Correa studied Charlotte, Paul Lewis and Marie Provine covered Phoenix, and Manuel Pastor, Rachel Rosner, Jennifer Tran, and Juan de Lara examined Los Angeles and San Jose.

Table 4-3. *Votes Cast, by Immigrant Generation and CBSA, November 2008*

| CBSA | Immigrant generation | | | | |
	Foreign-born	Second generation	2.5 generation	Native stock	Total
Los Angeles					
Principal cities	733,256	257,913	152,399	1,456,245	2,599,813
	28.2%	9.9%	5.9%	56.0%	100.0%
Remainder of CBSA	507,232	337,009	92,307	1,374,770	2,311,318
	21.9%	14.6%	4.0%	59.5%	100.0%
New York					
Principal cities	655,710	276,632	194,232	1,642,726	2,769,300
	23.7%	10.0%	7.0%	59.3%	100.0%
Remainder of CBSA	548,286	397,392	285,497	3,090,571	4,321,746
	12.7%	9.2%	6.6%	71.5%	100.0%
Chicago					
Principal cities	78,801	76,945	74,019	1,134,950	1,364,715
	5.8%	5.6%	5.4%	83.2%	100.0%
Remainder of CBSA	164,396	122,856	125,033	1,900,981	2,313,266
	7.1%	5.3%	5.4%	82.2%	100.0%
San Jose					
Principal cities	109,892	23,580	39,423	264,615	437,510
	25.1%	5.4%	9.0%	60.5%	100.0%
Remainder of CBSA	67,533	62,879	27,868	225,477	383,757
	17.6%	16.4%	7.3%	58.8%	100.0%
Charlotte					
Principal city	17,796	8,092	23,124	331,770	380,782
	4.7%	2.1%	6.1%	87.1%	100.0%
Remainder of CBSA	2,632	6,409	7,032	336,890	352,963
	.7%	1.8%	2.0%	95.4%	100.0%
Phoenix					
Principal cities	71,343	28,707	34,921	743,327	878,298
	8.1%	3.3%	4.0%	84.6%	100.0%
Remainder of CBSA	46,423	29,649	49,653	593,910	719,635
	6.5%	4.1%	6.9%	82.5%	100.0%

Source: November 2008 Current Population Survey.

conducted throughout 2009 and 2010, although some of the Charlotte summary is based on previous work.

Each group of researchers provided us with field notes and participated in debriefings with the whole team. In synthesizing and pulling common themes out of the case studies, we went back to the researchers with questions, did supplemental research, and sought feedback from the group about whether our preliminary conclusions reflected their field experience. Some of our conclusions are more speculative than others. These are, after all, just six cases, albeit complemented by our broader research experience in other settings. And we try to indicate clearly which we think are more established and which need further research.

Los Angeles

A significant presence of immigrant and immigrant-origin voters throughout the Los Angeles metropolitan region would seem to create the conditions for both a highly sympathetic and relatively uniform approach to immigrants all across the region. The region, however, is far from uniform and Los Angeles is, in some sense, an "underperformer." Given its long-established and large immigrant presence, one might expect an even more welcoming attitude, even in the central city. To explore both the general regional response and the variation by geography, we focused on three iconic (from an immigrant integration point of view) parts of metropolitan Los Angeles: the city of Los Angeles; the small, dense, heavily Hispanic municipality of Maywood in Los Angeles County east of the city; and the Inland Empire, the urban areas of San Bernardino Valley in the two counties east of Los Angeles County.

After a long history of white migration from the Midwest, which had contributed to its main demographic change and population growth, Los Angeles became a majority-minority city in the late 1980s, when people of Mexican descent came to constitute the largest ethnic group. And less than twenty years later, in 2005 Antonio Villaraigosa was elected the first Mexican American mayor of the modern era (son of an immigrant father and U.S.-born mother), defeating incumbent James Hahn with a broad coalition of Latino, African American, and white liberal supporters.[42] Of its fifteen city council members, four are Mexican American and three are African American. Several of the eight white council members are also grandchildren of immigrants. The two other citywide office holders are currently whites, although one recently succeeded a Mexican American.

As befits a city with such a large immigrant-origin population—and electorate—and an articulate and charismatic Mexican American mayor, the city of Los Angeles has adopted a number of pro-immigrant measures (table 4-3 shows that more than two-fifths of the voters in the region's principal cities, mainly Los Angeles, are immigrants or are children of immigrants, and while immigrant voters are less common in the suburban areas, their children make up a larger share).[43] The Los Angeles Mayor's Office of Immigrant Affairs works to provide

42. Sonenshein and Pinkus (2005).
43. Aside from Los Angeles, the principal cities include Long Beach, Santa Ana, Anaheim, Irvine, Glendale, Pomona, Pasadena, Torrance, Orange, Fullerton, Costa Mesa, Burbank, Compton, Carson,

translation services in city agencies and the Immigrant Advisory Council to the Human Rights Commission (HRC) enables immigrant advocacy organizations to have access to city officials. Since 1979, Special Order 40 has directed the Los Angeles Police Department not to determine immigration status in the course of routine stops. Education reform is a signature issue for Mayor Villaraigosa, and he uses the HRC to improve intergroup relations in troubled schools and has established district language assessment committees to provide non-English-speaking parents' input on procedures for educating English language learners. Mayor Villaraigosa also joined the campaign to boycott Arizona over its 2010 adoption of Senate Bill 1070.

At the same time, advocates sometimes criticize the city for being less systematic in its efforts than other locales with a far smaller stake in the immigrant population. For example, previous mayor James Hahn originated the Office of Immigrant Affairs but it floundered over the past few years of the Villaraigosa administration. Initial timidity may have been the problem: Villaraigosa worried about being seen as too active on immigration, particularly since one of his first acts was to welcome over half a million immigrants as they marched on City Hall in 2006 to protest anti-immigrant legislation in Congress. An ethnic mayor, particularly in today's political climate, may be more constrained than a white mayor in taking up the immigrant banner—at least compared to Mayor Bloomberg in New York and former mayor Daley in Chicago—although Villaraigosa did, as noted, take a leadership position against the Arizona legislation.[44]

In Los Angeles County, outside the city, conditions vary greatly. Although the five-member Los Angeles County Board of Supervisors includes only one Mexican American from East Los Angeles, Gloria Molina, its black member has taken pro-immigrant stances, as does a Jewish member with Russian immigrant ancestry. The other two members are white Republicans, and one has been particularly concerned about undocumented immigrants and what he claims is the use of welfare and health services by their children. This is significant because each supervisor holds a great deal of influence over county matters in his or her district, and thus the living conditions for immigrants can vary significantly.

The separately elected county sheriff, Lee Baca, a Republican, oversees law enforcement in the county's unincorporated areas and its many smaller municipal jurisdictions. The Los Angeles County Sheriff's Department maintains a

---

Santa Monica, Newport Beach, Tustin, Montebello, Monterey Park, Gardena, Arcadia, Paramount, Fountain Valley, and Cerritos.

44. Stepping into the gap, the California Community Foundation, headed by Antonia Hernandez, former executive director of the Mexican American Legal Defense and Educational Fund, launched an immigrant integration initiative, including the creation of a multisector Council for Immigrant Integration, a step recommended in Pastor and Ortiz (2009).

"287(g) agreement" with the federal Immigration and Customs Enforcement (ICE). Section 287(g) of the Immigration and Nationality Act was inserted by the 1996 Illegal Immigration Reform and Immigrant Responsibility Act. It authorizes the federal government to allow local law enforcement officers to identify and detain those without authorization during their normal duties. Immigrant rights activists claim these arrangements undermine community trust in the police and can lead to the deportation of otherwise law-abiding undocumented residents. While the city of Los Angeles is perceived as hospitable because its Special Order 40 limits police checks on documentation, the Los Angeles County Sheriff's Department polices the many unincorporated areas and has generated thousands of deportation referrals each year.

Maywood is an example of one of the small incorporated areas within Los Angeles County but outside the city of Los Angeles. This small town of about 45,000 people, almost entirely Latino, shelters many undocumented immigrants. Its elected leadership declared Maywood a sanctuary city in 2006 and went as far as eliminating its police department's traffic division for allegedly targeting undocumented drivers. Maywood's political leadership has embraced a range of immigrant integration policies, and Maywood advocates wish to use their municipal platform to develop an immigrant-based political movement in southeast Los Angeles County.

These moves have made Maywood a target for anti-immigrant activists, who use it as an example of the ill consequences of immigration. VDARE.com, an anti-immigrant, web-based news service, calls the city "occupied America." Anti-immigrant forces like the Minutemen and Federation for American Immigration Reforms routinely attack Maywood's policies. Some Latino politicians have also criticized Maywood's leadership for building its own immigrant-based political machine that sometimes refuses to cooperate with the Democratic Party establishment.

To the east of Los Angeles County, the San Bernardino Valley has a mostly conservative Republican political establishment that has adopted a consistently anti-immigrant approach to governance. Though immigrants make up less of the electorate than in Los Angeles, more than a quarter of the voters in Riverside and the area's other principal cities are immigrants or their children.[45] Nevertheless, Joe Turner, an aide to a San Bernardino County supervisor, is a leading anti-immigrant advocate who sought to ban private landlords from renting to tenants who could not prove legal residency. Local politicians have supported the repeal of citizenship for the U.S.-born children of undocumented immi-

---

45. The principal cities include Riverside, San Bernardino, Ontario, Victorville, Temecula, Chino, Hemet, Redlands, Colton, and Palm Desert. The data are not depicted in table 4-3 but are calculated in similar fashion.

grants. Prominent leaders of the Minutemen and white supremacist movements live in the region. This political climate makes it difficult for elected officials to show sympathy for pro-immigrant policies and puts immigrant advocacy organizations on the defensive.

Los Angeles and the Inland Empire therefore show quite different responses to immigration. The core city hosts a broad range of immigrant advocacy organizations, such as the Coalition for Humane Immigrant Rights in Los Angeles (CHIRLA), the Consejo de Federaciones Mexicanas en Norteamérica, the Koreatown Immigrant Workers Association, the National Association of Latino Elected Officials, and the Mexican American Legal Defense and Education Fund, which have access to decisionmakers and influence their key decisions. Some of them work beyond the city limits in the rest of Los Angeles County, but few have projected their influence in other counties in the region, particularly in the Inland Empire.

Recently, however, churches, labor unions, and community organizations have begun to test an immigrant rights agenda in the Inland Empire. The San Bernardino Catholic Diocese organized a Justice for Immigrants Coalition, while labor unions are attempting to organize immigrants in this region. Reform Immigration for America (RIFA) has also held training and informational meetings throughout Southern California, and both RIFA and CHIRLA have held community forums on immigration reform in the Inland Empire, although these activities were not based on strong connections with local immigrant rights leaders. Despite these efforts, however, the deep immigrant organizational infrastructure in the regional core does not reach outlying areas, especially those that display less receptivity.

The Los Angeles experience suggests that the highly fragmented political and social landscape of the region is also reflected in the fragmented response to immigrants. The long-standing immigrant population in the urban core, led by a mayor from an immigrant background, certainly suggests a pro-immigrant response in the most visible part of the region. But this varies greatly as one moves away from that core. In some places, such as Maywood, local fragmentation creates a space for pro-immigrant responses, but in many others, such as San Bernardino, the same fragmentation can promote negative responses. In the end, the organizational infrastructure for immigrant advocacy is strong in the core but fragmented and even weak elsewhere in the far-flung region.

New York

The thirty-county New York metropolitan region (CBSA) stretches from New Haven, Connecticut, in the northeast, down the coast through New York City, over the Hudson to Trenton, New Jersey, in the southwest and from the farthest eastern tip of Long Island to Pennsylvania border counties in the west. Despite the vast extent of this huge, 18-plus million-person region, New York City plays a highly central role, accounting for 44 percent of the total metropolitan area population, compared to 30 percent for Los Angeles and Chicago. Like those two other traditional receiving areas, however, the region presents a varied range of responses to immigrants. The region contains a number of significant principal cities such as New Haven, Bridgeport, Yonkers, Newark, and Trenton, each of which contains a particular mix of immigrant and native-born groups. Immigrant groups have settled in a number of suburban areas as well.

It is a challenge to consider this sprawling and complex metropolitan area in just a few pages. Somewhat arbitrarily, we analyze here dynamics in the central city and in Suffolk County on the east end of Long Island. There are certainly many other interesting stories in the region, such as New Haven's provision of a municipal identity card for its residents, including the undocumented, or how Teaneck, N.J., came to elect its first Indian American and Muslim mayor. And although the conflict over immigration in Suffolk offers one counterpoint, others may be found on the suburban New Jersey side of the region as well.

It has become politically obligatory in New York City to celebrate virtually every aspect of the immigrant experience. Native-born whites with native-born parents now make up less than one in five of the city's residents, while immigrants and their children are a majority. The city is overwhelmingly Democratic both in party registration and votes for most political candidates. (With 69 percent Democratic registration, the city gave 79.3 percent of its votes for Obama in the November 2008 presidential election.) Table 4-3 shows that naturalized foreign-born individuals provided 24 percent of the 2008 presidential votes in New York City and the region's other principal cities, while the children of immigrants provided another 17 percent. (The figures are comparable to those for Los Angeles and San Jose, but substantially higher than in Chicago, Phoenix, or Charlotte.)[46]

New York City may well have the deepest and widest array of immigrant service and advocacy organizations of any place in the United States, and it certainly has strongly pro-immigrant policies. This reflects both New York's long history as a major entry point for migration to the United States and the great variety of groups that have settled in the city. Unlike Los Angeles or San Jose, or even Chicago, where individuals of Mexican origin predominate, no single national origin dominates the city's immigrant population. Indeed, New York has attracted many black and white as well as Latino and Asian immigrants,

46. The principal cities, aside from New York City, are White Plains in New York and Newark, Edison, Union, Wayne, and New Brunswick in New Jersey.

with major groups hailing from the Dominican Republic, Colombia, Ecuador, Peru, the Anglophone West Indies, Haiti, West Africa, China, Vietnam, India, Pakistan, Bangladesh, and the countries of the former Soviet Union. Unlike Los Angeles, where Mexicans make up 38 percent of the immigrant population, Dominicans, at 16 percent, are the largest national origin group in New York City. As a result, while each group mobilizes along national lines, their relatively small individual size gives them an incentive to form coalitions across national borders, both in terms of creating panethnic identities and forming advocacy groups that span racial boundaries.

The city has faced a number of major immigration-related policy issues in recent years, particularly how the New York City Police Department treats the identification issue for undocumented individuals with whom its members come in contact as well as implementation of a new language access policy. Decades ago, the Koch administration adopted Executive Order 124, which prohibited city employees from volunteering information on anyone's immigration status to federal authorities unless required by law to do so—for instance, if the person was suspected of committing a crime. After the passage of the 1996 federal welfare and immigration reform laws, the city came under pressure to report immigration status on a regular basis, even when it involved an undocumented person who had not committed a crime. To clarify the matter, Mayor Bloomberg issued Executive Order 34, later modified by Executive Order 41, reiterating that city employees should not inquire about the documentation status of people with whom they were interacting, particularly if they are victims reporting a crime unless specifically required by law (to determine eligibility). It stipulated, however, that city employees would continue to cooperate with federal authorities in apprehending criminal aliens who may lack authorization to reside in the United States. It reaffirmed that undocumented immigrants were entitled to receive services (unless otherwise specifically deemed ineligible by federal legislation) and that the city would not treat one's undocumented status as a crime (in stark contrast to Arizona Senate Bill 1070).

In a city where more than half the people are foreign-born or grew up in an immigrant family, where one-fourth do not speak English at home, and where two-fifths of the public school students have language challenges, virtually every point of contact between city agencies and city residents raises issues relevant to immigrant status. A new executive order required city agencies to develop plans to improve accessibility to clients with limited English proficiency, to designate language coordinators to implement those plans, to make both published materials and translation services available in the most frequently used six languages other than English, and to train frontline workers to facilitate access by non-English speakers. By May 2009, thirty-nine agencies had filed accessibility-improvement plans with the Office of Operations at an estimated cost of $27 million.

As in the Los Angeles region, quite different attitudes and receptivity levels can be found sixty miles east of the city and its famous beacon, the Statue of Liberty. The population of Long Island is about 2.7 million: Suffolk County on Long Island has slightly more people, but only one-third the population density, of closer-in Nassau County. Since 1980 Suffolk's immigrant population has more than doubled to at least 465,000. This growth was faster in Nassau during the early part of the period, but faster in Suffolk more recently. Suffolk County is a heterogeneous mix of distant suburbs, small commercial centers, agricultural zones, and high-end summer home towns. Immigrants arrived in response to the high demand for low-skilled workers such as farm workers, landscapers, and dishwashers as well as potentially more skilled construction work.

As a middle- to upper-middle-class white area, Suffolk County mainly leaned Republican until 2003, when Steve Levy, a Democrat, won the county executive position. (Levy switched parties in 2010 in an unsuccessful quest to run for governor, but remains county executive.) Democrats have held a slight majority in the county legislature since 2005. The county is divided into ten towns and villages as well as various special districts. In contrast to the more immigrant-friendly Nassau County to the west, County Executive Levy and county legislators sponsored several anti-immigrant local laws, including an attempt to deputize Suffolk County police to be immigration agents in 2004 (not passed) and to require county contractors to demonstrate the legal status of their employees (passed). Several anti-immigrant hate groups emerged in the county, such as Sachem Quality of Life. The area has experienced several serious hate crimes, including the murder of Marcelo Lucero, an immigrant from Ecuador, by six teenagers in 2008. Earlier, Orlan Enrique Moreno-Zavala, a Honduran young man, was found dead in the woods near Huntington Station in 2007, and two Mexican day laborers were kidnapped and almost murdered in 2000.[47]

In response to these acts of violence, immigrant advocacy organizations founded the Long Island Immigrant Alliance (LIIA), an umbrella organization of nonprofit, social justice, labor, and religious organizations. The alliance grew quickly from twenty-five members to forty-four organizations. While this foundation-funded effort has only one permanent staff member, its executive director, it maintains a broad coalition, involving both representatives of Service Employees International Union 1199, one of the most influential unions in New York State, and Sister Margaret from the North Fork Hispanic Apostolate, a one-nun army leading a set of loyal volunteers. At the same time, the LIIA

47. Southern Poverty Law Center (2009).

mostly works from a defensive posture in opposition to anti-immigrant bills in the county legislature, though it did conduct a "Long Island Wins" campaign to present immigrant contributions in a positive light.

These two cases—New York City and its affluent far suburbs in Suffolk County—undoubtedly miss many aspects of the politics of immigrant integration in metropolitan New York. Many areas fall between these two examples. The region's highly variegated matrix of classes and ethnic groups intersect in many different ways, each potentially yielding important lessons. Still, these two cases do allow us to draw a few lessons. As in Los Angeles, regionwide efforts around immigrant integration issues are rare, even though a large, highly politicized, and pro-immigrant central city dominates the regional discourse. This urban core celebrates its past and contemporary immigrant heritages and the considerable influence of its immigrant service and advocacy organizations does extend to other parts of the metropolitan area, but this still leaves the region without a coherent regional response, and this arrangement has not been effective in countering anti-immigrant outbreaks. Receptivity can be strained in peripheral communities experiencing rapid immigrant influxes. In these instances, even in this traditional immigrant gateway, some civic leaders try to advance their agendas by mobilizing citizen anxieties over immigration.

Chicago

Like New York, the Chicago metropolitan region is also less fragmented and more focused on the central city than is Los Angeles. Chicago makes up half the population of Cook County. Yet the far-flung metropolitan area still reaches from the city of Gary in northwestern Indiana around Lake Michigan, through Chicago, and up to southern Wisconsin. As table 4-3 shows, immigrants and their children account for markedly fewer voters in greater Chicago than Los Angeles, New York, or San Jose. Indeed, their share in Chicago is roughly the same as in Phoenix, and the principal cities actually have a lower share of immigrant voters (less than 6 percent) than the Chicago suburbs (about 7 percent), a different pattern than the other metropolitan areas.[48] Yet the core of the region has been relatively supportive of immigrant issues because of its long history of immigration and its strongly Democratic political orientation.

The Chicago metropolitan area has seen a large influx of immigrants over the last decade. As the data in table 4-1 show, slightly fewer than 40 percent are of Mexican descent, many from the state of Oaxaca. Aside from Chicago, they have also moved to Lake, Will, McHenry, and DuPage counties, which have all

---

48. The principal cities are Chicago, Naperville, Joliet, Elgin, Arlington Heights, Evanston, Schaumburg, Skokie, Des Plaines, and Hoffman Estates in Illinois and Gary, Indiana.

seen double-digit increases in their immigrant populations. In general, the city of Chicago has responded by accommodating immigrant populations. City officials cooperate with nonprofit organizations on health, education, and literacy initiatives, and immigrant advocacy organizations have built multiethnic coalitions. In particular, efforts are being made to bridge the Latino and Asian immigrant communities, which had relatively little contact in the past.

One reason for these adaptive responses to immigrant integration lies in the vaunted Cook County Democratic organization—the Chicago Machine. At present, six of Chicago's fifty aldermen come from Latino backgrounds—three are Mexican and three Puerto Rican—a significant rise from the beginning of the decade but still below their share of voting-age citizens. Former mayor Richard Daley and his organization actively encouraged this increase. Indeed, Simpson and Kelly argue that he modernized that organization by incorporating Latino voters.[49] Although the machine's growing reliance on Latino votes to offset potential challenges from black or white liberal independents may ensure it frames relevant policy issues in a generally pro-immigrant way, it also means that future Latino empowerment will be accomplished through the machine, not by challenging the political establishment, as Antonio Villaraigosa did when he defeated an incumbent mayor in Los Angeles. Nonetheless, this strategy of incorporation from above has paved the way for immigrant-friendly policies.

Another reason for Chicago's relatively temperate response may be that while it has a large Mexican presence, many immigrants also hail from Europe, with that group constituting a larger share of recent immigrants (21 percent) than in any other metropolitan area in the study. As in San Jose (see later discussion), this has tended to "deracialize" the image of immigrants and encourage a welcoming attitude, particularly as this reflects an earlier view of who immigrants were in the Chicago context.

In any case, Chicago's thick network of immigrant rights and immigrant advocacy organizations has led to political influence with the city's Democratic machine to shape state policies. For example, the Illinois Immigrant Rights Coalition recently won the prestigious E Pluribus Unum Prize from the Migration Policy Institute for working with the state to implement an Immigrant Family Resource Program that reduces the barriers faced by low-income immigrants and their children when seeking public benefits and services and is seen as a model for cooperation between state agencies and the region's immigrant-serving organizations. The coalition has also made inroads into suburban poli-

49. Simpson and Kelly (2011).

tics by pointing out to civic leaders that immigrants are a growing presence and a potential swing vote.

As in New York, however, the periphery of the region does not always echo Chicago's pro-immigrant positions. While Mayor Richard M. Daley and Police Chief Jody Weis were critical of a 287(g) arrangement in Chicago, suburban jurisdictions have moved in the opposite direction on immigrant enforcement. The Waukegan City Council, for example, voted to endorse a 287(g) arrangement in 2007, with the two Latino council members on the losing side of an 8 to 2 vote. The Elgin School District has also threatened to cut bilingual education and English as a second language (ESL) classes that serve immigrant students.

At the same time, other suburbs have, after a period of adjustment, responded in a supportive manner. For example, under the New Americans Initiative, the village of Melrose Park lobbied the state of Illinois in 2007 to establish the first "welcoming center" to connect recently arrived immigrants to important human, educational, and employment services. Since 2005 the town of Cicero has set several programs in motion to create a hospitable environment for its immigrants, including a popular Department of Community Affairs and Special Projects initiative to assist Spanish-speaking business owners, many of them legal immigrants, with translation on procedures and regulations for becoming licensed. Stone Park has responded to its growing (primarily Latino) immigrant population with community events and festivals in local schools, cultural competency training for municipal employees who service immigrants, conflict resolution, and training (a financial literacy course and ESL) for immigrant parents.

It may be that the Chicago Democratic machine's control over Cook County has seemed to dampen (but not eliminate) the negative response of natives to immigrant "shocks" in the suburbs. It is also the case that Chicago may be different from New York and Los Angeles in its coordination of certain civic actions across jurisdictions. For example, Chicago Metropolis 2020, a business-led group, has tried to address regional issues of affordable housing and former Mayor Daley made a consistent effort to meet with his suburban counterparts on issues of concern. Although these regional approaches have not addressed immigrant integration per se, there may be some spillover from the regional visioning—a point we explore in the conclusion.

San Jose

Although the San Jose metropolitan region is a relatively new gateway, its immigrants have already become quite established. Silicon Valley, after all, has developed with the help of many immigrant entrepreneurs and, as noted, its immigrants include many Indians and Chinese who play key roles in high technology industries.[50] In terms of receptivity, the region most closely approximates the immigrant-friendly tenor of the urban cores of the three traditional receiving areas; indeed, it goes beyond them in some respects because San Jose's suburbs also have reacted positively.

One reason may be that naturalized immigrants already form an important part of the urban and suburban electorate, with some 40 percent of the voters in the principal cities of the metropolitan area being immigrants or their children.[51] As the region's immigrant communities matured, they have become civically engaged, electing a growing number of immigrant candidates. The city of San Jose is roughly one-third Latino, one-third Asian, and one-third white and has a history of progressive reform; San Jose's ten-member city council includes an Indian American, a Chinese American, a Vietnamese American, and two Mexican Americans.[52] The nearby city of Cupertino has a Chinese American mayor and three Asian members on a five-member city council.

Overall, the region trends Democratic, also lending a more supportive tone. But the voters also expect the region's politicians to pay attention to immigration in a positive way. One of the region's Democratic representatives in the U.S. Congress, Zoe Lofgren, was chair of the House Immigration Subcommittee and consistently took up the issue of temporary visas allowing high-tech immigrants to work in Silicon Valley and, more generally, comprehensive immigration reform. Another, Representative Mike Honda, is chair of the Congressional Asian Pacific American Caucus. He was interned (along with his family) during World War II and is considered a stalwart defender of immigrant rights.

Compared to other new destinations, the San Jose metropolitan area has a well-developed public and nonprofit infrastructure of immigrant services. Santa Clara County's Human Relations Council founded the Immigrant Relations and Integration Services (IRIS) in 1996. This publicly funded program promotes citizenship, provides legal services, and conducts outreach and leadership development. In 2000 IRIS hosted a conference, Bridging Borders in Silicon Valley: Summit on Immigrant Needs and Contributions, and the council published an accompanying report with hundreds of recommendations for improving immigrant lives around economic development, education, family support, and health. IRIS also coordinates an immigrant leadership course in collaboration with San Jose City College, helping to generate the kinds of civic infrastructure and activism that are missing in the Inland Empire (urban areas in the

50. Saxenian (1999).
51. The principal cities are San Jose, Sunnyvale, Santa Clara, Mountain View, Milpitas, Palo Alto, and Cupertino.
52. See Trounstine (2008) on the history.

two counties east of Los Angeles County), the far Chicago suburbs, or Suffolk County on Long Island.

This "warmth of the welcome," apart from modest tensions around day labor sites, is quite remarkable given that the San Jose metropolitan area saw the biggest percentage increase in the number of recent immigrants of any of our cases. With a higher share of Asian, high-skilled, and wealthy immigrants, it is harder to "racialize" immigrants as the "other" (something we also suggested was important in Chicago). More important, however, this positive framing seems to spill over to other populations. Even communities with many undocumented Mexicans, such as the Mayfair neighborhood in San Jose, receive positive attention and support from local authorities.

It also seems that another driving force in the "warmth of welcome" is that regional leaders can—and do—credibly argue that the region's ability to attract and retain immigrants is vital to its economic success. For example, the *Index of Silicon Valley* published by Joint Venture: Silicon Valley Network, a grouping of new economy business and civic leaders, describes immigrants under the rubric of "Talent Flows and Diversity"—and the *Index* writers express concern when the flow of foreign-born slows rather than rises. The labor movement's own think tank, Working Partnerships USA, also put out a celebratory analysis of immigrant contributions in 2004.[53] Both business and labor interests, therefore, have consistently emphasized the importance of immigrants to the region's social and economic health.

Charlotte

The Charlotte metropolitan region is less receptive than San Jose but much more so than Phoenix. As in San Jose, Charlotte includes a self-conscious business class that thinks of itself as building a regional metropolis (though in a more politically conservative mode). Yet unlike San Jose, and even unlike Phoenix, its immigrants are among the newest of any region. Table 4-3 shows that they and their children make up the smallest part of the city electorate relative to our other cases: just 13 percent.[54] It is not surprising, therefore, that, unlike in San Jose, no candidates from immigrant backgrounds have been elected to office in Charlotte.

Over the last three decades, Charlotte has undergone a dramatic economic restructuring, with downtown banking replacing previously dominant textile and furniture manufacturing. A "tight-knit, private-sector, philanthropic, economic growth machine" oversaw this transformation. NationsBank (now Bank of America) was a driving force behind Charlotte's downtown revitalization. It

---

53. Auerhahn and Brownstein (2004).
54. Charlotte is the only principal city in the CBSA.

underwrote the Corporate Center, Founders Hall, and the Blumenthal Perform-ing Arts Center.[55] It leased a large, centrally located parcel to the city to create a hub for the transit system. When the public failed to support a referendum for a sports arena, the private sector secured the financing. Charlotte's two major banks saw their success as intertwined with that of the new downtown. Its busi-ness leadership urged the city to pay attention to concentrated poverty in and near the downtown.[56]

The recent arrival of substantial numbers of Latino immigrants was perhaps an unexpected part of this shift. The foreign-born population is clustered on the Eastside and southwest side of downtown. The Eastside is a more "established" Latino community, having expanded from a small Asian immigrant settlement that formed in the 1980s. The position of this Latino neighborhood fits in between the larger pattern of black-white segregation in Charlotte and Mecklen-burg County. Charlotte's African American communities are concentrated to the north, surrounding "Uptown" (Charlotte's downtown). The city's older white residential neighborhoods are to the south of Uptown. The two areas are now partly separated by the new Latino immigrant population.

Pat McCrory, a Republican, served as mayor from 1995 through 2009, when much of this economic and demographic transformation occurred. As down-town was redeveloped, the city's population increased substantially and immi-grant settlement in the surrounding region increased exponentially. The govern-ing structures of the partially consolidated region are the city and county councils, now both headed by Democrats. They share oversight for key public agencies, such as the schools, which have worked to adjust to the influx of non-English-speaking immigrants, providing immigrants with a modicum of "bureaucratic incorporation."

However, there is still a significant "institutional mismatch" between the immigrant community needs and the services provided by public and nonprofit organizations. Institutional responses still lag behind demographic changes, while immigrant organizations are still in their infancy and immigrant political representation has yet to emerge. Indeed, local service providers have been on the defensive, trying not only to manage increased demands from new immi-grant clients, but to forestall negative reactions from native-born white and black residents. A 2007 immigration report commissioned by the former mayor

55. The business community as a whole was more engaged in Charlotte than in peer cities. See a report by the Tijeras Foundation ranking Charlotte among the ten most "giving cities" in the United States. In the foundation's survey, Charlotte is tied in fourth place for percent of household income given to philanthropy; residents in the city were estimated to give 3.1 percent of their household income to charity. See Chazwold, "Grand Rapids in Top Ten for Giving Hours and Dollars," June 10, 2008 (www.rightmichigan.com/story/2008/6/10/12915/7998).

56. Pastor and others (2000).

adopted a schizophrenic tone, veering from suspicion of the legitimacy of new arrivals to a bureaucratic accounting of the services that the city and county provided them.

Deaton and Furuseth and Smith suggest that the reception has chilled since 2006, partly because rapid growth of the immigrant population and early signs of its civic and political mobilization raised concerns among the native-born about new Latino political influence.[57] In 2006 the Mecklenberg County Sheriff's Department became one of the first in the country to train deputies under the 287(g) program. And former Mayor McCrory, once known for welcoming immigrants, raised concerns about illegal immigration in his 2008 campaign for governor (which he lost). Still, Charlotte has proven relatively welcoming to immigrants, particularly given the rapidity of the increase in the immigrant population.

The relative warmth of welcome in Charlotte suggests the importance of business leadership. As Furuseth and Smith note, "The Charlotte-Mecklenburg corporate community displayed little interest in targeting undocumented immigrants or designing strategies to punish or remove them from the area."[58] That leadership sees the need for immigrant labor and wants Charlotte to stand as a model of the tolerant "New South." At the same time, as shown in the suburbs of Los Angeles, New York, and Chicago, local political entrepreneurs can still whip up anti-immigrant sentiment in the pursuit of political advancement, but they at least encounter some degree of resistance from business forces concerned with the region's overall economy.

Phoenix

The Phoenix metropolitan region, which is largely contained within Maricopa County, is the twelfth most populous in the country.[59] At 1.5 million residents, Phoenix itself is the nation's fifth largest city. Though Maricopa County includes twenty-five municipalities, the city of Phoenix occupies 517 square miles and holds 40 percent of the county's population.

Although this political geography is less complex than that of the other regions, Maricopa County is by no means easily governed. Its five-member Board of Supervisors, elected by districts, is sometimes at loggerheads with the constituent cities. Rather than leading the region, Phoenix co-exists alongside the large suburban municipalities of Chandler, Gilbert, Glendale, Mesa, and

---

57. Deaton (2008); Furuseth and Smith (2010).

58. Furuseth and Smith (2010, p. 186).

59. The Census Bureau added Pinal County (with a population of 300,000 on the southeast border of Maricopa County) to the metropolitan area in 2000 due to significant commuting from that formerly rural area. Principal cities aside from Phoenix include Mesa, Scottsdale, and Tempe.

Scottsdale, which all have more than 200,000 residents. (Mesa alone has more than 450,000.) Though it has affluent and middle-class neighborhoods, Phoenix is also poorer than many of these suburbs.

Although Maricopa County as a whole is a Republican bastion, Phoenix leans Democratic. Immigrants, however, hold little electoral sway in either part of the region. As table 4-3 shows, they and their children make up only 15 percent of the voters in the principal cities and even less in the suburbs. Of all the nation's large metropolitan areas, Phoenix has the sharpest difference between the older, primarily native-born population and the more immigrant (and noncitizen) youth population.

This division has helped to fuel native Anglo angst about immigrants. White residents tend to equate "immigrant" with "Mexican immigrant" and specifically "illegal immigrant." Helping (or perhaps hurting) matters is the fact that undocumented Mexicans do indeed dominate the recent immigrant population (table 4-1). The high share of undocumented residents stems partly from the successful federal effort to fortify the California and Texas borders in the late 1990s, which pushed unauthorized immigration toward the northern Sonoran desert and Arizona and made Phoenix a flashpoint for frustrations about border control. Unauthorized immigrants, who may be 10 percent of the region's entire population and workforce, tend to keep a low profile. Black-market activities related to human smuggling are quite visible in Phoenix, however, and the crime and violence across the nearby border in Mexico heightens anxieties.

Police focus on locating and raiding drop houses where immigrants are held pending payment or transport. Many of these are in otherwise unremarkable residential neighborhoods. Kidnapping or assault of migrants by smugglers (*coyotes*) is common. At the beginning of the last decade, the Phoenix police department hired several hundred new officers who "were needed to directly combat crimes associated with illegal immigration—crimes like smuggling and kidnapping," according to Mayor Phil Gordon.[60] The local media extensively covered these "underground" activities, contributing to the crisis atmosphere and cementing the connection between immigrants and crime and disorder.

The state (as well as national) context has also politicized the landscape. Dominated by Republicans, the Arizona legislature's passage of SB 1070 sparked a great deal of controversy and a backlash against Phoenix in many other parts of the country, despite the fact that most Democratic legislators from Phoenix opposed the measure. While SB 1070 purports to avoid racial profiling, the state in fact has embraced a policy of attrition of undocumented immigrants through

60. Speech to Harvard Law School conference, The Localization of Immigration Law, February 5, 2010. Gordon has staked out a relatively supportive position on immigrants, but he also highlights the fiscal and human strains on public safety caused by unauthorized immigration.

enforcement. The Center for Immigration Studies, a Washington-based restrictionist organization, sees Arizona as a test case in reducing the unauthorized population by ratcheting up local enforcement, a "third way" between providing amnesty or undertaking a prohibitively expensive wholesale removal action.[61]

Phoenix is thus entangled in an intense and polarized debate over how to respond to unauthorized immigration from Mexico.[62] This furor has overshadowed and displaced the issues of immigrant integration and empowerment. Few organizations have attempted to build bridges between natives and immigrants or form coalitions in support of immigrant integration. Latinos are, nevertheless, a large and growing voting constituency in the region's principal cities, including Phoenix. Advocacy organizations, service providers, and Latino elected officials are attempting to speak for the interests of immigrants. However, they mostly find themselves on the defensive in the face of overwhelming popular hostility toward unauthorized immigration driven by publicity-grabbing efforts of anti-immigration political entrepreneurs at the county and state levels.

All the factors limiting receptivity are compounded in Phoenix. Immigration is highly racialized, regional fragmentation is high, the immigrant "shock" has been sudden, and many immigrants are, indeed, undocumented. The demographic distance between the new, younger immigrants and the older, native-born population is among the highest in the country. Many elected officials have sought to build their careers by tapping into the anxieties that these conditions create among the voters.[63] In San Jose and to a lesser degree in Charlotte, a broad business and civic leadership seems willing to say that efforts to heighten anti-immigrant sentiment run against the region's broader economic and social interests. This has not generally been the case in Phoenix—although sixty business leaders signed a letter in March 2011 arguing that Arizona's anti-immigrant legislation was hurting the state economically; this provided cover for state lawmakers to table a new set of anti-immigrant laws. In the general vacuum, however, the Phoenix police and the county sheriff have been bickering over the enforcement of immigrant policy, and local politicians continue to capitalize on public anxieties.

What Is to Be Learned?

These case studies—and other studies of metropolitan immigrants—point to several analytical lessons about the relationship between regional receptivity to immigrants and regional resilience. First, history matters; reception is more welcoming

61. Krikorian (2005).

62. It is interesting that Tucson, a more Democratic-leaning university town that more fully dominates its county, has had a much less negative reaction to immigrants than Phoenix.

63. Frey (2010).

in regions with long histories of immigrant integration. New York and Chicago both illustrate this, with New York priding itself as a city of immigrants and beacon of hope for many arriving from around the world. The history of Los Angeles has involved more conflict, including mass deportations of Mexican immigrants in the 1930s and the displacement of Mexican Americans from urban redevelopment projects in the 1950s and 1960s. However, the more recent past has included electing the son of a Mexican immigrant as mayor. Phoenix, on the other hand, has experienced a sharp buildup of recent immigrants in the context of little past immigration, contributing to a sense of dislocation and conflict. Demography is not destiny here, however, because San Jose and Charlotte have far more gracefully received immigrants despite very rapid recent increases in number.

The geography of reception also matters. The urban cores of all these regions tend to provide a more supportive context of reception featuring a legacy of immigrant service organizations, informal and formal modalities of representation for immigrant interests, and acceptance by the native-born establishment of a positive immigrant story. The peripheral parts of all the regions have less experience with immigration and greater demographic distance from them. They often have a cooler response to their newcomers.[64] They are less equipped to cope with the change and lean toward what De Graauw, Gleeson, and Bloemraad call "free riding," that is, relying on nearby central cities to provide needed immigrant services.[65] Other sympathetic suburban jurisdictions provide services quietly, hoping to avoid attention or provoke political conflict. In such areas, low levels of immigrant political mobilization may facilitate this approach. In any case, given the steady suburbanization of immigration, a better understanding of suburban responses—both by agencies and by immigrants—should be a research priority.

Race matters as well. Metropolitan areas with more diverse immigrant flows—by class as well as national origin—seem less likely to react negatively to immigration. Places where a single group is negatively framed—particularly poor, undocumented Mexicans—tend to view the whole phenomenon of immigration in that light. New York and Los Angeles have more varied flows than other regions, but New York's diversity is greatest. This, along with the fact that one of its main immigrant groups, Puerto Ricans, are citizens, may enable it to respond more positively to the challenges of immigrant integration. Immigration is also more deracialized in Chicago and San Jose, where Eastern Europeans in the former case and higher-skill and higher-income Asian immigrants in the

---

64. The regions also differ considerably in their concentration and spread. Silicon Valley and Charlotte are more consolidated and compact than the New York region, which crosses multiple cities, counties, and states. This has real implications for regional governance and immigrant service infrastructure.

65. De Graauw, Gleeson, and Bloemraad (2010).

latter have a prominent presence. Conversely, the fact that so many immigrants in Phoenix are undocumented Mexicans and recent arrivals has helped to foster a racialization that diminishes empathy for the immigrant experience.

Where immigration is racialized, the perception that immigrants are all recent and undocumented may be greater than the reality. The growth of recent Mexican migrants to Phoenix was, we think, perceived as a shock even though Mexican migration was low compared to other regions. San Jose saw the sharpest rise in percent foreign-born and now has the highest immigrant share of the regions discussed here—but its response was the most harmonious and embracing. Race matters in Chicago where the political machine has incorporated Mexican immigrants in the grand tradition of other ethnic groups. And race has a different importance in Charlotte because the region's business leadership wants to present it as a racially tolerant center of the New South, which has helped to keep the tone generally civil.

Indeed, the responses of San Jose and Charlotte suggest that regional business elites can be a critical counterweight—and that researchers need to better understand the role of business in regional responses to immigration. After all, fragmented metropolitan landscapes provide opportunities for anti-immigrant political entrepreneurs to gain ground. The combination of certain demographic antecedents—many new, undocumented, racialized immigrant populations in areas with little experience with them and large demographic distances between older natives and younger immigrants—poses a great temptation for politicians to polarize the issue. In so doing, they raise the level of controversy beyond what would have prevailed without them even as they advance their own political fortunes.

This suggests that efforts to portray residents of a region as sharing a common fate could be important. For example, in his most recent state of the city speech in January 2011, New York Mayor Michael Bloomberg noted, "The biggest single step we can take to promote innovation in New York City, and across this country, is to fix our broken immigration system. It's not only hurting national security; it's the most ruinous economic policy you could ever conceive of. It's destroying American jobs every single day. We've got to change it."[66]

Bloomberg has also organized a group of CEOs and big-city mayors, the Partnership for a New American Economy, to push for immigration reform. At the same time, the rest of the region does not always echo New York City's tone—and it has few vehicles, such as San Jose's Joint Venture, to push for a

---

66. See Momar Visaya, "Immigration Reform Needed for Economic Growth—Bloomberg," Asian Journal, January 21, 2011 (www.asianjournal.com/dateline-usa/15-dateline-usa/8584-immigration-reform-needed-for-economic-growth-bloomberg.html).

regional approach to immigration or any other issue.[67] As a result, the immigrant response within the New York City metropolitan area is sharply varied.

Los Angeles also exhibits much variation, with areas of significant immigrant organizing, particularly in the core city, coupled with equally large pockets of important anti-immigrant sentiment. This may be a general problem of fragmentation: the Los Angeles metropolitan area has been aptly described as "seventy-two suburbs in search of a city."[68] It is also noteworthy that the city of Los Angeles never managed to host a single one of the "regional collaboratives" supported by the Irvine Foundation in Southern California in the 2000s to promote the coming together of civic leaders around a shared regional destiny (even as a series of collaborations took place in the San Fernando Valley, the older industrial suburbs of the Alameda Corridor, and Orange County).[69] Finally, the leadership of Los Angeles on this issue may also be constrained by the fact that its mayor is a Mexican American: he may be seen as playing racial politics if his pro-immigrant stances are too strong and his progressive politics also may not play well in other parts of the metropolitan area.

Finally, we note that timing, in the context of national trends, also matters. San Jose's immigrant boom occurred after a Republican president had supported a means for integrating the undocumented (IRCA under Ronald Reagan). The tensions so apparent in Phoenix—and even the controversy over the Islamic Center proposed near Ground Zero in New York—occurred in a more politically polarized era. The national tenor of debate can influence how local regions respond and can offer up new opportunities for political entrepreneurs (for example, the way in which national anti-immigrant groups have been working to promote "attrition through enforcement" by seeding Arizona-style legislation). However, our cases suggest that local and regional leadership can either dampen or fan the flames.

What Is to Be Done?

The national gridlock around immigration reform has shifted the geographic focus of debate to the states and metropolitan areas. When Congress failed to pass the DREAM Act in December 2010, immigrant advocates started to think about moving parallel legislation at the state level. Meanwhile, restrictionist forces are not only hoping SB 1070 copycat legislation will lead to "self-deportation," but its proponents are trying to end birthright citizenship for the children of undocu-

67. The Regional Plan Association, a New York–based nonprofit organization, has promoted regional integration since 1922, but its influence mainly takes the form of putting issues on the public agenda.

68. The quote is widely attributed to American poet and satirist Dorothy Parker.

69. See Innes and Rongerude (2005) and Jonas and Pincetl (2006).

mented immigrants. As the fights move down the geographic scale, some may think the time for new federal policies has passed. Although we concur that regions vary greatly in terms of the actual process of integrating immigrants (including the undocumented) and that much can be done to improve the situation at the urban and regional levels, the federal government can still play a major role in shaping this new landscape.

The federal government, in particular U.S. Citizenship and Immigration Services (USCIS), should help develop, expand, and support the welcoming and forward-looking civic leadership profiled in the best of our case study regions. The receptivity of a region should not be left purely to its preexisting combination of immigrant-friendly business leaders, opportunity-seeking politicians, or legacies of regional collaboration. USCIS can spur regional leadership by developing indicators of immigrant integration, supporting research on immigrant contributions to regional economies, and convening regional actors to talk through the challenges of welcoming and integrating immigrants.

Newer receiving areas need particular attention because they face a bigger challenge with fewer supports. This holds not just for new receiving regions but for new suburban destinations within the older receiving areas (for example, the Inland Empire, Suffolk County, and the Chicago suburbs). The shock of a big new population seems to trigger a more negative reaction than an equivalent addition to a large existing immigrant base (though this may be attenuated by other factors, as in San Jose). Nevertheless, the immigrant integration component of any eventual national policy reform will need to include special resources and training for newer receiving areas, and available statistics give us a reasonable initial guide to those places.

Our case study regions and others provide numerous positive examples for state and local policy. Municipal and metropolitan leaders are sharing best practices, for example, through the National League of Cities immigrant integration initiative. The J. M. Kaplan Fund and other supporters are seeking to expand Welcoming America, a grassroots effort to build positive understanding toward immigrants in the newer receiving communities. The Haas Foundation in California has been supporting efforts to consider another sort of new receiving area—black communities that have seen a significant influx of immigrants. Further support for sharing real-world scenarios and creating a broad consensus on what works would be useful.

Expertise also needs to be spread within regions. As noted earlier, the historic pattern of spatial assimilation involves immigrants first concentrating in the urban cores and then moving outward to suburbs as their socioeconomic standing improves. Today, more new immigrants are moving directly to the suburbs. Suburban jurisdictions have less experience and fewer support organizations for responding to these immigrants. Although regional coordination can help them by extending capacities that have already developed in central cities, they need to be encouraged to move beyond "free riding" to develop their own capacities for receiving and integrating immigrants.

Immigrants, of course, need not be constrained by the environments they enter. They can also devise strategies for political advancement and policy development to make these environments more responsive (or in some cases develop political defenses to make them less hostile). The shape of immigrant political mobilization cannot be deduced simply from the political opportunity structure in which immigrants find themselves. Individual and organizational activists in these communities can draw on a repertoire of possible political actions, resources, and strategies to reframe those political opportunities.[70]

New York, Los Angeles, and Chicago all have vibrant immigrant rights communities. They should be challenged and helped to extend their reach into the new suburban destinations. The immigrant rights groups in San Jose are quite active—they fielded 100,000 marchers on May 1, 2006, proportionately far larger than the Los Angeles marches. Phoenix and Charlotte both have relatively non-mobilized immigrant populations. This does not undermine Charlotte's immigrant integration efforts but does facilitate anti-immigrant responses in Arizona.

By mobilizing for better services and policy changes to facilitate immigrant and regional adjustment, immigrants are contributing to metropolitan resilience. Newer destinations typically lack this type of mobilization and their service infrastructure engages immigrants as clients, not civic actors.[71] Although the simple delivery of services is important, mobilized populations create a new voice in civic debate and deliberation that can set a different tone, create new opportunities for pro-immigrant political entrepreneurs, and help to hold systems accountable. We would, therefore, recommend that noncitizen immigrants be encouraged to participate in local planning exercises, school councils, and other forms of active "citizenship," partly as preparation for eventual naturalization and voting. Although we recognize that this could provoke short-term anxieties among the native-born, it will also facilitate long-run political incorporation.[72]

---

70. Bada and others (2010) review Latino civic engagement in nine U.S. cities, including four— Charlotte, Chicago, Los Angeles, and San Jose—that anchor the metropolitan areas we explore.

71. Given the potential for conflict over providing immigrant services in new receiving areas, some argue that a "depoliticized" strategy is the best way to achieve a minimum service level. This, however, can lead to a truncated form of immigrant integration with shallow political roots.

72. Immigrant integration also involves considering the impacts of immigrants on more general public systems, a topic we do not explore here due to constraints of space. See, for example, Fix's (2009) analysis of the failure to redesign systems with immigrants in mind during the 1996 welfare reform. Capps and others (2009) also explore how to adjust Workforce Investment Act funding to better respond

Conclusion

America is at a demographic crossroads. Even if we could slow immigration through tougher enforcement and more restrictions, our current immigrants and their families will still turn us into a majority-minority nation in the due course of time.[73] Far more likely is that economic and demographic needs will prevail and we will continue to rely on immigration to address issues raised by aging baby boomers and a consequent increase in the so-called dependency ratio (the percentage of those too young or too old to work over the age-eligible workforce).[74] Either way, America will face an important test in coming decades about how well we will adjust to those changes.

The six metropolitan regions we have profiled here provide a foretaste of what it will mean for the nation to cope with this immigrant "shock." Some have managed to create a welcoming atmosphere, while others have not—and the responses nearly all vary within their regions. Whether the resilience demonstrated by some with regard to new immigrants will spill over to resilience along other dimensions, such as economic sustainability, remains to be seen and should be the subject of future research. Also to be studied are the interactions between immigrants and African Americans as well as the intriguing—but not fully demonstrated—relationship between business and civic elite commitment to a regional perspective and more positive overall responses to immigrants and immigrant integration.

Despite the need for further work, we trust that this analysis provides an initial guide to the factors that drive receptivity and resilience and the policy strategies that follow for those interested in furthering immigrant integration. For example, rapid increases in immigration in newer areas seem to trigger concern; perhaps any national immigration policy reform should include special resources and training for newer receiving areas, including new suburban destinations. A high concentration of poorer, less-skilled Mexican immigrants seems to drive negative reactions; since altering the flow is difficult, perhaps metropolitan leaders can work more on healing racial relations and projecting a civil tone. Political entrepreneurs can often take advantage of anti-immigrant sentiment to further their own goals; encouraging civic engagement, leadership development, and naturalization among immigrants can help shift the political cost-benefit

---

to adult English learners of varying levels of education, while Batalova and Fix (2008) describe ways to address "credentialing" and other challenges facing skilled immigrants in the United States.

73. Recent unofficial census projections have taken into account the slowdown in immigration stemming from the 2008–09 financial crisis and slowing birthrates in Mexico, but this only pushes the date when America becomes a majority-minority nation back to 2050. The official midrange estimate still indicates 2042 as the threshold date.

74. Myers (2007).

calculus and help extend and protect services crucial for new immigrants to becoming full participants in American democracy.

Finally, we believe that regional leaders who want their metropolitan areas to weather the country's inevitable economic and demographic changes will likely need to weave immigrants into their regional narratives and visions for their regional futures. By highlighting how immigrants and their children can be assets rather than problems, they can work to calm the political waters and facilitate a broad recognition that a region's resilience is based not on struggling with strangers, but rather on helping the newcomers maximize their contributions to our country's metropolitan future.

References

Alba, Richard D., and Victor Nee. 1997. "Rethinking Assimilation Theory for a New Era of Immigration." *International Migration Review* 31, no. 4: 826–74.

Auerhahn, Louise, and Bob Brownstein. 2004. "The Economic Effect of Immigration in Santa Clara County and California." San Jose, Calif.: Working Partnerships USA.

Bada, Xóchitl, and others. 2010. "Context Matters: Latino Immigrant Civic Engagement in Nine U.S. Cities." Washington: Woodrow Wilson International Center for Scholars.

Batalova, Jeanne, and Michael Fix. 2008. "Uneven Progress: The Employment Pathways of Skilled Immigrants in the United States." Washington: Migration Policy Institute.

Blackwell, Angela B., Stuart Kwoh, and Manuel Pastor. 2010. *Uncommon Common Ground: Race and America's Future*. New York: W. W. Norton.

Bohn, Sarah. 2009. "New Patterns of Immigrant Settlement in California." San Francisco: Public Policy Institute of California.

Capps, Randy, and others. 2009. "Taking Limited English Proficient Adults into Account in the Federal Adult Education Funding Formula." Washington: Migration Policy Institute.

Catanzarite, Lisa. 2004. "Occupational Context and Wage Competition of New Immigrant Latinos with Minorities and Whites." In *The Impact of Immigration on African Americans*, edited by Steven Shulman, pp. 59–76. New Brunswick, N.J.: Transaction Publishers.

Clark, William A. V., and Sarah A. Blue. 2004. "Race, Class, and Segregation Patterns in U.S. Immigrant Gateway Cities." *Urban Affairs Review* 39: 667–88.

Deaton, Joyce. 2008. "Charlotte: A Welcome Denied." Washington: Woodrow Wilson International Center for Scholars.

De Graauw, Els, Shannon Gleeson, and Irene Bloemraad. 2010. "Immigrant Suburbs and Central Cities: Understanding Differences in Municipal Support for Immigrant Organizations and Suburban Free-Riding." Unpublished article, April 29.

Fiscal Policy Institute. 2009. "Immigrants and the Economy: Contribution of Immigrant Workers to the Country's 25 Largest Metropolitan Areas." New York.

Fix, Michael, ed. 2009. *Immigrants and Welfare: The Impact of Welfare Reform on America's Newcomers*. New York: Russell Sage.

Frey, William H. 2010. "Age." In *State of Metropolitan America: On the Front Lines of Demographic Transformation*. Metropolitan Policy Program, Brookings.

Furuseth, Owen J., and Heather A. Smith. 2010. "Localized Immigration Policy: The View from Charlotte, North Carolina, a New Immigrant Gateway." In *Taking Local Control:*

Immigration Policy Activism in U.S. Cities and States, edited by Monica W. Varsanyi, pp. 173–92. Stanford University Press.

Hochschild, Jennifer, and John Mollenkopf, eds. 2009. *Bringing Outsiders In: Transatlantic Perspectives of Immigrant Political Incorporation*. Cornell University Press.

Hopkins, Daniel J. 2010. "Politicized Places: Explaining Where and When Immigrants Provoke Local Opposition." *American Political Science Review* 104, no. 1: 21–39.

Iceland, John. 2009. *Where We Live Now; Immigration and Race in the United States*. University of California Press.

Iceland, John, and Melissa Scopilliti. 2008. "Immigrant Residential Segregation in U.S. Metropolitan Areas, 1990–2000." *Demography* 45, no. 1: 79–94.

Innes, Judith, and Jane Rongerude. 2005. "Collaborative Regional Initiatives: Civic Entrepreneurs Work to Fill the Governance Gap." Working Paper 2006-04. Institute for Urban and Regional Development, University of California–Berkeley.

Jonas, Andrew E. G., and Stephanie Pincetl. 2006. "Rescaling Regions in the State: The New Regionalism in California." *Political Geography* 25, no. 5: 482–505.

Jones-Correa, Michael. 2008. "Immigrant Incorporation in the Suburbs: Differential Pathways, Arenas and Intermediaries." In *Immigration and Integration in Urban Communities: Renegotiating the City*, edited by Lisa M. Hanley, Blair A. Ruble, and Allison M. Garland, pp. 19–47. Johns Hopkins University Press and Woodrow Wilson Center Press.

Kasinitz, Philip, John Mollenkopf, and Mary Waters, eds. 2004. *Becoming New Yorkers: Ethnographies of the New Second Generation*. New York: Russell Sage.

Katznelson, Ira. 2005. *When Affirmative Action Was White: An Untold History of Racial Inequality in Twentieth-Century America*. New York: W. W. Norton.

Keely, Charles B. 1971. "Effects of the Immigration Act of 1965 on Selected Population Characteristics of Immigrants to the United States." *Demography* 8, no. 2: 157–69.

Krikorian, Mark. 2005. "Downsizing Illegal Immigration: A Strategy of Attrition through Enforcement." Washington: Center for Immigration Studies.

Light, Ivan. 2006. *Deflecting Immigration: Networks, Markets, and Regulation in Los Angeles*. New York: Russell Sage.

Marcelli, Enrico. 2004. "From the Barrio to the 'Burbs? Immigration and the Dynamics of Suburbanization." In *Up against the Sprawl: Public Policy in the Making of Southern California*, edited by Jennifer Wolch, Manuel Pastor, and Peter Dreier, pp. 123–50. University of Minnesota Press.

Massey, Douglas S. 1985. "Ethnic Residential Segregation: A Theoretical and Empirical Review." *Sociology and Social Research* 69: 315–50.

Massey, Douglas S., ed. 2008. *New Faces in New Places: The Changing Geography of American Immigration*. New York: Russell Sage.

Mehta, Chirag, and others. 2002. "Chicago's Undocumented Immigrants: An Analysis of Wages, Working Conditions, and Economic Contributions." University of Illinois at Chicago Center for Urban Economic Development.

Myers, Dowell. 2007. *Immigrants and Boomers: Forging a New Social Contract for the Future of America*. New York: Russell Sage.

Myers, Dowell, John Pitkin, and Ricardo Ramirez. 2010. "The New Homegrown Majority in California: Recognizing the New Reality of Growing Commitment to the Golden State." University of Southern California School of Policy, Planning, and Development.

Orfield, Myron. 2002. *American Metropolitics: The New Suburban Reality*. Brookings.

Pastor, Manuel. 2001. "Looking for Regionalism in All the Wrong Places: Demography, Geography, and Community in Los Angeles County." *Urban Affairs Review* 36, no. 6: 74–82.

————. 2011, forthcoming. "Spatial Assimilation and Its Discontents: The Changing Geography of Immigrant Integration in Metropolitan America." In *Handbook of Urban Economics and Planning*, edited by Nancy Brooks, Kieran Donaghy, and Gerritt Knaap. Oxford University Press.

————. 2012, forthcoming. "Keeping It Real: Demographic Change, Economic Conflict, and Inter-Ethnic Organizing for Social Justice in Los Angeles." In *Black and Brown Los Angeles: A Contemporary Reader*, edited by Josh Kun and Laura Pulido. University of California Press.

Pastor, Manuel, and Enrico Marcelli. 2004. "Somewhere over the Rainbow? African American Immigration, and Coalition-Building." *Review of Black Political Economy* 31, nos. 1–2.

Pastor, Manuel, and Rhonda Ortiz. 2009. "Immigrant Integration in Los Angeles: Strategic Directions for Funders." University of Southern California, Program for Environmental and Regional Equity (PERE) and Center for the Study of Immigrant Integration (CSII).

Pastor, Manuel, and Deborah Reed. 2005. "Understanding Equitable Infrastructure Investment for California." San Francisco: Public Policy Institute of California.

Pastor, Manuel, and others. 2000. *Regions That Work: How Cities and Suburbs Can Grow Together*. University of Minnesota Press.

Pumak, Ayse. 2004. "Geography of Immigrant Clusters in Global Cities: A Case Study of San Francisco." *International Journal of Urban and Regional Research* 28, no. 2: 287–307.

Putnam, Robert. 2007. "E Pluribus Unum: Diversity and Community in the Twenty-First Century—The 2006 Johan Skytte Prize Lecture." *Scandinavian Political Studies* 30, no. 2: 137–74.

Ramakrishnan, Karthick, and Tom K. Wong. 2010. "Partisanship, Not Spanish: Explaining Local Ordinances Affecting Undocumented Immigrants." In *Taking Local Control: Immigration Policy Activism in U.S. Cities and States*, edited by Monica W. Varsanyi, pp. 73–93. Stanford University Press.

Ready, Timothy, and Allert Brown-Gort. 2005. "The State of Latino Chicago: This Is Home Now." University of Notre Dame, Institute for Latino Studies.

Saxenian, AnnaLee. 1999. "Silicon Valley's New Immigrant Entrepreneurs." San Francisco: Public Policy Institute of California.

Simpson, Dick, and Tom Kelly. 2011. "The New Chicago School of Urbanism and the New Daley Machine." In *The City Revisited: Urban Theory from Chicago, Los Angeles, and New York*, edited by Dennis Judd and Dick Simpson, pp. 205–19. University of Minnesota Press.

Singer, Audrey. 2004. "The Rise of New Immigrant Gateways." Brookings.

————. 2007. "Twenty-First-Century Gateways: An Introduction." In *21st Century Gateways: Immigrant Incorporation in Suburban America*, edited by Audrey Singer, Susan W. Hardwick, and Caroline B. Brettel, pp. 3–20. Brookings.

————. 2010. "Immigration." *In State of Metropolitan America: On the Front Lines of Demographic Transformation*. Brookings Metropolitan Policy Program.

Sonenshein, Raphael J., and Susan H. Pinkus. 2005. "Latino Incorporation Reaches the Urban Summit: How Antonio Villaraigosa Won the 2005 Los Angeles Mayor's Race." *PS: Political Science & Politics* 38, no. 4: 713–21.

Southern Poverty Law Center. 2009. *Climate of Fear: Latino Immigrants in Suffolk County, N.Y.* Montgomery, Ala.

Telles, Edward Eric, and Vilma Ortiz. 2008. *Generations of Exclusion: Mexican Americans, Assimilation, and Race.* New York: Russell Sage.

Trounstine, Jessica. 2008. *Political Monopolies in American Cities: The Rise and Fall of Bosses and Reformers.* University of Chicago Press.

Varsanyi, Monica W., ed. 2010. *Taking Local Control: Immigration Policy Activism in U.S. Cities and States.* Stanford University Press.

Zhou, Min. 1999. "Segmented Assimilation: Issues, Controversies, and Recent Research on the New Second Generation." In *The Handbook of International Migration: The American Experience,* edited by Charles Hirschman, Philip Kasinitz, and Josh DeWind, pp. 196–211. New York: Russell Sage.

Zúñiga, Víctor, and Rubén Hernández-León, eds. 2005. *New Destinations: Mexican Immigration in the United States.* New York: Russell Sage.

5

Bringing Equity to Transit-Oriented Development: Stations, Systems, and Regional Resilience

ROLF PENDALL, JULIET GAINSBOROUGH,
KATE LOWE, AND MAI NGUYEN

As the United States prepares for the next fifty years of growth, many observers hope that transit-oriented development (TOD) will make regions more resilient in the face of rising fuel prices and demographic change. In some metropolitan areas, the number of households living within a quarter-mile of existing or proposed transit stations is already expected to double. In addition, competition among regions for federal funding to support new fast-rail systems has become increasingly fierce.[1]

But new regional rail systems also pose threats and challenges to low-income people. They can divert scarce resources from other important infrastructure investments and lead to reductions in bus service and gentrification of low-income neighborhoods. This chapter explores how transit-oriented development can make U.S. metropolitan areas both more equitable and more resilient in the face of the challenges facing the nation in the next fifty years; we also reiterate, however, that fixed-route transit and TOD pose challenges for low-income communities and people of color. Our case studies examine whether and how government, civil society, and business institutions in four regions have planned their rail investments and modified land use and community development interventions.

After reviewing our research questions, data, and methods, we turn to case studies of transit and development in Denver, Charlotte, Miami, and Boston.

1. Dittmar and Ohland (2003); Center for Transit-Oriented Development (2007a).

These cases suggest that surprising new alliances can arise that help maximize the benefits of and minimize the disruption caused by new rail stations for low-income people, African Americans, and Hispanics. But such alliances are tenuous and their successes fragile.

In our conclusions, we find grounds for both optimism and caution. Three main findings stand out. First, mixed-income development in TOD will result mainly from a broader commitment to affordable and mixed-income housing in a city or region. Second, especially in fragmented metropolitan areas, the politics of ballot campaigns to fund and implement rail transit—which usually require commitments for suburban commuter service—can threaten investment in low-income neighborhoods. Third, however, those campaigns can offer unique opportunities to broaden coalitions supporting reinvestment in established urban areas, thereby helping to increase environmental quality, social equity, and economic vitality. In this way, rail transit promises to make metropolitan areas more resilient in the face of demographic change and growth challenges at least as much by helping shift the politics of development and planning as by changing land values and developer decisionmaking.

Suburbia, Transit-Oriented Development, Social Equity, and Resilience

Resilience is, for us, "success through time." Success, in turn, means the attainment of social equity, environmental quality, economic vitality, and civic engagement, which also are critical elements of sustainability.[2] Decisionmakers rarely aspire to build sustainable cities for contemporary society; on the contrary, most plans for U.S. cities and regions have privileged economic growth at the expense of environmental quality and have delivered disproportionate advantages to upper-income and white households while disproportionately harming African Americans, Hispanics, and low-income people. Rarer still are attempts to plan cities that will be sustainable for the society that will inherit them. Yet such efforts are emerging in both Europe and the United States, reflecting the popular desire for better cities and growing diversity, technological advances, and climate change. The most resilient regions will, we think, be those whose political institutions allow them to invent and reinvent urban infrastructure as a technology to deliver social justice, environmental sustainability, economic vitality, and civic engagement. Regional resilience is not a consequence of any particular urban form but an outcome of political institutions that both respond to current needs and anticipate change.

2. Campbell (1996).

The current pattern of land use and transportation in U.S. metropolitan areas is a product of at least seventy-five years of land development based on automobiles. Most metropolitan areas are dominated by low- to moderate-density development facilitated by government subsidies for highways, water systems, sewage treatment facilities, and mortgage interest. By 2000, two-thirds of U.S. households owned their own houses, most of them in suburbs, and almost three-fifths of households had at least two cars; only 8 percent had no cars.[3] Sensibly, advocates for suburban development justify it—and even justify subsidies to it—by citing consumer sovereignty and democracy.[4] Consumers make big sacrifices to buy suburban houses, and voters support elected officials who make driving easier. Americans who live in single-family detached houses (regardless of tenure) and those who live in uniformly low-density neighborhoods are more satisfied with their housing units and their neighborhoods than those living in any other housing type.[5]

Suburbia does not work for everyone, however. Non-whites have faced numerous hurdles in employment, housing markets, and transportation that have reduced their homeownership level and made it difficult for them to live in single-family houses, especially in suburbia.[6] Seniors, single-parent households, single-person households, nontraditional households of many kinds, immigrants, and people with disabilities may find low-density suburbia inconvenient, uncomfortable, or just too expensive. Had the nation's heavy investment in and subsidies for low-density development patterns been matched by investments in and careful stewardship of housing and neighborhoods that suit these other households, then perhaps they, too, would be quite satisfied with their neighborhoods and houses. But such has not been the case. The choices available to these households often are limited, and too often they must pay more than they can afford to live in dwellings that are either too big or too small, surrounded by neighborhoods with numerous problems, poor facilities, and limited access to employment and even stores where they can buy healthful food.

Over the next fifty years, the conditions in which urban development takes place are likely to differ considerably from those of the late twentieth century, raising increasingly grave concerns about the resilience of metropolitan areas whose urban form continues to be dominated by low-density, auto-oriented development. First, the households that suburbia has served poorly have already become majorities in several states and in over 500 counties, a trend that will

3. U.S. Department of Transportation (2010).
4. Gordon and Richardson (1997).
5. Yang (2008).
6. Jackson (1985); Pendall (2000).

sweep the nation in the decades to come.[7] We are increasingly a nation of "immigrants and boomers."[8] Disability rates will rise along with the senior population. Second, between the years 2030 and 2050 millions of baby boomers will sell their suburban housing units, but in many metropolitan areas demand will be too weak to absorb the supply.[9] The fate of suburban single-family housing—both new and existing—will also depend on national economic performance, energy prices, and incomes. Wages have grown slowly and gasoline prices have soared, raising concerns that new households will be unable to earn incomes high enough to pay for suburban housing and transportation costs.

In light of these national changes and considering the durability of buildings and transportation infrastructure, planners and alternative transportation advocates have redoubled their efforts to build more balance into metropolitan America. One key component of their strategy is transit-oriented development, an urban form that unites fixed-route mass transportation with mixed-use, walkable, moderate- to high-density neighborhoods.[10] Creating TOD requires, perforce, investment in transit (usually light rail, but increasingly streetcars and occasionally busways), but rail alone does not consistently affect local land use.[11] Rather, TOD necessitates concerted regulatory action (often deregulation) and ancillary investment in the other infrastructure necessary to support concentrations of workers and residents. In our view, such efforts to prepare for a very different metropolitan America will help regions perform better in the face of the most likely demographic, economic, and environmental future. Their residents will have more choices of neighborhood, and with TOD (and other mixed-use, walkable areas) they will have access to a larger number of destinations. Local governments in such regions will spend less on the many public services that become more expensive as density falls.[12] And metropolitan areas built on smaller land areas that also have an extensive and dependable transit infrastructure inarguably will produce lower greenhouse gas emissions.[13]

Building both light rail itself and development along with it may help long-run resilience, but it may also be disruptive on several counts, at least in the short term. It must therefore be considered a potential shock that can threaten vulnerable people and their neighborhoods. We identify three key equity-related challenges that civic, government, nonprofit, and for-profit actors will often face as they try to build their new transit-oriented regions.

7. Lichter and others (2010).
8. Myers (2007).
9. Myers and Ryu (2008).
10. Dittmar and Ohland (2003); Center for Transit-Oriented Development (2007a).
11. Giuliano and Agarwal (2010).
12. Carruthers and Úlfarsson (2008).
13. Transportation Research Board (2009).

First, at the broadest (citywide or regional) scale, rail and TOD may foreclose other choices. Most important, the rail systems that TOD advocates strongly prefer are exceptionally expensive—usually costing billions of dollars—and usually involve construction periods of decades or longer.[14] To the extent that decisionmakers see transit as a single pot, every dollar spent on rail is a dollar made unavailable for buses. To maximize the financial and political appeal of rail, transit operators and local governments often extend lines to new suburban areas; select politically acceptable and inexpensive routes through unpopulated areas and along highways; deliver more frequent and reliable service to high-density business districts; and build enough parking to obviate the need for costly feeder bus service. In the absence of additional funds, capital expenditures on rail may starve reinvestment in buses, and when operating revenues tighten, transit agencies often find it easier to reduce bus service than to cut back on rail service.

Such conflicts were at the root of the now-famous Bus Riders' Union lawsuit against the Los Angeles County Metropolitan Transportation Authority.[15] Activists have filed other civil suits highlighting disparate funding among agencies or services.[16] While courts have weakened the prospects of these civil suits, their very existence reminds us that some advocates for low-income people and communities of color still think "equitable TOD" is a contradiction in terms. Fixed-route advocates might reasonably respond that buses are easier to eliminate than rails or that rail builds long-term political support for all mass transit, but these arguments about a hypothetical better (and more secure) future for transit appeal little to advocates for bus riders who are facing real, and immediate, degrading of their transportation options.

Therefore the first progressive strategy for capturing the maximum value of rail—assuming that rail or bus rapid transit (BRT) will, in fact, be built—is to win routes and station sites that benefit low-income riders. In one example, residents of East St. Louis demanded and got a stop on the new light-rail transit (LRT) line built between downtown and the airport.[17] Otherwise, however, such campaigns have not yet been well documented, but this chapter presents one such story, about the Fairmount Corridor in Boston.

A second challenge of LRT/TOD is maintaining or creating mixed-income housing. When fixed-route transit comes to established low-income neighborhoods, it often raises property values. Sitting tenants (whether residents or small businesses) may enjoy improvements in their transit service, but they may also

14. Rubin, Moore, and Lee (1999).
15. Grengs (2002, 2004).
16. Transit Cooperative Research Program (2008).
17. Reardon (2003).

face higher rents, overcrowding, and involuntary displacement. Property owners can benefit substantially from new transit, but they may feel compelled to sell prematurely if their property taxes rise beyond their ability to pay. To the extent that a city or a metropolitan area has limited numbers of low-cost neighborhoods, an improvement in transit service may lead to gentrification, reducing the overall supply of reasonably priced locations or at least shifting the landscape of choices for low-income households and small business operators.

A progressive national response to the displacement induced by gentrification has emerged thanks in part to PolicyLink, an Oakland-based advocacy and research organization formed specifically to bring social equity into the smart growth and TOD debate. In PolicyLink's campaign responding to gentrification, the organization developed an online "toolkit" of over a dozen strategies aimed at capturing the benefits of rising property values instead of stopping increases in values. In several states, inclusionary zoning (IZ) has become standard operating procedure, allowing and sometimes obliging private sector developers to provide affordable housing (or fees in lieu of units) as a condition for development.[18] But IZ remains controversial and has become the target of concerted opposition by housing developers and apartment owners. In the past decade, online advice about building equitable and mixed-income TOD has proliferated, building on PolicyLink's successful toolkit. The main source of more recent publications is the Center for Transit-Oriented Development (CTOD), a joint project of Reconnecting America, the Center for Neighborhood Technology, and Strategic Economics. This partnership has become—in the absence of strong federal leadership—a national policy entrepreneur, preparing not only consultancies for local transit agencies, municipalities, and metropolitan planning organizations but also evaluations funded by the Federal Transit Administration.

Part of the affordability challenge in transit-rich areas, as CTOD has documented in a project for the American Association of Retired Persons, is the preservation of affordable housing. Even with value-capture strategies in place, advocates have come to understand that additional public subsidies will be necessary to preserve affordability in newly transit-rich neighborhoods. The picture is especially acute when it comes to the preservation of federally subsidized but privately owned apartments. CTOD's 2009 report on twenty major metropolitan areas found over a quarter-million such units built within one-half mile of "high-quality" transit; four-fifths have contracts that will expire by 2014, and contracts have already expired on over 80,000 units since 2000 alone.[19] Many nonprofit owners will maintain low rents even after the subsidy contracts expire,

18. Pendall (2008); Schuetz, Meltzer, and Been (2009).
19. Harrell, Brooks, and Nedwick (2009).

but others will undoubtedly convert to market rents that have become increasingly unaffordable in many metropolitan areas.

A third potential challenge relates to the difficulties of *any* TOD, especially in infill situations. Property ownership often is highly fragmented and lots very small in built-up, low-income areas.[20] In the 1950s, government used eminent domain, sometimes ruthlessly, to assemble parcels for anticipated development that all too often failed to meet expectations. By the 2000s, government had mostly lost its appetite for eminent domain, and in recent years some states have prohibited the use of eminent domain for purposes of private development. While this has reduced some threats to low-income people and property owners, it has also eliminated important potential benefits. Many low-income neighborhoods already have more than their share of absentee owners and speculators. Absent alternative tools for property assembly and public-private development ventures, announcement of plans for fixed-rail transit may ironically lead to disinvestment in the built environment as speculators wait for the market to catch up to their expectations. In the meantime, sitting tenants and residents of nearby neighborhoods may suffer both higher rents and lower neighborhood quality—and then be faced with eviction notices when property owners think that the market is finally ready for high-end townhouses, condominiums, offices, and shopping. Another element of equitable TOD, therefore, will incorporate community development and other strategies that bolster neighborhood quality and protect long-time residents from the negative short- and medium-term impacts of infrastructure construction.

Research Questions, Data, and Methods

While CTOD and PolicyLink point to best practices, challenges, and opportunities at many different levels, urban planners and policymakers still need to know more about the conditions under which local and regional actors support equity (or fail to do so) in developing their fixed-route transit systems. We organized our reporting of four case studies (described below) based on the three challenges described above, in response to the following sets of research questions.

First, what does the history of the development of fixed-rail transit tell us about the challenges of developing routes and stations that serve low-income neighborhoods? Who fought for the routes and stations? How did they fit into the overall regional transportation system? To what extent did, and could, equity advocates shift the service to provide better service for low-income people and communi-

20. Hess and Lombardi (2004).

ties of color? Who fought against fixed-route transit, and were their arguments honestly based on concerns about social equity? How did state and federal rules, policies, and institutions influence the extent to which the new and expanded systems serve transit-dependent populations?

Second, what are the principal obstacles to development near transit stations? How have local governments tried to shift the balance so that more development can occur? Considering the issues of fragmented land ownership, speculation, and possibly even the sudden appearance of more stations than the local "TOD market" can bear, will station areas really develop into high-quality neighborhoods? Or will they be yet another overhyped example that defenders of low-density suburbia can use to undermine further the broader agenda of high-density, mixed-income, mixed-use, walkable urban areas? If development does have good prospects, what institutional actions have helped to overcome the many challenges to infill development?

Third, what attempts have been made to increase benefits and avoid costs of rail stations (existing and new) for low-income people and people of color? In particular, what evidence is there of a systematic effort to ensure the long-term incorporation of affordable housing in station areas? This single indicator is the main sign thus far that equity matters and that local actors have agreed that low-income people deserve to benefit from massive investments in transit.

In seeking to answer all these questions, we go beyond the analyses of single stations that characterized some previous studies of mixed-use TOD to take a more systemwide view. That is, we look for—and find, to a certain extent— ways in which broader public policy, civic efforts, and private sector interventions help or harm the prospects for equitable LRT/TOD. In the answers to these three questions we also see an emergent, unanticipated story of potential resilience: as regional actors in the four metropolitan areas that we analyzed have engaged in planning rail transit and TOD, they have increasingly focused on critical concerns about social equity. This is a consequence of the political environment, in which actors who previously focused exclusively on efficiency have been forced by local politics and federal requirements to account for the distributional implications of transit investment.

We employed a qualitative, comparative case study approach, relying on semi-structured key informant interviews; document review; and mapping and census data analysis. Our interview questions were designed to elicit information about

—the design and histories of the transit systems themselves
—broader local and regional efforts to ensure affordability in housing
—key opponents of rail and their reasons for opposition
—state and federal obstacles and encouragement for more equity in TOD.

The responses to these questions and our interpretation of our data are (as is always the case for such qualitative research) intended to reflect on theory and to provide better insight into politics and policy. The case studies, though not statistically representative, offer insights about how local and regional actors can be expected to interact to produce (or fail to produce) equitable TOD given the state and federal incentives to which they respond and given common features of infill development and transit system deployment.

We conducted our interviews in person in four regions and did some follow-up interviews by telephone. Interviewees include a cross-section of stakeholders from government, business, and civil society. We selected informants for comparability across sites and for responsiveness to their region's unique set of stakeholders. We selected three regions—Denver, Charlotte, and Miami—because they have recently experienced, and will probably experience in the future, very fast growth but have substantially different urban forms, government structures, and racial-ethnic compositions. All three have built fixed-route transit systems since 1980; Denver and Charlotte are reputed to be successful cases of both rail development and TOD, whereas Miami has a much weaker reputation. For our fourth case, we chose to focus on a completely different urban and transit environment: Boston, where—like a few other long-standing transit locations—advocates have pressed for a new line within a mature transit network. We selected Boston mainly to learn how the politics and mechanics of equitable TOD work at the corridor, or "meso," scale. Boston also offers intriguing lessons about how community actors can lead, not just follow, in responding to the threats and opportunities presented by new fixed-route transit. After reviewing our findings in each of the cases, we return to the broader level to focus on lessons from all four cases.

Denver: Consensus Building, Regional Governance, and the Emergence of Equitable TOD

Denver is perhaps the most successful of the four cases that we examined. Its success is all the more remarkable because it was the result not solely of one-city politics but of a regional effort. In fragmented metropolitan areas, complex regional politics complicate the effort to connect low-income communities to transit. That was true in Denver, where it took officials many years of getting used to working across local government boundaries through the Metro Mayors Caucus to get agreement on transit. The agreement included attention to equity issues, in part because the low-income population in the Denver region is spread across multiple jurisdictions, thereby increasing the number of players with an incentive to focus on this issue. Furthermore, the Denver case is distinguished by the involvement of local public housing authorities in affordable housing development at station sites. In particular, the Denver Housing Authority has used federal HOPE VI grants to redevelop housing projects near LRT.

Development of the Rail System

Between 1970 and 1995, Denver's Regional Transportation District (RTD) pushed unsuccessfully, nearly by itself, for a comprehensive fixed-route transit network connecting the region's five far-flung activity centers. It failed twice (in 1980 and 1997) to convince voters to fund the network,[21] but it proceeded incrementally to complete a downtown and suburban segment by 2000. In the late 1990s, rail became part of a broader regional agenda championed by regional business leaders and local elected officials, who had been forging consensus on regional issues since 1993 through the Metro Mayors Caucus (MMC).[22] In 1997, actors from both business and government formed the Transit Alliance to educate the public and press for a regional fast transit system and to groom future RTD board members who supported rail and TOD. The pro-rail coalition won voter approval in 1999 for two additional transit lines; one of these, the Southeast Corridor, became part of the highly successful T-REX project, which also added highway lanes and improved interchanges on I-25 between downtown and the region's biggest "edge city," the Denver Tech Center. All told, the four LRT "starter lines" now provide about thirty-five miles of LRT; as of 2010, about 65,000 passengers rode the rails each weekday. In 2004, the coalition won the approval of 58 percent of regional voters for a 0.4-cent sales tax increase for "FasTracks," which promised seventy additional stations, 122 miles of new rail, and eighteen miles of BRT. Between 2007 and 2011, sales tax revenues declined and construction costs increased substantially, making delays certain and a new tax referendum likely in 2012, according to recent newspaper accounts.[23]

Planning, Development, and Equity on RTD's Rapid Transit Lines

Reflecting elected officials' and landowners' desire to promote infill and redevelopment projects, cities throughout the region have undertaken a flurry of station area planning and zoning exercises, aided in part by grants from the region's metropolitan planning organization, the Denver Regional Council of Governments. As a consequence, many of the ninety-four stations that will constitute

21. Alan Prendergast, "One-Track Minds: Rail-Happy RTD Candidates Want to Solve Denver's Traffic Nightmare. Are They Just Spinning Their Wheels?" *Westword*, October 29, 1998, p. 1.

22. Personal communication, Peter Kenney, Metro Mayors Caucus, July 2009.

23. Jeffrey Leib, "Denver Metro Mayors Wrangle over 2012 Ballot Measure for FasTracks Tax Increase," *Denver Post*, September 20, 2011; Jeffrey Leib, "Metro Mayors Task Force Wants 2012 Ballot to List All Transit Corridors That Would Benefit from Tax Hike," *Denver Post*, September 21, 2011.

the built-out RTD rapid transit system now are surrounded by prospective TOD sites. Denver, where most of the stations will be located upon buildout, developed a typology of station areas to allow common approaches across seven neighborhood types. Lakewood and Denver worked together on a plan for the West Corridor to avoid a plethora of "plain vanilla" TOD sites. Most of the other cities have also done TOD plans, though generally one station at a time.

The plans are not all hype; to the contrary, station area development accounts for a very large share of the region's recent growth. As of 2009, RTD estimated that over 16,000 new housing units and nearly 20 million square feet of employment and hotel space had been built within a half-mile of working stations since either the start of rail service or the FasTracks vote.[24] Even with this wave of construction, people active in real estate in the area feel confident that TOD will not be overbuilt because so many projects require public investment and approvals, both of which require greater scrutiny. The heightened attention slows development down, preventing some projects from even getting under way before the end of a hot business cycle and thereby reducing harmful levels of overbuilding. Perhaps a greater remaining obstacle to TOD is RTD's emphasis on intercepting suburban commuters at convenient and free park-and-ride lots. Once completed, the rail/BRT network will include 21,000 parking spaces in lots and structures that often dominate station areas. When RTD acquires these lands using eminent domain, it may not dispose of them for private redevelopment.[25] TOD and equity supporters are working to reduce this constraint, but thus far their efforts have not borne fruit.

The area's leadership has become more serious about ensuring affordability in TOD based on the unpromising results of the redevelopment of closed Stapleton Airport into a 4,700-acre new urbanist development along the East Corridor. At completion late in the 2010s, Stapleton will include 8,000 for-sale dwellings in a range of densities and styles, 4,000 apartments,[26] 10 million square feet of commercial space, 2 million square feet of retail centers, and more than 1,100 acres of new open space. An official affordable housing plan calls for 10 percent of the for-sale and 20 percent of the rental housing to be "income qualified," with the for-sale units to be affordable for households earning 80 percent or less of area median income (AMI) and the rentals for those earning 60 percent or less of

24. The initiation dates and the starting year of RTD's tracking both vary: 1996 for the Central Corridor, 1999 for the Southeast Corridor, 2000 for the Southwest Corridor, 2001 for the Central Platte Valley spur, and 2004 for the FasTracks corridors. Rapid Transit District (2010, p. A-1).

25. Personal communication, July 2009.

26. Estimates on the mix of houses and apartments vary. Most sources suggest that the area will have 30,000 residents and up to 35,000 jobs when completed; in other words, it will have a substantial net surplus of jobs, occasioning substantial in-commuting.

AMI.[27] The most recent "comprehensive snapshot" of housing and affordable housing at Stapleton (from August 2008) indicates that even less housing than proposed in this fairly undemanding plan has been built.[28]

New TOD captures attention and headlines in Denver and undoubtedly represents an opportunity for new housing development, but RTD's rapid-transit system also serves (and will serve in the future) many established neighborhoods. The concern is not just about building new affordable housing but also about preserving options that low-income and minority households already enjoy. In 2000, according to our analysis of U.S. Census data, about a tenth of the residents and housing in the metropolitan area's six core counties lived within a half-mile of the ninety-four stations on the complete system. About 52 percent of the station area households were renters, while the comparable regionwide figure was 33 percent.[29] Renter occupancy in station areas was especially pronounced in suburban Aurora, Thornton, Arvada, Littleton, Northglenn, and Golden, all of which have homeowner majorities. In Denver, by contrast, the station area homeownership rate matched the citywide rate of about 54 percent, but Denver still accounts for 30 percent of the 41,000 renter households who lived in and around current and future station areas in 2000. Whether they live in single-family houses, small multi-unit buildings, or older large structures, low-income renters are the most threatened residents of station areas. Homeowners, by contrast, will mainly benefit from rising land values, due to Colorado's low property tax rates. In some neighborhoods, cities have blocked increased development by reducing permitted density.

The new transit system therefore poses both an opportunity and a threat for social equity in metropolitan Denver. As the lines connect multiple growing job destinations, residents in intervening neighborhoods will have more affordable and secure transportation options. But established neighborhoods will not stay affordable for long in the absence of institutional action. New development in TODs will require extensive investment in infrastructure, and the construction costs of this high-density development will make market-rate housing more expensive. Land costs, too, have risen dramatically throughout the region in the

27. As of April 16, 2010. Stapleton Affordable Housing Plan, January 29, 2001 (http://stapleton denver. com/data/uploads/Stapleton_Affordable_Housing_Plan_0.pdf).

28. Housing Diversity Committee of the Stapleton Development Commission's Citizen Advisory Board, "A Comprehensive Snapshot of Where Housing and Affordable Housing Stands at Stapleton, Compiled by Forest City Stapleton with Review and Comments by Stapleton Development Corporation Stapleton Citizens Advisory Board and Citizen Advisory Board Housing Diversity Committee," on file with the authors. See also Naomi Zeveloff, "Affordable Housing a Tough Sell in Stapleton: There's Room for Everyone in Stapleton, but After Five Years, Developers Are Having Trouble Finding Room for Affordable Housing," *Westword*, November 8, 2007, p. 1.

29. Adams, Arapahoe, Boulder, Denver, Douglas, and Jefferson Counties.

past fifteen years. The transit corridors—which RTD first staked out over thirty years ago—must by now contain some of the most expensive land in the region.[30] In the face of these challenges, local and regional actors have made efforts to ensure affordability.

Bolstering Affordability in Station Areas: State Context, Local Actions

Colorado presents a challenging environment for development of affordable housing. The state devotes very little money to affordable housing, and well-connected and financed interests have thus far blocked proposals for a housing trust fund. Consequently, Colorado ranks between 45 and 50 among all states on spending on housing.[31] State statute bars the use of rent control.[32]

Despite these obstacles, a variety of stakeholders have worked hard to craft responses to maintain affordability in established station areas and build it into the new TOD. These efforts have been unusually well publicized and coordinated, due again in part to the Metro Mayors Caucus. In 1996, the caucus highlighted the region's growing affordability problems and forged a position supporting "workforce housing." Decisionmakers have taken two broad but shallow approaches that, if effective, will introduce a modest amount of affordable housing into quite a few station areas. Two intense, focused strategies, by contrast, will build significant affordability into new mixed-income developments around a small number of station areas.

The first broad and shallow approach—the TOD bond fund—grew out of the Metro Mayors Caucus itself, which developed an arrangement to pool local housing bond allocations in the late 1990s.[33] In 2003, the caucus decided to direct the funding pool to station areas and persuaded the Colorado Housing Finance Authority to join the pool.[34] All told, this pool makes $62 million (in 2009) in low-cost financing available each year to private sector developers who agree to make at least 20 percent of their units affordable to low-income renters. The TOD fund has seen little use thus far because private mortgages carried lower interest rates than the more restrictive TOD fund.[35] After the mortgage meltdown, the pool may have more appeal.

---

30. Center for Transit-Oriented Development (2007b).

31. Personal communication, Alana Smart, Housing Colorado, July 2009.

32. Colorado Revised Statutes, 38-12-301, "Control of Rents by Counties and Municipalities Prohibited."

33. Half of Colorado's private activity bond cap is allocated to larger cities, providing each the ability every year to float bonds that subsidize housing and industrial development projects.

34. Ann Schrader, "Metro Cities Aim to Boost Housing Near Light Rail," *Denver Post*, July 28, 2003, p. B-01.

35. Personal communication, Milroy Alexander, Colorado Housing Finance Agency, July 2009.

In a second broad approach, Boulder, Longmont, and Denver all have adopted inclusionary zoning, though they all have limitations. First, a 2000 state supreme court ruling ruled out the use of IZ for rental housing, interpreting rental IZ as a form of rent control.[36] In Boulder, which has the strongest ordinance, residential growth controls have limited overall housing production (and affordable housing along with it). Denver has a very moderate IZ program; it applies only to developments over thirty units and requires only that 10 percent of owner-occupied units be affordable at between 80 and 95 percent of the area median income. Longmont's program may work better than either Boulder's or Lafayette's, but it will make little impact in station areas since only one station is planned there.

The most significant and potentially lasting effort to build affordability into TOD (the first of two intense and focused approaches) has come from an unexpected quarter: the local public housing authorities. Many of the oldest properties of the Denver Housing Authority (DHA) sit near LRT stations. Predictably, federal HOPE VI and low-income housing tax credit programs both became available just as LRT plans got under way. In 1998, DHA received a federal HOPE VI grant to help redevelop the relatively low-density 286-unit Curtis Homes and Arapahoe Courts projects at the northernmost station of the downtown rail line. The new mixed-income development, Curtis Park, opened in 2002, with 550 mixed-income housing units. The revitalization and gentrification of Five Points after (though not entirely because of) Curtis Park led the DHA's board to rethink the agency's mission and strategies, adding a comprehensive and capable affordable housing development team and a new executive director with background in both the private sector and the nonprofit sector.[37] This team led the agency in its next HOPE VI development, Park Place, which will also increase the area's residential density in a mixed-income project. DHA's next redevelopment will replace the 270 apartments in South Lincoln Homes with up to 900 units of mixed-income housing as part of a broader station area plan for the 10th and Osage station on the Southeast Corridor. DHA may turn next to the redevelopment of its 324-unit Sun Valley project, close to the Federal station on the West Corridor. Both the Aurora Housing Authority and the Lakewood Housing Authority have also established capable real estate development functions.

36. *Lot Thirty-Four Venture, L.L.C. v. Town of Telluride*, 976 P.2d 303 (Colo. App. 1998), aff'd, 3 P.3d 30 (Colo. 2000). A Denver representative introduced a bill in 2010 (HB 1017) to assert that nothing in the state's rent control laws restricts property owners from voluntarily entering into an agreement that controls rent; the state's apartment owner association is fighting the bill.

37. Personal communication, Ismael Guerrero, Denver Housing Authority, July 2009.

The final intervention—one unique to the Denver area so far—is the Urban Land Conservancy (ULC), a land bank founded in 2003 by local philanthropies to purchase at-risk properties that benefited low-income communities. In 2007, the ULC began to focus primarily on station area properties. Funds come from a mix of public, private, and foundation sources; the city and county of Denver provided the largest amount ($2.5 million), and the MacArthur Foundation provided $1 million.[38] Thus far ULC has acquired eight properties, all of them inside Denver and most in partnership with other nonprofits and local government.

Charlotte

Though not as far along as Denver, Charlotte is expected to be a success because it has strong potential both to build TOD and to offer at least some affordable housing within the TOD. Simplifying the process of consensus building in Charlotte is the fact that the development of rail has occurred within a single political jurisdiction. The city's elected officials—especially the mayor—and business elites have been important in supporting the development of rail and setting the stage for affordability. The expectation that TOD in Charlotte will include equity considerations is bolstered by the city's existing commitments to affordable and mixed-income housing through policies that limit the concentration of affordable housing in particular neighborhoods and target the most distressed neighborhoods to receive city resources. At the same time, the lack of specific mandates to include affordable housing in TOD raises questions about the extent to which the general commitment to equity expressed by elected officials and planners in Charlotte will be enough to ensure that the interests of low-income residents and neighborhoods are reflected in future station development.

Development of the Rail System: LYNX

North Carolina's first modern-day light-rail system, LYNX, opened in Charlotte on November 24, 2007, and has been hailed as a model nationwide.[39] The 9.6-mile, fifteen-station Blue Line, which cost $462.7 million, runs from Charlotte's central business district, also known as Uptown, to the southern edge of the city, providing an alternative mode of transport from homes to jobs. With the system

---

38. Disclosure: The MacArthur Foundation provided funding for the research for this chapter.

39. Josh Voorhees, "A Southern Success Story for Public Transportation Offers Lessons in Livability," *New York Times*, April 5, 2010.

in place, transit (including buses) is expected eventually to capture between 25 and 40 percent of the total number of commuters to Uptown.[40]

Contemporary efforts to bring light rail to Charlotte began in the 1980s. Unlike the other systems under consideration here, Charlotte's has been linked from the start with the desire to spur development rather than with efforts to reduce traffic congestion. From the beginning, the key proponents have been the city's planners and mayors, starting in 1984 with Harvey Gantt. The city council rejected Gantt's proposal for a study of a single LRT line, however. Sue Myrick, who succeeded Gantt, appointed a task force in 1988 that recommended—based on a detailed $185,000 study—an eight-line, half-billion-dollar system connecting Uptown with smaller suburban cities throughout the metropolitan area (including Rock Hill, South Carolina). The city council again balked, and in any event federal funds may not have been available considering low prospective ridership on those lines. In the ensuing years, the Charlotte Area Transit System (CATS) spent $14 million to acquire rights-of-way, anticipating that the region would eventually build LRT.

In 1998, Mecklenburg County voters overwhelmingly approved a half-cent sales tax to be used toward the 2025 Integrated Transit/Land Use Plan. This plan tied land use planning to transit station locations, increasing residential density in planned station areas in order to qualify for grant money based on the cost-benefit formula prescribed by the Federal Transit Administration (FTA). With these two funding sources—the half-cent sales tax and New Starts funding from the FTA—Charlotte built the first segment of the Blue Line.

The first rail corridor runs along abandoned streetcar rails through a blighted industrial corridor that includes very few residential neighborhoods. The 1994 "Centers, Corridors, Wedges Growth Framework" study conducted by the Charlotte-Mecklenburg Planning Commission aims to guide development to this corridor; it increases permitted residential densities to make transit both accessible to new residents and viable in terms of receiving federal funding.[41]

There has been no neighborhood resistance to the siting of LRT routes; on the contrary, neighborhoods have tried hard to win routes and stations. The Centers and Corridors study identified five primary corridors where transportation infrastructure (for example, highways and transit lines) already existed or were planned and where future public transit routes could be located. Charlotte won its New Starts bid in part because it directed development toward proposed

40. Charlotte Area Transit System, "Comments on David Hartgen's 'For the Record' Piece, Which Appeared in the *Charlotte Observer* on August 8, 2007," August 9, 2007 (http://charmeck.org/Departments/CATS/Home.htm).

41. Charlotte-Mecklenburg Planning Commission (2008).

transit stations. Another major urban area in North Carolina, Raleigh–Durham–Chapel Hill, by contrast, failed because of its weak integration of land use and transportation planning.[42]

Rather than having a contentious relationship with the public, transit planners and local officials have viewed the public as a partner in the planning process. For example, once routes and stations were planned, transit planners held meetings where the public helped to refine the plans. According to a transit planner in Charlotte, hundreds of meetings were held with the public in order to designate specific routes and to select transit technologies.[43]

Ridership on the Blue Line, which was projected to make 9,100 passenger trips on an average weekday, has far exceeded expectations. By November 2009, due partly to historically high fuel costs (hovering at $4.00/gallon), the average number of weekday trips reached 16,000. Although average weekday trips have dropped somewhat with fuel price reductions, they are still well above projections, considering that the average number was projected to be 18,100 in 2025. Also impressive is that 70 percent of rail riders are new to transit, according to CATS. These claims are debated by LYNX's critics, who argue that as many as half of the riders are switching from buses, thereby having minimal impact on traffic congestion or pollution.[44]

The success of the Blue Line, in terms of ridership and private investment, has made subsequent transit station planning more contentious. Rail is considered the preferred mode for transit, with buses viewed as less desirable, creating political pressure from local elected officials to build rail where the density, ridership, and cost estimates may not justify it. Therefore, moving forward, the politics and planning of rail stations and development surrounding them may be driven in large part by those who have the greatest financial and political stake. If decisions are based on political pressure and not cost efficiency and equity, Charlotte's rail system may not retain its successful reputation.

Opposition to Rail: Libertarians, Not Social Justice Advocates

The forces fighting LRT in Charlotte have not aligned with social justice concerns (as in Los Angeles) but with the same national anti-planning, libertarian agenda whose proponents fought against LRT in Denver. In the beginning, the main point of contention was whether rail or bus operation was more cost effective and flexible with respect to change. Proponents for each of these modes fall into traditional political camps: libertarians prefer bus over rail, whereas local

42. Ernest Robl, "Where Rail Succeeds and Where It Doesn't," *Metro Magazine*, July, 2007, pp. 16–20.
43. Personal communication, March 2010.
44. Hartgen (2008).

elected officials and business leaders, dominated in Charlotte by the financial sector, prefer rail.

Nearing the completion date of the first rail line, the ballooning cost of construction raised consternation among some residents, prompting the organization of a group called Sensible Charlotte Area Transportation (SCAT). This group collected 63,000 signatures to call for a referendum on a proposal to repeal the 1998 half-cent sales tax during November 2007 elections.[45] Private sector firms—including Wachovia, Bank of America, and Duke Power—helped fund a campaign in favor of the line. Although the passage of the proposal would not have stopped the opening of the Blue Line, it would have eliminated funds for future expansion of rail and decreased bus funding. A remarkable 70 percent of voters decided to keep the half-cent sales tax, thereby defeating SCAT's initiative and keeping the momentum alive for public transit investments in Charlotte. Even so, local libertarians (under the aegis of the John Locke Foundation) continue to disseminate anti-rail op-ed pieces and are poised to fight extensions, supplemented by national anti-planning and anti-LRT observers.

Development Trends on the LYNX Corridor

The LYNX corridor has been transformed from deserted warehouses and vacant industrial land into new residential, mixed-use, and adaptive re-use developments with new infrastructure, bringing life to an area that was sorely underutilized. The transit stops on the edge of the city now have large park-and-ride structures that are overflowing with downtown commuters. While the recession has slowed construction along the corridor, construction cranes still dot the landscape and development continues today.

The rail system has been touted at least as much for its prospective boost for development as for its effects on congestion. An estimated $1.4 billion has been privately invested near the Blue Line, and property values have increased by 52 percent near the corridor.[46] Locating the rail line along an abandoned trolley line and underutilized industrial corridor has created a "rebirth of economic opportunity" with very little residential displacement or gentrification, according to Charlotte's city planners.[47] The corridor has seen the development of new condos, shops, and restaurants. There has also been increasing investment in home renovations.

45. Steve Harrison, "Light-Rail Petition Has 63,000 Signatures," *Charlotte Observer*, April 3, 2007, p. 1B.

46. Charlotte Area Transit System, "2009 Annual Report" (http://charmeck.org/Departments/CATS/Home.htm).

47. Personal communication, March 2010. For background on the location of the route, see Ernest H. Robl, "Returning to the Rails: Charlotte, N.C., Prepares to Launch Commuter Light-Rail Service—on a Right-of-Way Still Intact after 60 Years," *Trains Magazine*, October 2004, p. 50.

Background for Equity: Citywide Policies for Deconcentrated Affordable Housing

The city of Charlotte has a strong record of promoting equity through public policy and provision of social services. In attempts to deconcentrate poverty, the city has adopted a policy that restricts the quantity of multifamily rental housing developed in any single neighborhood. The policy also identifies priority areas where subsidized housing is absent and therefore new units can be built.[48] This policy seeks to avoid the negative consequences associated with the overconcentration of low-income populations (for example, increased crime, blight, and gangs). The city has also been successful in bids for HOPE VI funds, garnering four grants that have allowed the Charlotte Housing Authority to transform large, crime-ridden, blighted public housing structures into mixed-income, mixed-tenure communities where a diverse population now resides.[49] The city recently received its fifth HOPE VI grant to tear down a 301-unit distressed public housing community named Boulevard Homes in order to rebuild a mixed-income community rich in education facilities that will serve both children and adults.

Another innovative initiative, the Charlotte Quality of Life Study, measures neighborhood indicators to classify all of the city's neighborhoods into three broad categories: stable, transitioning, and challenged. The challenged neighborhoods are those that are most distressed socially, physically, and economically and have the highest crime rates.[50] Neighborhood action plan teams, consisting of city staff from a variety of departments, give priority to services and investments that help revitalize challenged neighborhoods, thereby channeling more resources into the neighborhoods that need it the most.

According to high-level planning staff, the philosophy of serving those with the greatest needs while also serving the public good is also applied to public transit planning. Staff working in the planning department and the housing authority believe that local politicians lend substantial support to the development of affordable and workforce housing. There is a sense that equity considerations are a part of the city's institutional culture; therefore they transfer to the arena of transportation planning as well.[51] While the city has invested in building and renovating affordable housing citywide, little affordable housing has been built around rail stations, raising questions about the reality of equitable TOD.

48. Neighborhood Development Department, City of Charlotte (2008).
49. Charlotte Housing Authority, "Written Testimony of Charles Woodyard, President/CEO of the Charlotte Housing Authority, Submitted to the U.S. House of Representatives Committee on Financial Services, Subcommittee for Housing and Community Opportunity," June 21, 2007 (www.cha-nc.org/realestate/hopevi.asp).
50. Neighborhood Development Department, City of Charlotte (2008).
51. Personal communication, March 2010.

Government officials and planning staff in Charlotte express the belief that research and analysis coupled with an open and transparent public participation process will lead to equitable planning outcomes. But even with extensive outreach and public participation, there are no clear mandates to build affordable housing or to provide social services near transit stations. The city contends that it will

> aggressively pursue opportunities to develop assisted housing within a quarter-mile of transit stations when participating in joint development projects such as building or providing loans for infrastructure, acquiring land, and/or other economic development initiatives.[52]

Another weak attempt at encouraging affordable housing development involves applying a point system in the zoning process whereby extra points are awarded to developers for affordable housing, neighborhood walkability, and access to schools; this system gives developers incentives to consider social equity that they otherwise would not have. But it remains unclear whether the incentives will result in the construction of affordable housing since they provide only guidelines—not specific goals.[53]

Will Charlotte Deliver on Its Equity Promise?

A consistent theme that emerged from the interviews is that public transit must create a benefit for the city of Charlotte and the region, not just for the areas surrounding the transit lines. How can that be achieved? According to city planners, if transit can improve mobility for both transit riders and auto users by getting more people off the roads and also provide more choices, giving people greater flexibility, it would improve general social welfare. Moreover, when a greater number of people benefit from transit, it is more equitable. Terms such as "fairness" and "value" for all residents were repeated among interviewees. But if we look at our main measure of equity, the production of affordable housing near rail stations, Charlotte has not yet delivered on its promise of equity.

Unlike in other cities, in Charlotte equity considerations have not explicitly targeted disadvantaged groups or neighborhoods that would benefit the most by access to transit and the infusion of public and private investment. Instead of a narrow constituency, planners and public officials in Charlotte seek to serve the greatest number of residents and minimize the negative consequences that can result from the construction of rail and TODs. Building the first extension of the rail along a historic streetcar line and underutilized industrial corridor gave the

---

52. Neighborhood Development Department, City of Charlotte (2008).
53. Personal communication, March 2010.

city a good head start in avoiding some typical pitfalls, such as residential displacement and gentrification. Formalizing equity principles—such as encouraging the private development of affordable housing around transit stations, promoting mixed-use and mixed-income developments, and acquiring parcels of land to help facilitate the construction of affordable housing—in planning documents and city policies provides opportunities for greater equity. But, without mandates or specific goals in place to ensure that benefits accrue to low-income residents and neighborhoods, it is still too early to know whether those principles and guidelines will allow Charlotte to deliver the equity that it promised.

Miami

Miami is the least successful of the four cases examined in this chapter. Given rapid population growth (at least until recently) and consequent severe levels of traffic congestion, most Miami interviewees cited improved mass transit as a critical regional need. The extremes of wealth and poverty that coexist in Miami also put the provision of affordable housing high on the list of regional challenges. These factors, together with the long-standing desire for economic development in the severely depressed, predominantly African American communities north of the central business district, suggest that Miami might be ripe for discussion of transit-oriented developments with strong equity components. To date, however, that has not occurred.

In Miami as in Denver, the effort to incorporate the interests of low-income communities into rail transit plans and station area development are complicated by complex regional politics. Unlike those in Denver, local governments in the Miami region have not developed a significant level of comfort working across their boundaries, and the problems of low-income populations are largely seen as concentrated in a few distinct areas. In fact, the need to garner support for regional transit projects from suburban jurisdictions led to the development of a "people's transportation plan" that made too many promises and ultimately foundered, failing to deliver significantly better service to established neighborhoods. While low-income tax credits have been used to build some affordable housing adjacent to stations, few incentives exist to ensure that jurisdictions plan mixed-income housing near their stations, and no political leadership has evolved to promote a systemwide vision of mixed-income TOD.

Development of the Rail System: Metrorail

The primary rail system serving Miami–Dade County is the elevated rapid transit system known as Metrorail. The system, which began operating in 1984, covers 22.6 miles and has twenty-two stations that stretch from Kendall in the southwest of the county and move north through downtown and communities north of downtown, such as Overtown and Liberty City, before heading west through Hialeah. In addition to Metrorail, the downtown area is served by the 4.4-mile-long monorail, Metromover, which is elevated and automated. The initial 1.9-mile downtown loop of the Metromover opened in 1986, and two additional extensions (1.4 miles north and 1.1 miles south) were added in 1994.[54] In addition, the Miami–Fort Lauderdale–West Palm Beach metropolitan area (Dade, Broward, and Palm Beach Counties) is served by a seventy-two-mile, eighteen-station commuter rail system, Tri-Rail, which is managed by the South Florida Regional Transportation Authority.[55] Although ridership on Metrorail has increased over the years, it has consistently underperformed initial projections.[56] Currently, Metrorail averages approximately 61,700 daily boardings.[57]

Ongoing concerns about the need for improved transportation infrastructure in the county have lead to periodic attempts to generate additional revenue for the transit system. In 1999, a proposed one-cent sales tax increase to fund new transportation initiatives was overwhelmingly defeated at the polls, in part because of organized opposition from the mayor of the city of Hialeah, Raul Martinez, as well as an anti-tax, anti-corruption campaign funded by a local businessman.[58]

In 2002, Miami–Dade County mayor Alex Penelas again pushed for passage of a dedicated sales tax increase to fund transportation improvements. This time, however, the People's Transportation Plan (PTP), as it was called, was designed to overcome the opposition that had emerged in 1999. In particular, the mayor emphasized the plan's grassroots nature by holding eighty public meetings and two transportation summits.[59] In addition, the plan included lists of specific rail, bus, and road improvements that would be financed by the tax, and it promised 20 percent of the revenue to thirty municipalities within the county boundary. The measure was approved by voters in November 2002 by a 2 to 1 margin.

54. Miami-Dade Transit, "Metromover Facts" (www.miamidade.gov/transit/about_metromover.asp [April 5, 2010]).

55. South Florida Regional Transportation Authority, "South Florida Transit Resource Guide," September 2008 (www.sfrta.fl.gov/docs/planning/Existing%20System/TransitResourceGuide.pdf [April 5, 2010]).

56. Gatzlaff and Smith (1993, p. 57); Associated Press, "Miami's Metrorail Chugs On Despite Critics, Empty Seats," *Sarasota Herald-Tribune,* May 20, 1985, p. 8B. When the system was under development, officials predicted average daily ridership of more than 200,000 after the first few years of operation. Once the system opened, that projection was downgraded to 50,000; after its first year in operation, the transit agency expressed hopes for an average of 21,000 riders.

57. Miami-Dade Transit, "Metrorail Facts" (www.miamidade.gov/transit/about_metrorail.asp [April 5, 2010]).

58. Andres Viglucci, "Low-Key Campaign Pursues Transit Tax," *Miami Herald,* October 17, 2002, p. 1B.

59. Miami-Dade Transit, "People's Transportation Plan Resource Guide," p. 23; Karl Ross,"Voters Handed Yes/No Power on Transit Tax," *Miami Herald,* July 10, 2002, p. 1B.

The PTP included 88.9 miles of new rail lines, including two corridors that were "ready to enter into final design and construction—the North Corridor and the East-West Corridor."[60] The proposed North Corridor runs through the heart of the African American community in Miami and was widely viewed as fulfilling a long-standing promise to the community, first made in the 1970s when Metrorail was under development.[61] At that time, the Metrorail line went west toward the largely Hispanic community in Hialeah but not north toward the largely African American areas of the county.[62]

Almost immediately after passage, however, the People's Transportation Plan was criticized for promising more than it could deliver. The cost of implementing all the components of the plan would clearly exceed the revenue generated by the half-cent sales tax. While the tax revenue was supposed to support new projects, huge annual deficits in the transportation budget meant that there was immediate pressure to divert the revenue to cover existing operations.[63] In 2009, the Miami–Dade County Commission voted to fold the PTP funds into the general operating budget for Miami-Dade Transit.

As of 2011, neither the North Corridor nor the East-West Corridor, which the county has now combined as one proposal (the Orange Line), was anywhere near becoming a reality. Although the sales tax increase was supposed to satisfy federal requirements for matching funds, the federal government has repeatedly found that the county does not have a realistic plan in place to finance the operation of the new rail corridors. The only rail project included in the PTP that is moving forward is the Earlington Heights station connector to the new Miami Intermodal Center, adjacent to the Miami International Airport. For advocates of the North Corridor extension, the failure to move forward on this project is viewed as another in a long line of transit-related betrayals of the African American community in Miami.[64]

TOD in Miami-Dade County

Discussion of transit-oriented development in Miami began early in the history of Metrorail. From the very beginning, Miami-Dade officials viewed develop-

---

60. Miami-Dade Transit, "People's Transportation Plan Resource Guide," p. 32.

61. *Miami Herald*, "Editorial: Don't Abandon North Corridor Rail," February 8, 2008.

62. Personal communication, December 2009; *Miami Herald*, "Editorial: Don't Abandon North Corridor Rail," February 8, 2008.

63. Larry Lebowitz, "Tax and Fail," *Miami Herald*, June 8, 2008, p. 1A. This point was also made by several interviewees in the region. As of the end of 2009, Metrobus service was operating at 11 percent above pre-PTP levels. Alfonso Chardy. "Bus Service Cut Again, Almost to Pre-Half-Penny Tax Level," *Miami Herald*, December 12, 2009, p. 1B.

64. This point was made forcibly at a community meeting attended by one of the authors in December 2009.

ment around stations as an essential tool for financing the system.[65] Beginning in the 1980s, the agency pursued joint development opportunities on county-owned land around the stations, which are designated as "rapid transit zones." This designation is intended to facilitate the development process by "giving the developer a single jurisdiction to work with," since the county and relevant municipality are supposed to develop joint standards for the area, and by providing flexibility to adjust the zoning codes to match the proposed development.[66] The transit agency identified total TOD development in Miami-Dade as of 2008 as including over 2.3 million square feet of office space, 400,000 square feet of retail space, 570 dwelling units (412 of which were affordable), nearly 5,000 parking spaces, and 300 hotel rooms. The transit agency leases the land on which these projects sit, generating over $2 million in revenue for the agency by 2008.[67]

In addition to joint development around transit stations, some station areas have experienced private residential and commercial development. Most notable is a surge of residential condominium construction in the central business district, much of which is adjacent to transit. Although much of that development occurred at least a decade or more after the opening of the transit stations, developers have suggested that rail access has increased the sales potential of the units.[68] As that suggests, a significant amount of the transit-adjacent development in Miami has occurred in reaction to market demand rather than being actively shaped or directed by local government.[69]

TOD and Affordability

As the county's figures for existing TOD joint development illustrate, housing has been a relatively small component of the projects that have been developed to date. However, to the extent that housing has been constructed, it has been predominantly affordable housing (412 of 570 total units). The affordable housing is part of two rental apartment buildings (a nine-story, 208-unit building and a seventeen-story, 204-unit building) at the Santa Clara Station in the Allapattah neighborhood of Miami-Dade. The county points to a 90 percent

---

65. Craig Gilbert, "Metrorail Sites Draw Developers; Complexes Grow around Stations," *Miami Herald*, May 14, 1984.

66. Transit Cooperative Research Program (2004, pp. 269–70).

67. Information drawn from a Miami-Dade Transit presentation prepared for Federal Transit Adminstration/Partnership in Transit meeting, Dallas, October 2008.

68. Gena Holle, "Two of a Kind: Miami's Metrorail and Metromover," *Rail Magazine* 19 (2007), pp. 34–52.

69. Even the joint development that has occurred has been based more on responding to private initiative than on a countywide vision for TOD in station areas. Frank Talleda, MDT's former chief of joint development leasing, described the joint development to date as "retroactive. . . . First we put in the system and then we thought about joint development" but suggested that the county is becoming more proactive. Cited in Holle (2007, p. 40).

increase in ridership at this Metrorail station since construction of the buildings, although it also acknowledges that ridership rates were so low that a 90 percent increase is still not an enormous number of riders.[70] Projects now under way are projected to create even more affordable housing adjacent to Metrorail stops. The county predicts that future TOD will create over 1,200 residential units, of which almost all (1,190) will be affordable housing.[71]

To the extent that affordable housing is part of existing or planned developments at Metrorail stations, it is in existing low-income neighborhoods where market-rate development is less attractive to private developers. The county has generally not sought to encourage the inclusion of affordable housing in market-rate developments at station areas outside low-income neighborhoods. To construct affordable housing projects in low-income neighborhoods, the county works with large developers who specialize in affordable housing, funded primarily through the federal government's low-income housing tax credit program, with some additional revenues provided by local government subsidies. Community development corporations (CDCs) have been involved as official partners on some of these projects; however, their role in project design and scope is described as minimal.[72]

TOD as Economic Development

The low-income, African American community of Overtown is an example of both the desire to use TOD to revitalize neighborhoods in Miami and the difficulty of realizing that desire. Once a thriving community adjacent to downtown, Overtown has a troubled relationship with transportation policy. Highway construction in the mid-1960s is widely seen as a key factor in the community's decline.[73] The construction of interstates 95 and 395 split the community into four quadrants, making it hard for residents to traverse their neighborhood. At the same time, urban revitalization efforts cleared large swaths of land without much accompanying redevelopment. In the five-year period from 1965 to 1970, "40 percent of the population [in Overtown was] displaced . . . the number of business establishments drop[ped] by half . . . and the rate of homeownership decline[d] over 60%."[74] As a consequence, Overtown became the poorest neighborhood in one of the country's poorest cities.[75]

---

70. Personal communication, March 2010.

71. Personal communication, March 2010.

72. This description of the joint development process for affordable housing was echoed in multiple interviews with private developers and CDCs.

73. Mohl (1993); Dluhy, Revell, and Wong (2002).

74. Dluhy, Revell, and Wong (2002, p. 84).

75. Transit Cooperative Research Program (2004, p. 272).

When Metrorail was being constructed in the 1980s, government and non-profit officials suggested that the "planning and development of Metrorail's Overtown station . . . presented the neighborhood with an unprecedented opportunity to attract new investment and restore vitality to the struggling commercial strip."[76] However, despite several planned developments that were heralded as the beginning of significant revitalization in Overtown, relatively little transit-related development has occurred.[77] To date the most significant developments adjacent to transit are county office buildings that include parking garages as well as ground-floor retail space, the first of which was constructed in 2005.[78] The county transit agency offices are now located in this Overtown building.[79]

Two other redevelopment proposals for Overtown incorporate a vision of transit-oriented development. The 9th Street pedestrian mall extends from the Overtown Metrorail station north; the Overtown Folklife District aims to build on the area's historic connection to the arts, including the Metrorail-adjacent Lyric Theater.[80] A version of the Overtown Folklife District appeared as early as 1983 in redevelopment plans for Overtown, and the 9th Street pedestrian mall was first developed in 1994.[81] More recently a coalition of community-based groups led by the Mt. Zion CDC has worked to promote the Folklife District vision with proposals for coordinated mixed-use and mixed-income development within district boundaries.[82]

One explanation for the limited success of the Overtown station as a catalyst for more significant development is the competing location of the Government Center Metrorail station, which, "just two short blocks away [from the Overtown station], connects directly to a major mixed-use office and retail development serving thousands of office workers, commuters, and shoppers."[83] An ultimately unsuccessful multiyear (2006–08) battle to develop a mixed-income residential and commercial property in the heart of Overtown illustrates additional challenges. The project was initially delayed and ultimately halted in response to conflict within the community over how to balance the desire for revitalization with the fear of gentrification. Conflict between Miami–Dade

76. Transit Cooperative Research Program (2004, p. 272).

77. Andres Viglucci, "Will Overtown Get Its Piece of Miami's Pie?" *Miami Herald*, January 13, 2008; Transit Cooperative Research Program (2004, p. 274); Also interviews with CDCs.

78. Personal communication, March 2010.

79. Personal communication, March 2010.

80. Gale (1999); Personal communication, April 2010.

81. Trust for Public Land, "Overtown Greenway Plan," 2002 (www.ci.miami.fl.us/cra/files/Plans/Overtown_Greenway_Plan082002.pdf).

82. Personal communication, April 2010; personal communication, December 2009.

83. Transit Cooperative Research Program (2004, p. 274).

County and the City of Miami also complicated the efforts to develop the county-owned land in the station area.[84]

Continuing Challenges

Fragmented local government and divisions along racial, ethnic, and socioeconomic lines have complicated efforts to expand the transit system in Miami-Dade. The same factors, as well as the relatively limited capacity of CDCs and organized equity advocates, have impeded efforts to use TOD around Metrorail stations as a tool for significant economic development. Affordable housing has been part of some joint development projects at rail stations but primarily at stations that are located in existing low-income communities. The future challenges are whether current plans to develop transit-oriented projects in Overtown can succeed where others have failed, and, more broadly, whether the county can maintain its commitment to expand transit options and TOD in the face of the economic downturn and the public's disenchantment with the results of the PTP.

Boston: The Fairmount/Indigo Corridor

Boston is a successful case, but here affordable housing advocates led the push for rail investment. The rail system is mainly built out; the Massachusetts Bay Transportation Authority (MBTA) operates the Boston area's extensive rail service of three heavy rail lines, five streetcar branches, and thirteen commuter rail lines, which, along with 183 bus routes, averaged nearly 1.3 million unlinked trips each weekday in 2008.[85] The moderate transit improvement linked to transit-oriented development in this case was the addition of four stops on an atypically short, urban commuter rail line: nine miles entirely within the city of Boston. Adding these stops brought thousands into close proximity to rail service in the largest section of Boston that lacked it. The impetus for the improvement came from community groups that fought for the service in 1987 and began mobilizing for improved service around 2000, compelling the MBTA and the state of Massachusetts to commit to add stations. Community development corporations, with support from local and national foundations, have led efforts for station area planning and affordable, mixed-use development. The central role of established CDCs and their explicit focus on realizing revitalization

84. Andres Viglucci, "Conflict Slows Overtown Project," *Miami Herald*, August 7, 2006; Michael Vasquez, "Ruling to Delay Crosswinds Start," *Miami Herald*, July 14, 2007; Michael Vasquez, "City, County Battle on Crosswinds Land," *Miami Herald*, January 1; 2008. This point was also made by several interviewees in the region.

85. National Transit Database (2009).

opportunities and mitigating displacement risks in the corridor has meant that equity considerations are at the heart of TOD plans. In addition, the CDCs operate within a city and state environment that supports affordable housing provision with policies like inclusionary zoning and an affordable housing trust fund. At the same time, questions remain about the possibilities for TOD along the corridor, given the number of alternative TOD sites around the city.

The Development of Rail Transit

The Fairmount Line connects downtown Boston's South Station to Hyde Park, a moderate-density neighborhood within city boundaries. It traverses the denser, less affluent neighborhoods of Dorchester and Mattapan, where large shares of low-income and African American residents live. Passenger operations ceased in 1944, but commuter trains returned to the track in 1979 when the Massachusetts Bay Transit Authority rerouted trains there from its Southwest corridor because of major construction.[86]

In 1987, as the MBTA prepared to return commuter trains to the Southwest corridor and take them off the Fairmount Line, community organizations demanded train service, contending that their neighborhoods had borne the noise and pollution of passing commuter trains without any benefits.[87] The MBTA agreed to continue service on the nine-mile commuter rail line, with the addition of one station each in Mattapan and Dorchester.[88] While the addition of the stops enabled some residents to ride the commuter rail, the distance between stops and the infrequent service meant limited mobility benefits to the area.

Community leaders led a new effort for improved transit service beginning in the late 1990s. The Four Corners Action Coalition, which focuses on community organizing, along with the MBTA advisory board, proposed that the Fairmount Corridor host a new hybrid rapid transit service. The proposed service—dubbed the Indigo Line—would make more stops, operate at higher frequency, and charge fares equivalent to those for subway service. As community support grew and the media noticed, the Massachusetts Bay Transportation Authority agreed to conduct a study. After receiving the completed report in 2002, the MBTA's general manager became enthusiastic about the corridor's potential, seeing it as an affordable opportunity to maximize ridership along an existing line and improve service for

86. The SW corridor construction included the creation of a linear park and heavy rail line parallel to the commuter rail tracks in the corridor. The land was assembled for the expansion, later aborted, of an interstate highway. With the opening of the new SW subway/heavy rail line (the Orange Line), the elevated rail that served Roxbury to the east was torn down in 1987. For more information, see KKO and Associates and HNTB Companies (2002).

87. Peter Howe, "Mattapan Rapid Transit Service Sought, T [the MBTA] Urged to Convert Commuter Rail Line," *Boston Globe*, May 6, 1987, p. 32.

88. Goody Clancy, KKO Associates, and Byrne McKinney (2006).

an underserved area.[89] The relationship between neighborhoods of color and the MBTA has been tense at times. Unmet promises to and inadequate service in nearby Roxbury, a largely African American neighborhood where an elevated line was dismantled in 1987, has generated anger and mistrust. Government agencies see the Fairmount Corridor as a feasible, cost-effective project that can address environmental justice concerns and maximize existing infrastructure.[90] Soon after the release of the 2002 report, the MBTA pledged to add four more stops—one component of the broader vision for the Indigo Line—and improve some of the line's infrastructure.

In 2004, four community development corporations came together with several other community organizations to form the Fairmount/Indigo Coalition.[91] CDC leaders created the coalition in response to the revitalization opportunities and displacement risks associated with transit investment as well as to ensure follow-through on the pledged improvements. Because of community activism, educational outreach, and leadership by the area's state legislators, in 2005 the Massachusetts legislature approved $43.5 million in state funds for corridor improvements, including four new stations. Next the state added the Fairmount Corridor to its Big Dig mitigation plan, replacing another transit project. The Environmental Protection Agency approved the change, and the Conservation Law Foundation also consented to the replacement as part of its agreement with the Commonwealth on Big Dig mitigation.

The MBTA and the state have completed station rehabilitation at the existing Dorchester and Mattapan stops and committed funds for four new stops. The MBTA emphasizes that its current dire financial condition makes any significant increase in service unlikely in the near term and that South Station, the line's downtown terminus, lacks capacity for more frequent service.[92] Both the MBTA and Massachusetts Department of Transportation avoid use of the Indigo Line moniker, which connotes a commuter rail–rapid transit hybrid. The MBTA sees existing service as underused, as the Fairmount Line has the lowest ridership among commuter rail lines. However, adding stops may increase ridership, and projections suggest that one stop (Four Corners) may become the busiest stop in the commuter rail system outside of downtown Boston. TOD could bolster ridership numbers, but it faces challenges, discussed below. The Federal Transit Administration might be able to encourage increased frequency, a key element

89. Mac Daniel, "More Trains, Stations in Fairmount Plan," *Boston Globe*, August 31, 2002, p. A1.

90. Personal communication, March 2010.

91. The CDCs were the Dorchester Bay Economic Development Corporation, the Codman Square Neighborhood Development Corporation, Mattapan CDC, and Southwest Boston CDC.

92. Personal communication, March 2010. Peak hour service now runs every half-hour and off-peak service every hour, with no weekend trains.

in transformation to the Indigo Line, by directing attention to it through the Department of Housing and Urban Development–Department of Transportation–Environmental Protection Agency Interagency Partnership for Sustainable Communities (HUD-DOT-EPA Interagency Partnership) and identifying potential funding sources for increased service.[93]

Increasing Benefits and Avoiding Costs of Rail Stations

Activism to increase transit benefits for low-income neighborhoods and communities of color has led to allocation of public funds to transit, and community organizations lead the efforts to maximize development benefits and prevent displacement. To cooperate on corridor development, the four CDCs created a collaborative that receives support from local foundations—such as the Barr Foundation, the Hyams Foundations, and the Boston Foundation—and from national organizations, specifically the Local Initiatives Support Corporation (LISC) and the Surdna Foundation. Encouraged by their funders, the CDC Collaborative conducted corridor planning and in 2006 released a plan that presents the area as "Boston's Newest *Smart Growth* Corridor."[94] The plan describes a vision of mixed-use transit villages with commercial activity and housing and states its commitment to affordability and diversity without displacement. It suggests that new stops "could stimulate the creation of 3,000–5,000 new housing units" and that "1,200 to 1,400 low- to moderate-income multifamily housing units can be built near current and future stops."[95]

Since the corridor planning effort, the CDC Collaborative has led the execution of redevelopment. Given the mission of these CDCs, affordable housing is a key component of redevelopment, and their vision of mixed-use transit villages has led them to incorporate retail and community space. Dorchester Bay Economic Development Corporation has already completed its first TOD project (Dudley Village) near an existing stop, with fifty units of affordable housing and more than 6,000 square feet of retail space. Near a future stop, the Codman Square Neighborhood Development Corporation has begun construction on a project combining twenty-four affordable units with commercial space. In combination, the CDCs own or have development rights to enough property to allow construction of 312 housing units and 101,500 square feet of commercial space, while approximately 673 housing units and 268,000 square feet of commercial space are currently in the earlier stages of development.[96]

93. An FTA deputy administrator and other federal officials toured the corridor in spring 2010. The corridor was also the subject of a webinar for the tri-agency partnership.
94. Goody Clancy, KKO Associates, and Byrne McKinney (2006).
95. Goody Clancy, KKO Associates, and Byrne McKinney (2006).
96. Personal communication, May 2010.

The public sector has provided tools for TOD without leading efforts along the corridor. Neither the city nor the Boston Redevelopment Authority, which has control over zoning and responsibility for planning, has formally adopted the corridor vision or sought to pursue it through direct involvement.[97] Both do support the CDCs' affordable housing efforts, for example, through funds and property acquisition assistance.[98] The city has demonstrated increased interest in the Fairmount/Indigo Corridor, inviting the corridor partners in spring 2010 to meet with the mayor's economic development subcabinet, but it has yet to fully embrace it as a strategy to pursue multiple goals.[99] Likewise, the state supports the effort by contributing funds for transit and providing affordable housing tools. Massachusetts is known for supporting affordable housing through a variety of regulatory tools (for example, Chapter 40B) and a dedicated funding stream (Massachusetts Affordable Housing Trust Fund). More recently, it has developed programs to encourage TOD/smart growth with affordability provisions, but the programs support locally led efforts.[100]

Obstacles to Any Development

Achieving the CDCs' vision of transit-oriented development and ensuring that development and transit benefits minority and low-income populations will be challenging. Even high-capacity CDCs face obstacles to producing affordable housing, especially under current economic conditions. The aim of "scaling up" to be a catalyst for TOD requires that CDCs, which typically lack reserves to hold and acquire property, increase their emphasis on assembling land—which requires "patient capital." Under current economic conditions capital is more scarce and risk-averse, and developing affordable ownership units is less feasible for CDCs.[101]

In the Fairmount Corridor, CDCs have acted as community organizers, planning leaders, and developers. Stoecker describes the conflicts that may result when CDCs take on multiple roles, although his focus is on the dilemma that they face as both landlords and community organizers.[102] In the Boston case, the

---

97. Center for Transit-Oriented Development (2007a).
98. Center for Transit-Oriented Development (2007a).
99. Personal communication, March 2010.
100. The state provides funds to municipalities that adopt transit, downtown, or node overlay districts that allow more housing units. The Commercial Area Transit Node Housing Program is a bonding program for first-time homeowner housing (rehab or new construction) near public transit in which at least 51 percent of units are affordable. Another bonding program, the TOD Infrastructure and Housing Support Program, can fund bike/pedestrian facilities or housing in which at least 25 percent of units are affordable at 80 percent of AMI. Center for Transit-Oriented Development (2007a, p. 55).
101. Personal communication, March 2010.
102. Stoecker (1997).

roles of community planner and organizer could conflict or at least compete for resources and staff time with the role of developer. One confidential interviewee suggested that the CDCs' desire to acquire land at low cost has inhibited their promotion of the corridor. However, that may be a resource constraint issue, as one CDC leader noted her need for specialized staff precisely so that she could better promote the corridor.

Private investment is necessary to some extent for successful transit-oriented development in the United States. Attracting investment and managing it to achieve the CDCs' vision may prove difficult along the Fairmount/Indigo Corridor. As one interviewee noted, the CDCs cannot take on all the redevelopment proposed in the corridor plan, and a number of macro and neighborhood factors present challenges to securing private investment to do so. Research has yet to untangle the ways in which investment in transit infrastructure interacts with the web of factors that shape for-profit development choices. The Fairmount Corridor exists within an extensive metropolitan transit system that offers numerous other locations for TOD; many of those locations are closer to urban activity centers and/or have transit service that is vastly more convenient than any service that the corridor will offer in the near term. One interviewee suggested that gentrification—one indication of private investment—was less likely to sprout up near the new stations than to spread from a neighborhood west of the corridor, where subway service is only one among numerous urban amenities. Even before the housing crisis and economic downturn, private development in the corridor was limited.[103]

Given the current level of local government involvement, few comprehensive measures exist to channel development toward the corridor and prevent displacement. It may seem contradictory, yet barriers to generating sufficient redevelopment exist simultaneously with the risk of escalating land values and displacement. Urban living in Boston continues to attract professionals, middle-class households, and recent graduates of elite universities and colleges; the demand for housing that they create combined with continued high housing costs in the metropolitan area cause ongoing gentrification in major portions of the urban core. Compared with many community-based actors, the CDCs have significant support and capacity to develop affordable housing, but unless stronger public sector mechanisms emerge, affordability will depend on their combined output. The corridor's location within one municipal jurisdiction should offer an advantage and arena for comprehensive action, but the city of Boston oversees neighborhood development while the Boston Redevelopment Authority controls planning and zoning. Some locals criticize the redevelopment authority for favoring

103. Center for Transit-Oriented Development (2007a, p. 58).

certain projects and having a fragmented, project-by-project approach.[104] Community actors may, however, be able to foster a city role in helping to manage development more comprehensively, given the recent interest of the mayor. State responsibilities also are fragmented, with separate agencies overseeing community development, housing, and transportation, but Massachusetts still offers significant affordable housing tools and shows increasing interest in overcoming fragmentation through state support for TOD and smart growth.

Answering the Research Questions

Here, we return to our research questions to reflect on the lessons of the case studies and their implications for federal policy.

—What does the history of the development of fixed-rail transit tell us about the challenges of developing routes and stations that serve low-income neighborhoods?

These cases all suggest that *if new fixed-route transit serves established low-income neighborhoods, it will be the exception, not the rule,* until the rules of the game change. Many of the routes currently under development or in the planning stage have a very long history behind them, and that history connects to the metropolitan reality of the 1970s, not the 2010s. The transit goals of the 1970s were, first, to move middle- and upper-income suburbanites to job centers and second, to connect job centers to one another. To the extent that new rail and BRT projects yield fixed-route transit service for low-income neighborhoods, they tend to do so more by accident than by design. The exception that proves the rule here is the project that almost did not happen: the Fairmount Corridor/Indigo Line. The People's Transportation Plan, which in fact did not come to fruition (and probably never will), also helps prove the rule: it simply proposes service to too many neighborhoods to be financially feasible. Current incentives do not make it sensible for transit providers to improve service to transit-dependent neighborhoods, whose residents would have to ride—and pay—even if their current service deteriorated. The incentive structure for selecting fixed-route transit routes will have to tilt considerably more toward improving service for transit-dependent neighborhoods before transit agencies will do so for more than coincidental reasons.

At the same time, thinking about changing the incentive structure to improve service in transit-dependent neighborhoods also requires thinking about the complex regional political terrain in which decisions about fixed-route transit

104. Center for Transit-Oriented Development (2007a, p. 46).

routes are being made. Improving service for transit-dependent populations may be easier when decisions about transit service are being made within a single political jurisdiction. In Charlotte, the division of the spoils (routes and stations) plays out within the familiar arena of local politics. Although mayors, planners, and community advocates must work to build support for development of the transit system and for routes that service some communities and not others, they do so within the context of centralized political leadership and established relationships among private and public sector groups.

In fragmented metropolitan areas, elected officials in many jurisdictions must support development and extension of a transit system. The concerns of equity advocates are weighed not only against those of other organized interests within the same city but also against the needs and desires of other local governments in the region. When other local governments contain smaller shares of transit-dependent populations, the concern for equity may be swept aside in the pursuit of regional consensus. That may mean less service for transit-dependent communities and more stations in the suburbs. In Denver, that tendency was held in check because the metro Denver region contains several large jurisdictions with low-income populations. Denver therefore is not the only jurisdiction in the region with a stake in connecting low-income residents with transit and an interest in developing affordable neighborhoods. In Miami, the problems of political fragmentation and concentrated poverty are further compounded by racial and ethnic divisions; equity considerations therefore struggle for sustained attention within the regional context.

In addition to the special challenges that multiple-jurisdiction regions may face in maintaining a focus on transit-dependent neighborhoods, the complex politics of these regions pose special challenges for successful rail initiatives more generally. Multiple political leaders with distinct constituencies must be able to forge a shared vision of transit in the region. Doing so is almost always a slow process, and it may require some decisionmaking on transit that reflects political rather than planning imperatives. In Denver, the Metro Mayors Caucus supported rail only after the mayors built trust working together on other issues. In addition, they backed FasTracks only after long negotiations over who would get rail lines. Consequently, some of the corridors may not be obvious choices based on planning criteria alone, but the need to build regional consensus means that the design of a transit system must include clear local benefits. In Miami, the two-tier county government structure could in theory provide a mechanism for coordinated regional transportation planning. In practice, however, the fragmented and conflicted nature of local politics in the region means that planning across Miami–Dade County requires a complex effort to forge regional consensus. In order to build support for the People's Transportation Plan, for example, the county initiative promised to give 20 percent of the new revenue to cities to use for their own transportation-related projects, and the plan included more transit improvements for more communities than the remaining revenue could realistically fund.

IMPLICATIONS FOR FEDERAL POLICY: On one hand, the federal government can create incentives that facilitate the difficult task of forging regional consensus in complex regions by specifying that transit proposals that are truly regional will be looked on favorably in the competition for federal dollars. This carrot has been shown to work in terms of overcoming resistance to regional cooperation in fragmented metropolitan areas and improving the prospects for coordinated regional action.[105] At the same time, the federal evaluation of regional transit proposals may need to account for the political transaction costs of achieving regional consensus. One concern is that these costs may initially facilitate consensus but may pose problems for successful rail initiatives later on. For example, in Denver, FasTracks is now threatened, and all the projects proposed in the PTP in Miami will probably never be built.

Furthermore, the effort to facilitate regional transit planning also needs to consider the particular challenges that regional coalition building poses for efforts to serve transit-dependent neighborhoods. Incentives for regional coordination are an important tool to enable multi-jurisdiction regions to plan for transit projects. But those incentives need to account for the possibility that equity considerations may struggle for attention in transit plans that are developed in multijurisdiction metropolitan areas where the emphasis is on securing support from suburban governments. Federal policy could help moderate that tendency if it integrated additional equity criteria in federal assessments of local and regional mass transit capital proposals. For example, a project could be assessed on the degree to which it reduces combined housing and transit costs for low-income residents; the extent to which it connects underserved populations to job centers; its safeguards against displacement; and its expected economic development benefits. The current HUD-DOT-EPA Interagency Partnership, which emphasizes an integrated approach to the assessment of transit projects, indicates a move in this direction. Both DOT (TIGER II planning grants) and HUD (sustainable community challenge grants) have recently awarded grants to projects that combine goals related to housing, transportation, and jobs. The upcoming reauthorization of the surface transportation program is an opportunity to build on this momentum and increase the extent to which equity considerations are an explicit component of federal transportation policy.

105. Alpert, Gainsborough, and Wallis (2006).

A final observation on federal transportation policy is also in order here. The current structure of federal transit finance is tilted in favor of capital investment and against operating expenditures.[106] As long as that is true, elected officials and transit agencies will be induced to build new lines, even when it might make more sense to improve service on the existing infrastructure instead. Since existing riders are so often low-income, transit-dependent people, a more socially equitable federal transit policy would look for a better balance between operating and capital subsidies.

— Are the obstacles to any development so great that we expect to see slow or no development in station areas at all?

Nothing in any of these cases persuades us that private sector actors view the obstacles to development as insuperable. In Denver, Charlotte, and Boston, the actors that have pushed hardest for the transit improvements have been those with the greatest stake and interest in transit-oriented development. The same actors have been instrumental in overcoming the obstacles of speculation, small and fragmented parcels, and neighborhood resistance. In Denver and Charlotte, rail routes traverse underdeveloped parcels alongside railroad tracks and in light-industrial zones and sometimes abut public housing projects, meaning that many station areas have few (if any) prospective development opponents, and in many cases the parcels are not too small to accommodate medium-sized and large projects. Furthermore, the most vocal and concerned local residents and business owners in all cases have been worried not about land development— mostly, the active residents would prefer to see rising property values—but about how construction will disrupt their lives.

On the Fairmount Corridor and in some parts of Miami, by contrast, the obstacles to development seem significant to us, but community-based actors are working, with public and private sector support, to generate development in these neighborhoods, where transit alone would not. Boston's extensive transit system creates TOD opportunities in numerous neighborhoods, many of which offer more amenities and have attracted far more private investment than Fairmount Corridor neighborhoods, and that fact may prove the greatest challenge to attracting private development to the corridor. The efforts of CDCs, however, may mean the gradual transition of an established built environment through moderate-scale projects rather than the construction of entirely new neighborhoods. Over time and with more city leadership, CDCs' direct redevelopments could create attractive opportunities for private investment. Miami's Overtown neighborhood, despite being immediately adjacent to downtown, has

106. Garrett and Taylor (1999); Taylor (2004).

not sparked investment, perhaps due to the appeal of nearby Government Center for transit-oriented development or the draw of other Miami neighborhoods with strong livability conditions (for example, Coconut Grove) and transit access (for example, Brickell). Furthermore, developers may be weary of community opposition to market-rate housing development in Overtown, especially given the recent Crosswinds conflict. Past discussions of using TOD to transform Overtown have had some community support, and it remains to be seen whether current community-based leadership on the Folklife District will result in greater community confidence in development proposals and ultimately in mixed-used, mixed-income development.

Some observers have questioned the prospects of TOD because they maintain outmoded stereotypes about how homeowners will respond to high-density and mixed-use development proposals. While some homeowners do oppose densification and development, the TOD formula offers enough benefits to win over other suburbanites. In fact, our case studies lead us to believe that *the participatory process that accompanies station development and TOD may yield broader acceptance for a new kind of urbanism, even outside TODs.* Contemporary rail planning, as in the case of Charlotte and Denver, is conducted in an era in which engaging with the public before, during, and after a project is implemented is essential to its success. Planners in Charlotte, for example, held hundreds of public meetings while planning the first 9.6-mile segment of the Blue Line. The outreach and engagement process has more lasting consequences than merely planning the rail system; it broadens the public consciousness about a new kind of urbanism, one that incorporates accessible public transit, pedestrian-scale urban design, and modern amenities that improve livability. With increasing demand for urban living, especially among aging baby boomers and young professionals, there is renewed interest in having easy access to jobs and amenities, reducing greenhouse gases, and living more sustainably. While the public can easily express its new set of values and demands, it often does not have the tools to visualize how those values can be translated into the built environment.

Therefore, TOD projects and the public participation process involved in planning them present planners with an opportunity to offer the public a vision of an alternative lifestyle and living environment for both cities and suburbs. With early successes in private investment and economic development around rail stations and glimpses of what TOD will ultimately bring to station areas in cities such as Charlotte and Denver, residents are clamoring for transit stations. In these places, the mantra for the siting of transit stations is not NIMBY but YIMBY ("yes in my backyard"). The wild popularity of rail and TOD in these places suggests that the principles guiding transit station development may filter into the broader regional development environment.

IMPLICATIONS FOR FEDERAL POLICY: The interest in transit-oriented development in our case study regions supports the idea that value-capture strategies can offer an additional funding mechanism for transit in an era of limited federal funds; they also can increase the incentives for local governments, working with transit agencies, to develop supportive land use policies and undertake joint development at station sites.[107] While these strategies often depend on action at the local level (and supportive state policies), the Federal Transit Administration can also facilitate TOD development planning by ensuring that projects that incorporate TOD at stations are not disadvantaged in the competition for federal funding. For example, there have been concerns about the extent to which TOD hurts eligibility for New Starts funding if it increases the upfront land acquisition costs associated with a project.[108] Weakening the cost-effectiveness criteria associated with New Starts and delinking those criteria from the economic development criteria are two ways to begin addressing that concern. In general, incorporating more of the HUD-DOT-EPA livability principles into the New Starts funding criteria would help encourage additional TOD planning with new rail projects.

—How has income mixing become part of the TOD agenda?

Want mixed-income TOD? Build support for mixed-income housing in general. In all three of the cases in which mixed-income TOD is either under way or is well supported by public policies, consensus had already been achieved on the importance of affordability and the development of mixed-income communities and workforce housing in general. In Miami, where it had not, affordability has not been as strong a part of the civic or government agenda and there appears to be much less support for mixed-income development.

Affordability has become important in transit-oriented development in Denver, Boston, and Charlotte through distinct avenues. In Denver, the issue arose most strongly within the Metro Mayors Caucus. In fact, the MMC devoted itself to affordable and workforce housing before it took up rail transit. When MMC became the primary channel for rail advocacy, affordable housing appeared more naturally within the TOD agenda. Since the MMC had already raised awareness and generated commitment among the region's mayors, it became easier for nonprofits (Mercy Housing), foundations (Enterprise), and public housing authorities (Denver, Aurora Housing, MetroWest Housing) to enter the TOD conversation. The funders and providers of housing did not have to plead their own cases; they could just get to work and build their credibility and

---

107. General Accounting Office (2010).
108. General Accounting Office (2010, pp. 34–38).

capacity by delivering excellent new developments. And with their strong commitment to both affordability and TOD, the mayors could create a potentially more effective partnership with the state's housing finance agency to build affordable housing in station areas.

Boston, too, is well known for its many far-reaching efforts to create affordable housing. It was among the first cities to use inclusionary zoning and linkage fees, and it has long supported exceptionally active CDCs. Communities were able to champion the Fairmount Corridor in the first place because of the background support for neighborhood-based affordable housing providers. Community actors have well-founded concerns about gentrification in the corridor; the entire city of Boston has upscaled in the past twenty years, and the corridor is not immune to those pressures. Building 100 percent affordable projects will help safeguard places for lower-income residents to live as the corridor becomes more accessible and better known to prospective middle-income households.

Charlotte, finally, has generally low-cost housing, with many market-rate apartment developments scattered around the city and inexpensive single-family housing at the urban edge. For Charlotte's middle-income households, affordability is simply a less pressing issue than it is in Denver and Boston. Even so, the city has maintained a commitment to multifamily development and to affordability near transit thanks to commitments by a series of mayors and business leaders (notably, a president of Bank of America). It is also possible that the dominance of banking in Charlotte's economic base makes affordable housing a higher priority on elites' civic agenda because of the Community Reinvestment Act–related requirement that banks show how they serve their communities.

Miami, by contrast, has less systematic support for affordable housing within the regional context. Ironically, Florida is the only one of these states in which a state law requires local governments to plan affordable housing. This mandate—part of the state's growth management act—requires local governments to plan new housing for low-income residents not on the basis of redistributive or fair-share principles but on the basis of historic shares of affordable housing. Consequently, it is easy for upper-income communities to reason that they have no responsibility for accommodating low-income people, leaving it all instead to the city of Miami. Florida also has a state housing trust fund, but most trust fund projects are built outside station areas for owner-occupiers.

Given the staunch (and well-publicized) rejection of market-rate development in Overtown and the state's process for tax-credit allocation (which allows reluctant cities to avoid affordable housing), the affordable housing development that has occurred in some station areas has generally been 100 percent affordable projects in already distressed areas rather than either mixed-income projects or affordable projects in middle- and upper-income communities.

IMPLICATIONS FOR FEDERAL POLICY: As discussed, interest in transit-oriented development on the part of private developers improves the prospects for development at stations in general. However, it does raise equity concerns. Private developers are unlikely to focus on affordability unless they are given incentives to do so. To the extent that TOD is seen as a value-capture strategy that generates revenue for the transit agency, it may reduce interest in including an affordability component in TOD plans. For that reason, federal policy needs to offer strong incentives to include affordable housing in TODs. Federal policy on the low-income housing tax credit, which is used in most of the nation's new affordable housing developments, could be applied specifically to encourage developments near transit. However, careful consideration would need to be given to the suitability of transit-station areas for families with children and potential conflicts between compact development and fair housing goals. In awarding grants, HUD could also give preference to developments that are close to transit and that address gentrification concerns in station areas. In general, the movement away from maintaining separate policies for affordable housing and transportation toward taking a more integrated approach in awarding federal funds will ensure that regional transportation planning includes attention to the housing and job needs of low- and moderate-income populations in the region.

Conclusion: Regions, Resilience, and Transit

We conclude by returning to the issue of regional resilience. Having reviewed these cases, how should we conceptualize light-rail transit and TOD within the resilience framework? While our initial impulse was to treat the coming of a station as a potential shock to low-income neighborhoods and to view affordable housing as a potential buffer in the face of that shock, we now think that is too narrow a view. The fixed-transit systems that we studied were the product of such protracted negotiations and discussions that by the time that stations were finally built, the shock to neighborhoods would have been lessened by years of land speculation, reinvestment, and disinvestment within a changing regional context. Furthermore, the new routes and stations seldom go to and through low-income neighborhoods at all, and when they do so, the neighborhoods often are already on the path of development and redevelopment.

Moving away from our "shock" orientation, we consider it useful to view transit, equity, and regional resilience within the framework of complex adaptive systems. Our cases persuade us that rail transit offers a unique opportunity for constructing a more *sustainable* region, in the sense that Campbell proposes: one in which advocates for equity, environmental quality, and economic development not only find common ground but build mutual dependence.[109]

The Denver, Charlotte, and (to an extent) Boston cases all offer evidence that the success of rail and the interjection of equity considerations in development are mutually supportive. Rail advocates in all three cases needed to appeal to some extent at least to social equity arguments to advance their agenda past the first halting efforts to build extensive and expensive passenger rail systems. This was most necessary, of course, in Boston, where equity advocates took the lead on the Fairmount Corridor. But in Denver and Charlotte too, equity became important in rebranding rail. Such rebranding helps counter charges that rail does not address a pressing public problem but only enriches a few at the expense of the many. Opinion leaders can now build a case for publicly supported rail as a legitimate city-building move on at least three fronts. First, TOD delivers benefits that the average voter might enjoy or at least might want as an option: a place where he or she could imagine living, even if not right now; an urban experience for recreation; and a workplace where lunch can involve a pleasant walk to a local deli instead of a car trip to a chain restaurant. Second, advocates for rail transit can bill TOD as part of a strategy to reduce air pollution and (for those who trust the majority of climate scientists) lower overall greenhouse gas emissions. Third, and most important for our argument, transit advocates can appeal to local and regional actors who care either personally or more broadly about income mixing and gentrification. While the numbers of voters with such concerns might be small, other regional actors—nonprofit builders, foundations, planning and environmental organizations, progressive political groups, and even labor-supported organizations like the Front Range Economic Strategies Council (FRESC) in Denver—can bring resources other than votes to the table. They can help raise funds for campaigns, create positive news about how rail improves the lives and neighborhoods of ordinary people, and sometimes help get out the vote in crucial elections.

The Miami case and the rail struggles of the 1990s in Los Angeles show that coalitions of equity, pro-rail, environmental, and development actors do not always fall into place easily or endure over time. In Miami, the People's Transportation Plan made too many promises to too many people, the system fell apart, and now neither fixed-rail transit nor TOD has much support. In fact, both face fairly widespread cynicism owing to the failure to deliver rail, on one hand, and massive speculative overdevelopment of condominiums on the other.

109. Campbell (1996).

In Los Angeles, by contrast, the first attempts at building rail failed to engage equity actors and were slowed down by several years as a consequence. While the Bus Riders' Union lawsuit occurred and was settled early in the latest round of rail development in Los Angeles and new alliances have emerged since then (including a strong coalition supporting extension of the Gold Line to East Los Angeles), the 1990s conflict over "white rail" still shapes public perceptions about rail transit, in both the city and the nation.

To some observers, coalition building may look like the co-opting of equity and environmental advocates. From their perspective, the "growth machine" has expanded enough to quiet the voices calling for less development and slower growth by directing growth and development in ways that benefit previously ignored constituencies.[110] Of course, the TOD/transit agenda does promote development of the ultimate attributes of at least one version of the growth machine: a strong downtown; a photogenic and appealing national and international image; and new opportunities to develop real estate near rail stations and in other infill locations. However, the most likely alternative to this version of the growth machine is not an anti-growth, redistributive coalition that has collective land ownership; on the contrary, it is another growth machine whose stake is in low-density peripheral development. Rail's high profile and continued appeal as a development strategy offers a secondary benefit.[111] It may capture the attention of stakeholders who previously were unsupportive of or unengaged with alternative metropolitan growth strategies. By broadening stakeholders and coalitions, debates and partnerships on rail transit could shift the regional political will toward building a more sustainable region.

We think it matters *which pro-growth coalition dominates over the next fifty years.*[112] While the compact-development version might threaten equity interests (with unwanted impacts on low-income neighborhoods), it threatens equity less than the low-density suburban model that dominated in the twentieth century. While that model elevated homeownership and provided cheap housing, it also fostered and ultimately required excessive dependence on individual automobiles, separated people geographically by income and race, and allowed many high-income people to disengage from responsibility for meeting social needs.

We therefore think that the kind of region that can result from coalition building on rail transit will be more *resilient* in the face of myriad challenges than the metropolitan region of the twentieth century would be. That model—useful though it was in the construction of a prosperous nation—cannot now promise prosperity and general welfare. It separates people by race, class, occupation, age,

110. Logan and Molotch (1987).
111. Giuliano and Agarwal (2010).
112. The conflict here is especially sharp in Houston, a case that we explore in future research.

and activity; it spreads them over too wide an expanse; and it presents too few choices. In light of climate change, the growth in the senior population, the world's uncertain economic future, and intensifying social and cultural diversity, the United States will need to invest wisely and compactly in its infrastructure systems and to create metropolitan areas with a rich and diverse array of neighborhoods, business areas, and transportation systems. Delivering an equitable transit-oriented metropolis now appears to require and motivate coalition building among the very groups that must contribute more broadly to civic life in the next half-century. Hence we see the politics of equity in transit and TOD as a bright thread in the narrative on building resilient regions.

References

Alpert, Lenore, Juliet F. Gainsborough, and Allan Wallis. 2006. "Building the Capacity to Act Regionally: Formation of a Regional Transportation Authority in South Florida." *Urban Affairs Review* 42, no. 2: 143–68.

Campbell, Scott. 1996. "Green Cities, Growing Cities, Just Cities? Urban Planning and the Contradictions of Sustainable Development." *Journal of the American Planning Association* 62, no. 3: 296–312.

Carruthers, John I., and Gudmundur F. Úlfarsson. 2008. "Does 'Smart Growth' Matter to Public Finance?" *Urban Studies* 45, no. 9: 1791–823.

Center for Transit-Oriented Development. 2007a. *Realizing the Potential: Expanding Housing Opportunities near Transit.* Oakland, Calif.

———. 2007b. "The Case for Mixed-Income Transit-Oriented Development in the Denver Region." Report commissioned by Enterprise Community Partners, Denver. Oakland, Calif.: Center for Transit-Oriented Development.

Charlotte-Mecklenburg Planning Commission. 2008. "Centers, Corridors, Wedges Growth Framework: Draft." Charlotte, N.C.

Dittmar, Hank, and Gloria Ohland. 2003. *The New Transit Town: Best Practices in Transit-Oriented Development.* Washington: Island Press.

Dluhy, Milan, Keith Revell, and Sidney Wong. 2002. "Creating a Positive Future for a Minority Community: Transportation and Urban Renewal Politics in Miami." *Journal of Urban Affairs* 24, no. 1: 75–95.

Gale, Dennis E. 1999. "Miami. The Overtown Neighborhood: A Generation of Redevelopment Strategies Gone Awry." In *Rebuilding Urban Neighborhoods: Achievements, Opportunities, and Limits,* edited by W. Dennis Keating, Philip Star, and Norman Krumholz, pp. 159–176. Thousand Oaks, Calif.: Sage Publications.

Garrett, Mark, and Brian Taylor. 1999. "Reconsidering Social Equity in Public Transit." *Berkeley Planning Journal* 13: 6–27.

Gatzlaff, Dean H., and Marc T. Smith. 1993. "The Impact of the Miami Metrorail on the Value of Residences near Station Locations." *Land Economics* 69, no. 1: 54–66.

General Accounting Office. 2010. "Public Transportation: Federal Role in Value-Capture Strategies for Transit Is Limited, but Additional Guidance Could Help Clarify Policies." Washington.

Giuliano, Genevieve, and Ajay Agarwal. 2010. "Public Transit as a Metropolitan Growth and Development Strategy." In *Urban and Regional Policy and Its Effects,* vol. 3, edited by Nancy Pindus, Howard Wial, and Harold Wolman. Brookings.

Goody Clancy, KKO Associates, and Byrne McKinney. 2006. "Boston's Newest *Smart Growth* Corridor: A Collaborative Vision for the Fairmount/Indigo Line." Boston: Fairmount/Indigo Line CDC Collaborative.

Gordon, Peter, and Harry W. Richardson. 1997. "Are Compact Cities a Desirable Planning Goal?" *Journal of the American Planning Association* 63, no. 1: 95–106.

Grengs, Joe, 2004. "The Abandoned Social Goals of Public Transit in the Neoliberal City of the USA." *City* 9, no. 1: 51–66.

———. 2002. "Community-Based Planning as a Source of Political Change: The Transit Equity Movement of Los Angeles' Bus Riders Union." *Journal of the American Planning Association* 68, no. 2: 165–78.

Harrell, Rodney, Allison Brooks, and Todd Nedwick. 2009. *Preserving Affordability and Access in Livable Communities: Subsidized Housing Opportunities near Transit and the 50+ Population.* Washington: AARP Public Policy Institute.

Hartgen, David. 2008. "Charlotte's LYNX Line: A Preliminary Assessment." Raleigh, N.C.: John Locke Foundation.

Hess, Daniel Baldwin, and Peter A. Lombardi. 2004. "Policy Support for and Barriers to Transit-Oriented Development in the Inner City: Literature Review." *Transportation Research Record: Journal of the Transportation Research Board* 1887: pp. 26–33.

Jackson, Kenneth. 1985. *Crabgrass Frontier: The Suburbanization of the United States.* Oxford University Press.

KKO and Associates and HNTB Companies. 2002. "Fairmount Line Feasibility Study: Final Report, Executive Summary." Boston: Massachusetts Bay Transportation Authority.

Lichter, Daniel T., and others. 2010. "Residential Segregation in New Hispanic Destinations: Cities, Suburbs, and Rural Communities Compared." *Social Science Research* 39: 215–30.

Logan, John R., and Harvey L. Molotch. 1987. *Urban Fortunes: The Political Economy of Place.* University of California–Berkeley.

Mohl, Raymond A. 1993. "Race and Space in the Modern City: Interstate 95 and the Black Communities in Miami." In *Urban Policy in Twentieth-Century America*, edited by A. R. Hirsch and R. Mohl, pp. 1–45. Rutgers University Press.

Myers, Dowell. 2007. *Immigrants and Boomers: Forging a New Social Contract for the Future of America.* New York: Russell Sage Foundation.

Myers, Dowell, and SungHo Ryu. 2008. "Aging Baby Boomers and the Generational Housing Bubble: Foresight and Mitigation of an Epic Transition." *Journal of the American Planning Association* 74, no. 1: 17–33.

National Transit Database. 2009. "Transit Profile: Top 50 Agencies for the 2008 Report Year." Washington: Federal Transit Administration (www.ntdprogram.gov/ntdprogram/data.htm).

Neighborhood Development Department, City of Charlotte. 2008. "Charlotte Neighborhood Quality of Life Study 2008." Charlotte, N.C..

Pendall, Rolf. 2000. "Local Land Use Regulation and the Chain of Exclusion." *Journal of the American Planning Association* 66, no. 2: 125–42.

———. 2008. "From Hurdles to Bridges: Local Land-Use Regulations and the Pursuit of Affordable Rental Housing." In *Revisiting Rental Housing,* edited by Nicolas Retsinas and Eric Belsky, pp. 224–73. Brookings.

Rapid Transit District. 2010. *Transit-Oriented Development Status Report: 2009*. Denver, Colo.: Rapid Transit District.

Reardon, Kenneth M. 2003. "Riding the Rails for Social Justice." *Shelterforce* 128: 1–3.

Rubin, Thomas A., James E. Moore II, and Shin Lee. 1999. "Ten Myths about U.S. Urban Rail Systems." *Transport Policy* 6, no. 1: 57–73.

Schuetz, Jenny, Rachel Meltzer, and Vicki Been. 2009. "31 Flavors of Inclusionary Zoning: Comparing Policies from San Francisco, Washington, D.C., and Suburban Boston." *Journal of the American Planning Association* 75, no. 4: 441–56.

Stoecker, Randy. 1997. "The CDC Model of Urban Redevelopment: A Critique and an Alternative." *Journal of Urban Affairs* 19, no. 1: 1–22.

Taylor, Brian D. 2004. "The Geography of Urban Transportation Finance." In *The Geography of Urban Transportation*, edited by S. Hanson and Genevieve Giuliano, pp. 3–29. New York: Guilford Press.

Transit Cooperative Research Program. 2008. "Civil Rights Implications of the Allocation of Funds between Bus and Rail." *Legal Research Digest* 27 (http://onlinepubs.trb.org/online pubs/tcrp/tcrp_lrd_27.pdf).

———. 2004. *Transit-Oriented Development in the United States: Experiences, Challenges, and Prospects*. Washington: Transportation Research Board, pp. 269–70.

Transportation Research Board, Committee for the Study on the Relationships among Development Patterns, Vehicle Miles Traveled, and Energy Consumption. 2009. *Driving and the Built Environment: The Effects of Compact Development on Motorized Travel, Energy Use, and CO_2 Emissions*. Transportation Research Board Special Report 298.

U.S. Department of Transportation, Bureau of Transportation Statistics and Federal Highway Administration. 2010. *National Household Travel Survey: Preliminary Data Release, Version 1*.

Yang, Yizhao. 2008. "A Tale of Two Cities: Physical Form and Neighborhood Satisfaction in Metropolitan Portland and Charlotte." *Journal of the American Planning Association* 74, no. 3: 307–23.

6

Economic Shocks and Regional Economic Resilience

EDWARD HILL, TRAVIS ST. CLAIR, HOWARD WIAL,

HAROLD WOLMAN, PATRICIA ATKINS, PAMELA BLUMENTHAL,

SARAH FICENEC, AND ALEC FRIEDHOFF

Economic shocks to metropolitan economies occur periodically, although the effects of the shocks vary from region to region, as do regions' adjustment to and recovery from them. In this chapter we examine the nature and extent of the shocks, their effects on regional economies (some regional economies are resistant to shocks while others suffer substantial downturns), and the resilience of regional economies to shocks. We are particularly concerned with regional economic resilience: why are some regional economies that are adversely affected by shocks able to recover in a relatively short period of time while others are not?

Economic resilience is a concept that is frequently discussed but rarely well defined. Pendall, Foster, and Cowell posit two separate, though not necessarily unrelated, concepts. The first is based on "equilibrium analysis," in which resilience is the ability to return to a preexisting state in a single equilibrium system. The second defines resilience in terms of complex adaptive systems and relates to the ability of a system to adapt and change in response to stresses and strains.[1] In this chapter we focus on the first definition of resilience.

In regional economic analysis, perhaps the most natural meaning of economic resilience, and the one we use, is the ability of a regional economy to maintain or return to a preexisting state (typically assumed to be an equilibrium

1. Pendall, Foster, and Cowell (2010, pp. 2, 6).

193

state) in the presence of some type of exogenous (externally generated) shock.[2] Although only a few studies explicitly use the term "resilience," the economic literature that deals with the idea of resilience typically is concerned with the extent to which a regional or national economy is able to return to its previous level and/or rate of growth of output, employment, or population after experiencing an external shock.[3]

A related concept of resilience is the extent to which a regional economy avoids having its previous equilibrium state disrupted by an exogenous shock. This could involve avoiding the shock altogether (for example, by having a regional economy that is not dependent on an industry that is likely to experience a negative demand shock) or withstanding the shock with little or no adverse impact (for example, by having an economy that is diversified enough that the shock has little macroeconomic effect).[4]

We conceptualize regional economic resilience as the ability of a region (defined for the purpose of this chapter as a metropolitan area as delineated by the Office of Management and Budget) to recover successfully from shocks to its economy that throw it substantially off its prior growth path and cause an economic downturn.[5] Shocks can be of three kinds: shocks caused by downturns in the national economy (national economic downturn shocks); shocks caused by downturns in particular industries that constitute an important component of the region's export base (industry shocks); and other external shocks (a natural disaster, closure of a military base, movement of an important firm out of the area, and so forth).[6] These shocks are not mutually exclusive; a regional economy may experience more than one simultaneously.

Not all shocks throw an economy substantially off its prior growth path. When a shock occurs that does not cause the region to be thrown off its prior growth path—that does not cause it to experience an economic downturn—we term the region "shock resistant." If the region is adversely affected by the shock, we consider it "resilient" if it returns to at least its prior growth path within a relatively short period of time. If it does not, we consider it "nonresilient." (See

2. Note that this "shock-related" definition of resilience does *not* include consideration of regional response to long-term economic stagnation or persistent slow growth. This is clearly an important concern, but one that we do not consider in this chapter.

3. See, for example, Blanchard and Katz (1992), Rose and Liao (2005), Briguglio and others (2006), and Feyrer, Sacerdote, and Stern (2007). Although these macroeconomic indicators are commonly used, it is also possible to apply this and other resilience concepts to other measures of regional economic performance, such as wage inequality or measures of environmental sustainability.

4. Briguglio and others (2006).

5. This chapter uses the 2003 metropolitan statistical area definitions unless otherwise indicated.

6. In this chapter, we follow common usage in regional economics and use the term "export," at the regional level, to refer to goods and services that are produced in a region but consumed mainly by people who live in other regions. Those other regions may be located in either the United States or other countries.

Figure 6-1. *Resilience Concepts*

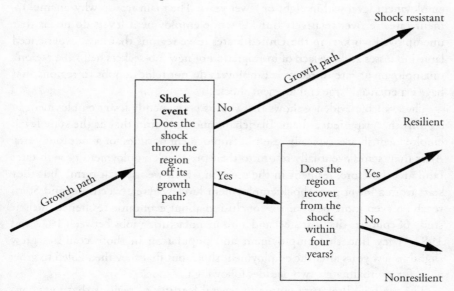

figure 6-1.) We operationalize these concepts below. Being shock resistant is the best outcome for a regional economy, followed by being resilient. Being nonresilient is the least desirable outcome.

Note that economic resilience can occur because the region's economy simply bounces back (for example, because of a favorable shift in demand for its products), because the region's industry or occupational structure undergoes change, or because less radical economic changes take place (for example, existing firms adopt better technologies or organizational forms or produce new products). The key question is what happens to the competitive position of the region's economic base and how the region responds to changes in the competitive position of its base. Note also that returning to its prior growth path is not necessarily a good thing for a region, particularly if its growth was low or stagnant (although that is presumably better than stabilizing at an even lower level).

Understanding and Accounting for Regional Economic Resilience: Reviewing the Literature

Research describing determinants and patterns of shock resistance and/or economic resilience is sparse. The descriptive literature finds that U.S. states, counties, and metropolitan areas that experience employment shocks generally recover to their pre-shock unemployment rate but not to their pre-shock employment level within eight or fewer years. The main reason why unemployment rates recover relatively quickly while employment levels do not is that unemployed workers in the United States leave regions that have experienced large job losses and the lack of in-migration of new job-seekers helps the region's unemployment rate to recover. Employers do not relocate jobs to regions that have experienced large employment shocks.[7]

The available evidence shows that shocks permanently lower employment in regions that experience them. Blanchard and Katz find that at the state level, employment shocks typically result in employment declines for about four years. After that, states eventually return to their pre-shock employment growth rates (and are, therefore, resilient in the sense in which we use that term), but they start from a lower post-shock employment level.[8] Feyrer, Sacerdote, and Stern reach an even more pessimistic conclusion about economic resilience in their study of counties that lost steel and auto manufacturing jobs between 1977 and 1982. They find that employment and population in those counties grew slightly a few years after the employment shock but that they then failed to grow at all for approximately two decades following the shock.[9]

The regional literature points to several features of regions that may contribute to either shock resistance or resilience.[10] With respect to industrial structure, Feyrer, Sacerdote, and Stern find that counties that experienced auto and steel job losses in the late 1970s and early 1980s had higher post-shock population growth if they had warm, sunny climates and were located near large metropolitan areas.[11] Kolko and Neumark, in a study of the impact of regional and industry shocks on employment within business establishments, find that employment in corporate headquarters and, to a lesser extent, in small locally owned chains is less likely to decline in response to those shocks.[12] Therefore, high concentrations of such types of business would be expected to make regions more shock resistant. Chapple and Lester find evidence that regions in which technology and knowledge-based work are growing rapidly exhibit greater resilience in terms of average earnings per worker. They also find that regions attracting highly skilled workers have greater increases in average earnings per worker.[13]

7. See Blanchard and Katz (1992); Bartik and Eberts (2006); and Feyrer, Sacerdote, and Stern (2007).
8. Blanchard and Katz (1992).
9. Feyrer, Sacerdote, and Stern (2007).
10. See Ficenec (2010) for a review of the literature.
11. Feyrer, Sacerdote, and Stern (2007).
12. Kolko and Neumark (2010).
13. Chapple and Lester (2007, 2010). See also Christopherson, Michie, and Tyler (2010).

Other literature on regional economic growth, although not about resilience per se, suggests hypotheses that may be relevant to the analysis of resilience. One strand of research emphasizes the role of product and profit cycles in regional growth; it suggests that regional economies can be renewed if their firms introduce new goods or services for export from the region or use new technologies to produce such goods and services.[14] A second strand examines the unresolved question of whether industrial specialization or industrial diversification better promotes growth.[15] It has also been suggested that the quality and age of a region's public and private infrastructure is related to cyclical volatility and to growth. Howland finds that states with new private capital stocks experience more severe recessions. She reasons that such states have a larger proportion of newer and smaller firms and that such firms are more susceptible to bankruptcy during a recession.[16] That contradicts earlier findings by Varaiya and Wiseman, who argue that regions with older capital stock may experience more severe regional recessions because older (and more obsolete) capital is most likely to be retired during a recession.[17] However, Howland also finds that once small firms are eliminated from the sample, states with older capital stock experience more severe recessions.[18] Age of the metropolitan area is sometimes used as a proxy for the condition of both private and public capital infrastructure as well as a proxy for the match between an area's urban form and modern transportation needs (the implication being that older areas are likely to have less effective and efficient infrastructure, which is more prone to break down and to need repair).[19] In the case of both public and private infrastructure, older areas are hypothesized to be less "resilient." A small literature explores whether local government fragmentation within a metropolitan area promotes or inhibits growth, although the findings tend to be inconclusive.[20]

Another line of research suggests that human capital (the educational attainment or skills of the region's workforce) is a major driver of growth.[21] Some accounts of the revitalization of New England in the 1980s posit that low wages for skilled workers were necessary to restart the region's growth.[22] Some research

14. Desmet and Rossi-Hansberg (2009); Duranton and Puga (2001); Markusen (1985); and Norton and Rees (1979).

15. Glaeser and others (1992); Henderson, Kuncoro, and Turner (1995); Harrison, Kelley, and Gant (1996); and Henderson (2003).

16. Howland (1984).

17. Varaiya and Wiseman (1978).

18. Howland (1984).

19. See Blumenthal, Wolman, and Hill (2009).

20. Carr and Feiock (1999) and Hamilton, Miller, and Paytas (2004).

21. Glaeser and Saiz (2004); Glaeser, Scheinkman, and Shleifer (1995); Gottlieb and Fogarty (2003); and Simon (1998).

22. Flynn (1984) and Harrison (1984).

has linked regional economic growth to a low level of income inequality within a region.[23] Finally, some literature suggests that the domination of regional labor markets, suppliers, research and development pipelines, or channels of informal business association and communication by a few large, vertically integrated firms may inhibit the growth of other firms.[24] All of these potential determinants of regional growth may be determinants of regional economic resilience as well.

The literature on international economic development may also contribute some insights that are relevant to regional economic resilience. Duval, Elmeskov, and Vogel, in a study of the reasons why shocks to national economies occur and persist, find that public policies that restrict firms' ability to lay off or reassign workers make shocks less severe but also make them last longer.[25] At the regional level, that may suggest that state and local policies that inhibit layoffs or promote unionization have similar effects. Briguglio and others develop an index of national economic resilience based on several hypotheses about resilience, including the hypothesis that concentration of a nation's exports in a few industries inhibits resilience.[26] That suggests a similar hypothesis for regional export industries (distinct from the hypotheses about overall regional economic diversification noted above). Finally, there is a growing body of international quantitative evidence that national and regional institutions, behavioral norms and customs, knowledge, and technology have long-lasting impacts on the economic development of countries and regions.[27] Although these concepts are difficult to apply in quantitative studies of regional economies within the United States, they are relevant to regions' ability to avoid or recover from economic shocks.

The broader literature on regional resilience, especially the literature on resilience to natural disasters, also offers insights that may be relevant to regional economic resilience. For example, a common finding in that literature is that access to economic resources promotes regional or community resilience in the face of natural disasters.[28] That suggests that regions with higher average incomes or wages (independent of human capital) may recover more quickly from economic shocks.

In this chapter we draw on the literature surveyed above to examine various potential determinants of regional economic resilience. We do so through quantitative analysis when possible and supplement that analysis with insights from

23. Pastor and Benner (2008) and Morrow (2008).
24. Chinitz (1961); Safford (2009); and Christopherson and Clark (2007).
25. Duval, Elmeskov, and Vogel (2007).
26. Briguglio and others (2006).
27. For a survey of recent studies, see Nunn (2009).
28. Paton and Johnston (2001); Rozario (2005); and Norris and others (2008).

qualitative case studies of six metropolitan areas. The case studies enable us to look at the role of institutions, norms, and other potential influences on resilience for which we have no quantitative data.

Research Design and Concept Operationalization

We first present simple descriptive statistics on economic shocks, their effects on regional economies, the extent to which regions are resistant to various types of shocks, and if they are not shock resistant, whether they are resilient or nonresilient after suffering the adverse effects of the shocks. We then present four analytical models. We attempt to explain the likelihood of a region experiencing a downturn in response to a shock in a given year; whether individual shock episodes resulted in downturns or not; whether individual regions were resilient or nonresilient to downturns; and the time it took for regions, once adversely affected by a shock, to recover.

To accomplish those tasks we operationalize our key concepts—economic shocks, shock resistance, downturns, and resilience—as well as terms that are related to those concepts, such as "prior growth path."

We begin with economic shocks, of which there can be several kinds. A *national economic downturn shock* is a shock that results from a downturn in the national economy as a whole. We define such a shock as having occurred when in any year (which we call the base year) the national growth rate (separate for employment and for gross metropolitan product) declines by more than 2.0 percentage points from the annual growth rate over the previous eight years.[29]

An *industry shock* affects one or more of a region's major export industries.[30] A region suffers an industry shock when the job loss experienced by export industries in a particular year represents a one-year annual decline of more than 0.75 percent of aggregate metropolitan employment. Our use of the term "shock" thus refers to an inferred shock; we conclude that a shock occurred based on patterns in our data. Industry shocks can be national (a shock to an industrial sector at the national level) or local (a shock that occurs to an industry at the regional but not the national level).

---

29. The previous eight-year growth rate is measured by the slope of the regression line of the natural logarithm of employment on a time trend for the previous eight years. If the prior eight-year growth rate is 4.0 percent or higher, then the growth rate in the base year must decline by the number of percentage points equal to more than half of the prior eight-year growth rate. Our use of a decline in the growth rate to measure shocks is analogous to Hausmann, Pritchett, and Rodrik's use of an increase in the growth rate to measure growth accelerations. See Hausmann, Pritchett, and Rodrik (2004).

30. For a given year, a three-digit NAICS industry is defined as a major export industry in a region if its share of regional employment is at least 1.0 percent and at least 80 percent above the same industry's share of national employment.

—A *national industry shock* occurs if the three-digit North American Industry Classification System (NAICS) industry that contributes the largest share of employment loss to the region's export base when the region experiences an industry shock is also in shock at the national level.[31]

—A *local industry shock* occurs if the three-digit industry that contributes the largest share of employment loss to the region's export base when the region experiences an industry shock has not experienced a shock at the national level.

We define gross metropolitan product (GMP) shocks in the same way as employment shocks, but we use GMP data. Non-economic shocks to a region's economy can result from natural disasters, terrorist attacks, or other non-economic events that have the potential to affect the regional economy adversely. However, as these shocks are unobserved in the data, we confine our discussion of shocks within this section to the types of shocks discussed above. Some of our case study findings will touch on shocks that are not directly observable in the data.

Not all shocks adversely affect regional economies. A region is adversely affected by a shock if in the year of the shock or the year thereafter, its economy experiences a substantial economic downturn, defined as a decline of more than 2.0 percentage points from the annual regional growth rate over the previous eight years.[32] However, if the eight-year growth rate was 4.0 percent or higher, then the region's growth rate had to decline by more than half of the previous eight-year average growth rate. If the region did not undergo a downturn in the year of the shock or the year thereafter, it is considered shock resistant.[33]

A region that undergoes an economic downturn as a result of a shock can be either resilient or nonresilient to the shock. A region is resilient if, within four years of the onset of the downturn, its annual growth rate returns to the eight-

31. An industry is considered to be in shock at the national level if it meets the same criteria as a national downturn shock: the industry's annual employment growth rate declines by more than 2.0 percentage points from its eight-year growth rate.

32. In the case that two separate industry shocks occur in the years preceding and concurrent with a downturn, one a national industry shock and one a local industry shock, we look at the first year of the shock to determine whether the shock was local or national in nature.

33. Note that our definition of an economic downturn is thus similar to our definition of an economic shock. The difference is that an economic downturn results from a decline in the growth rate of the metropolitan area's economy. Shocks reflect declines in either the national economy or specific industries.

year growth rate prior to the year the downturn occurred.[34] If it does not do so within four years, we term it nonresilient.[35]

Counting Shocks and Their Effects on Regions

Using our operational definition and employing metropolitan-level employment data from the economic forecasting firm Moody's Analytics for 1970–2007, we identify 1,476 distinct employment shocks to regions between 1978 and 2007. (See table 6A-1 in the appendix. An employment shock refers to a shock evident in employment data. GMP shocks refer to GMP data and are presented in appendix table 6A-2. We confine the discussion in this section to employment data.) Of these, national economic downturn shocks, which occurred during 1981, 1990, and 2000–01, accounted for 661 instances, of which 82 occurred in conjunction with a local industry shock and 173 occurred with a national industry shock.[36] There were 663 instances of local industry shocks and 407 instances of national industry shocks to regions. In addition, there were 292 downturns due to unidentifiable causes (that is, cases in which a region's employment growth rate declined by 2 or more percentage points from that of the prior eight-year average even in the absence of a national economic downturn or a national or local industry shock).

Of the 1,476 identifiable employment shocks, regions were resistant to almost half (47 percent): they did not suffer a serious economic downturn as a result of the shock. Regions were less likely to be resistant to national economic downturn shocks and national industry shocks than to local industry shocks. Not surprisingly, they were also less likely to be resistant to multiple shocks—that is, when two types of shocks occurred simultaneously. Regions were adversely affected—that is, they suffered a substantial economic downturn—in 775 (53 percent) of all identifiable shock incidents.

Regions suffering a downturn as a result of a shock were "resilient" 65 percent of the time—that is, they returned to at least their prior eight-year average

34. If a new "secondary" downturn begins before a region has been deemed resilient or nonresilient to the previous downturn, the region will have four years from the end of the secondary downturn in which to return to its eight-year growth rate from prior to the original downturn year.

35. We also ran separate models in which regions had five years in which to recover from a downturn. This had almost no impact on our quantitative findings.

36. There were three national economic shocks during the 1978–2007 period: 1981, 1990, and 2000–01. Since there are 361 metropolitan areas, that should have resulted in nearly 1,000 shock instances. However, we have not counted as shock instances those shocks that occurred while a region was still being affected by a prior shock. As a result, the total number of national economic shocks amounted to only 661 instances.

employment growth rate within a reasonably short period (four years). The average length of time from the onset of the downturn to recovery for a region was 2.9 years.

As table 6A-1 indicates, regions that were adversely affected by a shock were less likely to be resilient if the shock was a national economic downturn alone (to which 55 percent of adversely affected regions were resilient) than if it was a national industry shock alone (80 percent resilient) or a local industry shock alone (77 percent resilient).

There was virtually no regional variation in the extent to which metropolitan areas were resistant to shock or, once adversely affected, they were resilient. The one exception was that the percentage of metropolitan areas in the Northeast that were likely to be resilient in the face of an economic downturn (53 percent) was less than the national average (65 percent).

Explaining Shock Resistance and Resilience

We now move from description to analysis. We consider four questions:

—What accounts for economic downturns as we have defined them—that is, how do characteristics associated with areas that experience downturns of their regional economies compare with those of areas that do not?

—Why are some regions adversely affected when an economic shock occurs (that is, experience an economic downturn as we define it) while others are not (that is, are shock resistant)?

—Why are some areas resilient when experiencing an economic downturn, in that they return to their previous growth rate within a relatively short period of time, while others are not?

—What accounts for the length of time that it takes a region that is experiencing an economic downturn to recover (that is, to become resilient by our definition)?

We specify and estimate economic models addressed to each of these questions.

Data and Analysis

Our data for all of the models consist of total employment from 1970 through 2007 and gross metropolitan product from 1978 through 2007 for the 361 metropolitan statistical areas in the United States.[37] Since our definition of an economic downturn requires eight prior years of employment data, the years available for analysis are limited to the thirty years from 1978 through 2007 for

---

37. Since the Office of Management and Budget (OMB) has changed its definition of metropolitan areas over time, we aggregated our data from the county level when necessary to ensure consistency. The metropolitan area definitions that we use are from 2003.

total employment and to the twenty-two years from 1986 through 2007 for GMP. Each of the models includes only a subset of observations depending on the variable of interest.

The literature review presented earlier guides the selection of variables that we test for the models, though we were unable to find data to test all of the hypotheses. We employ a series of independent variables in the regressions that attempt to capture features of the different regions' economic structure, labor force, and demographic and other characteristics that, based on the literature related to economic resilience reviewed above, might be related to shock resistance and/or resilience. Our dependent variable in each case is a dummy variable that takes on a value of 1 when the event of interest—either an economic downturn or a recovery, depending on the model—takes place in a given year; the dummy variable takes a value of 0 when it does not. (See the appendix for data definitions and sources, regression results, and summary statistics.)

To test whether regional economic resilience is related to characteristics of the region's economy, we include the percentages of regional employment in selected major export industries: durable manufacturing, nondurable manufacturing, health care and social assistance, and tourism-related industries.[38] While we were unable to include data on employment in higher education (another export industry), we do include a variable consisting of a count of the number of research universities in the metropolitan area involved in high and very high research activity (according to the Carnegie Foundation's classification system). We also include two measures of industrial diversity—a Herfindahl index (which measures the extent to which the regional economy is concentrated in a few industries or diversified among many) and the number of export industries in the region—to assess the frequently asserted proposition that more diverse and less concentrated regional economies are more resilient. Finally, we also include a variable capturing the rate of growth prior to a downturn to test whether previously rapidly growing regions are more likely to experience economic downturns, to be susceptible to shock, and/or to be less resilient.

To examine the effect of labor force and labor market institutions, we include a skill variable—the percentage of the population aged twenty-five years and older who possess no more than a high school education—to assess whether areas with a higher proportion of low-skilled labor are likely to be more susceptible to economic downturns and less resilient in terms of recovery; we also assess demographic characteristics, including the percentage of the population that is

---

38. Health care is combined with social assistance at the two-digit NAICS level. We originally included professional, scientific, and technical services as another category of employment, but removed it from the model when it was found to be highly correlated with other variables and not statistically significant.

non-Hispanic black or Hispanic.[39] As one indicator of labor market flexibility, we include a variable for whether the region is wholly or predominantly in a state that has a right-to-work law, since, as noted above, such laws may make labor markets more flexible in a way that makes regions both more resilient and less shock resistant.[40]

We also include background characteristics of metropolitan areas that might affect shock resistance and/or resilience. To determine whether the size of a region matters (and also to standardize other variables for size differences), we include a lagged employment variable (lagged GMP in the case of the GMP models). Since some literature suggests that resilience is related to resource capacity, we include a variable on wages per employee as a proxy for regional personal income. We also include a variable on the age of the metropolitan area (as expressed by the number of years since the principal city attained a population of 50,000) as an indicator of infrastructure age. The proportion of the metropolitan population residing in the central city is used as a rough proxy for the influence of the central city in regional decisionmaking. Since some of the literature reviewed above argues that income inequality makes flexible regional responses more difficult, we use a variable that is the ratio of the income of high-income households to that of low-income households in the region.[41]

We also include variables capturing the three different kinds of shocks (national economic downturn shock, national industry shock, and local industry shock as previously defined) in tandem with each other or alone to test whether shock resistance and/or resilience are related to shock type.[42] Finally, to capture the effect of omitted variables that might vary by region, we include variables for each of the four regions of the country (Northeast, Midwest, West, and South); the West is the baseline region with which the other regions are compared.[43]

EXPLAINING THE OCCURRENCE OF REGIONAL ECONOMIC DOWNTURNS. Our first model examines the regional characteristics that influence whether or not a region suffers a downturn. The following are the main results from this model (shown in detail in tables 6A-3 and 6A-4):

39. For those demographic variables that we obtained from census data, we applied linear interpolation to obtain estimates for non-census years. See the appendix for summary statistics.

40. See Blumenthal, Wolman, and Hill (2009).

41. Technically, we measure the ratio of a region's household income at the 80th percentile to that of its household income at the 20th percentile.

42. It is, of course, possible to model each of the shocks separately to assess whether the relationship of the independent to the dependent variables differs by type of shock. Initial efforts to do so suggest that this may well be the case.

43. We also collected data on average July temperature. We discarded the temperature variable because we found it to be highly correlated with the regional dummies.

—A region's industry structure affects the probability that the region will experience a downturn. Higher employment in durable goods manufacturing as a percentage of total employment makes a region more susceptible to downturns in both employment and GMP, while higher employment in health care and social assistance makes it less so. A 1 percentage point increase in a region's employment in durable manufacturing increases a region's risk of seeing an employment downturn in a given year by 2.8 percentage points and increases its risk of GMP downturn by 2.4 percentage points, all else equal.[44]

—Having a large number of major export industries makes a region less likely to experience a downturn in both employment and in GMP, suggesting that the less concentrated the export sector (that is, the larger the number of industries that are major exporters), the more protected the region is from economic shocks.

—Regions in which a large share of the population has a low level of formal schooling (no more than a high school diploma) are more susceptible to downturns. An increase of 1 percentage point in population with a high school education or less was associated with an increase of 4.9 percentage points in the risk of experiencing a downturn in employment and 5.6 percentage points in the risk of experiencing a downturn in GMP.[45]

—Regions experiencing a national industry shock are more likely to have a downturn in employment and in GMP than regions facing other types of shocks.

—Metropolitan areas in the Northeast and South are less susceptible to downturns in employment than those in the West, but there is no significant difference among the regions with respect to downturns in GMP.

—A region in a state with a right-to-work law is 23.5 percentage points less likely to experience a downturn in GMP than one without such a law, all else equal. However, there is no relationship between right-to-work laws and employment downturns.

—Regions with large income gaps between high- and low-income households are more susceptible to downturns in employment (but not GMP) than those with lower levels of income inequality.

Most of these results make sense in light of the cyclical nature of employment and output patterns. Durable goods manufacturers will produce more and hire

44. See the appendix for additional notes on interpreting the results of a hazard model.

45. Endogeneity may be a concern insofar as the model does not account for migration. More working-age, educated adults may flee from regions that are hard hit in favor of regions that are doing well. To account for that, we also ran a specification that included a variable for lagged net migration as a percentage of the population. Migration data are available only since 1991, which severely limits the number of observations. When the model was run, all the variables discussed above retained their signs except for the number of export industries, which was no longer statistically significant.

more workers when demand for such goods rises and lay them off when demand falls (a cyclical effect). Export industries, many of which are in manufacturing, may have output and employment patterns that are more cyclical than those in other industries, but except in a general national economic downturn, they are unlikely to follow similar cycles. Thus, the more major export industries a region has, the less likely it is that all or a large number of those industries will suffer industry shocks simultaneously; lack of concentration in a small number of export industries protects regions against industry shocks substantial enough to trigger a regional economic downturn (a portfolio diversification effect). The findings on our education/human capital measure are also as expected. In response to a decline in the demand for their products or services, employers of all types are more likely to lay off nonprofessional and nonmanagerial workers, who typically have lower levels of formal education than professionals and managers.

Explaining Shock Resistance. Our second model examines what makes regions shock resistant once they have experienced a shock (that is, they do not suffer an economic downturn). In contrast to the first model, this model includes only instances in which a region has experienced some sort of identifiable shock. The principal results of this model (shown in detail in tables 6A-5 and 6A-6), are as follows:

—Some of the regional characteristics that make a region more or less likely to experience a downturn also affect the region's chances of being shock resistant once a shock has occurred. Regions with a high proportion of employment in durable goods manufacturing and a less educated population are less likely to be resistant to an employment shock, while regions with a large number of major export industries are more likely to be resistant to such a shock. These relationships are similar to those found in our first model for the occurrence of downturns, likely for the same reasons. A less educated workforce affects resistance to a GMP shock in the same way that it affects resistance to an employment shock. However, durable goods manufacturing and a large number of export industries do not make the region more resistant to a GMP shock.

—Regions whose export base is more diverse are more likely to be resistant to employment shocks.[46]

---

46. To allow for easier substantive interpretation, tables 6A-5 and 6A-6 display discrete effects, which measure the change in probability that occurs from increasing a variable from half a unit below its mean value to half a unit above while keeping all other variables at their means. For example, an increase in the number of export industries from 4.5 to 5.5 (half a unit below the mean to half a unit above), holding all other variables constant at their means, results in a decrease in the probability of being adversely affected by an employment shock by 2.3 percentage points. See the appendix for additional notes on interpreting the discrete effects of the logit models.

—Regions experiencing a national economic downturn shock in tandem with a local or national industry shock are more likely to experience an economic downturn.

—Regions that pay higher average wages are more likely to experience both employment and GMP downturns, all else equal.

EXPLAINING REGIONAL RESPONSES TO ECONOMIC SHOCKS. Our third model examines the regional characteristics that influence whether a metropolitan area economy that experienced an economic downturn was resilient—that is, whether it rebounded to its annual average eight-year growth rate prior to the downturn.

The results for this model are presented in tables 6A-7 and 6A-8. For employment they are broadly similar to those of the first model, the model accounting for regional economic downturns. Having a large percentage of the population with a high school education or less and having a large percentage of employment in durable manufacturing make metropolitan areas resilient to employment downturns caused by shocks. Just as cyclical demand for durable goods makes employment in that sector susceptible to downturns, the eventual uptick in demand allows it to be resilient. These variables may simply express the cyclical nature of durable goods manufacturing and of employment of low-skilled labor.

However, the results for GMP are quite different. There is no relationship between durable goods employment and GMP resilience, nor is there a relationship between educational attainment and GMP resilience. Taken together with the employment results, that suggests that regions with lower levels of education (and substantial employment in durable goods) were resilient as a result of employment rebounds (presumably during cyclical upswings in which employment in durable goods rebounded) but that they did not experience a major change in productivity.

The following are other important findings from the model:

—Right-to-work laws appear to have a positive effect on resilience with respect to both employment and GMP downturns. Regions with more flexible labor markets may be more likely to recover employment after it has been temporarily lost. The probability of a region being resilient to employment downturns is 8.3 percentage points greater and to a GMP downturn 5.1 percentage points greater if it is located in a state with a right-to-work law than if it is located in a state without such a law, all else equal.[47]

—Regional income inequality reduces employment resilience (that is, the greater the extent of income inequality, the less likely the region is to be

47. This is calculated with all other variables set to their mean values.

resilient) but increases GMP resilience (the greater the income inequality, the more likely the region is to be resilient).

—Having a large percentage of employment in health care and social assistance makes a region less resilient to both employment and GMP downturns. Because employment in these industries is not especially cyclical, a large share of health care and social assistance employment makes a region less susceptible to downturns (as shown above) but also makes it more difficult for the region to recover from downturns once they occur.

—Metropolitan areas in the West, while more likely to experience employment downturns, are significantly more likely to be resilient in the face of employment downturns than are other regions.

EXPLAINING LENGTH OF TIME TO RESILIENCE. In our fourth model the concern is not what determines whether a region is resilient but what determines how long it takes after a downturn occurs for a region to become resilient. The results are presented in tables 6A-9 and 6A-10.

Some of the results of this model are the same as those of the third model. A high percentage of the population with no more than a high school education, a high percentage of employment in durable manufacturing, a low percentage of employment in health care and social assistance, the presence of right-to-work laws, and low levels of income inequality all reduce the amount of time that it takes a region to become resilient following a regional employment downturn. For GMP downturns, as in the previous model, low health care and social assistance employment, right-to-work laws, and high inequality reduce the amount of time to become resilient.[48] In addition:

—For both employment and GMP downturns, the higher a region's pre-downturn growth rate, the longer it takes the region's economy to become resilient.

—Neither the degree of concentration of a region's economy as measured by its Herfindahl index nor the diversity of its export sector is significantly related to the time that it takes the region to become resilient to either employment or GMP downturns.

—The presence of a large number of research universities appears to enable a region's economy to recover more quickly from employment, but not GMP, downturns.

48. As with the first model, we re-estimated the fourth model, adding a variable for lagged net migration as a percent of the population. That enabled us to address potential sources of simultaneity, though the decreased number of observations made it more difficult to achieve statistically significant results. All the variables discussed achieved the same sign in the re-estimated model, with the exception of the 80–20 percentile income ratio.

Summary of the Quantitative Analysis

Our analysis shows that there are no "magic bullets" that both insulate regions from the harmful impacts of economic downturns and help them recover quickly from downturns. No regional characteristics or public policies do everything that one might like with respect to both employment and GMP. (Tables 6A-11 and 6A-12 present summary statistics for the data used in the employment and GMP models, respectively.) Table 6-1 summarizes our major findings on the impacts of regional characteristics and public policies on regions' vulnerability and resilience to downturns. It shows that some characteristics make regions less susceptible to downturns but also make it more difficult for them to recover. For example, a high percentage of employment in durable manufacturing and a poorly educated population make a region more likely to suffer from an employment downturn but make it easier for the region to recover from such a downturn, while a high percentage of employment in health care and social assistance has the opposite effects. The table also shows that some regional characteristics that have desirable impacts on employment have negligible or even undesirable impacts on GMP, and vice versa. For example, low educational attainment promotes employment resilience but has no effect on GMP resilience, while a high degree of income inequality promotes GMP resilience but actually undermines employment resilience. Finally, every regional characteristic or policy shown in table 6-1 affects some outcomes but has no meaningful impact on others.

There are two regional characteristics or policies that seem to have some desirable impacts and no undesirable ones: export industry diversity and right-to-work laws. However, it is difficult to diversify a region's export base through intentional action, especially in a short period of time, and a diversified export base is more likely to be attainable in a large metropolitan area than in a small one. Our findings on right-to-work laws suggest that labor market flexibility is beneficial, but there are forms of labor market flexibility besides the wage flexibility that may exist in nonunion firms. Those other forms of flexibility may exist independently of unions or right-to-work laws but be geographically correlated with them.[49] In addition, right-to-work laws may be undesirable for other reasons (such as their impact on worker representation or wage inequality) even if they are beneficial for resilience outcomes. Therefore, our findings on right-to-work laws should not be interpreted as an endorsement of those laws.

49. For extended discussions of alternative forms of labor market flexibility, see Piore (1986) and Piore and Schrank (2008).

Table 6-1. *Major Impacts of Regional Characteristics and Public Policies on Resilience Outcomes*[a]

Regional characteristic or public policy	Immunity to downturn		Shock resistance		Resilience		Speed of resilience	
	Employment	GMP	Employment	GMP	Employment	GMP	Employment	GMP
Durable manufacturing employment	−	−	−	0	+	0	+	0
Low educational attainment	−	−	−	−	+	0	+	0
Export industry diversity	+	+	+	0	0	0	0	0
State right-to-work law	0	+	0	0	+	+	+	+
High income inequality	−	0	0	−	−	+	−	+

Source: Tables 6A-3–6A-10 of this chapter.

a. Plus sign (+) indicates a positive impact that is substantively significant and statistically significant; minus sign (−) indicates a negative impact that is substantively significant and statistically significant; zero (0) indicates an impact that is not statistically significant or, if statistically significant, not substantively important.

Case Studies of Regional Resilience and Nonresilience

The quantitative analyses presented above describe and explain regional economic downturns, shock resistance, and resilience after a downturn. But they do not provide information on the processes that occurred, on the nature of interventions or changes in behavior, or on their effects. In short, the quantitative analysis lacks depth and context. To provide a richer understanding of economic shock and resilience, we undertook intensive case studies in six regions: Charlotte, Cleveland, Detroit, Grand Forks, Hartford, and Seattle. We chose regions to reflect different kinds of shocks (cyclical shocks for Detroit and Cleveland; industry shocks for Charlotte, Hartford, and Seattle; and a major natural disaster shock and military base closing for Grand Forks) and different degrees of resilience in response to those shocks (from high resilience in Charlotte and Seattle to lack of resilience in Hartford in the 1980s, in Grand Forks in the 1990s, and in Cleveland and Detroit since 2000). While we make no claim that these six regions are representative of regions nationally, they do vary in the kinds of shocks that they have experienced and in their responses. Table 6-2 summarizes the major shocks and responses in the case study regions.

We made at least two trips to each of the regions, during which we conducted semi-structured interviews with individuals who were major "players" in area economic development (including important private firms in the region), were owners or managers of firms in the region's major export industries, or were reputed to be acute observers and/or analysts of the regional economy. We conducted additional telephone interviews with selected individuals whom we were unable to interview during our trips. We identified interviewees through a "snowball" process that began with the initial contacts that we had in each region and ultimately expanded the pool through referrals to other potential interviewees and organizations of interest. In most regions we interviewed representatives of organizations concerned with the region's economic future, including individuals from public and private economic development organizations, local and regional government, trade association or cluster association organizations, workforce development programs, universities (including both researchers, as observers and analysts, and officials, as participants), foundations, leading private sector firms in the export sector, and the business and economics desks of local newspapers.

Table 6-2. Case Study Regions

Region	Location	Major shocks	Response	Population (2000)[a]	Major export industries
Detroit	Midwest	National economic downturn shocks (auto sales)	Resilient to shocks in the early 1980s and early 1990s; nonresilient to the 2000 national economic downturn shock	4.5 million	Auto manufacturing
Cleveland	Midwest	National economic downturn shocks	Resilient to shocks in the early 1980s and early 1990s; nonresilient to the 2000 national economic downturn shock	2.1 million	Auto manufacturing
Charlotte	South	Industry shock (textile manufacturing in the 1980s)	Resilient; shifted away from textile manufacturing to banking	1.3 million	Textile manufacturing; banking
Grand Forks	Midwest	Natural disaster (1996 flood); military base closing	Nonresilient	100,000	Military; agriculture; higher education
Seattle	West	Industry shocks (aerospace in the 1980s; information technology in the 2000s)	Nonresilient in the 1980s; resilient in the 1990s and 2000s	3.0 million	Information technology; aerospace
Hartford	Northeast	Industry shocks (aerospace in the early 1980s; insurance in the late 1980s)	Resilient in the early 1980s; nonresilient in the late 1980s	1.1 million	Insurance; aerospace

Source: Authors' analysis.
a. Rounded to nearest 100,000.

Detroit

The Detroit region has been dominated for nearly 100 years by the "Big Three" automakers (now Ford, General Motors, and Chrysler) and their suppliers.[50] It now faces the decline of those companies and their supply chains as a result of increasing competition from abroad and from lower-cost production sites within the United States.

Periodic regional economic downturns as a result of economic shocks have been the norm for the Detroit region. National economic downturns are shocks that disproportionately affect the sales and therefore the production of motor vehicles as consumers cut back on their purchases of durable goods. During the economic downturn that Detroit experienced from 1979 to 1982, employment in the region declined by 276,660 jobs (15.2 percent) and employment in the automobile industry fell by 69,900 (33.9 percent). During a similar period of decline a decade later, the region's employment fell by 51,600 jobs (2.6 percent) between 1989 and 1991. The downturn that began in 2000, however, has been emphatically not normal; it has been far more severe and more prolonged. From 2000 through 2008, the Detroit region lost 304,670 jobs (13.7 percent) overall and employment in the automobile industry fell from 240,465 to 205,350 (or 14.6 percent).

REGIONAL ECONOMIC RESILIENCE/NONRESILIENCE. In the past, the Detroit region was resilient to economic shocks. When the national economy suffered, the automobile industry and thus the region suffered, and when the economy expanded, the auto industry and region grew. The region ultimately was resilient to economic downturns that occurred as a result of shocks in 1979 and 1989–90.[51] Total employment rebounded after each national recession and actually increased from its 1978 level to its peak of 2,223,000 in 2000.

However, the most recent shock and response has been a different story. Prior to 2000, the region averaged an eight-year annual employment growth rate of 1.9 percent. Between 2000 and 2001 employment fell by 3.0 percent

50. For purposes of the data presented in this chapter, the Detroit region consists of the Detroit Metropolitan Statistical Area (Wayne County, which includes the city of Detroit, plus the contiguous counties of Lapeer, Livingston, Macomb, Oakland, and St. Clair). However, Washtenaw County, home of Ann Arbor and the University of Michigan, is increasingly linked to the officially defined Detroit metropolitan area through economic ties, and our discussion acknowledges that link.

51. Prior to the 1979 shock, the Detroit region's average eight-year employment growth rate was 2.2 percent. However, the annual growth rate was -7.9 percent between 1979 and 1980 before rebounding by 14 percentage points by 1983 and by an additional 0.9 percentage point over the next year. Prior to the 1989 shock, the Detroit region's average eight-year employment growth rate was 3.0 percent. However, the annual growth rate was -0.4 percent between 1989 and 1990 before rebounding by 4 percentage points by 1993.

and continued to decline every year after that through 2009. Over that nine-year period, total employment in the region declined by 20.1 percent.

EXPLAINING RESILIENCE/NONRESILIENCE. The explanation for resilience to the earlier shock-induced downturns is obvious: the national economy simply recovered. There was virtually unanimous agreement among those we interviewed that the recovery had nothing to do with policy or strategic interventions but rather to the national economic turnaround. In effect, the region simply "held its breath" until things got better.

The Detroit region has not bounced back from the 2000–01 downturn as it did after the previous two economic downturns, and the effects of the national recession that began in 2008 have been piled on top of that. As one of our interviewees said, the region was hit by a truck, and no one is resilient when hit by a truck. The collective regional response has been characterized as a movement to hopelessness and despair from earlier denial in the face of trends that were long evident (indeed, during the past forty years regional leaders did little to adjust to trends in the automobile industry that some observers predicted would ultimately have a severe long-term effect on the region's economy).

Business and civic leaders now publicly state (and many political leaders believe, though they do not always say so publicly) that while the automobile industry still will play the major role in the regional economy, it is not going to be the job engine for the region that it has been in the past, at least with respect to providing substantial employment for relatively low-skilled workers. However, most of the people that we interviewed predicted (or hoped) that the region would remain the international center of automobile research, development, and engineering and that those parts of the industry would continue to be the major driver of the regional economy. No one that we interviewed thought that employment in motor vehicle production, particularly in automobile assembly work, was likely ever to return to anywhere close to pre-2000 levels.

The difficulty that the region has had in developing a collective response to and strategy for the downturn is, in part, a reflection of its historical legacy of adversarial and confrontational relationships. That legacy includes not only union-management conflict but also conflict between blacks and whites, the city of Detroit and its suburbs, and one county and another. As a consequence, positive social capital has been in short supply and there is little history of cooperation at the regional level or across jurisdictional or racial lines. Despite that, many interviewees agreed that the severity of the economic downturn has resulted in greater recognition of the need for cooperation and that some collaborative efforts are now taking place.

In addition, many of those we interviewed said that the prolonged domination of the Big Three created a "culture of dependence and entitlement." Area residents have long believed that they and their children will be able to find well-paid employment in the auto industry with relatively little education. Several of our interviewees said that suppliers to the auto industry were characterized by a "procurement culture": they have been able to prosper through procurement contracts from the Big Three and consequently did not try seriously to find other markets. This "culture," according to interviewees who mentioned it, has stifled entrepreneurship, risk taking, and small business creation not tied to the automobile industry in the region.

RESPONSES.   There have been efforts to devise strategies and responses, some by existing organizations and some by new or restructured ones. The Detroit Regional Chamber of Commerce runs several traditional business attraction and promotion programs, including the Detroit Regional Economic Partnership. The chamber of commerce, along with several other economic development organizations and local governments in the region, is also one of the leading promoters of a plan to develop "Aerotropolis," a major transportation and logistics center encompassing both Detroit's Metropolitan Airport and the Willow Run Airport in Ypsilanti and the surrounding areas. Detroit Renaissance, a CEO-led organization that emerged after the Detroit riot in 1967 and focused primarily on the city of Detroit for most of its history, launched a plan for regional economic development in 2006 ("Road to Renaissance"). However, the organization changed its name in 2009 to Business Leaders for Michigan and directed its concerns completely to the state level, with a focus on reducing business costs (particularly taxes) in the state. City and county economic development organizations (such as the Detroit Economic Growth Corporation in the city and similar county-level organizations) continue to perform their traditional functions of promoting and attracting economic development in their own jurisdictions. The most innovative of these is Ann Arbor Spark in Washtenaw County, which serves as the county's economic development and business attraction organization; however, while its goal is locating companies within the county, its leaders told us that they help businesses locate elsewhere in the region or state if a better location can be found.

Foundations have played an increasing role in the region. The New Economy Initiative for Southeast Michigan, sponsored by the Community Foundation of Detroit, was set up in 2008 to help the region shift to what the initiative termed the "new economy." It was funded with $100 million from ten foundations with links to the region, including the Ford and Kresge foundations—which, after the founding companies built their fortunes within the region, have until recently devoted most of their funding elsewhere. The Kresge Foundation also recently launched a new initiative, Re-Imagining Detroit 2020, an effort to coordinate the foundation's activities and those of other organizations focused on development in the city. Re-Imagining Detroit 2020, which has the support of Detroit mayor Dave Bing, is focused on nine modules—the green economy, entrepreneurial development, urban health care, land use reform, the Woodward Creative Corridor, mass transit, neighborhood strategies, education, and arts and culture.

The realization that the automobile industry is not going to bounce back as it has in the past has produced a variety of new proposals, some serious and some more fanciful, for regional development alternatives. They include proposals to promote the Detroit region as an amenity-rich area to attract highly educated professionals (since high levels of human capital are now seen as critical to the economic development of the region); a potential leader in wind power and water resources; a region well-placed to produce the next generation of batteries for electric automobiles; a major supplier in the defense production industry through diversification of automobile production technologies and facilities; a major medical center and exporter of health care services (building on the presence of several major research hospitals and medical centers and the legacy of extensive health insurance benefits provided by the automobile industry); and an international transshipment center (because of its location on the border with Canada, the presence of major highways used to ship cargo across the NAFTA corridor, and the presence of an airport with direct flights to China and other developing economies). However, virtually all of these proposals are either at the very beginning of the implementation stage or are still being developed. Every one of the plans will require long-term commitment and development before it yields visible economic results.

The region's economic development policymakers and practitioners have few overarching goals or strategies that could show immediate effects on the economy, outside of efforts to promote entrepreneurship in the region, most notably through the establishment of TechTown, a small business incubator with a wide variety of services located on the campus of Wayne State University. TechTown has a variety of partners and funders, including the New Economy Initiative, the Ewing Marion Kauffman Foundation, and the city of Detroit. Efforts are also under way to encourage collaborative research and the commercialization of resulting concepts and products among the three major universities in or near the region, Wayne State University, the University of Michigan, and Michigan State University.

Many proposals are designed to deal with the problems of the city of Detroit rather than those of the region. Kresge's Re-Imagining Detroit, for example, focuses almost exclusively on the city, which everyone that we interviewed agreed is in desperate shape. While the city suffers from population loss, poverty, and crime, the concern most often expressed by those we interviewed was the dysfunctional school system. Interviewees described Detroit public schools as some of the worst in the nation, although many noted that recent actions taken by Robert Bobb, an emergency financial manager appointed by the governor for a year and subsequently reappointed, were at last beginning to show hope.

At the rhetorical level most (but not all) of the people that we interviewed emphasized that while the economic problem is a regional one, it cannot be solved without successfully addressing the severe social, economic, and fiscal problems of the city of Detroit. However, some argue that it is unclear whether improving the condition of the city is indeed a precondition for regional economic revival. As one interviewee observed, until recently the region was doing very well thanks to the automobile industry while the city had been declining for decades. It is unknown whether the new focus on the importance of the city to the region is a late recognition of the city's role or a matter of "political correctness" and political necessity that provides actors with the political legitimacy to participate in regional interactions—which, nonetheless, will not bring the city many benefits.

The most important activities related to the region's economic future are being undertaken by the individual Big Three auto firms and their suppliers as they struggle to maintain their viability. While some suppliers have made inroads in diversifying to meet the needs of related industries (such as defense), those efforts have been limited, especially because of the past rebounds in the auto industry, which drew suppliers' attention away from needed changes. Other industries, notably health care and higher education, have achieved greater importance, both in their impact on the regional economy and as explicit targets of area decisionmakers for leveraging economic development.

RESULTS. Currently there are few, if any, tangible effects of the above actions on Detroit's regional economy. Most of those interviewed acknowledged that the current economic situation was the result of the region's long-term dependence on the automobile industry, which had brought them unparalleled (though somewhat cyclical) prosperity but was now coming to an end. Most interviewees did not regret that dependence and the benefits that it brought, although many did regret regional leaders' inability to see some time ago that the region's motor vehicle industry would decline. Even the most optimistic felt that the effects of any changes will take years to show substantial results.

Cleveland

The Cleveland region was traditionally a manufacturing powerhouse, but between 1980 and 2005 it lost 42.5 percent of its manufacturing jobs (over 110,000).[52] Because many of its primary industries have been related to automobile and truck manufacturing, Cleveland, like Detroit, is susceptible to regional economic downturns when national downturns occur. Thus, the Cleveland region experienced downturns during the national economic shocks around 1981, 1990, and 2000. It did not experience additional local industry shocks. It lost 98,500 jobs between 1979 and 1982. The 1991 downturn was smaller, with the region losing 24,450 jobs between 1990 and 1992. Each year from 2000 through 2007, the Cleveland region experienced a loss in employment, losing a total of 64,000 jobs over the period.

REGIONAL ECONOMIC RESILIENCE/NONRESILIENCE. Is the Cleveland region resilient to economic shocks? Its similarity to Detroit continues: when the national economy suffered, the region followed, and when the national economy expanded, regional employment increased. The region ultimately was resilient to economic downturns that occurred as a result of shocks in 1979 and 1990. Total employment rebounded after each national recession downturn, increasing to a new peak. Although it took ten years for the region to regain its 1979 level of employment, by 1983 it had regained its prior growth rate and employment was increasing by 3.7 percent. The recovery from the 1990 downturn occurred even more quickly. However, the downturn that began as a result of the 2000 shock has been different. The region has yet to recover and has been fighting to remain on a positive trajectory. The eight-year average employment growth rate for Cleveland between 1979 and 2006 ranged from −0.85 percent to 1.85 percent.[53] And despite its former resilience, Cleveland is no longer winning the fight to bounce back: employment growth has been negative every year but one since 2000.

EXPLAINING RESILIENCE/NONRESILIENCE. The Cleveland region's resilience to previous shock-induced downturns, like Detroit's, reflected the recovery of the national economy. The regional economy is driven by manufacturing,

52. The Cleveland region is the Cleveland-Elyria-Mentor Metropolitan Statistical Area, which consists of five counties: Cuyahoga, Geauga, Lake, Lorain, and Medina. In 2000, almost two-thirds of the region's 2.1 million population was contained in Cuyahoga County (1.39 million residents/65 percent), with 478,403 located in the city of Cleveland (22 percent of the region). Prior to 1993 the metropolitan area consisted of only four counties; Lorain was not included.

53. It is important to note that the first eight-year average employment growth rate in our study, for 1970–78, was just under 1 percent a year for the Cleveland region. By 1979, Cleveland's growth trajectory had already slowed; at no time during our study did it reach 2 percent.

with its strength in producers' durables, making it susceptible to national shocks. It has, however, avoided local industry shocks.

Leaders in the region recognized as early as 1980 the need to engage in economic development to diversify and expand the local economy, hiring both the RAND Corporation and McKinsey and Company to conduct studies on the economy and to propose strategies. Numerous studies have been conducted since that time to assess the economy and recommend actions to make Cleveland more competitive. Unlike Detroit, this is a region whose leaders understood that an economic transition was occurring and that they needed to respond. Foundations, corporations, and governments spent significant sums during the last twenty-five years to address the region's challenges. Despite their efforts, Cleveland has continued to struggle.

In 1992 an editorial stressed the important role of manufacturing to the Cleveland economy:

> Manufacturing matters to Cleveland, and it is a major reason why it has survived the current recession as well as it has. The recessions of 1979 and 1982 flushed out uncompetitive firms and disciplined labor and, more importantly, management. The result is a highly competitive manufacturing segment, where productivity continues to grow.[54]

While that was accurate in 1992, when Cleveland was able to recover from the national downturn of 1991, more recent experiences suggest that changes in national and international markets have left Cleveland with a mix of firms and industries that make the region especially susceptible to downturns.

RESPONSES. The Cleveland region has experience with the "typical" range of responses. Its business leaders asked both academics and consultants to provide analyses and recommendations. It has created, restructured, and merged economic development organizations. A strong philanthropic community, led by the Gund and Cleveland foundations, has invested in the community, funding community development, physical redevelopment, research studies, and many other types of contributions. Despite the steps that its leaders took, the region continued to experience slow job growth. Beginning in 2000, that turned into a slow decline in employment, with virtually no growth in real gross regional product (2.7 percent from 2000 to 2007) and in wages per worker (1.3 percent over the same seven-year period).

Two notable sets of responses occurred. The first was in the early 1980s in the wake of the 1979 recession with the election of George Voinovich as mayor;

---

54. Hill (1992).

the formation of Cleveland Tomorrow by the CEOs of the fifty largest Cleveland businesses; and the funding of studies conducted by RAND and McKinsey on the Cleveland economy and projects resulting from these activities. The second major phase, which occurred in the early 2000s, involved consolidation and coordination. Foundations across a broader seventeen-county region, which included the Cleveland region, began coordinating their resources and focusing on a regional approach. Meanwhile, the business organizations in the city of Cleveland consolidated to remove duplication, improve coordination, and lower their combined operating costs as they created a renewed set of economic development intermediaries with a narrower agenda.

After its formation in 1981, Cleveland Tomorrow focused on jobs and economic vitality.[55] Some of the initiatives that Cleveland Tomorrow supported included the following:

—Work in Northeast Ohio Council, an independent labor-management organization established in 1981 that promoted productivity programs and quality of work life programs in manufacturing industries.

—Cleveland Advanced Manufacturing Program (CAMP), a partnership among the state government, Cleveland Tomorrow, local universities, and the community college to expand research and services to promote advanced manufacturing, beginning in 1984. CAMP was later incorporated into the federal Manufacturing Extension Partnership's network of manufacturing assistance centers and in 2006 was renamed the Manufacturing Advocacy and Growth Network (MAGNET).

—Center for Venture Development, created and funded with grants from the Cleveland and Gund foundations and the Greater Cleveland Growth Association to assist entrepreneurs with developing business plans, building their boards, identifying professional services, and finding funding.

—Technology Leadership Council, established in 1988 to coordinate development activities across the region's highest-potential technology sectors: bioscience and health care, information technology, electronics, polymers and advanced materials, and power and propulsion. This organization was succeeded by NorTech in 1999.

Although our interviewees generally identified Cleveland Tomorrow as an "effective" and "impactful" organization, it was unable by itself to put the Cleveland region on the path to sustained higher growth or to avoid the major downturn in the regional economy that began in 2000 and continues today. While

55. Cleveland Tomorrow Committee (1981).

the effort of Cleveland Tomorrow on the regional economy is difficult to assess, its impact declined over time. Many of the founding CEOs were with companies that subsequently were acquired and/or moved. The CEOs had more demands on their time, decreasing the time that they had to devote to civic causes and weakening the personal connections among them. The leaders had less autonomy over corporate money as their firms became branches of larger firms. As the CEOs of the large companies became less available, smaller firms became more important in the economy and nonprofit organizations, particularly universities and hospitals, also became more important to both the economy and civic leadership.

Partly as a response to the sustained downturn after 2000, Cleveland Tomorrow and two other regional business groups, the Greater Cleveland Growth Association and the Greater Cleveland Roundtable, merged in 2004 to form the Greater Cleveland Partnership (GCP). The stated rationale for the merger, according to one of the board members, "was to use savings from removing duplication to expand economic development activities." However, the new organization also reflected the change in composition of Cleveland's regional leadership. Whereas Cleveland Tomorrow consisted of CEOs from the fifty largest companies, the sixty board members of the Greater Cleveland Partnership included twenty-six members from large firms, fourteen from small firms, three from mid-sized firms, eight from professional services, three from higher education (Case Western Reserve University, Cleveland State University, and Cuyahoga Community College), and six others. The new organization reflects the growing role of nonprofit institutions as well as banks and law firms. One interviewee explained that banks have replaced utilities and manufacturers as the "go to" companies.

The Greater Cleveland Partnership decided to adopt a focused, holistic economic development strategy. It supports five intermediary development organizations that now work on a broad regional scale that includes the Cleveland, Akron, and Youngstown metropolitan areas and much of nonmetropolitan northeast Ohio. Two of the intermediaries are from the original set established by Cleveland Tomorrow: NorTech and MAGNET. BioEnterprise grew out of a NorTech initiative on bioscience.

Foundations have always played an important role in the Cleveland area, but their role has increased markedly in the economic development arena during the past decade. The two primary foundations in the region are the Cleveland and Gund foundations, which have supported economic development by funding research, supporting initiatives introduced by Cleveland Tomorrow, and participating in other regional projects. For example, the Gund Foundation funded the 1980 Cleveland Tomorrow Committee and McKinsey study and the Cleveland

Foundation funded the 1980 RAND study to develop regional economic indicators and evaluate economic development opportunities for the Cleveland region.

After many years of struggling to make a difference in economic development in the region, often supporting bricks-and-mortar projects as well as various business-led initiatives, the Cleveland and Gund foundations, together with the GAR Foundation of Akron, were instrumental in creating the Fund for Our Economic Future, a collaboration of philanthropic organizations in Northeast Ohio. Formed in 2004, this collaboration of seventy private and corporate foundations in sixteen Northeastern Ohio counties adopted a larger regional focus, incorporating all of Northeast Ohio rather than the Cleveland region alone. The fund's goal is to frame a regional economic development agenda "that can lead to long-term economic transformation," track overall regional progress, and financially support highly promising initiatives. It brings more foundation players to the table and gets them to agree on a common strategy. The fund follows a strategy similar to that of Cleveland Tomorrow by using its resources to fund intermediary organizations. As mentioned above, many of the organizations that it funds are entities that grew out of Cleveland Tomorrow's initial programs.

Five intermediary organizations are supported by both the Greater Cleveland Partnership and the Fund for Our Economic Future: Team NEO, NorTech, JumpStart, MAGNET, and BioEnterprise. The most important departure from previous efforts is a determined concentration on a regional approach and the creation of a set of intermediaries, each with a fairly narrow focus and a commitment to performance measurement.

Team NEO was formed in 2003 to market the greater Northeast Ohio region and attract firms. As an interviewee explained, the group was formed to respond to the common complaint that marketing organizations focused on specific jurisdictions instead of the entire region.

NorTech is the successor organization to the Technology Leadership Council, established in 1988 by Cleveland Tomorrow. NorTech supported the creation of BioEnterprise, facilitated the formation of the Ohio Polymer Strategy Council, and was a founding member of the Ohio Technology Partnership. This set of programs is intended to increase entrepreneurial support and activity substantially, drawing on Northeast Ohio's technological strengths in biosciences and health care, polymers, advanced materials and manufacturing, electronics, information and communications technology, and advanced energy.

JumpStart was formed in 2002 to stimulate early-stage business development and investment by providing financial, technical, and managerial support to new and promising enterprises. It has three primary tasks: to connect new entrepreneurs with successful entrepreneurs, provide technical assistance, and assist with venture development. The programs provided by JumpStart are designed to address some of the challenges to entrepreneurship, such as establishing personal connections and securing adequate capital.

MAGNET, the Manufacturing Advocacy and Growth Network, assists small and medium-size manufacturers with technological modernization, work reorganization, product quality, and innovation. Its goal is to support, educate, and champion manufacturing to transform the region's economy into a powerful, global player. It provides manufacturing process and productivity improvement services, product design and development services, and fee-for-service training. It also brokers commercial and university intellectual property in selected manufacturing areas and delivers federal and state assistance programs for small and medium-sized manufacturers.

BioEnterprise (BioE), created in 2002, provides management counsel, clinical access, business development, and capital access services to newly forming bioscience companies, with the aim of accelerating their growth. The Cleveland Clinic, University Hospitals Health System, Case Western Reserve University, and Summa Health System jointly committed to raising a half-billion dollars to support new ventures in the biosciences. By 2005, the joint initiative had raised more than half of the necessary funds and had created, recruited, and accelerated expansion of more than forty companies. As with JumpStart and TeamNeo, BioE was the outgrowth of a McKinsey report that recommended that the entity be a catalyst for health care services and innovations and proposed two primary strategies: focus on small private companies that need funding to grow and promote broader health care initiatives across the region. That included supporting research institutes, attracting larger companies, helping companies expand, addressing workforce development, and advocating for changes in state policy.

RESULTS. Cleveland's leaders have reorganized Cleveland's economic development institutions, focused on the macro-region, and undertaken the series of initiatives described above, which can be considered at the forefront of current economic development strategy and thinking, but it is too soon to assess the effectiveness of their activities. One area of concern with respect to future outcomes is an incipient split in the Fund for Our Economic Future. The Cleveland Foundation was the largest investor in the fund and supported the broad regional effort through two rounds of funding. In 2009 it largely pulled out of the fund in a very public manner. The Cleveland Foundation's withdrawal may be the result of the fund's insistence on regional funding approaches combined with the foundation's desire to be more directly active in investing in development activities in the city of Cleveland and to support development activities that are responsive to strategies developed by its leadership and board.

The region's economy continues to stagnate, but the economic development activities described in this case study may have softened the blow and laid the groundwork for future growth. However, even the most aggressive and innovative approaches to regional economic development may be insufficient to address a forced economic transformation on the scale of that facing Cleveland.

Charlotte

The economic face of the Charlotte region during much of the twentieth century was manufacturing, which accounted for about one-third of the region's jobs in 1980.[56] Textile mills, textile product manufacturing, and apparel manufacturing accounted for more than half of manufacturing jobs and just under one-sixth of all jobs in 1980. Global competition eroded the profitability of those three subsectors between 1980 and 2005, when they collectively shed 49,800 jobs, declining 82 percent, even as the region as a whole had a net gain of 393,032 jobs over the period, for a 96.3 percent gain.

While the manufacturing sector was in decline, Charlotte banks grew, and in the wake of federal banking deregulation Charlotte became the nation's second-largest financial center (measured by assets).[57] Bank mergers and acquisitions allowed the region to prosper even as employment in its textile and apparel industries declined at a precipitous rate. By 2005, manufacturing had dropped to 10 percent of regional employment (from over 30 percent in 1980) and finance and insurance had doubled (from 3.7 to 7.4 percent).[58] Jobs in credit intermediation and related activities (commercial banking and related industries, such as mortgages and credit cards) increased 287 percent during 1980–2005, growing from 9,000 to 35,000.

The Charlotte region experienced four shocks over the period that we examined. Three of them included national economic downturn shocks in 1981, 1990, and 2000, each of which resulted in a regional downturn in the Charlotte economy. In each case, Charlotte never lost more than 1.3 percent of employment (5,000 jobs, 7,000 jobs, and 2,000 jobs, respectively), and the region proved resilient to the shock within three years. The other shock, to which the region was resistant, was an industry shock that occurred in 1984 as a result of

56. The Charlotte Metropolitan Statistical Area includes York County in South Carolina and five counties in North Carolina: Anson, Cabarrus, Gaston, Mecklenburg, and Union.

57. The ranking of the top ten banking centers appears on the Charlotte Chamber of Commerce website in a table titled "Major Banking Centers" (www.charlottechamber.com/business-profile/leading-financial-center/ [April 30, 2010]). The source for the table is SNL Securities, December 2008. The asset totals include Bank of America's acquisition of Merrill Lynch.

58. Some manufacturing firms have replaced a segment of their permanent manufacturing positions with temps in order to better handle shifts in demand, suggesting that the decline of employment within manufacturing may not be as drastic as it appears.

transformations occurring in textiles and apparel manufacturing. The textile mills industry also had an industry shock in 1981, but that was piggybacked on the national economic downturn shock.

The decline in total manufacturing employment resulted primarily from the decline of the textile and apparel industries. Textile and apparel manufacturers, unable to integrate advanced machinery and move into higher value-added product lines, struggled to keep their firms afloat; many did not survive. A few manufacturing sectors with at least 6,000 employees in 2005 had major employment gains during 1980–2005, including plastics and rubber products (58.6 percent), fabricated metal products (61.7 percent), and transportation equipment (94.9 percent). Their growth was connected to the expansion of motorsports in the region.

The most recent national recessionary period, beginning in the late 2000s, resulted in the collapse of large financial corporations across the nation, and the dependence of the Charlotte region's economy on financial institutions made it especially vulnerable to the recession. The Bureau of Labor Statistics showed a decline of 5.7 percent in jobs for the region between 2007, the beginning of the financial crisis, and 2009.

In December 2008, San Francisco–based Wells Fargo took over Charlotte-based Wachovia. Bank of America, another local presence, acquired Merrill Lynch in the fall of 2008. The acquisitions by Wells Fargo and Bank of America gave them redundant employees in some divisions, leading to employment reductions. Wachovia, weakened by the troubled mortgages that it inherited in its 2006 acquisition of Golden West Financial, had begun employee reductions even before its takeover by Wells Fargo. The cumulative effect for the Charlotte region of these financial upheavals was substantial employment loss. By mid-2009, mortgage-related jobs had declined from their 2006 high; employment in commercial banking declined from its 2007 peak; and jobs in administrative and support services fell significantly from their 2008 high point.[59] Job loss within the financial institutions in the region was one part of the recessionary picture. Reduction of past years' generous salaries and bonuses had additional recessionary effects on the regional economy.

REGIONAL ECONOMIC RESILIENCE/NONRESILIENCE. As noted above, the Charlotte region was resilient in the face of three national economic downturns between 1978 and 2007 and was resistant to a national industry shock that occurred in 1984. The region's downturns tracked national economic downturns,

59. Data in this paragraph are from Employment Security Commission of North Carolina, "Industry Information: Employment and Wages by Industry, 1990 to Most Recent" (www.ncesc1.com/lmi/industry/industryMain-NEW.asp).

and its recoveries tracked national upturns. Leading into the 1981 national economic downturn, the region's prior average eight-year employment growth rate was 3.1 percent. Between 1981 and 1982, employment declined by 1.3 percent, but by 1983 the economy was growing again, at an annual rate of 7.4 percent. The region's annual growth rate did not turn negative again until the 1990–91 national economic downturn, when employment declined by 1.2 percent before rebounding to 4.3 percent two years later. Employment was essentially flat between 2000 and 2002. In 2005, growth had returned to a healthy 4.4 percent. Much of the regional resilience throughout those twenty years was a function of the shift from manufacturing to tradable services, which both financed the national recoveries and insulated the regional economy.

EXPLAINING RESILIENCE/NONRESILIENCE. The transformation of the regional economy was not the result of conscious policy or planning by the public sector or by civic alliances. Instead it was largely due to the success of Charlotte's banking sector. Beginning in the 1980s, the region's banks experienced explosive growth, and they became the region's new economic engine, cushioning manufacturing's decline. Two interacting factors accounted for Charlotte's rise in banking and finance: favorable state laws and two entrepreneurial corporate banking CEOs who took advantage of them.

Historically, branch banking had not been allowed in most U.S. states; the fear of monopoly by the large Northeastern banks led most states to prohibit branching.[60] Given the legal authority by their state legislature to branch statewide, North Carolina banks learned how to acquire other banks, merge their operations, and run the merged bank as a branch facility, exhibiting expansion-minded behavior as early as the 1950s. In 1982, North Carolina National Bank was expanding beyond state lines fully two years ahead of any competitors and before the Supreme Court ruled that interstate banking compacts were permitted. Southeastern states' legislatures, including North Carolina's, passed permissive regional reciprocal banking bills, the most uniform collection of state banking laws that existed in 1984, providing a common banking market. Experience with handling multiple branches statewide and the Southeastern compact's protection of interstate expansion gave North Carolina banks yet another advantage in going nationwide when interstate banking was declared constitutional by the U.S. Supreme Court in 1985.[61] Although it would be a decade before Congress passed the Riegle-Neal Interstate Banking and Branching Efficiency Act of 1994, repealing restrictions on interstate banking, banks were allowed before then to service large

60. Roussakis (1997, p. 43).
61. Frieder (1988).

borrowers through loan offices outside of their state and to conduct nationwide advertising for deposit customers.[62]

While the Southern state laws permitting branch banking provided the opportunity for expansion of Charlotte's financial sector, two visionary figures, Hugh McColl and Edward Crutchfield, seized that opportunity. McColl was named CEO of North Carolina National Bank in 1983. Crutchfield became CEO of First Union Bank in 1985. Both McColl and Crutchfield pursued an aggressive strategy of consolidation, buying banks in large and fast-growing markets such as Florida, Texas, and Georgia. More conservative banks that did not follow a similar growth strategy were acquired or disappeared.[63]

Interviewees told us that as the banking industry grew, McColl, Crutchfield, and other financial sector leaders feared downtown Charlotte was not an attractive destination for new financial talent (particularly during the national economic downturn of 1981). Thus, even as they began their aggressive bank expansion strategies in the mid-1980s, McColl and Crutchfield, along with Bill Lee, the head of Duke Power (a regional energy company), pushed a downtown development strategy, using their relationships with city officials to forge public-private partnerships and a division of labor whereby the city government handled crime-prevention and infrastructure such as street lighting and parks while the private sector assumed a role in developing amenities, providing housing, engaging in commercial construction, and marketing the region. From all accounts, the public and private sectors in Charlotte worked remarkably well together over that period, and the open display of harmony reduced transaction costs, including lost time, waste of political capital, and public ill-will.

Many of those interviewed asserted that the region's residents held to some common principles that characterized public and private activities, including effective use of social networking; civic optimism; careful strategizing that left nothing to chance, thus reducing risk; and a sense of stewardship.

As the community reinvented the Charlotte region as an attractive location, banking talent from outside the region settled in Charlotte. That in-migration enabled the financial industry to mitigate the effects of a lack of skilled administrative workers in the region and a public education system that may have otherwise prevented the banking sector from obtaining the number and level of educated workers that it required.

RESPONSES. The public sector's response to massive losses in textile and apparel firm employment was simply not to respond. In the 1980s, as such

62. Bernstein (1987).

63. Dan Fitzpatrick, "Charlotte Reveling in Its Role as a Giant; How It Outpaced Pittsburgh Banks," *Pittsburgh Post-Gazette*, June 25, 2006, p. A-1.

firms diminished, there were no deliberate public policies to confront the economic loss, such as reports or agendas for programs to help larger textile and apparel firms shore up core competencies or strengthen their supply chains.[64] Some officials acknowledged being taken off guard by the sudden unwinding of the industry, but there was little that could have been done to preserve the sector in the face of international competition at lower wages.

In 1991 McColl, Crutchfield, Lee, Stuart Dickson (Ruddick Corporation), and John Belk (Belk department stores) formed the Charlotte Regional Partnership, a public-private organization with a mandate to attract firms (especially foreign) and investment to the sixteen counties in the broader Charlotte region (including some that were not a part of the strictly defined metropolitan area).

The Charlotte Chamber of Commerce, which served the city and Mecklenburg County, was another visible public agency. It campaigned on bond sales, advocated for the business community, and focused on attraction and retention of businesses with such programs as its 2006 initiative called Business First. In 1998, the Charlotte chamber initiated the Advantage Carolina project. A total of seventeen key initiatives would grow out of the project, including Pathways to Employment, a three-month welfare-to-work program managed by Central Piedmont Community College. McColl led the chamber's efforts to hire students from the program, and 76 percent of chamber members participated.

The civic elite recognized the importance of a research university, but in 1989 Charlotte was the largest metropolitan area without a doctoral degree–granting university. With help from McColl and Crutchfield, officials of the University of North Carolina–Charlotte started a capital campaign to fund the offering of doctoral degrees, and by 2005 the Carnegie Foundation classified the University of North Carolina–Charlotte as a research-intensive institution.

The motorsports industry expanded in the region, most recently with the NASCAR Hall of Fame in 2010, which was brought to the region through public-private efforts. Earlier, the Charlotte Motor Speedway coordinated with area jurisdictions to establish a garage tour of the race cup teams headquartered in the region, and the Speed Channel's headquarters, originally in Chicago under a different name, expanded in Charlotte in 2008, assisted by the state's One North Carolina Fund.

No overarching public sector economic development strategies or public policy decisions explained the region's phenomenal growth. Rather, the attitude within the public sector, which took pride in its own businesslike demeanor, was that "the business of Charlotte is business." In 1993, the city government re-

64. Conway and others (2003).

organized itself to support an even more pronounced focus on business.[65] The public sector operated to help the business community thrive in the Charlotte region.

The recent takeover of Wachovia by Wells Fargo opened a new financial chapter for the region, where homegrown talent and homegrown philosophy might hold less sway. We were told, however, that Wells Fargo, unlike Wachovia, has a decentralized management style that retains more local management. Now that Charlotte employees have become the "local" employees of a distant corporate owner, the philosophy could work to reduce the impact of the bank's new ownership by outsiders.

Other financial institutions, including GMAC Financial, are picking up some of the newly unemployed financial talent pool. To show that the region was still open for business, the Chamber of Commerce mailed a pitch signed by McColl to several thousand financial institutions. Former First Union and Bank of America executives have filed paperwork to establish a new bank in Charlotte, looking to benefit from purchase of problem banks.[66]

RESULTS. This bank-led, business-friendly trajectory worked well for twenty-five years, and the Charlotte region nearly doubled its employment during that time, from 408,000 to 801,000 jobs. While a business-friendly attitude invited business, it did not require public economic development policy efforts. With the private sector putting its own funds into job training and recruiting many of its employees from elsewhere, there was little incentive for the public sector to worry about taking such initiatives.

Charlotte's resilience was thus a product of the strategy and fortunes of its major private sector firms and the entrepreneurs who led them. Its "resilience strategy" was ultimately dependent on two very large banking firms and the power company. Wells Fargo (a presence through its Wachovia takeover) and Bank of America now face difficult and changed environments. Duke Power, the member of the triumvirate that maintained the lowest profile during the growth years, is emerging out of the Great Recession as a major national and international policy leader in green energy and in nuclear power. Under Lee's guidance, Duke Power established the World Association of Nuclear Operators and has taken a major role in the Carolinas' Nuclear Cluster Group.

The energy sector may be the emerging face of a new regional economy for Charlotte, because the financial crisis has created retrenchment and uncertainty in the banking world. Through local eyes, the Great Recession in the Charlotte

65. City of Charlotte, "The Charlotte Story: Public Service Is Our Business," April 2000, p. 13.

66. Rick Rothacker, "Former First Union, Bank of America Execs Organizing New Bank," *Charlotte Observer*, April 26, 2010.

region was "like nothing we have ever seen before. These jobs are not coming back." Observers believe that the region's "new normal" will no longer exhibit unprecedented growth in the financial sector. How resilient the financial sector proves to be in the face of the Great Recession, how well the energy sector performs in carrying an economy bolstered by niche industries like motorsports, and whether the qualities said by residents to underpin the region's economic bounce still come into play—all of these factors will tell the future of the Charlotte region's resilience following the Great Recession.

Grand Forks

Grand Forks is a small region that encompasses portions of two states (North Dakota and Minnesota) and has a population of slightly less than 100,000, of which about 67 percent is on the North Dakota side.[67] The region has historically had an agricultural economy, with major crops of wheat (largest crop by acreage), sugar beets (largest cash crop), potatoes, and soybeans. Other large employment sectors have been the military, specifically Grand Forks Air Force Base, established in 1955, and state government, which includes the University of North Dakota. In 1980, the region's economic drivers were the military (14.5 percent of the region's employment in 1980), state government (13 percent of employment), and agriculture (12 percent of employment). The region thus is susceptible to shocks resulting from decisions at the national level (for example, military base reductions) and the state level as well as natural events. The regional economy is diverse, but local policymakers have few levers to respond to economic shocks.

The Grand Forks region experienced a large number of shocks during our period of study, including local industry shocks in 1978, 1980, 1985, and 1996; national industry shocks in 1983 and 1989; and a national economic downturn shock in 2000. Nearly all of the industry shocks involved shocks to its military employment sector. The region was shock resistant to the 1978, 1983, 1985, and 2000 shocks, but it experienced economic downturns as a result of shocks in 1980, 1989, and 1996. The region was resilient to the first of the downturns but not to the second two.

The 1980 shock-induced downturn appears to have been primarily the result of the national recession rather than local events. Thus, when the nation rebounded, so did the Grand Forks region. In 1989–90, however, the region suffered a one-year loss of 7 percent of its military employment (likely a result of the deactivation of some missile wing units), followed by a 4 percent employ-

---

67. The Grand Forks region is defined in this chapter as the Grand Forks metropolitan statistical area, which consists of Grand Forks County, North Dakota, containing the city of Grand Forks, and Polk County, Minnesota, containing the city of East Grand Forks. The Red River divides the states.

ment loss in state government in 1991. The region was not resistant to those shocks. The 1996 downturn involved an additional 7 percent decrease in military employment (1,500 employees), this time the result of the 1995 round of military base closings. Contributing to this downturn was the flood in April 1997, which damaged 83 percent of homes and 62 percent of commercial units in the city of Grand Forks and all but eight homes in East Grand Forks, resulting in almost $2 billion of damage in the Grand Forks area. The agricultural industry suffered distress, presumably related to the flood, particularly with the spring wheat crop.[68] In 1997 alone, the region's total employment fell by 2 percent, the region's largest decrease in our study period.

REGIONAL ECONOMIC RESILIENCE/NONRESILIENCE. Grand Forks differs from the other case study regions profiled in this chapter because it has a small economy, with regional employment below 60,000 and a GMP of $3.6 million. Downturns in Grand Forks reflect, for example, only a 2 percent employment decline, but that means 1,200 people losing their jobs. Another difference is that while Grand Forks experienced a decline in its annual employment growth rate in 1989, its employment otherwise continued to increase until the greater downturn of 1996 occurred.[69] At that point, it experienced an immediate and drastic decline.[70] Finally, the kinds of shock that Grand Forks experienced were different from those experienced by the other case study regions. In Grand Forks the shocks were military base closings brought about by the Defense Base Realignment and Closure Commission, followed by a major natural disaster (the 1997 flood).

Is the Grand Forks region resilient to economic shock-induced downturns? The data indicate that while it was resilient to the 1981 recession, it has not been resilient otherwise. Prior to the 1980 shock, the Grand Forks region's average eight-year employment growth rate was 1.6 percent. While the annual growth rate fell to –1 percent in 1980, it rebounded to its prior level within two years. However, the region was, by our definition, not resilient to the downturn caused by the 1989 shock; it did not return to its prior growth rate within a four-year period. Nonetheless, employment continued to increase every year for the next six years—until the year of the flood and the base reduction. Prior to the 1996 downturn, the Grand Forks region's average eight-year employment

---

68. Another factor mentioned by some interviewees was reduced retail sales from the rise of the U.S. dollar in relation to the Canadian dollar, which discouraged Canadians from shopping in the region.

69. Similarly, Grand Forks recovered quickly from GMP downturns in 1988 and 1993, rebounding within a year. However, it was not resilient to the shock in 1997, when GMP fell from $3.4 million to $3.1 million and then continued to fall, dropping to $2.9 million in 1999.

70. Pendall, Foster, and Cowell (2010).

growth rate was 1.8 percent. In 1996, the annual growth rate fell to -2.2 percent and remained negative or under 1 percent until 2002, when the annual employment growth rate was 1.3 percent. From 2002 to 2006 the average annual employment growth rate was 1.5 percent. In short, the Grand Forks region seems to have established a new equilibrium at a growth rate of about 0.3 percentage point below its prior rate.

While Grand Forks was nonresilient based on annual and eight-year growth rates, the region's leaders view it as resilient because it ultimately recovered from the flood and other shocks of 1997, with population, employment, and GMP all having surpassed their pre-1997 levels. During and after the Great Recession (from late 2007 through mid-2010), the Grand Forks region's unemployment rate was low, peaking at just over 5 percent. In addition, inflation-adjusted wages per worker increased by 17.7 percent between 1995 and 2007.

EXPLAINING RESILIENCE/NONRESILIENCE. Although the flooding of 1997 was only one of the shocks to the Grand Forks region that year, our interviewees saw it as a catalyst for change in the region, in particular by improving the relationships between the Grand Forks and East Grand Forks governments and the self-image of residents throughout the region. When asked how they perceived the region after 1997, interviewees consistently responded that the region was better, for two reasons: increased collaboration among the different groups in the area, particularly the business community and local government in the city of Grand Forks, as well as improved interaction between Grand Forks and East Grand Forks; and the belief that, working together, they can improve their community. A third reason often mentioned was the huge influx of money, primarily from the federal government, which enabled new investment in the region. Reliance on federal funding, which often takes several years to disburse, may be part of the explanation for the region's recovery time frame exceeding that of our "resilience" definition.

RESPONSES. Since the Grand Forks region spans two states, the need for a cross-state regional approach is evident. East Grand Forks has a population of fewer than 8,000, leaving it with little power in Minnesota politics; in contrast, Grand Forks is the third-largest city in North Dakota. In addition, during the flood recovery, the two cities were served by different Federal Emergency Management Administration and Economic Development Administration field offices, and Grand Forks was a community development block grant (CDBG) entitlement city while East Grand Forks received its CDBG funds through the state. That meant that as Grand Forks and East Grand Forks engaged in rebuilding, they had different directions and restrictions from their federal partners. As one of our respondents observed, "You could do things in Minnesota that you couldn't do in North Dakota, and vice versa, which pulled us apart instead of putting us together." Although the river separates the cities, it also brings them together with a shared greenway (funded as a state park by each state).

Recovering from the flood required reinvestment in the region, but investment requires security. That was accomplished through the flood protection programs implemented by each of the cities. Grand Forks residents paid $92 million toward its flood protection system, in three tax assessments. After enhancing the flood protection system, state and local governments and businesses were able to rebuild the region with the help of federal funds. As one person explained, "We did about 20 years of redevelopment in five years." Similarly, "that flood did in a week what urban renewal couldn't do in 40 years." Almost every person interviewed noted that the physical redevelopment of the region represented an important symbol of its recovery; evidence of what the communities could accomplish when working together and an incentive to continue striving for improvement; and a source of important amenities to make the region more attractive to both existing and potential residents (including University of North Dakota graduates).[71]

Both cities redeveloped their downtowns, which, because they were located along the river's banks, were destroyed by the flood. East Grand Forks was able to take an industrial downtown, populated by old railroad tracks and dilapidated warehouses, and create an area for retail, restaurants, and a movie theater. It used CDBG funds to attract Cabela's, an outdoor specialty store. According to one city official, an area that previously had $500,000 in taxable value now has a value of $12 to $15 million. In Grand Forks, Mike Maidenburg, publisher of the *Grand Forks Herald* at the time, drove the revitalization of the downtown. In addition to convincing the city to invest in the downtown, he pledged to maintain the newspaper in its downtown location, although that resulted in bifurcated operations, with production occurring elsewhere in the city. Brownstones and condominiums were built and occupied, creating a residential presence downtown, which had been missing prior to the flood.

In both cities, federal and state funds enabled redevelopment, which increased amenities in the region; interviewees consistently commented on the improved quality of life following the flood. Yet as one person said, "The basics remained. Agriculture and the university didn't go away." The flood response/recovery was a small piece of a larger, longer-term economic development approach in the city

71. Several interviewees mentioned that it was difficult to attract educated workers to the Grand Forks region, with the harsh winters being only part of the problem. Some companies, we were told, had moved certain functions to Minneapolis, where it is easier to attract workers, because of the greater amenities of the Twin Cities.

of Grand Forks, which appears to seek growth and diversification of the region's economic drivers by pursuing manufacturing, encouraging entrepreneurship and innovation through centers affiliated with the university, and re-envisioning the region as a "destination" location. The larger economic development effort of which the rebuilding was a part built on the region's existing institutions and initiatives:

—*General economic development*: Although some interviewees credited the flood with fueling economic development activities in the Grand Forks region, many of the economic development activities were under way prior to 1997. The flood served as a reminder of the importance of economic development as the region struggled to stem population loss, employment loss, and revenue loss. One of the means by which the city of Grand Forks supports economic development is through its Growth Fund. Adopted in 1988, the fund is supported in part by 0.25 percent of retail sales tax revenues. The fund provides gap and early-stage financing of construction and capital costs for new and expanding firms. For example, the Growth Fund contributed $500,000 toward the Research Enterprise and Commercialization Center.[72] In April 2010, the Growth Fund Committee approved loans to three manufacturers, LM Wind Power, a wind turbine manufacturer; Ideal Aerosmith, which makes testing equipment for aircraft and missiles; and American Defense, which makes metal components for military vehicles.[73] Ideal Aerosmith came to East Grand Forks in 1984 as the first occupant of a new industrial park that had been built with federal funds and tax-increment financing.

—*Destination city*: In his 2003 State of the City address, Mayor Mike Brown stated, "My vision is that we become a destination city," a great place not only to live and do business but to visit. He asked for an increase in the sales tax, which was defeated, as well as a commitment to the greenway, the water park, and the community center by the Alerus Center, Grand Forks' entertainment and convention facility. This vision, according to interviewees, gave leaders and residents a direction as they left the flood behind them. The goal is to attract visitors from Winnipeg, a city of 800,000 located 145 miles to the north. Part of that strategy builds on promoting air service to Phoenix and Las Vegas (popular vacation spots), which is cheaper from Grand Forks than from Winnipeg because of Canadian taxes and fees. Grand Forks recently attracted Allegiant Air, which runs a few flights a week between Grand Forks and these other locations.

—*University*: The University of North Dakota plays a major role in the region, not just as an employer but as a source of innovation. The university was

72. State, federal, and foundation funds accounted for the remainder of the $8.75 million to build the center.

73. Tu-Uyen Tran, "GF Loans for Manufacturers on Track," *Grand Forks Herald*, April 21, 2010.

able to maintain its enrollment of over 10,300 students following the flood, and it has experienced continued growth in enrollment, which increased 25 percent between 1998 and 2003 (when enrollment reached over 13,000). Between 2009 and 2010, enrollment increased over 7 percent, from 13,172 students to 14,194 (with the city of Grand Forks having a population of 51,000 in 2009, university students are a significant portion of the population). The university is affiliated with four independent research centers: the Energy and Environment Research Center (which has ten "Centers of Excellence"); the Innovation Center; the Odegard School of Aerospace Sciences; and the newest addition, the University of North Dakota Research Foundation's Research Enterprise and Commercialization Park, which houses the state's Center of Excellence in Life Sciences and Advanced Technologies.

—*Military*: The most recent shock to the community was the loss of its last tanker group at the Air Force base as part of the 2005 round of military base closings. In its place, the base was to prepare itself for an unmanned aerial systems (UAS) mission, in anticipation of receiving Predator and Global Hawk unmanned aerial vehicles. Regional leaders' response to this shock was to embrace the change and proactively develop a community plan to support the new mission. The activities that have occurred in the Grand Forks region with respect to the UAS mission suggest that changes that occurred following the flood have been institutionalized, resulting in a new culture within the community. That includes recognition of the importance of understanding the region's strengths and weaknesses. For example, the UAS mission builds on the region's competitive advantage in energy research (conducting cold weather testing of unmanned aircraft, renewable energy, and tactical fuels); engineering (developing payloads and sensors); pilot training programs; and the Minnesota community college's aircraft maintenance program (with its new certificate in unmanned aircraft vehicle maintenance). It also benefits from the base's location in a sparsely populated area with uncrowded airspace.

RESULTS. The economy resembles its traditional roots to an extent. Trains rumble through town pulling freight. Sugar beet trucks head to Crystal Sugar in East Grand Forks. The air base is once again threatened. While the methodology that we used indicates a region that is not resilient, perhaps because of the few local levers available to a region of under 100,000 people, the region of Grand Forks is weathering the current economic environment well.

In 1980, three sectors alone—military, state government, and agriculture—made up at least twice as large a share of Grand Forks employment as of nationwide employment. In 2007, food manufacturing and mining had joined the original three. Yet each of the growing industries employs fewer than 5 percent of the region's workers (1,400 and 675 employees, respectively). The original three export industries continue to be economic drivers, with the university the largest employer in the region (6,385 employees in 2009).

Seattle

The Seattle region has two major export industry clusters.[74] The first, consisting of aerospace manufacturers and suppliers, is anchored by Boeing, which has had its major production facilities (and, until 2001, its headquarters) in the region since 1916. The second, consisting of information technology developers, manufacturers, suppliers, and major users, is anchored by software giant Microsoft, which moved to the region in 1979. Other major firms that use information technology intensively were started in the region between the 1970s and 1990s, including coffee retailer Starbucks, warehouse club Costco, and online bookseller Amazon. In addition, new export industries that draw on the skill and technology bases of the aerospace and information technology clusters, notably medical device production, have begun to develop in the region.

Employment growth downturns in the Seattle regional economy have occurred around the time of national recessions. The region experienced shock-induced employment growth downturns in 1980–81, 1990, 1993, and 2000–01. The region's GMP growth downturns occurred in 1990, 1994, 1999–2000, and 2003. The regional economic development policymakers and practitioners whom we interviewed perceived the Great Recession as the region's most severe economic downturn since the early 1970s. When we conducted our interviews (July 2009 and July 2010) the region's employment was lower, as a percentage of pre-recession employment, than at the same time after any of the previous three recessions, although by mid-2010 it had begun to rebound from its post-recession employment trough.

Employment growth downturns in the region's major export industries preceded or accompanied the aggregate regional employment growth downturns. Wood products (a major regional export industry prior to the mid-1980s) suffered employment growth downturns in 1978–79. Software had such downturns in 1993 and 2000–01, although they appeared as sharp reductions in the industry's employment growth rate rather than as job losses. (Microsoft, the region's largest information technology employer, laid off workers for the first time during the Great Recession.) Aerospace experienced downturns in 1980–82, 1990–93, 1998–99, and 2002, all of which were employment declines. However, their impact on the region as a whole probably became less severe over time because the share of the region's employment accounted for by

74. The region is the Seattle-Tacoma-Bellevue, Washington, metropolitan statistical area, which consists of King, Snohomish, and Pierce counties.

Boeing, the region's largest manufacturer, was declining (though still substantial). Moreover, downturns in industry employment growth were mostly not severe enough to qualify as shocks by our definition.[75]

Seattle experienced rapid growth of employment and near-average growth of its average wage between 1980 and 2005. The total number of jobs rose by 78 percent during that time, well above the national average job growth rate of 43 percent. The average inflation-adjusted wage rose by 27 percent, just below the national average of 28 percent.

During the late twentieth and early twenty-first centuries, the region's export base became less centered on wood products and (to a lesser extent) aerospace and more centered on information technology. Wood products manufacturing jobs, which made up nearly 3 percent of total jobs in the region in 1980, fell by 30 percent between 1980 and 2005 and accounted for less than 0.5 percent of total employment in 2005. Jobs in transportation equipment manufacturing (overwhelmingly aerospace) were 25 percent of regional employment in 1980, fell by 20 percent during 1980–2005, and were only 4 percent of regional employment in 2005. The number of jobs in publishing (most of which were in software in the Seattle area) grew by 555 percent during 1980–2005, accounting for just under 1 percent of regional employment in 1980 and just under 3 percent in 2005.

REGIONAL ECONOMIC RESILIENCE/NONRESILIENCE. Seattle had been very resilient and shock resistant since 1980 and became increasingly so over time, at least until the Great Recession. The region was resilient to the 1993 and 2000–01 shock-induced employment downturns but not resilient to the 1980 downturn. The region was also resilient to the 1994 GMP downturn. (There was little opportunity to demonstrate resilience to the 1990 employment and GMP downturns and the 2000–01 GMP downturn because other downturns occurred so soon afterward, and our data series ends too soon to permit an assessment of the response to the 2003 GMP downturn.)

As noted above, the region experienced export industry employment growth downturns that were, for the most part, not very severe. Seattle was shock resistant to the one export industry downturn (aerospace in 1998) that was severe enough to count as an industry shock.

The Great Recession of 2007–09 had relatively little impact on the region's aerospace industry because Boeing was completing the development of a new

75. Of the region's industry employment downturns, only the 1982 and 1998 aerospace downturns were large enough to meet our definition of a shock, and because the 1982 aerospace downturn occurred in the midst of an overall regional shock, it did not count as an industry shock by our definition. Therefore, the region's only industry shock occurred in aerospace in 1998.

airplane model (the 787 Dreamliner) at the time and therefore was ramping up employment and supplier orders for the project. That compensated for the loss of aircraft demand from airlines experiencing a decline in air travel.

The 2008 failure of Seattle-based Washington Mutual, which was the largest bank failure in U.S. history, cost the region about 4,500 jobs. However, banking has never been a major export industry in Seattle, and the collapse of the bank does not seem to have had major regional implications according to either our interviews or our data analysis.

EXPLAINING RESILIENCE/NONRESILIENCE. Seattle's economic resilience was mainly a result of two things. The first was the absolute and relative decline in the importance of its most shock-prone major export industries, wood products and aerospace. The second was the absolute and relative rise in the importance of the software industry. As a newer industry built around a relatively new technology and lacking the high fixed costs of durable manufacturing industries, the software industry was less prone to job growth downturns than the other major export industries, and its downturns were less severe. As a consequence of both the decline of wood products and aerospace employment and the rise of software, the region's export base became more diversified; as our quantitative analysis shows, a diverse export base contributes to regional economic resilience.

Diversification of the region's export base came about not as a result of any deliberate policy or strategy but because of a historical accident: Bill Gates moved Microsoft to the region in 1979. Other information technology–intensive firms (Starbucks, Amazon, and Costco, as well as their suppliers and Microsoft's suppliers) sprang up subsequently, in part to take advantage of proximity to Microsoft and the large pool of information technology workers that it attracted to the region. Additional local information technology companies were then founded by former Microsoft managers or engineers.

The presence of both aerospace and information technology in the region may have contributed to regional economic resilience by helping to spur the growth of new export industries such as medical device production. The two core export industries employ many mechanical and electrical engineers, who sometimes form new firms that apply their skills outside of the core industries. Layoffs of engineers from Boeing and, more recently, from Microsoft have been a source of new firm formation. The wealth generated by the region's information technology industry has helped support a local venture capital industry, which has been a source of funding for these new firms.

Both the region's overall export base and its aerospace suppliers have become more diversified since the 1990s. In the past Seattle's aerospace suppliers mainly supplied components to Boeing, but over time they gained an increasing share of their business from other aircraft manufacturers located outside the region and even outside the United States. Thus, the suppliers are now more insulated from downturns in Boeing's business than they once were.

RESPONSES. After the severe early 1970s recession, policymakers perceived a need to diversify the region's economy away from its strong reliance on aerospace manufacturing in general and Boeing in particular. The Chamber of Commerce accelerated its business recruitment efforts. Local government and business leaders created the King County Economic Development Council, now called Enterprise Seattle, to recruit new firms to the region. In the wake of the 1970s recession the organization conducted a major campaign to market Seattle to businesses located elsewhere. Enterprise Seattle continues to recruit businesses but now also commissions reports on the region's economy and connects businesses to sources of public and private financial and technical assistance to help them get established, remain in business, or expand in the region.

Although regional leaders do not consider further diversification of the regional economy to be as high a priority today as it was in the 1970s, some still think that the region is too dependent on Boeing and Microsoft. In 2008 the state established the Economic Development Commission to promote an innovation-based economy that was less dependent on Boeing and Microsoft. The commission has recommended that the state Commerce Department expand its traditional focus on attracting and retaining businesses by trying to increase the educational attainment of state residents, bring entrepreneurially oriented faculty to state universities, promote electric car usage, and boost exports by improving transportation links between Seattle and the East and Midwest. The Commerce Department has reorganized to enable it to carry out this strategy.

Many of our interviewees thought that rather than diversifying away from reliance on Boeing, retaining Boeing's aircraft production in the region was necessary to preserve the regional economy's strength, at least in the short run. Many interviewees told us that the biggest threat to Seattle's economy was the possibility that Boeing would increasingly move production to lower-wage parts of the United States or abroad. The move of Boeing's headquarters to Chicago in 2001 and a recent history of strained union-management relations at Boeing exacerbated fears that Boeing would leave the area. When Boeing considered the possibility of building some of its new 787 airplanes outside the state, local governments and economic development agencies lobbied Governor

Gary Locke and the state legislature for a tax incentive package to retain production of the new aircraft. The package was enacted into law, but Boeing nevertheless decided to build some (but not all) of its 787s at a newly acquired plant in South Carolina.

Another response to the threat of Boeing's relocation of production was the formation of the Prosperity Partnership in 2003. This joint initiative of the region's metropolitan planning organization and its economic development district mainly conducts research on and planning for five of Seattle's industry clusters and activities: aerospace; information technology; international trade (including the Port of Seattle and logistics, transportation, and related support services); biotechnology and life sciences; and clean technology (energy efficiency, renewable energy generation, environmental remediation, and green building). The partnership also does some public policy advocacy for these clusters and has started membership organizations for the aerospace and clean technology clusters. The partnership's goal is to support all five clusters, neither focusing exclusively on retaining aerospace jobs nor on further diversifying the economy away from aerospace.

In addition to policies and strategies designed to preserve or increase the region's economic resilience, Seattle has several economic development organizations that target specific industries or other activities in the regional economy. None of the organizations was established with the goal of making the regional economy more resilient or of responding to specific economic shocks. The Trade Development Alliance—jointly sponsored by local governments, the Chamber of Commerce, the Port of Seattle, and unions—promotes international trade in the heavily trade-dependent Seattle area by sponsoring trade missions for regional business and government leaders, promoting Seattle exports abroad, and providing local businesses with information about trade. The Washington Technology Industry Association, founded in 1984, is the regional trade association for high-technology businesses (initially software companies, but now also telecommunications and medical device firms). It engages in lobbying at the state and federal levels and provides members with business networking opportunities and discounted services. The Technology Alliance, founded in 1996 by Bill Gates Sr., is a statewide organization that advocates for state-level public policies to improve K-12 and higher education, research capacity, technology transfer and commercialization of inventions, and the entrepreneurial climate. The Pacific Northwest Aerospace Alliance, an organization of primarily small and medium-size aerospace suppliers that was founded by the Prosperity Partnership, is a trade association that provides its members with information, business networking opportunities, and industry advocacy. The Center for Advanced Manufacturing Puget

Sound is a similar membership organization that was founded in 2008 with the specific goal of helping small and medium-size manufacturers (primarily in aerospace) succeed in the face of international competition. It emphasizes information and services related to innovation, business development, and supply chain positioning.

RESULTS. It is difficult to evaluate the success of any of the specific policies and strategies that Seattle's leaders have undertaken to diversify the region's economy, respond to the threat of Boeing's departure, or promote specific industries or activities in the region. The region's export base has diversified since the 1970s but, as noted above, that diversification came about for reasons that were unrelated to any regional policies or strategies. Boeing maintained its existing production capacity, including one production line for its new 787 airplane, in the Seattle area, while opening a second 787 production line in South Carolina. We have no evidence on whether either the tax incentives that the state provided to Boeing or the recent creation of organizations to improve the competitiveness of Seattle's aerospace suppliers had any role in inducing Boeing to maintain production in Seattle.

As of July 2009, no public or private organization had undertaken or planned any policy or strategy to restructure the regional economy in response to the Great Recession. Our interviewees did not think any such restructuring was necessary. They viewed the regional economy as sufficiently diverse because it is built around two large firms, Boeing and Microsoft, which have steadily introduced new products and around which distinct industry clusters (in aerospace and information technology, respectively) have formed. Our interviewees believed that the region's eventual recovery from the Great Recession would be a continuation of pre-recession trends, including further growth of the information technology industry and the gradual movement of Boeing away from the region (which began with the relocation of the firm's headquarters to Chicago and the opening of a new aircraft production line in South Carolina, its first outside the Seattle area). They also anticipated further growth of the nonprofit sector, which has been fueled largely by funding from current and former Microsoft executives.

Hartford

The economy of the Hartford region is propelled by its strengths in insurance and aerospace manufacturing.[76] Hartford, which has long been called "the insurance

---

76. The Hartford metropolitan area consists of the Connecticut counties of Hartford, Middlesex, and Tolland.

capital of the world," is home to the headquarters of many large insurance companies, such as the Hartford Financial Services Group, Aetna, Phoenix, and major
operations of Travelers, CIGNA, and MetLife. The region's aerospace manufacturing industry is anchored by the family of companies owned by the United Technologies Corporation, including Pratt & Whitney, known primarily for its production of aircraft engines; aerospace systems manufacturer Hamilton
Sundstrand; and helicopter manufacturer Sikorsky Aircraft.[77] These firms, especially Pratt & Whitney, support a large network of aerospace component manufacturers throughout the region that form the region's aerospace supply chain. The
region has had slow overall job growth and extremely fast wage growth, which
reflect its concentration of jobs in industries and firms producing high-value-
added but mature products that have not generated rapid job growth.

Employment growth downturns in the Hartford region have generally coincided with national recessions, although the region's downturn in the late 1980s
preceded the 1990 national recession by two years and its job losses following
that downturn persisted well beyond the period of the national recession. It
experienced downturns in 1980 and 1988 and a shock-induced downturn in
2001, with the 1988 downturn registering as the most severe in terms of job
loss. Our analysis did not reveal any local or national industry shocks affecting
the Hartford region during our study period.

Employment in Hartford transportation equipment manufacturing (which
includes aerospace manufacturing) has been cyclical, with the industry shedding
large numbers of jobs during the years 1974–78, 1980–84, and 1991–95.[78] The
early 1990s downturn, which was the most severe of the three industry downturns, followed several years of relatively moderate job losses. From 1987 to
1991, the industry lost 2,400 jobs (a decline of 5.7 percent), while from 1991 to
1995 it lost an alarming 16,800 jobs, cutting the number employed in the
industry by 41.4 percent in just four years. By comparison, the 1974–78 downturn resulted in a loss of 12,900 jobs and the 1980–84 downturn resulted in the
loss of 7,900 jobs. None of the recoveries that followed those downturns was
sufficient to regain what had been lost.

Employment has been less cyclical in Hartford's insurance industry than in
its aerospace industry. The region's insurance industry had consistent job gains
during much of the 1970s and 1980s, before large-scale job losses led to the
industry's downsizing in the 1990s.[79] Employment in insurance declined by

77. Sikorsky is headquartered in Stratford, Connecticut, just outside the Hartford metropolitan area.

78. None of the region's industry employment downturns was large enough to meet our definition of
an industry shock.

79. The insurance industry lost 1,200 jobs from 1973 to 1975, which coincided with a national
recession, in addition to losing 2,200 jobs from 1987 to 1990, before the 1990 national recession.

2,200 jobs (or 3.4 percent) from 1987 to 1990, increased slightly from 1990 to 1991, and then declined from 1991 to 1996 by 19,800 jobs (or 31.1 percent). As in transportation equipment manufacturing, job levels in insurance remained relatively stable from the late 1990s onward.

The impact of the Great Recession in Hartford was not as severe as that of the early 1990s or early 2000s recession. By the third quarter of 2010 (eleven quarters after the official start of the Great Recession), the region had gained jobs for two consecutive quarters and its employment was higher, as a percentage of pre-recession employment, than at comparable points following the start of the 1990 and 2001 recessions. The early 1980s recession in Hartford was comparable in its depth to the Great Recession, but recovery in the early 1980s was much swifter than the current recovery.

By the end of our study period Hartford's economy was more industrially diverse than in 1980, due primarily to its loss of manufacturing jobs. Manufacturing accounted for 11.9 percent of Hartford's jobs (1.16 times manufacturing's nationwide share), down by 14.4 percentage points from 1980. The share of jobs in health care and social assistance had increased by 5.4 percentage points since 1980. By the early twenty-first century, health care and social assistance employed more people than any other major industry in Hartford. The share of jobs in finance and insurance was down modestly (0.4 percentage point), while shares in administrative services and professional and business services increased by 2.3 and 1.6 percentage points, respectively.

REGIONAL ECONOMIC RESILIENCE/NONRESILIENCE. Hartford was resilient to two of the three downturns that it experienced since 1980. It was nonresilient to the third, which severely altered its growth path for many years. The downturn experienced in 1980 was relatively mild, and the region was resilient to it by 1983. From 1980 to 1982, the region lost 7,300 jobs (a decline of 1.3 percent), but by the following year it had more than made up for those losses. The 1988 downturn was far more severe, and the region proved nonresilient to it. From 1988 to 1993, Hartford lost 68,000 jobs (a decline of 10.2 percent), and it continued to slowly lose jobs for another two years. While the region subsequently gained jobs from 1995 to 2000, it failed to reach its 1988 level of employment before the 2001 downturn halted its recovery.[80] Hartford lost 20,600 jobs (decline of 3.2 percent) from 2001 to 2003, but the region proved resilient to this downturn by 2004. By 2007, employment in the region

---

80. Hartford actually lost jobs from 2000 to 2001, but that decline did not mark a large enough departure from its prior growth trend to qualify as the beginning of an employment shock by our definition.

had nearly returned to its 2000 level, but it was still well below its 1988 level, illustrating the tremendous impact of the 1988 downturn.

EXPLAINING RESILIENCE/NONRESILIENCE. Hartford's economic resilience has reflected national economic cycles, except the early 1990s recession, when downturns in aerospace and insurance combined to prolong that regional downturn.

During the 1980–82 downturn, aerospace manufacturing lost more jobs than any other industry. Transportation equipment manufacturing lost 5,000 jobs, while the related industries of fabricated metal products and machinery manufacturing lost 2,500 and 2,300 jobs, respectively.[81] However, during the same period the insurance industry added 4,100 jobs. While growth in insurance was not enough to offset the losses in aerospace, it was substantial enough to dampen the impact of the recession.

The early 1990s recession was a different story. The timing and magnitude of losses in insurance and aerospace contributed to an aggregate economic downturn in the region that occurred earlier and lasted longer than the nationwide recession that began in 1990. Aerospace manufacturing was especially hurt by decreased demand for spare parts due to the nationwide recession as well as cuts in defense spending.[82] Hartford's insurance companies, which had invested heavily in commercial real estate during the 1980s, were hurt by the bursting of the commercial real estate bubble of the late 1980s and early 1990s. A cycle of strong hurricanes in the early 1990s, including Hurricane Andrew, also harmed the region's insurance companies. Furthermore, insurers were shedding jobs in Hartford as structural changes enabled firms in the insurance industry to outsource jobs to lower-cost regions.

Hartford's 2000–03 downturn, which began before and ended later than the nationwide recession, affected a broad swath of industries. State government was hit the hardest, but fabricated metal products manufacturing and administrative and support services each lost more than 3,000 jobs during that period. Health care, education, and leisure and hospitality added the most jobs.

RESPONSES. Hartford is notable for its lack of large-scale responses to either short-term economic shocks or the long-term decline of its major industries. One possible reason, which interviewees frequently mentioned, is that the Hartford region has had very high median income and productivity and that those measures of economic success led to policymakers' inaction. Another rea-

81. Not all of the jobs in these industries were tied to aerospace manufacturing, but it is probably safe to assume that many, if not most, were tied to the aerospace supply chain in some way.

82. Jonathan Hicks, "United Technologies' Bumpy Ride," *New York Times*, May 1, 1991.

son for the lack of large-scale response might be the region's highly fragmented local government structure, which has made cooperation on regionwide efforts very difficult. Yet a third possibility is that for much of our study period, the region lacked a unified business leadership that was substantially engaged in the region's economic and political arenas. Until the early 1980s, an informal group of insurance executives referred to as "the Bishops" did fill that role, but their influence waned as firms from outside the region acquired locally owned insurance companies and as politicians and corporate leaders left their posts.[83] Consequently, major economic development efforts in the region have been primarily the responsibility of the state government. Hartford is also notable for its many small to medium-size economic development organizations, the size and number of which mirror the political fragmentation in the region. Although these organizations have helped individual firms in certain industries, they do not appear to have been large enough to shift the economic trajectory of the region.

In the late 1990s, Governor John Rowland's administration (1995–2004) launched a major economic development initiative that sought to develop formal, statewide industry clusters. The Rowland administration began the cluster initiative on the heels of the wrenching 1990s downturn, which resulted from what the administration called the state's "'three eggs in one basket' economy."[84] The administration identified six broad industry groupings for the initiative to target—financial services, telecommunications and information, health care services, manufacturing, high technology, and tourism—and convened industry cluster advisory boards for each. The boards were expected to develop recommendations to enhance the global competitiveness of Connecticut's firms and residents. They also were asked to determine whether or not a state cluster initiative should be formalized.[85] The industry groupings selected by the administration were intentionally very broad, "so as not to 'pick winners.'"[86] After a year of deliberation, the advisory boards concluded that the broad industry groupings should be formalized as industry clusters and that additional clusters should be encouraged. The summary report of the boards' recommendations described two general principles necessary for any cluster strategy to succeed: "Firms within a cluster must cooperate to identify problems and generate solutions; and [g]overnment, academia, and regional/local organizations in economic development must become full partners within the cluster and work toward common goals."[87]

83. Burns (2002).
84. Ellef (1997).
85. Connecticut Department of Economic and Community Development (1998).
86. Dan Haar, "State Convenes Economic Board," *Hartford Courant*, February 26, 1997.
87. Connecticut Department of Economic and Community Development (1998).

The statewide cluster initiative was relevant for the Hartford region because it targeted its two key export industries. After the report was released, the aerospace components manufacturers (ACM) and the insurance and financial services (IFS) clusters were formalized. ACM began as an alliance of fewer than ten aerospace suppliers, which initially joined to address common workforce issues. In 1999, the group sought funding from the state Department of Economic and Community Development (which administered the cluster program) and formally became the state's aerospace cluster. One interviewee familiar with the cluster told us that it was founded with the mission to counter offshoring trends present since the early 1990s. The cluster's members are mainly small to medium-sized firms. One interviewee told us that lean manufacturing was not widely implemented in 1999 and that it has been one issue tackled by the cluster, which does not do training itself but works with outside consultants and with the region's Manufacturing Extension Partnership affiliate, ConnStep. ACM also addresses basic workforce issues by arranging customized training courses for its members. In addition, it assists through providing consolidated purchasing agreements as well as a roundtable forum to discuss business development. One interviewee told us that "the greatest advantage of ACM is peer-to-peer support."

Evidence from our interviews suggests that the ACM cluster has been the most successful in terms of the support that it has brought to its members. The general view expressed by many of our interviewees was that the mission of the clusters was not well defined and that most simply devolved into trade organizations shortly after they were formed. For example, it is unclear how the clusters were supposed to interface with and become "full partners" with government, higher education, and other economic development organizations, as initially envisioned. After Rowland resigned from office in 2004, his successor's administration inherited the program. Although the program continued under that administration, interviewees suggested that the program suffered as a result of the discontinuity in leadership.

The ACM and IFS clusters are part of a dense landscape of economic development organizations operating in the Hartford region. There are two active chambers of commerce in Hartford, though they differ in terms of geographic scope and services provided. The MetroHartford Alliance, created in response to the region's economic downturn in the late 1980s and early 1990s, focuses on traditional economic development activities, such as business attraction and retention, talent attraction, entrepreneurship, and marketing. The statewide Connecticut Business and Industry Association lobbies to influence public policies affecting the state's business climate (for example, tax policy). Since 1983 it has also undertaken workforce development initiatives.

Hartford also is home to multiple organizations that have tried to increase the technological sophistication of the state's industries. The Connecticut Center for Advanced Technology helps aerospace suppliers implement both lean production and "hard" technologies that increase productivity. The Connecticut Technology Council, a statewide trade association, facilitates high-technology business networks between the state's metropolitan areas and lobbies the state government on issues related to innovation. The Beacon Alliance promotes medical device manufacturing in the region and helps aerospace suppliers who are interested in diversifying into medical device manufacturing. None of the organizations was founded in response to an economic shock, and none has viewed its role as helping the region's economy avoid, adjust to, or mitigate economic shocks.

Downtown Hartford revitalization became a focus of the Rowland administration, which unveiled its Six Pillars initiative in 1998. The governor cited the weakness of local government and the void left by the Bishops as reasons to give special attention to the city of Hartford.[88] The Six Pillars included "a rejuvenated civic center," "a highly developed waterfront," "a downtown higher education center," "a convention center and sports megaplex," "the demolition or redevelopment of vacant buildings and the creation of downtown housing units," and "an increase in the number of well-located and inexpensive parking spaces."[89] The state envisioned spending $350 million in the hope that accompanying federal and private investments would reach $1 billion.[90] It is not clear how Governor Rowland viewed the initiative in terms of regionwide economic impact, but the "suburbs also strongly supported the plans to redevelop Hartford," believing that the city's "dismal national reputation" was an impediment to attracting people to the region.[91]

RESULTS. The impacts of the industry clusters initiative and the Six Pillars initiative are not clear, but they appear to have been relatively minor. The efforts of Hartford's many economic development organizations appear to have aided many of the region's firms, especially aerospace manufacturers, but when taken together their efforts do not appear to have been successful in changing the economic trajectory of the region. Consequently, the evolution of Hartford's economy, including its response to economic shocks, has been shaped primarily by

88. Bloom (2004).
89. "Governor Rowland Offers Plan to Promote the Redevelopment of Downtown Hartford,"press release, March 19, 1998 (www.ct.gov/governorrowland/cwp/view.asp?A=1331&Q=256160).
90. "Governor Rowland Offers Plan to Promote the Redevelopment of Downtown Hartford,"press release, March 19, 1998 (www.ct.gov/governorrowland/cwp/view.asp?A=1331&Q=256160).
91. Burns (2002).

broad economic forces, including declines in defense spending; Pratt & Whitney's loss of market share in commercial aviation; large aerospace assemblers seeking lower-cost markets to source parts; the globalization of customers and, in turn, parts of the supply chain; woes in the air travel industry; and increases in productivity that were not offset by increases in sales. Structural changes in the insurance industry led to the outsourcing of many jobs to lower-cost regions, such as Scranton and metropolitan areas in the Great Plains.

As of the fall of 2010, no public or private organization had undertaken or planned any policy or strategy to restructure the regional economy in response to the Great Recession. Some of our interviewees thought such restructuring was necessary, but none thought it possible within the region's existing structure of governments and private organizations. They believed that the region's eventual recovery from the Great Recession would depend on continuation of pre-recession trends, including continued high wages and productivity, gradual loss of aerospace manufacturing jobs to productivity growth and relocation abroad, and loss of back-office insurance jobs to other U.S. regions.

Summary

What have we learned about regional resilience to economic shock? Through our quantitative work, we were able to test some but not all of the hypotheses suggested by the literature that we cited and reviewed in the first part of this chapter. Regional economic structure mattered. Regions that had a higher proportion of their employment in durable goods manufacturing were likely to experience more downturns and to be less shock resistant with respect to both employment and GMP. However, they were also more likely to be resilient after experiencing a downturn and to take fewer years to become resilient. As we observed, these results make sense in light of the cyclical nature of employment patterns. Industrial concentration also mattered: the greater the number of major export industries in a region, the less susceptible the region was to a downturn and the more shock resistant it was.

However, human capital also played a role. Regions that had a higher proportion of working-age residents with a high school diploma or less were likely to experience more downturns and to be less shock resistant. However, they were also more likely to be resilient after experiencing an employment downturn and to take fewer years to become resilient. The latter finding is surprising, since it is generally assumed that better-educated individuals adapt more easily to economic transformations that require changes in behavior and skill sets. However, if resilience is simply the "bouncing back" of a region due to downturns caused by national economic shocks, there is little need for such adaptive behavior. Other findings that emerged from our analysis included the following:

—Labor market flexibility is related to resilience, at least to the extent that right-to-work laws are an indicator of flexibility. Regions in states with right-to-work laws are likely to be more resilient after experiencing a downturn than other regions and also to take less time to return to their prior growth rates.

—The greater the income disparities in a region, the more likely it is to experience an employment downturn and the longer it takes to return to its prior growth rate. However, income disparities were positively related to resilience in the face of GMP downturns and to the speed with which resilience occurred.

The quantitative work that we report above provides descriptive results about the frequency of shocks, shock resistance, and resilience and evidence about what regional characteristics are associated with shock resistance and resilience. They tell us little, however, about the processes whereby regional actors protected their regions from or responded to downturns caused by economic shocks. Those processes remained a "black box." To gain insight into them, we turned to our case studies.

We can characterize Detroit and Cleveland, over the course of the nearly thirty-year period that we examined, as regions that until the turn of the twenty-first century simply rode out downturns without changing their economic structure. During the same period, Charlotte was resilient as the result of an economic transformation in which finance and insurance replaced textiles as the primary economic drivers of the regional economy. Seattle's regional economy was successfully transformed twice, first from wood products manufacturing to aircraft manufacturing and then to software. Hartford and Grand Forks, which suffered industry shocks to which they have not been resilient, seem to have established new equilibriums at lower levels of employment growth, but Hartford had rapid GMP growth despite its slow employment growth.

Why did these differing experiences play out as they did? Our first conclusion is that in virtually all cases, the region's resilience or lack thereof was primarily a product of what was happening to its major export industries, both nationally and locally, and the behavior of individual firms within the region. Within the region, the strategic decisions of individual firms and their leaders as well as decisions by entrepreneurs in the area were the key actions that affected the region's economy and determined whether it proved resilient. Charlotte's transformation to a financial center was largely a result of decisions made by the dynamic leaders of two financial institutions headquartered there. Seattle's transformation to a software-based economy was virtually a historical accident—Bill

Gates's decision to move there in the late 1970s and the subsequent birth of Microsoft and other information technology–intensive firms around it (although the region's educated labor force and amenities undoubtedly attracted other educated in-migrants, facilitating the growth of this sector). Detroit's economy reflected decisions that the Big Three auto firms made as the auto industry globalized that ultimately reduced their competitiveness and thus the region's economy.

The various shock-induced downturns were often met with public concern and public activity, except in Detroit, where people believed that the regional economy would simply recover when the national economy recovered. New organizations and new programs were formed with goals related to diversification, promoting entrepreneurship and innovation, and marketing an area more intensively. Cleveland's economic development leaders tried the full panoply of organizations and programs, following recommendations from RAND, McKinsey, and Deloitte in their quest to restructure the region's economy to be more robust. In Detroit, a variety of recent efforts have been made in which foundations have played an important if not the lead role, such as the New Economy Initiative. Charlotte's Chamber of Commerce initiated the "Advantage Carolina" project in 1998. In the wake of a serious recession, Seattle created Enterprise Seattle to recruit new firms to the region. In response to the 1990 recession and the industry shock to the insurance industry, the Greater Hartford Chamber of Commerce created a regional economic development (business recruitment and retention) agency. However, there has been little or no public or civic response in the Hartford region in terms of creating or restructuring organizations or a regional strategy to respond to the downturns related to the recessions of 2000 or of 2008.

Creating and restructuring organizations were frequent "responses" to shock. So, in some cases, were increased efforts to collaborate across previously impervious boundaries or to create networks of firms belonging to similar sectors or engaged in similar kinds of activities. Many people that we interviewed in the Detroit area noted the increased efforts at regional collaboration during the past several years, an activity that was nearly absent prior to the 2000 economic downturn, from which the region has not yet recovered. Similarly, the twin shocks of military base closings and the 1997 flood triggered substantial increases in collaboration in the Grand Forks region; as we noted earlier, community leaders saw these shocks as a catalyst, changing how the community interacted and its self-image. In the Hartford region several industry-specific organizations, some supported by the state cluster initiative, were founded during the 1990s and early 2000s to spur development in particular industries, but they were responses to the region's long-term economic stagnation rather than responses to specific shock-induced downturns.

What effect did these explicit efforts to promote economic growth have? First, while policymakers in all of the six regions engaged in traditional economic planning and development activities (for example, marketing and promotion, tax subsidies, and job training programs), there is no reason to believe that those activities played a major role in determining whether the region was shock resistant or resilient to downturns caused by shocks. That is not to say that the programs were ineffective or that they were not better in some places than in others; however, virtually no one that we interviewed thought that they played a major role in the region's resilience, and we find no reason to quarrel with that assessment.

The effect of other explicit responses is difficult to gauge. Some reflected a reasonable understanding of the region's economic condition and long-term prospects better than others. To the effect that they reflect community concern, cohesion, and concerted activity, they are probably a good thing. But there have been no serious efforts at evaluation; indeed, it is difficult to evaluate responses that were multifaceted and would have been expected to take a long time to have an impact. That is true in particular when other major forces are involved—the activities of the area's existing firms. Perhaps the strongest evidence of policy impact that we observed was Grand Forks policymakers' pursuit and support of manufacturers, which probably helped lead to an increase in specialization in the region's manufacturing sector. However, even that evidence is only suggestive.

Our focus to this point has been on responses. Do policymakers in some regions engage in precautionary planning that makes it less likely that their economies experience shock-induced downturns or make them more resilient in the face of downturns? We found little evidence of that kind of advance planning. Indeed, in many cases the response to shock-induced downturns included expressions of regret at not having taken precautionary actions. A frequent question was why a region—Detroit is an especially good example—had failed to diversify its export base to avoid the problems associated with concentration in one sector. In fact, there are good—or at least plausible—answers to that question. First, as some of the people in Detroit observed, dependence on the auto industry had brought them prosperity for nearly a century; they may be paying for that now, but a century is a pretty good run for a regional economy. Second, even if they had wanted to diversify, what could or should they have done? Expressing the desirability of diversification is not the same as actually doing it; what are the leverage points in the regional economy that could have been manipulated to bring about diversification?[92]

92. The six case study regions had quite varied trends. Detroit, which had the second-highest index of concentration in 1980, actually increased its degree of concentration by 2000, as did Cleveland, which had the lowest concentration index in 1980. The two regions with the most rapid job growth over that

Grand Forks is especially interesting in that our interviewees stressed how resilient the area was and how successful its recovery was from the industry shock and flood of 1996–97. Yet our data show that the region was nonresilient to that shock and, indeed, seems to have established a new equilibrium at an employment growth rate somewhat lower than its previous rate. But perhaps the evaluation of the Grand Forks community is at least as relevant as the picture presented by our data. Regional economic resilience inevitably has a subjective component, and the perception of regional economic resilience that our definition incorporates need not reflect the perceptions of leaders in every region. The Grand Forks region has continued to grow and prosper, and those whom we interviewed said that the community seems happy with the results. In 1995, the year prior to the onset of the regional downturn, wages per worker in Grand Forks amounted to $24,414 in 2005 dollars; in 2007 wages per worker had increased by 17.7 percent, to $28,726, also in 2005 dollars. However, that increase was considerably less than the 24 percent increase in national wages per worker during the same period.

Hartford presents a different scenario. Employment in the region was actually nearly 30,000 jobs less in 2007 than it was in 1988. Yet wages per worker in 2005 dollars had increased by 35.9 percent, from $39,019 per worker in 1988 to $53,030 in 2007. It appears that the Hartford region has shed a large number of low-income workers, including many back-office workers in the insurance industry, and has retained or added high-wage workers to its economy. Hartford was the only one of the six case study regions where income inequality (as measured by the ratio of the income of the household at the 80th percentile of the income distribution to that of the household at the 20th percentile) actually increased (from 3.74 in 1980 to 4.13 in 2000).

Conclusion

This chapter offers several lessons to regional economic development policymakers. First, they should understand the ways in which their regions are vulnerable to downturns or likely to have trouble recovering from them. Detroit, for example, is especially vulnerable to employment and GMP shocks because of its dependence on durable goods manufacturing; large population of less educated workers; undiversified export base; high degree of income inequality; and less flexible labor market; however, the first three of these characteristics also make it quick to recover from employment shocks and its high degree of inequality makes it quick to recover from GMP shocks.

---

time period, Charlotte and Seattle, both had greater industrial diversity in 2000 than they had in 1980, but so did Hartford, one of the regions with the slowest job growth.

Because it takes a long time to change the regional characteristics that affect resilience-related outcomes, policies and strategies that are put in place after a region has experienced an economic shock are likely to be of little value, as our case studies suggest. Thus, to the extent that they can, policymakers should undertake precautionary planning to make regions less vulnerable to downturns or more likely to rebound from them. Unfortunately our research has very little to say about what kind of precautionary planning works to increase shock resistance or resilience to shock. We found no evidence of such effective precautionary and preventive planning. However, our research has given us the ability to predict the likelihood that different kinds of regions will be adversely affected by different kinds of shocks as well as the length of time that it will take them to recover. This suggests that regional leaders have the ability, if they wish to use it, to plan for the adverse effects that shock-induced downturns will have on their residents and governments and to put in place efforts to cope with them, even if they are unable to prevent them.

However, our findings suggest that some of the regions that could benefit most from such planning may be ones in which regional actors are least equipped to carry it out effectively. In metropolitan areas with long histories of specialization in durable manufacturing and with large shares of less educated workers (such as Detroit and Cleveland), residents and businesses may come to believe that their regional economies will always bounce back from shocks even when those shocks are due more to fundamental, long-term changes in the regional economy (such as the decline of the auto industry) than to the ordinary ups and downs of the business cycle. In such regions, economic development policymakers may either perceive no need to plan for the restructuring of the regional economy (as in Detroit) or carry out plans that are not sufficient to cope with the challenges of restructuring (as in Cleveland).

In addition to industrial and demographic characteristics, the social organization of business in a region can impede planning to mitigate shocks. In regions such as Detroit, where a few large firms from the same industry or related industries dominate the economy and civic life, other public and private actors may be unable to plan or carry out plans on a regional basis, simply because they never needed to do so in the past. Workers, for example, may not believe that shocks to the dominant firms could be permanent because those shocks had never been permanent in the past. Suppliers may lack the design and marketing capacities that they would need to compete for other business because the dominant firms had always provided them with ready markets. Local business and economic development groups may lack the capacity to respond because they have neither the experience in bringing together the necessary resources nor the ability to cooperate to do so. Local governments may also lack such experience and ability.[93] Regional leaders in post-2007 Charlotte, which had long been dominated by a few large banks as Detroit was by automakers, may or may not suffer the same inability to plan in the face of the current shock to their region's dominant industry. At the opposite extreme, regions such as Hartford have such fragmented business communities and local public sectors, with so little communication or coordination among them, that there is simply no organization capable of planning to mitigate economic shocks.

In addition to precautionary planning, which may be difficult or impossible in some regions, what else can regional economic development policymakers do to improve the economic resilience of their regions? As our Cleveland case study suggests, policymakers' efforts to improve existing industries and grow new ones may at least cushion the blow of an economic shock. They may also lay the foundation for an eventual return to more robust economic growth.

93. See Atkins and others (2011).

Appendix

Model 1: Explaining the occurrence of regional economic downturns. We employ a hazard model, in which the dependent variable measures the duration of time that an entity spends in a steady state before experiencing a particular event.[94] A hazard model estimates when the event is likely to occur, and the independent variables in the model measure the effect of each on the probability that it will occur in a given year. The event of interest in this case is a regional economic downturn, defined as a decline of at least 2 percentage points in the prior eight-year average annual growth rate. Model 1 thus estimates how much time passes until a metropolitan area experiences a downturn. This is equivalent to asking what conditions contribute to an area suffering a downturn in a given year.

The unit of analysis is a regional economy-year (that is, each of the 361 metropolitan areas in each of the thirty years is a separate observation).[95] Since the model seeks to answer the question of how much time passes until a metropolitan area experiences a downturn, we used only those observations made when a metropolitan area was not already in a downturn and thus was capable of suffering from a new one.

Model results are presented in tables 6A-3 (for employment) and 6A-4 (for GMP). Positive coefficients on a variable indicate an increase in the risk that a metropolitan area will experience a downturn, given that one has not already occurred.[96] Negative coefficients indicate a decrease in the risk of occurrence of a downturn. The results can also be discussed in terms of hazard ratios, which allow for easier substantive interpretation. A hazard ratio of 1 suggest that a one-unit increase in a variable does not change the risk of experiencing the event in question, given that it has not already occurred. A hazard ratio of 2

---

94. Specifically, we use the Cox proportional hazards model. The Cox model is different from parametric models in that it leaves the hazard rate unparameterized; that is, it makes no a priori assumptions about the shape of the hazard. The hazard rate represents the risk of experiencing an event, given that the entity in question has not experienced it yet. Box-Steffensmeier and Jones (2004) argued that in most settings the Cox model is preferable to parametric alternatives due to its less strict assumptions about the data-generating process.

95. We apply the conditional gap time correction to the standard Cox model as recommended by Box-Steffensmeier and Zorn for sequential repeated events, using the Efron method to account for coterminous event occurrences or "ties." The model stratifies by the order in which the event (in this case, a downturn) occurs and uses robust variance estimates. See Box-Steffensmeier and Zorn (2002). Standard errors are clustered by metropolitan area.

96. If a metropolitan area experienced a downturn previously, then this can be taken to mean that a downturn has yet to occur in the years *since* a previous downturn. In other words, after a downturn occurs and is resolved, the area can once again experience another downturn.

Table 6A-1. *Employment Shocks by Type and Their Effects on Regions*

	Shock type and effect			Regional outcome of shocks resulting in downturns		
Type	*Number of shocks that did not result in downturn (percent)*	*Number of shocks that resulted in downturn (percent)*	*Total number of shocks (percent)*	*Region was resilient (percent)*	*Region was nonresilient (percent)*	*Average time to recovery for resilient regions (years)*
National economic shock	221 (33)	440 (67)	661 (100)	245 (56)	195 (44)	2.8
Alone	183 (45)	223 (55)	406 (100)	122 (55)	101 (45)	2.8
With local industry shock	9 (11)	73 (89)	82 (100)	44 (60)	29 (40)	3.0
With national industry shock	29 (17)	144 (83)	173 (100)	79 (55)	65 (45)	2.6
Local industry shock	383 (58)	280 (42)	663 (100)	204 (73)	76 (27)	2.9
Alone	374 (64)	207 (36)	581 (100)	160 (77)	47 (23)	2.8
With national economic shock	9 (11)	73 (89)	82 (100)	44 (60)	29 (40)	3.0
National industry shock	135 (33)	272 (67)	407 (100)	181 (67)	91 (33)	2.9
Alone	106 (45)	128 (55)	234 (100)	102 (80)	26 (20)	3.1
With national economic shock	29 (17)	144 (83)	173 (100)	79 (55)	65 (45)	2.6
Total shocks (not double-counting)	701 (47)	775 (53)	1,476 (100)	507 (65)	268 (35)	2.9

Source: Authors' analysis.

Table 6A-2. *GMP Shocks by Type and Their Effects on Regions*

Type	Shock type and effect			Regional outcome of shocks resulting in downturns		
	Number of shocks that did not result in downturn (percent)	Number of shocks that resulted in downturn (percent)	Total number of shocks (percent)	Region was resilient (percent)	Region was nonresilient (percent)	Average time to recovery for resilient regions (years)
National economic shock	233 (55)	188 (45)	421 (100)	148 (79)	40 (21)	2.3
Alone	178 (74)	62 (26)	240 (100)	45 (73)	17 (27)	2.3
With local industry shock	24 (32)	50 (68)	74 (100)	42 (84)	8 (16)	2.0
With national industry shock	31 (29)	76 (71)	107 (100)	61 (80)	15 (20)	2.5
Local industry shock	414 (58)	297 (42)	711 (100)	258 (87)	39 (13)	2.4
Alone	390 (61)	247 (39)	637 (100)	216 (87)	31 (13)	2.4
With national economic shock	24 (32)	50 (68)	74 (100)	42 (84)	8 (16)	2.0
National industry shock	184 (42)	258 (58)	442 (100)	226 (88)	32 (12)	2.4
Alone	153 (46)	182 (54)	335 (100)	165 (91)	17 (9)	2.4
With national economic shock	31 (29)	76 (71)	107 (100)	61 (80)	15 (20)	2.5
Total shocks (nor double-counting)	776 (56)	617 (44)	1,393 (100)	529 (86)	88 (14)	2.4

Source: Authors' analysis.

Table 6A-3. *Likelihood of a Metropolitan Area Experiencing an Employment Downturn in a Given Year (Model 1)*

Variable	Cox regression: conditional gap time model			
	Coefficient	Standard error	Hazard ratio	Standard error
Percent of population with high school education or less	0.048***	0.008	1.049***	0.008
Lagged employment	0.000	0.000	1.000	0.000
Wages per worker	0.002	0.012	1.002	0.012
Percent of employment in durable manufacturing	0.028***	0.008	1.028***	0.008
Percent of employment in non-durable manufacturing	0.013	0.013	1.013	0.013
Percent of employment in health care and social assistance	−0.083***	0.027	0.921***	0.025
Percent of employment in tourism-related industries	−0.015	0.013	0.985	0.013
Number of major export industries	−0.076***	0.023	0.927***	0.022
Herfindahl index	0.028*	0.015	1.028*	0.015
Eight-year growth rate	0.211***	0.033	1.235***	0.041
National economic downturn shock	1.027***	0.078	2.791***	0.219
Local industry shock alone	1.227***	0.107	3.410***	0.363
National industry shock alone	1.538***	0.135	4.655***	0.631
National economic downturn shock and local industry shock	1.220***	0.136	3.386***	0.462
National economic downturn shock and national industry shock	1.506***	0.091	4.509***	0.411
Northeast	−0.791***	0.212	0.453***	0.096
Midwest	−0.091	0.169	0.913	0.154
South	−0.867***	0.163	0.420***	0.068
MSA age	0.003**	0.001	1.003**	0.001
Percent of population in principal city	−0.002	0.003	0.998	0.003
Number of research universities (2010)	0.002	0.079	1.002	0.079
Right-to-work law	0.148	0.127	1.159	0.147
Percent of population non-Hispanic black	−0.000	0.006	1.000	0.006
Percent of population Hispanic	−0.011***	0.004	0.989***	0.004
Income ratio 80–20	0.274**	0.111	1.315**	0.146
Chi^2	887.13			
Probability > Chi^2	0.0000			
N	6,518			

Source: Authors' analysis.
*** $p < 0.01$; ** $p < 0.05$; * $p < 0.1$.

Table 6A-4. *Likelihood of a Metropolitan Area Experiencing a GMP Downturn in a Given Year (Model 1)*

Variable	Cox regression: conditional gap time model			
	Coefficient	Standard error	Hazard ratio	Standard error
Percent of population with high school education or less	0.054***	0.009	1.056***	0.010
Lagged GMP	−0.000	0.000	1.000	0.000
Wages per worker	0.021*	0.012	1.022	0.012
Percent of employment in durable manufacturing	0.024**	0.010	1.024***	0.010
Percent of employment in non-durable manufacturing	−0.001	0.014	0.999	0.014
Percent of employment in health care and social assistance	−0.039*	0.023	0.961*	0.022
Percent of employment in tourism-related industries	−0.004	0.012	0.996	0.012
Number of major export industries	−0.083***	0.022	0.920***	0.020
Herfindahl index	0.010	0.019	1.010	0.019
Eight-year growth rate	0.186***	0.031	1.205***	0.037
National economic downturn shock	0.071	0.121	1.073	0.13
Local industry shock alone	0.773***	0.093	2.167***	0.202
National industry shock alone	1.067***	0.104	2.906***	0.302
National economic downturn shock and local industry shock	0.848***	0.155	2.334***	0.362
National economic downturn shock and national industry shock	0.962***	0.126	2.618***	0.330
Northeast	−0.080	0.248	0.923	0.229
Midwest	−0.025	0.195	0.976	0.190
South	−0.136	0.194	0.873	0.170
MSA age	−0.001	0.001	0.999	0.001
Percent of population in principal city	0.007**	0.003	1.007**	0.003
Number of research universities (2010)	0.135	0.083	1.144	0.095
Right-to-work law	−0.268**	0.133	0.765**	0.101
Percent of population non-Hispanic black	0.012	0.008	1.012	0.008
Percent of population Hispanic	−0.019***	0.006	0.981***	0.006
Income ratio 80–20	−0.059	0.104	0.942	0.098
Chi^2	378.30			
Probability > Chi^2	0.0000			
N	5,025			

Source: Authors' analysis.

*** $p < 0.01$; ** $p < 0.05$; * $p < 0.1$.

suggests that a one-unit increase in a variable doubles the risk of experiencing the event, given that it has not already occurred. Variables that are expressed as a percentage have been standardized so that their values fall between 0 and 100 (rather than 0 and 1.0), allowing for more meaningful interpretation of the hazard ratios.

Model 2: Explaining Shock Resistance. Model 2 is a logistic regression that examines what makes regions shock resistant. It differs conceptually from model 1 because it considers only instances in which a region has experienced some sort of identifiable shock, while model 1 includes all metropolitan areas in all years, regardless of whether a shock has occurred in a metropolitan area. Each observation represents a year in which a region suffered from at least one type of shock. As with the previous model, we exclude observations made when a region was already in a downturn and thus could not be adversely affected by further shocks. We exclude national economic downturn shocks from the model. Thus, the results for the other types of shocks should be interpreted as the probability of a type of shock causing a downturn *relative to* the probability of a national economic shock causing a downturn.

To make for easier substantive interpretation, we calculate discrete effects for each variable, which can be interpreted as the increase in the probability of an event occurring produced by a one-unit increase in the independent variable (from half a unit below its mean value to half a unit above), holding all other variables at their mean values. If the variable in question is a dummy variable, then the discrete effect represents the effect of the dummy changing from 0 to 1, holding all other variables at their mean values. Model results are shown in tables 6A-5 (for employment) and 6A-6 (for GMP). Standard errors are robust and clustered by metropolitan area.

Model 3: Explaining regional responses to economic shocks. Model 3 is a logistic regression that examines the regional characteristics that influence whether a metropolitan area economy that experienced an economic downturn was resilient. This model treats each of the downturns that metropolitan areas experience as separate observations and looks at the factors that contribute to whether a metropolitan area is resilient to a particular downturn. Model results are presented in tables 6-A7 (for employment) and 6-A8 (for GMP). As with the previous model, standard errors are robust and clustered by metropolitan area.

Model 4: Explaining length of time to resilience. Model 4, a hazard model in the form of model 1, explains what determines how long it takes after a downturn occurs for a region to become resilient. This model is limited to observations when a metropolitan area is already in a downturn and excludes years

Table 6A-5. *Did Shock Result in an Employment Downturn? (Model 2, Logit)*

Variable	Coefficient	Standard error	Discrete effect
Percent of population with high school education or less	0.040***	0.009	0.010
Lagged total employment	0.000	0.000	0.000
Wages per worker	0.076***	0.019	0.019
Percent of employment in durable manufacturing	0.034***	0.012	0.008
Percent of employment in nondurable manufacturing	0.027*	0.015	0.007
Percent of employment in health care and social assistance	0.005	0.026	0.001
Percent of employment in tourism-related industries	−0.032	0.023	−0.008
Number of major export industries	−0.094***	0.033	−0.023
Herfindahl index	0.028	0.018	0.007
Eight-year growth rate	0.755***	0.079	0.185
Local industry shock alone	−0.379**	0.169	−0.094
National industry shock alone	−0.041	0.203	−0.010
National economic downturn shock and local industry shock	2.328***	0.410	0.400
National economic downturn shock and national industry shock	1.540***	0.250	0.322
Northeast	0.208	0.359	0.051
Midwest	0.430*	0.259	0.105
South	−0.483*	0.276	−0.119
MSA age	0.004*	0.002	0.001
Percent of population in principal city	−0.008*	0.004	−0.002
Number of research universities (2010)	0.072	0.157	0.018
Right-to-work law	0.084	0.169	0.021
Percent of population non-Hispanic black	0.026***	0.007	0.007
Percent of population Hispanic	0.004	0.006	0.001
Income ratio 80–20	0.140	0.145	0.035
Chi^2	328.87		
Probability > Chi^2	0.00		
Pseudo R^2	0.27		
N	1,476		

Source: Authors' analysis.
*** $p < 0.01$; ** $p < 0.05$; * $p < 0.1$.

Table 6A-6. *Did Shock Result in a GMP Downturn? (Model 2, Logit)*

Variable	Coefficient	Standard error	Discrete effect
Percent of population with high school education or less	0.037***	0.011	0.009
Lagged GMP	−0.000	0.000	0.000
Wages per worker	0.110***	0.022	0.027
Percent of employment in durable manufacturing	0.015	0.015	0.004
Percent of employment in nondurable manufacturing	−0.019	0.019	−0.004
Percent of employment in health care and social assistance	0.001	0.025	0.000
Percent of employment in tourism-related industries	−0.032	0.021	−0.008
Number of major export industries	−0.044	0.031	0.011
Herfindahl index	0.021	0.028	0.005
Eight-year growth rate	0.436***	0.053	0.107
Local industry shock alone	0.784***	0.198	0.191
National industry shock alone	1.365***	0.205	0.328
National economic downturn shock and local industry shock	2.314***	0.342	0.470
National economic downturn shock and national industry shock	1.870***	0.278	0.413
Northeast	0.090	0.306	0.022
Midwest	0.307	0.263	0.076
South	0.204	0.253	0.050
MSA age	−0.002	0.002	0.000
Percent of population in principal city	0.010**	0.004	0.002
Number of research universities (2010)	−0.012	0.175	0.003
Right-to-work law	−0.204	0.178	−0.050
Percent of population non-Hispanic black	−0.002	0.008	0.001
Percent of population Hispanic	−0.010	0.007	−0.002
Income ratio 80–20	0.262**	0.130	0.064
Chi^2	206.46		
Probability > Chi^2	0.00		
Pseudo R^2	0.16		
N	1,393		

Source: Authors' analysis.
*** $p < 0.01$; ** $p < 0.05$; * $p < 0.1$.

when a metropolitan area is in a growth period.[97] The results are presented in tables 6A-9 (for employment) and 6A-10 (for GMP). By exploiting the full

97. We censor observations in which a metropolitan area is deemed nonresilient to a downturn; that is, the full amount of time that it takes for those regions to recover from the downturn, if they do recover, is considered to be unobserved in the data.

Table 6A-7. *Was Metropolitan Area Resilient to Employment Downturn?*
(Model 3, Logit)

Variable	Coefficient	Standard error	Discrete effect
Percent of population with high school education or less	0.076***	0.011	0.016
Lagged total employment	−0.000	0.000	0.000
Wages per worker	−0.034*	0.020	−0.007
Percent of employment in durable manufacturing	0.032**	0.016	0.007
Percent of employment in nondurable manufacturing	−0.032	0.020	−0.006
Percent of employment in health care and social assistance	−0.083*	0.043	−0.017
Percent of employment in tourism-related industries	0.039**	0.018	0.008
Number of major export industries	−0.022	0.043	−0.005
Herfindahl index	0.053	0.044	0.011
Pre-downturn growth rate	−0.384***	0.054	−0.080
Number of years in downturn	−0.132	0.126	−0.028
National economic downturn shock	0.039	0.220	0.008
Local industry shock alone	0.043	0.248	0.009
National industry shock alone	0.098	0.289	0.020
National economic downturn shock and local industry shock	−0.719**	0.331	−0.165
National economic downturn shock and national industry shock	−0.591**	0.252	−0.133
Northeast	−1.301***	0.374	−0.305
Midwest	−0.885***	0.283	−0.197
South	−0.684**	0.316	−0.145
MSA age	−0.001	0.002	0.000
Percent of population in principal city	0.003	0.006	0.001
Number of research universities (2010)	0.048	0.142	0.001
Right-to-work law	0.398*	0.214	0.083
Percent of population non-Hispanic black	0.007	0.012	0.001
Percent of population Hispanic	0.007	0.007	0.001
Income ratio 80–20	−0.349**	0.152	−0.073
Chi^2	206.41		
Probability > Chi^2	0.00		
Pseudo R^2	0.20		
N	1,076		

Source: Authors' analysis.
*** $p < 0.01$; ** $p < 0.05$; * $p < 0.1$.

Table 6A-8. *Was Metropolitan Area Resilient to GMP Downturn (Model 3, Logit)*

Variable	Coefficient	Standard error	Discrete effect
Percent of population with high school education or less	−0.007	0.019	0.000
Lagged GMP	0.000	0.000	0.000
Wages per worker	0.045	0.030	0.003
Percent of employment in durable manufacturing	0.015	0.028	−0.001
Percent of employment in nondurable manufacturing	−0.016	0.033	−0.001
Percent of employment in health care and social assistance	−0.116*	0.060	−0.009
Percent of employment in tourism-related industries	0.017	0.030	0.001
Number of major export industries	0.018	0.048	0.001
Herfindahl index	0.003	0.044	0.000
Pre-downturn growth rate	−0.726***	0.082	−0.055
Number of years in downturn	−0.500**	0.195	−0.038
National economic downturn shock	−0.664*	0.361	−0.063
Local industry shock alone	−0.367	0.310	−0.030
National industry shock alone	−0.095	0.357	−0.007
National economic downturn shock and local industry shock	−0.668	0.518	−0.064
National economic downturn shock and national industry shock	−0.181	0.389	−0.014
Northeast	−0.838*	0.476	−0.083
Midwest	0.421	0.466	0.029
South	0.118	0.451	0.009
MSA age	−0.008**	0.003	0.000
Percent of population in principal city	0.004	0.008	0.000
Number of research universities (2010)	−0.267	0.210	−0.020
Right-to-work law	0.703**	0.337	0.051
Percent of population non-Hispanic black	−0.041**	0.017	−0.003
Percent of population Hispanic	0.012	0.014	0.001
Income ratio 80–20	0.519**	0.243	0.039
Chi^2	192.02		
Probability > Chi^2	0.00		
Pseudo R^2	0.28		
N	952		

Source: Authors' analysis.
*** $p < 0.01$; ** $p < 0.05$; * $p < 0.1$.

Table 6A-9. *Did Metropolitan Area Recover from an Employment Downturn in a Given Year? (Model 4)*

Variable	Cox regression: conditional gap time model			
	Coefficient	Standard error	Hazard ratio	Standard error
Percent of population with high school education or less	0.031***	0.009	1.032***	0.010
Lagged employment	−0.000*	0.000	1.000*	0.000
Wages per worker	−0.062***	0.017	0.939***	0.016
Percent of employment in durable manufacturing	0.027***	0.010	1.028***	0.010
Percent of employment in non-durable manufacturing	−0.003	0.012	0.997	0.012
Percent of employment in health care and social assistance	−0.092***	0.028	0.912***	0.025
Percent of employment in tourism-related industries	0.043***	0.012	1.044***	0.012
Number of major export industries	−0.013	0.026	0.987	0.025
Herfindahl index	−0.003	0.024	0.997	0.024
Pre-downturn growth rate	−0.408***	0.041	0.665***	0.027
Number of years in downturn	−0.777***	0.077	0.460***	0.035
National economic downturn shock	0.350**	0.166	1.419**	0.236
Local industry shock alone	0.294*	0.169	1.341*	0.227
National industry shock alone	0.162	0.185	1.176	0.218
National economic downturn shock and local industry shock	0.349*	0.192	1.418*	0.272
National economic downturn shock and national industry shock	0.463***	0.168	1.590***	0.267
Northeast	−0.715***	0.242	0.489***	0.118
Midwest	−0.751***	0.201	0.472***	0.095
South	−0.399*	0.210	0.671*	0.141
MSA age	0.002	0.001	1.002	0.001
Percent of population in principal city	0.001	0.004	1.001	0.004
Number of research universities (2010)	0.204**	0.094	1.226**	0.115

(continued)

time-series/cross-sectional nature of the data, the hazard model includes more observations than does the logit model used for model 3. Thus, more variables attain statistical significance.

Tables 6A-11 and 6A-12 present summary statistics for the data used in the employment and GMP models, respectively.

Table 6A-9. *Did Metropolitan Area Recover from an Employment Downturn in a Given Year? (Model 4) (Continued)*

| Variable | Cox regression: conditional gap time model | | | |
	Coefficient	Standard error	Hazard ratio	Standard error
Right-to-work law	0.292**	0.132	1.339**	0.177
Percent of population non-Hispanic black	0.005	0.008	1.005	0.008
Percent of population Hispanic	0.007	0.006	1.007	0.006
Income ratio 80–20	−0.323***	0.121	0.724***	0.087
Chi^2	503.75			
Probability > Chi^2	0.00			
N	5,018			

Source: Authors' analysis.
*** $p < 0.01$; ** $p < 0.05$; * $p < 0.1$.

Table 6A-10. *Did Metropolitan Area Recover from a GMP Downturn in a Given Year? (Model 4)*

| Variable | Cox regression: conditional gap time model | | | |
	Coefficient	Standard error	Hazard ratio	Standard error
Percent of population with high school education or less	0.008	0.011	1.008	0.011
Lagged GMP	−0.000	0.000	1.000	0.000
Wages per worker	−0.028	0.020	0.972	0.019
Percent of employment in durable manufacturing	0.000	0.011	1.000	0.011
Percent of employment in non-durable manufacturing	−0.023	0.016	0.977	0.016
Percent of employment in health care and social assistance	−0.081***	0.027	0.922***	0.025
Percent of employment in tourism-related industries	−0.014	0.022	0.986	0.021
Number of major export industries	0.005	0.024	1.005	0.024
Herfindahl index	−0.006	0.027	0.994	0.026
Pre-downturn growth rate	−0.380***	0.033	0.684***	0.022
Number of years in downturn	−1.439***	0.101	0.237***	0.024
National economic downturn shock	0.266	0.222	1.304	0.290
Local industry shock alone	−0.070	0.170	0.933	0.159
National industry shock alone	0.051	0.172	1.052	0.181

(continued)

Table 6A-10. *Did Metropolitan Area Recover from a GMP Downturn in a Given Year? (Model 4) (Continued)*

Variable	Cox regression: conditional gap time model			
	Coefficient	Standard error	Hazard ratio	Standard error
National economic downturn shock and local industry shock	0.018	0.193	1.018	0.197
National economic downturn shock and national industry shock	0.213	0.174	1.238	0.216
Northeast	−0.616**	0.258	0.540**	0.139
Midwest	0.011	0.200	1.011	0.203
South	−0.232	0.227	0.793	0.180
MSA age	−0.000	0.001	1.000	0.001
Percent of population in principal city	0.006	0.003	1.006	0.003
Number of research universities (2010)	−0.002	0.116	0.999	0.116
Right-to-work law	0.419***	0.158	1.521***	0.240
Percent of population non-Hispanic black	−0.022***	0.007	0.978***	0.007
Percent of population Hispanic	−0.002	0.005	0.998	0.005
Income ratio 80–20	0.424***	0.103	1.528***	0.158
Chi^2	708.02			
Probability > Chi^2	0.00			
N	3,508			

Source: Authors' analysis.

*** $p < 0.01$; ** $p < 0.05$; * $p < 0.1$.

Table 6A-11. *Summary Statistics, Employment (1978–2007)*[a]

Variable	Source	Mean	Minimum	Maximum
Percent of population with high school education or less	Census/DataFerrett/GeoLytics	58	22	83
Lagged employment (thousands of jobs)	Moody's Analytics	271	5	8,532
Wages per worker (thousands of 2005 dollars)	Moody's Analytics/authors' calculations	31	18	87
Percent of employment in the following categories				
Durable manufacturing (NAICS 33)	Moody's Analytics/authors' calculations	9	0	43
Nondurable manufacturing (NAICS 31, 32)	Moody's Analytics/authors' calculations	6	0	38
Health care and social assistance (NAICS 62)	Moody's Analytics/authors' calculations	9	1	36
Tourism-related industries (arts, entertainment, recreation, accommodations, and food services) (NAICS 71-72)	Moody's Analytics/authors' calculations	9	3	41
Number of major export industries	Moody's Analytics/authors' calculations	5	0	15
Herfindahl index	Moody's Analytics/authors' calculations	5	2	42
Eight-year growth rate	Moody's Analytics/authors' calculations	0.02	–0.06	0.15
Number of years in secondary downturn	Moody's Analytics/authors' calculations	0.29	0	4
National economic downturn shock	Moody's Analytics/authors' calculations	0.06	0	1
Local industry shock alone	Moody's Analytics/authors' calculations	0.09	0	1
National industry shock alone	Moody's Analytics/authors' calculations	0.03	0	1

Variable	Source			
National economic downturn shock and local industry shock	Moody's Analytics/authors' calculations	0.01	0	1
National economic downturn shock and national industry shock	Moody's Analytics/authors' calculations	0.02	0	1
Northeast	Census	0.12	0	1
Midwest	Census	0.25	0	1
South	Census	0.41	0	1
West	Census	0.22	0	1
MSA age (numbers of years since principal city passed 50,000 in population in a decennial census)	Historical census data	52	0	210
Percent of population in principal city	Census /DataFerrett/GeoLytics	44	10	100
Number of research institutions (universities classified by the Carnegie Foundation as involved in either high or very high research activity)	Carnegie Foundation	0.51	0	13
Right-to-work state	National Right to Work Legal Defense Foundation	0.43	0	1
Percent of population non-Hispanic black	Census /DataFerrett/GeoLytics	10	0	48
Percent of population Hispanic	Census /DataFerrett/GeoLytics	7	0	94
Income ratio 80–20	Census /DataFerrett/GeoLytics	4.17	2.94	7.95

Source: Authors' analysis.

a. Statistics are for fully pooled data. Models will exclude certain observations.

Table 6A-12. *Summary Statistics, GMP (1986–2007)*[a]

Variable	Source	Mean	Minimum	Maximum
Percent of population with high school education or less	Census/DataFerrett/GeoLyrics	52	22	76
Lagged employment (thousands of jobs)	Moody's Analytics	23	0.5	1,110
Wages per worker (thousands of 2005 dollars)	Moody's Analytics/authors' calculations	32	20	87
Percent of employment in the following categories				
Durable manufacturing (NAICS 33)	Moody's Analytics/authors' calculations	8	0	41
Nondurable manufacturing (NAICS 31, 32)	Moody's Analytics/authors' calculations	6	0	38
Health care and social assistance (NAICS 62)	Moody's Analytics/authors' calculations	10	2	36
Tourism-related industries (arts, entertainment, recreation, accommodations, and food services) (NAICS 71-72)	Moody's Analytics/authors' calculations	9	3	41
Number of major export industries	Moody's Analytics/authors' calculations	6	0	16
Herfindahl index	Moody's Analytics/authors' calculations	5	2	38
Eight-year growth rate	Moody's Analytics/authors' calculations	0.03	-0.11	0.12
Number of years in secondary downturn	Moody's Analytics/authors' calculations	0.22	0	3
National economic downturn shock	Moody's Analytics/authors' calculations	0.05	0	1
Local industry shock alone	Moody's Analytics/authors' calculations	0.14	0	1
National industry shock alone	Moody's Analytics/authors' calculations	0.06	0	1\

National economic downturn shock and local industry shock	Moody's Analytics/authors' calculations	0.02	0	1
National economic downturn shock and national industry shock	Moody's Analytics/authors' calculations	0.02	0	1
Northeast	Census	0.12	0	1
Midwest	Census	0.25	0	1
South	Census	0.41	0	1
West	Census	0.22	0	1
MSA age (numbers of years since principal city passed 50,000 in population in a decennial census)	Historical census data	52	0	210
Percent of population in principal city	Census /DataFerrett/GeoLytics	43	10	100
Number of research institutions (universities classified by the Carnegie Foundation as involved in either high or very high research activity)	Carnegie Foundation	0.50	0	13
Right-to-work state	National Right to Work Legal Defense Foundation	0.44	0	1
Percent of population non-Hispanic black	Census /DataFerrett/GeoLytics	10	0	48
Percent of population Hispanic	Census /DataFerrett/GeoLytics	8	0	94
Income ratio 80–20	Census /DataFerrett/GeoLytics	4.18	2.98	7.95

Source: Authors' analysis.

a. Statistics are for fully pooled data. Models will exclude certain observations.

References

Atkins, Patricia, and others. 2011. "Responding to Manufacturing Job Loss: What Can Economic Development Policy Do?" Brookings.

Bartik, Timothy J., and Randall W. Eberts. 2006. "Urban Labor Markets." In *A Companion to Urban Economics*, edited by Richard J. Arnott and Daniel P. McMillen, pp. 389–403. Malden, Mass.: Blackwell.

Bernstein, Mark. W. 1987. "Banking Law: Developments in Interstate Banking." In *1985 Annual Survey of American Law*, edited by Christopher J. Mahon and Joseph R. Profaci, pp. 113–36. Dobbs Ferry, N.Y.: Oceana.

Blanchard, Olivier, and Lawrence F. Katz. 1992. "Regional Evolutions." In *Brookings Papers on Economic Activity*, no. 1, edited by William C. Brainard and George L. Perry, pp. 1–75. Brookings.

Bloom, Nicholas Dagen. 2004. *Merchant of Illusion*. Ohio State University Press.

Blumenthal, Pamela, Harold Wolman, and Edward Hill. 2009. "Understanding the Economic Performance of Metropolitan Areas in the United States." *Urban Studies* 46: 605–27.

Box-Steffensmeier, Janet, and Bradford Jones. 2004. *Event History Modeling*. Cambridge University Press.

Box-Steffensmeier, Janet, and Christopher Zorn. 2002. "Duration Models for Repeated Events." *Journal of Politics* 64: 1069–94.

Briguglio, Lino, and others. 2006. "Conceptualising and Measuring Economic Resilience." In *Building the Economic Resilience of Small States*, edited by Lino Briguglio, Gordon Cardigan, and E. J. Kisanga, pp. 265–87. Malta: Islands and Small States Institute.

Burns, Peter. 2002. "The Intergovernmental Regime and Public Policy in Hartford, Connecticut." *Journal of Urban Affairs* 24: 55–73.

Carr, Jered B., and Richard C. Feiock. 1999. "Metropolitan Government and Economic Development." *Urban Affairs Review* 34: 476–88.

Chapple, Karen, and T. William Lester. 2007. *Emerging Patterns of Regional Resilience*. Berkeley, Calif.: Building Resilient Regions Network.

———. 2010. "The Resilient Regional Labour Market? The U.S. Case." *Cambridge Journal of Regions, Economy, and Society* 3: 85–104.

Chinitz, Benjamin. 1961. "Contrasts in Agglomeration: New York and Pittsburgh." *American Economic Review* 51: 279–89.

Christopherson, Susan, and Jennifer Clark. 2007. "Power in Firm Networks: What It Means for Regional Innovation Systems." *Regional Studies* 41: 1223–36.

Christopherson, Susan, Jonathan Michie, and Peter Tyler. 2010. "Regional Resilience: Theoretical and Empirical Perspectives. *Cambridge Journal of Regions, Economy, and Society* 3: 3–10.

Cleveland Tomorrow Committee. 1981. *Cleveland Tomorrow: A Strategy for Economic Vitality*. Cleveland.

Connecticut Department of Economic and Community Development. 1998. "Partnership for Growth: Connecticut's Economic Competitiveness Strategy at a Glance." Hartford.

Conway, Patrick, and others. 2003. "The North Carolina Textiles Project: An Initial Report." *Journal of Textile and Apparel, Technology and Management* 3: 1–12.

Desmet, Klaus, and Esteban Rossi-Hansberg. 2009. "Spatial Growth and Industry Age." *Journal of Economic Theory* 144: 2477–502.

Duranton, Gilles, and Diego Puga. 2001. "Nursery Cities: Urban Diversity, Process Innovation, and the Life Cycle of Products." *American Economic Review* 91: 1454–77.

Duval, Romain, Jorgen Elmeskov, and Lukas Vogel. 2007. "Structural Policies and Economic Resilience to Shocks." Economics Department Working Paper 567. Paris: Organisation for Economic Cooperation and Development.

Ellef, Peter N. 1997. "Industry Clusters Shape New CT Economy." *Connecticut Economy* 5 (Summer).

Feyrer, James, Bruce Sacerdote, and Ariel Dora Stern. 2007. "Did the Rust Belt Become Shiny? A Study of Cities and Counties That Lost Steel and Auto Jobs in the 1980s." In *Brookings-Wharton Papers on Urban Affairs*, edited by Gary Burtless and Janet Rothenberg Pack, pp. 41–102. Brookings.

Ficenec, Sarah, 2010. "Building Regional Economic Resilience: What Can We Learn from Other Fields?" Working Paper 2010-06. Berkeley, Calif.: Building Resilient Regions Network.

Flynn, Patricia M. 1984. "Lowell: A High Technology Success Story." *New England Economic Review* (September-October): 39–49.

Frieder, Larry A. 1988. "The Interstate Banking Landscape: Legislative Policies and Rationale." *Contemporary Economic Policy* 6: 41–66.

Glaeser, Edward L., and Albert Saiz. 2004. "The Rise of the Skilled City." In *Brookings-Wharton Papers on Urban Affairs*, edited by William G. Gale and Janet Rothenberg Pack, pp. 47–94. Brookings.

Glaeser, Edward L., Jose A. Scheinkman, and Andrei Shleifer. 1995. "Economic Growth in a Cross-Section of Cities." *Journal of Monetary Economics* 36: 117–43.

Glaeser, Edward L., and others. 1992. "Growth in Cities." *Journal of Political Economy* 100: 1126–52.

Gottlieb, Paul D., and Michael Fogarty. 2003. "Educational Attainment and Metropolitan Growth." *Economic Development Quarterly* 17: 325–36.

Hamilton, David K., David Y. Miller, and Jerry Paytas. 2004. "Exploring the Horizontal and Vertical Dimensions of the Governing of Metropolitan Regions." *Urban Affairs Review* 40: 147–82.

Harrison, Bennett. 1984. "Regional Restructuring and 'Good Business Climates': The Economic Transformation of New England since World War II." In *Sunbelt/Snowbelt*, edited by Larry Sawers and William Tabb, pp. 48–96. Oxford University Press.

Harrison, Bennett, Maryellen Kelley, and Jon Gant. 1996. "Specialization versus Diversity in Local Economies: The Implications for Innovative Private-Sector Behavior." *Cityscape* 2: 61–93.

Hausmann, Ricardo, Lant Pritchett, and Dani Rodrik. 2004. "Growth Accelerations." NBER Working Paper 10566. Cambridge, Mass.: National Bureau of Economic Research.

Henderson, Vernon. 2003. "Marshall's Scale Economies." *Journal of Urban Economics* 53: 1–28.

Henderson, Vernon, Ari Kuncoro, and Matt Turner. 1992. "Industrial Development in Cities." *Journal of Political Economy* 103: 1067–90.

Hill, Ned. 1992. "Perspective: Contested Cleveland." *Urban Affairs Association Newsletter* (Winter).

Howland, Marie. 1984. "Age of Capital and Regional Business Cycles." *Growth and Change* 15: 29–37.

Kolko, Jed, and David Neumark. 2010. "Does Local Business Ownership Insulate Cities from Economic Shocks?" *Journal of Urban Economics* 67: 103–15.

Markusen, Ann. 1985. *Profit Cycles, Oligopoly, and Regional Development.* MIT Press.

Morrow, Betty. 2008. *Community Resilience: A Social Justice Perspective.* CARRI Research Report 4. Oak Ridge, Tenn.: Community and Regional Resilience Initiative, Oak Ridge National Laboratory.

Norris, Fran H., and others. 2008. "Community Resilience as a Metaphor, Theory, Set of Capacities, and Strategy for Disaster Readiness." *American Journal of Community Psychology* 41: 127–50.

Norton, R. D., and J. Rees. 1979. "The Product Cycle and the Spatial Decentralization of American Manufacturing." *Regional Studies* 13: 141–51.

Nunn, Nathan. 2009. "The Importance of History for Economic Development." NBER Working Paper 14899. Cambridge, Mass.: National Bureau of Economic Research.

Pastor, Manuel, and Chris Benner. 2008. "Been Down So Long: Weak-Market Cities and Regional Equity." In *Retooling for Growth*, edited by Richard M. McGahey and Jennifer S. Vey, pp. 89–118. Brookings.

Paton, Douglas, and David Johnston. 2001. "Disaster and Communities: Vulnerability, Resilience, and Preparedness." *Disaster Prevention and Management* 10: 270–77.

Pendall, Rolf, Kathryn Foster, and Margaret Cowell. 2010. "Resilience and Regions: Building Understanding of the Metaphor." *Cambridge Journal of Regions, Economy, and Society* 3: 1–14.

Piore, Michael J. 1986. "Perspectives on Labor Market Flexibility." *Industrial Relations* 25: 146–66.

Piore, Michael J., and Andrew Schrank. 2008. "Toward Managed Flexibility: The Revival of Labour Inspection in the Latin World." *International Labour Review* 147: 1–23.

Rose, Adam, and Shu-Yi Liao. 2005. "Modeling Regional Economic Resilience to Disasters: A Computable General Equilibrium Analysis of Water Service Disruptions." *Journal of Regional Science* 45: 75–112.

Roussakis, Emmanuel N. 1997. *Commercial Banking in an Era of Deregulation*, 3rd ed. Westport, Conn.: Praeger.

Rozario, Kevin. 2005. "Making Progress: Disaster Narratives and the Art of Optimism in Modern America." In *The Resilient City*, edited by Lawrence J. Vale and Thomas J. Campanella, pp. 27–54. Oxford University Press.

Safford, Sean. 2009. *Why the Garden Club Couldn't Save Youngstown.* Harvard University Press.

Simon, Curtis J. 1998. "Human Capital and Metropolitan Employment Growth," *Journal of Urban Economics* 43 (1998): 223–43.

Varaiya, Pravin, and Michael Wiseman. 1978. "The Age of Cities and the Movement of Manufacturing Employment: 1947–1972." *Papers in Regional Science* 41: 127–40.

7

Building a Resilient Social Safety Net

SARAH RECKHOW AND MARGARET WEIR

A half century ago, when poverty stood atop the nation's policy agenda, the federal government launched a remarkable period of institution building. With the declaration of the War on Poverty in 1964, the Office of Economic Opportunity oversaw the creation of community action agencies in cities across the country. The delegation of a national goal to nonprofit neighborhood-based organizations marked a new form of social policy. The organizations created during these formative years became the forerunners of the wide array of community-based nonprofit organizations whose numbers grew dramatically in the subsequent decades. Especially in the fields of affordable housing development, human services, and job training, urban nonprofits took the lead in addressing the needs of the poor. In city after city, as the number of community nonprofits grew, they drew strength from their ties with the political, philanthropic, religious, and other organizations that made up the distinctive urban social ecology in each city. Even as nonprofits began to rely on federal and state contracts to support their activities, these local ties remained essential to sustaining nonprofits.

The rapid growth of poverty in suburban areas over the past fifteen years now raises questions about the ability of this locally rooted infrastructure to adapt to the changing geography of poverty. Moreover, the passage of federal welfare reform legislation in 1996 substantially reduced the number of families qualifying for cash assistance, making services provided by nonprofits—such as child

The authors are especially indebted to Ryan Hunter, who assembled the database of foundation grants and conducted interviews in Atlanta. Teresa Gonzales and Gregory Elinson also provided expert research assistance. We would also like to thank Jennifer Tran and Mirabai Auer for their work on the maps. We thank Scott Allard, Linda Thompson, Nancy Fishman, and Steven Rathgeb Smith for valuable comments. The authors gratefully acknowledge the support of the MacArthur Foundation's Network on Building Resilient Regions for financial support. We would particularly like to thank Erika Poethig, whose support and ideas were instrumental in launching this research.

275

care and job training—even more essential. Nonprofits have become the main providers of social services in local communities, but these nonprofits often are not located in the areas with the greatest need.[1] As the pattern of poverty has become more dispersed, has the organizational infrastructure of nonprofit service provision kept pace? How has the distinctive social, political, philanthropic, and business organizational endowment of suburban areas affected their ability to create appropriate nonprofit capacities? Has a strong nonprofit sector in the city eased capacity building throughout the region or does the rootedness of existing nonprofits within specific urban contexts create obstacles to building regionwide capabilities?

Resilient regions, we argue, are regions in which institutions respond to increasing demands on social services and can adapt to the emergence of needs in new places. This perspective on resilience represents an adaptation of systems logic to incorporate the ability of actors to use "foresight and creativity" to "adapt to potential future states."[2] Thus, this is a forward-looking use of the concept of resilience, assessing whether actors and institutions in the region can detect growing needs and create new institutional capacities or adapt existing institutions to address these needs. Because most nonprofit service capacity has been created in cities, which have historically housed the majority of the region's poor, the emergence of poverty in suburbs poses questions about the actors and institutions that would respond to these new needs. We expect that regions with stronger regionwide organizations will be more likely to detect new needs in new places and will have a greater capacity to forge responses to these needs.

We explore these issues with a particular focus on the role of the philanthropic sector in fostering institutional adaptation to the new geography of poverty. Although the nonprofits with which we are concerned depend on government contracts for the bulk of their operating funds, local foundations are well situated to play a crucial role in developing new capacities, supporting the collection and dissemination of information about need, and promoting network building and system change among clusters of nonprofits. Focusing on four metropolitan areas—Atlanta, Chicago, Detroit, and Denver—we examine the extent to which local foundations are in fact supporting innovation and strengthening organizational infrastructure throughout the region. How do such efforts vary across metropolitan areas with distinctive patterns of poverty, diverse histories of political conflict, and an inherited institutional infrastructure related to poverty? Where foundations have sought to strengthen the regional nonprofit safety net, what has been the outcome? What barriers have they encountered

---

1. Allard (2009); Joassart-Marcelli and Wolch (2003); Murphy and Wallace (2010).
2. Pendall, Foster, and Cowell (2010, p. 78).

and how well were they able to overcome them? The answers to these questions will clarify how the model of nonprofit social provision that has developed over the past forty years is adapting to the new demands placed on it by the changing geography of poverty and the restrictions on cash assistance. It will also illuminate whether that model needs to be reconfigured, assessing, in particular, the implications for the state and federal roles in addressing poverty.

Challenges to the Nonprofit Safety Net

The more complex geography of poverty and the new demands on the nonprofit safety net related to welfare reform do not present the type of broad-based shock that is likely to attract widespread attention. Rather, many of these changes have been building in the decade and a half since welfare reform or are felt only in selected parts of a region. However, in places where new levels of poverty are associated with immigration or with racial change, trends may well command attention. In addition, the economic recession that began in 2007 strained the nonprofit safety net across the country, focusing more attention on the needs of low-income residents. A closer look at the broader context of changes in the geography of poverty, the key role of nonprofits, and the philanthropic sector's connection with nonprofit capacity building will set the stage for our analysis.

The New Geography of Poverty

Within metropolitan America, the poor have historically clustered in cities. A century ago, European immigrants flocked to cities, attracted by the prospect of jobs and new opportunities. Black migrants from the rural South followed a similar pattern, anxious to escape grinding poverty and propelled by hopes for building better lives in cities. By 1976 a majority of America's poor found their home in metropolitan areas, not rural ones.[3] Central cities bore a significantly greater burden for the poor within metropolitan areas at the time. Although the common image of the suburbs as strictly middle and upper income never reflected reality, 62 percent of the poor lived in central cities and 37 percent in the suburbs in 1976.

During the past thirty years, this balance between central city and suburb has slowly shifted, but in some metropolitan areas it has changed very rapidly. Census data show that the percent of the metropolitan poor who lived in suburbs

---

3. U.S. Census Bureau, 2008, "Table 8. Poverty of People, by Residence: 1959 to 2009," Historical Poverty Tables (www.census.gov/hhes/www/poverty/data/historical/people.html).

grew from 42 percent of the metropolitan population in 1990, to 46 percent in 2000, to 47 percent in 2008. Examining the largest metropolitan areas from 2000 to 2008, Brookings analysts Elizabeth Kneebone and Emily Garr found that in 2008 suburbs, for the first time, housed more poor people than the primary cities in their metropolitan areas.[4] Using the official federal poverty measure, they estimate that the primary cities of the ninety-five largest metropolitan areas were home to 10,969,243 poor residents, while the suburbs of these cities housed 12,491,486 poor people. Moreover, they show that between 2000 and 2008, poverty grew much faster in suburban areas than in cities.

The causes of this shift are complex and they vary by region. In many metropolitan areas, the influx of immigrants has played an important role in the growing numbers of suburban poor.[5] In contrast to the immigrants of a century ago, many recent immigrants have migrated directly to suburbs, reflecting the job growth in those areas. By the turn of the new century, the majority of immigrants lived in suburbs, not cities.[6] Yet, movement to the suburbs does not by itself guarantee an escape from poverty. In 2009, 41 percent of the nation's poor immigrants lived in suburbs of America's 100 largest metropolitan areas, not their cities; 15.9 percent of the suburban poor were foreign-born.[7] Immigration is only one component of the rise in suburban poverty. In many midwestern metropolitan areas, the growth of poverty in the suburbs reflects the rise in poverty more generally, as manufacturing has declined and jobs have become scarcer. In metropolitan areas that experienced sharp increases in urban property values in the 2000s, gentrification has contributed to the suburbanization of poverty. Faced with rising rents, displaced residents have moved in search of affordable housing. Although there are no precise estimates, it is clear that some of the displaced have made their way to the suburbs to find affordable housing.[8]

Underlying these broad trends are distinctive regional trajectories in the geography of metropolitan poverty. In the Midwest, which has struggled to recover from the recession of the early 2000s, poverty grew significantly both in cities and suburbs between 2000 and 2008. By contrast, in the Northeast, poverty increased by less than 1 percent in the suburbs and fell by 1.7 percent in cities. In the South, poverty grew by less than a percentage point in the cities and suburbs. In the West, where the divisions between city and suburb have typically been less pronounced, no significant change in the poverty rates occurred

4. Kneebone and Garr (2010).

5. Jason DeParle, "Struggling to Rise in the Suburbs Where Failing Means Fitting In," *New York Times*, April 19, 2009, p. A1.

6. Singer, Hardwick, and Brettell (2008, pp.15–16).

7. According to three-year estimates of the 2009 American Community Survey.

8. Sink and Ceh (2011).

either in cities or suburbs. However, the recession that began in 2007 has hit the West and South with particular force; poverty data for these areas will likely show significant increases in the future.[9]

As these regional patterns indicate, the growth in suburban poverty did not signal significant declines in urban poverty. With more than double the population of cities, suburban areas still display significantly lower rates of poverty despite the recent growth in their poor populations. Although gentrification has actually reduced the poverty rate in a handful of cities, such as New York City and Los Angeles, urban poverty rates remained well above those of the suburbs.

Thus, in most metropolitan areas, the rise in suburban poverty does not signal a major shift away from cities so much as it represents the greater dispersal of poor people throughout metropolitan areas. This new, more dispersed pattern of need presents metropolitan areas with the challenge of creating significant service capabilities in new areas or extending the existing service infrastructure to new locations at a time when these organizations are themselves strained in their traditional areas of operation. The recession intensifies this challenge, particularly in the southern and western regions, where the housing crisis hit hardest, and in midwestern metropolitan areas that have been pummeled by the decline of the auto industry.

The Growing Significance of the Nonprofit Service Sector for the Poor

In some respects, the greater dispersal of poverty can be seen as a positive development. Indeed, the large literature on urban poverty spawned by William Julius Wilson's *The Truly Disadvantaged* took the deconcentration of poverty as its major goal.[10] Yet, the institutional framework and policy context in which deconcentration occurs determines much about its consequences for the poor. Two features of that context are particularly relevant: the development of a nonprofit sector focused on poverty in cities over the past forty years and the move to restrict cash assistance as part of the 1996 welfare reform.

Since the War on Poverty, low-income Americans have come to rely on a vast network of nonprofit organizations. These organizations play multiple roles, including providing basic safety net services, connecting residents to the new opportunities, and serving as advocates (and sometimes as organizers) for low-income communities. Urban nonprofit organizations took on significant new responsibilities for the poor in the 1980s as the federal government devolved

---

9. Kneebone and Garr (2010, p.12).
10. Wilson (1990).

funding and considerable authority to state and local governments and promoted contracting out of social programs.[11] These twin developments spurred
the rapid growth in the nonprofit sector and, at the same time, drew nonprofits
into a closer relationship with government.[12] Nonprofits typically provide services within a specific neighborhood or community, sometimes accompanied by
community-building activities that aim to develop relationships among clients
and with neighboring organizations.[13]

Relying heavily on public sector funding, nonprofits have become the largest
sector of the interest group community in many cities.[14] According to Berry and
Arons: "The nature of interest group politics in local communities offers nonprofits (of all sizes, membership and nonmembership alike) an enormous opportunity. Relatively thin lobbying networks and few opponents give local nonprofits with the right political instincts a chance to exert real influence."[15]

A subset of urban nonprofits make political engagement a central focus of
their activities. These groups focus less on service provision, and more on coalition building and the development and promotion of policy proposals.[16] In
some cases, these organizations are created by or sanctioned by city officials to
fill a particular function in local governance such as regional planning or community development. Berry and Arons refer to these organizations as "super
nonprofits."[17] Thus, the long history of nonprofit activity in cities has given rise
to a sector with wide-ranging capacities. Most of these nonprofits focus on service provision, community building, and some local advocacy, but a few fill
quasi-governmental roles such as convening stakeholders and developing policy.

This role has become more important since the 1996 welfare reform
restricted cash assistance and placed new requirements for work on recipients.
The new needs of welfare recipients, including job search, job training, child
care, and transportation, were largely contracted out to nonprofit organizations.
As Scott Allard has noted, access to these services is now tantamount to receiving the basic provisions of American social welfare.[18] Research on the initial
devolution of welfare through waivers from 1992 to 1996 shows that the new
requirements for work resulted in an influx of new funds and the creation of
more nonprofit organizations.[19] Yet the growth in the number of new nonprofits

11. Allard (2009); Smith and Grønbjerg (2006).
12. Smith and Lipsky (1995).
13. Marwell (2004).
14. Berry and others (2006).
15. Berry and Arons (2003, p. 97).
16. Hula and Jackson-Elmoore (2001).
17. Berry and Arons (2003, p.116).
18. Allard (2009)
19. Twombly (2003).

tells us little about whether the organizations are effective in addressing the needs of their clients. Accessibility to clients is one key factor for assessing how effective these organizations have been. Scholars have shown that there is considerable variation within metropolitan areas in the accessibility of nonprofits to clients needing services such as child care and job training.[20]

Welfare reform emphasized work requirements, and many nonprofits focus on addressing needs related to job training and finding employment. Yet the impacts of the recession—including high rates of joblessness and growing poverty—highlight another consequence of welfare reform. With restricted cash assistance, poor families often turn to the nonprofit sector for basic services and emergency assistance. These types of social services play an important but often unacknowledged role in addressing poverty. Focusing on material deprivation rather than income, sociologist Lane Kenworthy shows that generous social services contribute to reducing material deprivation in two ways.[21] Services, such as medical care and child care, can increase the disposable income of the poor by providing free or reduced cost benefits; services can also help the poor enter and remain in paid employment.

Anti-Poverty Nonprofits and the New Geography of Poverty

Despite the key role of nonprofits in addressing the needs of the poor, we know relatively little about nonprofit capacities in suburban locations with high or growing levels of poverty. What studies do exist of these areas covering the relationship between need, income, and the presence of nonprofits indicate considerable variation in the creation of nonprofits in response to need. For example, Grønbjerg and Paarlberg found no relationship between need and the number nonprofits in Indiana.[22] Others have found a positive relationship between per capita income and the number of nonprofit social service agencies.[23] These finding suggest that the poor might be well served by nonprofits in some suburban areas but not in others. Indeed, in a study of the distribution of nonprofits that serve low-income clients in metropolitan Los Angeles, Joassart-Marcelli and Wolch found that long-established middle- and upper-income suburban cities tended to provide more services, while poor suburban cities fared worst of all when it came to developing nonprofit capacities to serve the poor.[24] These fiscally stressed localities, which were once solid working class suburbs, are now

20. Allard (2009); Joassart-Marcelli and Giordano (2006).

21. Kenworthy (2011)

22. Grønbjerg and Paarlberg (2001).

23. Corbin (1999).

24. Joassart-Marcelli and Wolch (2003, pp. 91–92).

deindustrialized areas where low-income people, many of them immigrants, have made their homes.[25] With weak public fiscal capacities and low per capita income, they suffer from poor access to public and private funding sources.

Research also suggests that efforts to promote robust nonprofit capacities in the suburbs will encounter difficulties. A strong nonprofit sector is typically associated with active government and generous public funding.[26] In contrast to the large cities, where nonprofits originated, suburban local and county governments have historically had little experience with public spending beyond traditional suburban concerns including roads and schools. Moreover, there is little evidence that suburban governments have the capacity or the inclination to detect new problems, particularly those connected with poverty.

The correlation between active government and a strong nonprofit sector creates something of a chicken-and-egg problem for the development of nonprofit capacities in suburban areas. To the extent that nonprofits themselves serve as advocates for detecting and addressing new needs, places with weak nonprofit capacity are likely to experience less local political pressure to create new capacities.[27] Even in suburban areas with some nonprofit capabilities, it may not be easy to build a broader set of services. The social safety net, as Allard has pointed out, is politically fragmented into its functional components, raising questions about whether the development of capacities in some areas, such as human services, translates into building capacity in other domains, such as housing provision.[28] Some research suggests that the concentration of nonprofits in a particular location may make a significant difference for the poor as more referrals across agencies and social connections open up opportunities.[29]

All of these challenges associated with building new nonprofit capacities are likely to be particularly acute in suburbs where growing poverty is related to large-scale immigration. Research shows that membership in voluntary organizations is more likely in stable communities; accordingly, communities with rapidly changing demography may be expected to have fewer nonprofits.[30] And, although immigrants have long formed local associations, in suburban areas immigrant organizations may be especially unlikely to develop the type of machine-style connections with local governments that characterized urban pol-

---

25. See Nicolaides (2002) on the history of these suburban areas.
26. Smith and Grønbjerg (2006, p. 235).
27. Joassart-Marcelli and Wolch (2003, p. 97).
28. Allard (2009).
29. Small (2010).
30. Grønbjerg and Paarlberg (2001, p. 701).

itics in the past. As a study of community-based organizations in Brooklyn shows, ties to strong political leaders can facilitate the flow of public dollars to nonprofit organizations.[31]

Local Foundations and Organizational Capacity Building

Among the groups that are well situated to address these gaps in the regional capacity of the anti-poverty nonprofit sector are those in the local philanthropic sector. For over a decade, leaders in the philanthropic world have encouraged the creation of local community foundations and have urged these organizations to assume central roles in strengthening nonprofit capacity and in system building. The question we pose in this chapter is whether local foundations have undertaken this effort and, if not, why not? Where foundations have taken on this role, we examine what their efforts reveal about the challenges involved in creating new nonprofit capacities in the suburbs.

Although the local philanthropic role in nonprofit development long predated federal and state engagement, local foundations are now much less important in funding nonprofits. Based on one estimate, foundations supplied only 6 percent of funding for nonprofit human service providers.[32] Although philanthropic funding for nonprofit human services has increased in inflation-adjusted dollars since the 1970s, it now composes a smaller share of the revenues of these organizations. At the organizational level, dependence on philanthropic funding varies widely. According to Allard's survey, although 80 percent of nonprofits receive grants from private donors, "only 14 percent of nonprofits are resource-dependent upon revenues from nonprofit grants or foundations."[33] As their role in the direct funding of services has diminished, large national foundations have taken on the role of organizational innovators. Since the Ford Foundation helped launch the organizational template for the War on Poverty in the early 1960s, national foundations have become sophisticated innovators of programs designed to assist the poor, often in conjunction with federal and state policies.[34] Many major metropolitan areas are home to large foundations that, while national and international in focus, also devote particular attention to the city of their origin.

Likewise, community foundations focus on particular geographic areas. In older cities, community foundations have amassed substantial resources. In

31. Marwell (2007).
32. Berry and Arons (2003, p. 9).
33. Allard (2009, p. 93).
34. The earned income tax credit provides a good example.

contrast to national foundations, however, these organizations have typically devoted less attention to organizational innovation. Many community foundations have mainly provided "donor services," acting as a conduit for individual donations.[35] As a result, significant parts of their endowment have been in restricted funds, limiting their ability to play a larger proactive philanthropic role.

Recently, however, national organizations and associations of foundations have aimed to carve out a new role for community foundations as system builders. Part of the reason for the new focus is competition from the private sector in providing donor services. Competition has come not only from private financial firms, such as Schwab and Fidelity, which set up their own donor-advised funds in the early 1990s, but also from direct giving to individual organizations through the Internet. One important element of the new vision for community foundations is that they serve as "change agents," by creating new partnerships and seeking to promote systemic reform. As part of this new approach, some studies urged community foundations to "reach across the boundaries of place" and work on "brokering regional solutions."[36] The growing interest in regionalism on the part of business groups and social equity advocates in many metropolitan areas has reinforced this call for community foundations to expand their focus to the regional level.[37]

Although local foundations provide only a small fraction of the funding for nonprofits, there are good reasons to suspect that they may be able to promote regional resilience in the face of the increased demands on the nonprofits and the growth of poverty in the suburbs. Nonprofits see foundations as a source of funding that allows them to go beyond the day-to-day provision of services and to think creatively about their activities. As one suburban service provider put it, "Foundation and corporate money is really different . . . foundation or corporate dollars give nonprofits room for creativity and ingenuity."[38] The long experience of community foundations in addressing urban poverty together with the recent attention to regionalism in the philanthropic sector may make foundations especially attuned to the emergence of needs in new places. By contrast, most suburban governments—county and local—have had little experience with poverty until recently. Thus, even with limited resources, local foundations can promote regional resilience by providing information about suburban poverty, supporting new organizations in the suburbs, assisting existing organizations to establish branches in new places, and setting up consortia or networks of organizations throughout the region.

35. Graddy and Morgan (2006).
36. Bernholz, Fulton, and Kasper (2005); Hamilton, Parzen, and Brown (2004, pp. 9–10).
37. Dreier, Mollenkopf, and Swanstrom (2001); Pastor, Benner, and Matsuoka (2009).
38. Quoted in Allard and Roth (2010, p. 18).

Building a Resilient Regional Safety Net

Have local foundations, including community foundations, taken on new regional system building roles? And, when they have, what can we learn from their efforts about the challenges to building a resilient regional safety net? Our research addresses these questions through a comparative case study of the Chicago, Atlanta, Denver, and Detroit metropolitan areas. We first examine the local foundation landscape with particular attention to the differences between urban and suburban philanthropic capacities. Next, we analyze the geographic patterns of investments that key local foundations have made in nonprofits that serve low-income people. Drawing on the same data, we evaluate the extent to which these foundations have sought to support system building in their grant making. Finally, we discuss the challenges that efforts to expand regional capacity have encountered. To understand these challenges, we interviewed local foundation officers concerned with poverty, leaders in suburban and urban non-profit organizations serving the poor, and representatives of the United Way. We conducted twelve interviews in Chicago in the summer of 2009, nine interviews in Atlanta in the summer of 2010, and three interviews in Detroit in the fall of 2010. We asked interviewees about the role their organizations play in addressing suburban poverty, what supports they have received in their efforts, and what obstacles they have confronted.

Our Cases

Our research questions focus on two distinct relationships. One is the relationship between the pattern of suburban poverty in the metropolitan area and the response of the philanthropic sector to the problem. The other is the relationship between the history of regional cooperation or institution building and the philanthropic response. Thus, the cases were selected to offer variation on two independent variables of interest—the nature of the problem and the region's institutional history.

In order to assess different patterns of suburban poverty, our cases include two fast-growing Sunbelt metropolitan areas—Atlanta and Denver—and two slow-growth Frostbelt metropolitan areas—Chicago and Detroit.[39] The Sunbelt metropolitan areas experienced booming regional population growth and increasing

39. We use the metropolitan statistical areas (MSAs) as defined by the Office of Management and Budget (OMB) to determine the geographic boundaries of the Atlanta, Chicago, and Detroit metropolitan areas. For Denver, we have added Boulder County to the OMB-defined MSA. Boulder is commonly viewed as a part of the Denver metropolitan region by the actors in our study; for example, the region's major community foundation, the Denver Foundation, includes Boulder in its service area.

immigration in the 1990s and early 2000s. Suburban poverty is a relatively new issue in these areas, though the challenge has been heightened by the recession that began in 2007. Atlanta's economy has suffered more than Denver's; metropolitan Atlanta had a 7.8 percent decrease in employment from peak levels to late 2009, compared to a 4.9 percent decrease in Denver.[40] In the Frostbelt regions, the growth in suburban poverty is tied to longer-term economic decline, particularly in the manufacturing sector. These regions are home to many inner-ring or "first" suburbs, with problems such as aging infrastructure, fiscal stress, and job loss.[41] Despite these challenges, Chicago has remained a major immigrant gateway, and increasingly immigrants are moving directly to the suburbs of Chicago.[42] In this respect, some Chicago suburbs that have attracted large numbers of immigrants may resemble Denver and Atlanta suburbs more than Detroit. Nonetheless, Frostbelt suburbs have gained more recognition than Sunbelt suburbs as troubled areas requiring new policies and new resources. For this reason, we would expect the philanthropic and nonprofit sectors to be more responsive to suburban poverty in the Chicago and Detroit regions.

Alternatively, perhaps philanthropy will be more responsive to suburban poverty in metropolitan areas with a history of collaboration and institution building at a regional level. Existing patterns of relationships and institutional arrangements can shape the development of new interactions in cities and regions. For example, Safford shows how civic relationships formed the basis for economic innovation and recovery in Allentown, Pennsylvania, but a different pattern of relationships hindered economic recovery in Youngstown, Ohio.[43] Similarly, a study comparing regional transportation networks in Chicago and Los Angeles finds that relationships between sustainability advocates and regional business and political institutions in Chicago enabled institutional reforms in transportation planning, but advocates in Los Angeles did not establish relationships to key regional institutions.[44] Existing regional institutions in Chicago became powerful players in transportation policy, which in turn built regional capacity to fight for reform at the state level.

To assess variation on this dimension, our cases include two regions with a stronger history of regional institution building—Chicago and Denver—and two cases which are known for institutional fragmentation and a stark city-suburban divide—Atlanta and Detroit. Admittedly, these characterizations are not comprehensive—they do not describe the institutional framework of each region for all

40. Wial and Friedhoff (2010).
41. Puentes and Orfield (2002).
42. Gupta (2004).
43. Safford (2010).
44. Weir, Rongerude, Ansell (2009).

issues at all times. In fact, all four regions have a history of sharp divisions between city and suburbs. In Chicago, Atlanta, and Detroit, charged racial divisions and the history of white flight have fueled bitter city-suburb antagonisms since the 1940s.[45] In Denver, although race did not play as prominent a role in city-suburb divisions, little love was lost between the city and its suburbs. However, more recently, Chicago and Denver have launched efforts at promoting regional cooperation. In Chicago, a 1999 report by the business-related civic organization Chicago Metropolis 2020 inspired political and civic leaders to initiate a variety of efforts to promote regional engagement.[46] These efforts included a long campaign to create the Chicago Metropolitan Agency for Planning (CMAP) and the formation of the Metropolitan Mayors Caucus as a venue for regional discussion. Denver has a history of regional engagement stemming from the deep recession of the early 1980s, when economic development agencies in the region formed the Denver Business Network. Mayors in the Denver area began meeting as a caucus beginning in 1986. This background of regional activity along with strong backing from the business community built support for a 2004 regional sales tax for transportation. Driving this effort was a Denver mayor dedicated to strengthening relationships with suburbs and business leaders actively supporting a new regional infrastructure to promote growth.[47]

By contrast, Atlanta and Detroit have made less headway in promoting regional cooperation. Neither Atlanta nor Detroit currently has a full-fledged regional transportation agency. In 1999 Georgia launched the Georgia Regional Transportation Authority only under the threat of losing its federal highway funds. Despite initial hopes that the authority would evolve into a strong regional transportation authority, it mainly operates as a partner to counties in creating bus services.[48] In Detroit the Southeast Michigan Council of Governments (SEMCOG) has responsibility for regional transportation planning. SEMCOG has disproportionately higher levels of representation for outer suburban areas than for the city of Detroit and inner suburbs. A regional faith-based organizing group, Metropolitan Organizing Strategy Enabling Strength (MOSES), led a lawsuit against SEMCOG's voting system, but the judge upheld SEMCOG's existing representation imbalance, arguing that the "one-person, one-vote" doctrine does not apply to agencies such as SEMCOG.[49]

45. See Kruse (2007) on Atlanta; Sugrue (2005) on Detroit; and Weir (1996) on Chicago.
46. Johnson (1999); Hamilton (2002).
47. Wallis (2008, pp. 112–13); J. Lieb, "Voters Climb Aboard: Fast Tracks Tax Boost Six New Metro Area Rail Lines," *Denver Post*, November 3, 2004, p. B-01.
48. Henderson (2006).
49. Joe Grengs, "Fighting for Balanced Transportation in the Motor City," Planners Network, 2005 (www.plannersnetwork.org/publications/2005_spring/grengs.html [May 9, 2010]).

Although Detroit's regional institutions have been slow to develop, MOSES does represent a key effort toward regional political organizing. MOSES advocates a regional agenda on issues like transportation, and it draws on a membership base of congregations in Detroit as well as Wayne, Oakland, and Macomb counties.[50] Thus, although Detroit and Atlanta have experienced some regional cooperation, they have not had the same kind of political and civic leadership around this issue as have Chicago and Denver. Given that the civic and political institutions in Chicago and Denver have stronger track records in responding to problems by building regional relationships, we propose that the philanthropic sector in these regions will be better equipped to respond to growing suburban poverty.

Defining the Challenge

Suburban poverty has grown in each of these metropolitan areas since 2000; in all four regions, the suburbs added more people in poverty between 2000 and 2008 than the primary cities. Table 7-1 summarizes the changes in urban and suburban poverty in each of the four metropolitan areas from 2000 to 2008, based on Kneebone and Garr's analysis using the 2000 U.S. Census and American Community Survey data. Kneebone and Garr define primary cities as cities that "(1) appear first in the official metropolitan area name, or (2) are listed second or third in the official name and contain a population of at least 100,000 (per 2007 Population Estimates)."[51] The remainder of the metropolitan area, outside the primary cities, was designated as suburb. Although suburban poverty increased in all four metropolitan areas, there is substantial variation across these metropolitan areas in the size of the increase in suburban poverty and the increase in suburban poverty relative to urban poverty.

Although suburban poverty has increased in all four metropolitan areas, urban poverty rates remain much higher than suburban poverty rates, particularly in Detroit, where the poverty rate of the primary cities is 30.7 percent. It is important to recognize that urban poverty is still a severe problem in each of these places. Nonetheless, the number of poor people living in suburban areas is greater than the number of poor in the city in two of the four metropolitan areas, Atlanta and Detroit. In Chicago and Denver, the number of poor people living in the primary cities is only slightly higher than the number in the suburbs.

The metropolitan area with the most dramatic contrast between the change in urban poverty and the change in suburban poverty is Atlanta. The number of

50. Rusch (2008); Pastor, Benner, and Matsuoka (2009).
51. Kneebone and Garr (2010, p. 3).

Table 7-1. *Changes in City and Suburban Poverty, 2000–08*

Metro area	Number of poor in primary cities, 2008	Change since 2000	Primary city poverty rate, 2008	Number of poor in suburbs, 2008	Change since 2000	Suburban poverty rate, 2008
Atlanta	95,484	–259	22.4	519,521	218,227*	10.7
Chicago	578,494	7,948	19.4	535,707	171,741*	8.3
Denver	155,100	53,062*	17.4	123,737	55,126*	7.8
Detroit	275,263	21,998*	30.7	330,922	119,545*	9.5

Source: Kneebone and Garr (2010).
*Statistically significant at the 90 percent confidence level.

poor people living in primary cities in the Atlanta region actually decreased from 2000 to 2008, while suburban poverty increased by more than 200,000. Atlanta now has the highest suburban poverty rate among the four metropolitan areas. Denver's suburban poverty rate is the lowest of the four metropolitan areas, and the number of poor living in the suburbs increased only slightly more than in primary cities. In Chicago the number of poor people increased in both the primary cities and the suburbs, though the increase was more than twenty times larger in the suburbs. Similarly, the number of poor people rose in both primary cities and suburbs in Detroit, although the growth in the suburbs was only about five times greater than in the primary cities.

Regional Philanthropic Resources

As the early engines of metropolitan growth as well as centers of poverty, cities became home to major philanthropic organizations, including the first community foundations, nearly a century ago. Reflecting this history, philanthropic wealth remains concentrated in cities today, despite recent efforts to create community foundations in suburban areas. This geographic pattern is evident in our four regions, based on the asset data we collected for community foundations and for the largest private foundation in the region.[52]

As figure 7-1 shows, the major private foundations in each region held assets that far exceeded those of the largest community foundations. Three of these private foundations—the MacArthur Foundation in Chicago, the Daniels Fund in Denver, and the Kresge Foundation in Detroit—are national in scope (and

52. There are, of course, national foundations, such as the Casey Foundation in Atlanta, that also focus on our areas but are not included in this analysis.

Figure 7-1. *Assets by Foundation Type, 2007*

Billions of dollars

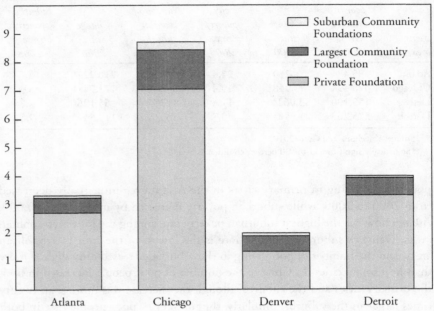

Source: Authors' analysis of Foundation Directory Online data.

international in the case of MacArthur); yet they regularly devote a portion of their giving to their home regions. The Woodruff Foundation provides grants within Georgia only. The MacArthur Foundation concentrates 13 percent of its total U.S. giving in Chicago; while Kresge awards 28 percent of its American grants in Detroit. Woodruff and Daniels focus their giving more heavily on their home regions, with Woodruff dedicating 75 percent of its total giving to the Atlanta region and the Daniels Fund allocating 50 percent of its total to metropolitan Denver.[53]

Community foundations in the core cities of our regions have far smaller endowments but devote all their giving to the region. These assets ranged from a high of $1.5 billion for the Chicago Community Trust to just over $500 million for the Community Foundation for Greater Atlanta and for the Community Foundation for Southeast Michigan.[54] Suburban community foundations are,

53. Data are from 2009. Data on the MacArthur and Kresge foundations are from the Foundation Center's online directory; the Woodruff data are from its website, and the Daniels data are from its website (www.danielsfund.org/Grants/index.asp).

54. Data are from 2009.

by contrast, much newer and smaller. In all four regions, most suburban community foundations began operating only in the 1990s, and have not accumulated significant asset bases. There are a few exceptions, most notably the Grand Victoria Foundation, which is a private independent foundation in Illinois with a statewide mission. The organization is headquartered in Chicago and has another office in Elgin, part of the Chicago metropolitan area. Relatively large for a community foundation formed in the 1990s, the Grand Victoria still had only 5 percent of the assets of the Chicago Community Trust.

The concentration of foundation assets in cities means that if the philanthropic sector is to help create a regional nonprofit safety net, the initiative will have to come from foundations that have long focused primarily on urban centers. During the 1990s, several of the community foundations in our study embraced a regional approach to their work. As part of its regional perspective, for example, the Community Foundation for Greater Atlanta made strengthening nonprofits throughout the region one of its central goals. The foundation now defines its service area as the twenty-three counties in metropolitan Atlanta, and throughout the 1990s it helped to establish affiliates across the region. As figure 7-1 shows, however, these suburban community foundations remain quite small. In 1998 the executive director summed up the foundation's regional approach, suggesting that the community foundation was "in an ideal position to act as a catalyst for collaboration across county and city boundaries—involving governments, businesses, nonprofit agencies and citizen groups. Unfortunately, greater Atlanta has very little tradition of true regional collaboration. In fact, in many respects our political and cultural heritage is anti-regional."[55]

The Chicago Community Trust also helped spawn numerous community foundations in the suburbs during the 1990s, but, as in Atlanta, these organizations have remained small. In contrast to Atlanta, the Chicago Community Trust's charter restricts its activities to Cook County, while a smaller affiliated Chicago Community Foundation can provide grants throughout the metropolitan region. These restrictions mean that the community foundation in Chicago can extend its reach to the growing poverty in the city's southern suburbs but has more limited resources available for exurban areas. The Grand Victoria Foundation, however, is explicitly focused on several areas of the state regions outside Chicago, creating some broader regional capacity. The foundation has invested in the financial and leadership development of existing community foundations, devoting more than $50 million in grants, coaching, organizational innovation, and network development for select community foundations in Illinois. The

---

55. Quoted in Maria Saporta, "Group Takes a Regional Approach to Philanthropy," *Atlanta Journal and Constitution*, October 13, 1998, p. B4.

effort to promote regional approaches in Chicago received a strong boost from the MacArthur Foundation, which launched a significant regional program in the mid-1990s.[56]

Similar to the Community Foundation for Greater Atlanta, the Community Foundation for Southeast Michigan defines its service area regionally, incorporating the city of Detroit and seven surrounding counties. Recently, there have been high profile efforts at regional collaboration within Detroit's philanthropic sector. For example, the Community Foundation for Southeast Michigan is now the home of the New Economy Initiative, a joint philanthropic effort started in 2008 involving ten local and national foundations, including Kresge, which have committed $100 million to the effort. The New Economy Initiative is focused on economic development in southeastern Michigan, such as supporting new entrepreneurs, building on regional assets, and developing the workforce. A recent article in the *Detroit News* highlighted the convergence of philanthropy in the region: "Detroit foundations used to speak politely to each other, once or twice a year; now they're divvying up projects according to their individual missions, cheering each other's successes and finding new ways to collaborate. . . . The unexpected emergence of such collective energy is being viewed as an exciting stimulus, or as a potential power grab by those outside the group."[57]

These developments in Detroit have occurred too recently to be captured by the data presented here. Nonetheless, this points to the potential for foundations to act as regional leaders despite a lack of strong public sector leadership around regional collaboration.

The Regional Distribution of Philanthropic Anti-Poverty Investments

To analyze the funding activities of philanthropies in each region, we assembled an original database of grants in each of the four metropolitan areas. We use these data to assess the extent of foundation support for safety net services and system building in each of our regions. First, we focus on the geographic patterns of grant making, particularly the amount of grant funding for suburban safety net service organizations. Second, we investigate whether grantees are located in high poverty areas within each region by mapping the location of human service grantees along with local poverty rates. Third, we identified large foundation grants that support system change in service areas targeting low-income people. These grants support regional networking, intermediaries, data

56. Sevin (2000).

57. Laura Berman and Christine MacDonald, "Foundations Take Action for Detroit," *Detroit News*, March 26, 2010.

gathering, and dissemination, among other activities. (See appendix B for a full description of the coding criteria.)

Our database includes grants distributed from 2003 and 2007 by urban and suburban community foundations and one major private foundation in each of our four regions.[58] A list of all of the foundations in our database is included in appendix A. The grants were collected using the Foundation Directory Online (FDO), which includes grants reported by foundations to the Foundation Center; the FDO provides the most current information available on foundation grant making in the United States. Our database includes 3,621 grants for Atlanta, 1,613 grants for Chicago, 6,077 grants for Denver, and 4,593 grants for Detroit, making a grand total of nearly 16,000 grants across the four regions. Interestingly, the number of foundation grants distributed in a region is inversely related to the amount of grant dollars distributed. Although fewer individual grants were distributed by Atlanta and Chicago foundations, these foundations distributed the most grant dollars in 2003 and 2007: $243 million in Atlanta and $187 million in Chicago. Meanwhile, the large numbers of grants distributed by Denver and Detroit foundations added up to fewer grant dollars: just $88 million in Denver and $133 million in Detroit. In total, our database includes more than $650 million in grants representing all the grants in our database, not only the grants to nonprofits that provide services to low-income people. Across the four metropolitan areas, the proportion of grants focused on low-income service providers varied widely. Combining the grants from 2003 and 2007, 60 percent of the Chicago foundation grant dollars were for organizations serving low-income people, 54 percent of grant dollars in Denver, 21 percent of Detroit grant dollars, and 19 percent of Atlanta grant dollars.

In addition to the coding for low-income grants and system change, each grant was coded by the location of the grantee as well as the grantee's policy area or type of service. For the analysis here, we focus on grantees working in three main policy areas that support low-income people: workforce training, housing, and human services.[59] The share of grants distributed in these three categories differs across the four regions, though the ranking of the regions mirrors the share of grants for low-income services generally. In Chicago, approximately

58. The database does not, therefore, capture the impact of larger funding collaboratives that include national foundations and other local philanthropic, private organizations, and public funds. Where such collaboratives exist, our data underestimate the degree of regional activity. For example, the National Fund for Workforce Solutions has supported a regional workforce collaborative in Chicago, for which the Chicago Community Trust and the MacArthur Foundation (two foundations in our database) are only two of twelve funders, including private and public sources of funding. For a description of the activities of the fund, see http://nfwsolutions.org/.

59. The two key areas that are excluded are health and education. We are continuing to verify our coding procedures in these areas.

Table 7-2. *Grant Dollars to City and Suburban Service Providers, 2007*

Millions of dollars

Type of provider	Atlanta		Chicago		Denver		Detroit	
	City	Suburbs	City	Suburbs	City	Suburbs	City	Suburbs
Human services	4.90	0.68	4.60	0.54	4.70	1.60	1.00	1.30
Housing	0.08	0.22	34.00	0.48	1.40	0.09	0.53	0.17
Workforce training	1.40	0.02	0.94	0.19	0.66	0.07	0.06	0.00
Total	6.30	0.90	39.50	1.20	6.80	1.70	1.60	1.50

Source: Authors' analysis of 2007 grants data.

27 percent of all the 2003 and 2007 grant dollars were in workforce, housing, and human services, and in Denver, these categories composed 14 percent of all grant dollars. In Detroit and Atlanta, workforce, housing, and human service grants were a much smaller share of all grant dollars—only about 5 percent in Detroit and 4 percent in Atlanta.

Across three of the regions, there was considerably more foundation grant making for workforce training, housing, and human services organizations based in the central city than provided by organizations based in the suburbs in 2007 (see table 7-2). Detroit is the one exception to this pattern; it is the only region where grant making to suburban-based human service providers is slightly higher than grants to those in the city, making the total grants for city- and suburban-based service providers relatively comparable. Given the high levels of need in the city of Detroit, this is surprising, but it may reflect the overall decline in the city's population. A recent article in the *Chronicle of Philanthropy* described the dire situation in Detroit.

> Detroit, whose population has been halved since the 1950s, is full of vacant land and foreclosed homes. The foreclosures, coupled with the nation's financial crisis, have crippled the city's community-development corporations, which focus on low-cost housing and economic development. At least two of the roughly 30 neighborhood-based charities have closed already, and several others shut down for a spell in the past year before reopening. A group of foundations is encouraging the neighborhood-based charities to consider merging to form regional organizations.[60]

60. Ben Gose, "Survival of the Fittest? Charities, Foundations, Struggle over Restructuring in a Sour Economy," *Chronicle of Philanthropy*, April 9, 2009.

These challenging circumstances for Detroit-based organizations may be playing a role in catalyzing a more regional approach within the philanthropic sector.

In both Chicago and Denver, city-based providers of workforce training, housing, and human services received at least twice as many foundation grant dollars as suburban-based providers. Housing particularly stands out in Chicago, with more than $30 million in grants for Chicago-based housing services. This is heavily influenced by a $26 million grant from the MacArthur Foundation to Local Initiatives Support Corporation (LISC) for the New Communities program, a housing and community development initiative in sixteen Chicago neighborhoods.[61] Excluding this grant, Chicago foundations gave more than $8 million in grants to city-based housing nonprofits, which is still more than the total in housing grants for the other three cities. Although Denver foundations gave considerably more to city-based service providers, Denver also has the highest total grant dollars for suburban-based service providers. In Atlanta, although grant dollars for human service and workforce nonprofits primarily supported city-based organizations, suburban-based housing nonprofits, including Housing Initiative of North Fulton, Initiative for Affordable Housing DeKalb, and Cobb Habitat for Humanity, received twice as many grant dollars as those in the city.

The results include one important caveat: many city-based nonprofit organizations do provide services in the suburbs. One example is ChildServ, a Chicago-based human services organization that offers services in Cook, Lake, and DuPage counties. Likewise, Families First, an Atlanta-based agency providing a range of family services, operates satellite programs in a number of suburban locations.[62] The reverse—suburban-based organizations providing services in the city—occurs less often, though there are a few examples. Gleaners Community Food Bank is located outside of Detroit in Oak Park, Michigan; the organization serves five counties in the region as well as the city of Detroit. Nonetheless, in three of the regions, the much smaller share of grant dollars for nonprofit service providers based in the suburbs suggests that philanthropies are primarily following well-established channels for grant making. In other words, foundations in these regions are devoting relatively fewer dollars to building new capacity in suburban-based organizations. Instead, to the extent that foundations are supporting services for low-income suburban residents, it is often through city-based organizations.

Yet these overall totals in foundation giving to suburban areas do not account for the potential need for services. We can assess this for suburban areas generally

61. See www.newcommunities.org/index.asp, 2010.
62. See www.familiesfirst.org/T80-home-page.

Table 7-3. *Suburban Grant Dollars and Foundation Assets per Poor Person*
Dollars

Grants/assets	Atlanta	Chicago	Denver	Detroit
Grants per poor person	1.78	2.28	11.20	4.48
Assets per poor person	168	523	659	205

Source: Authors' analysis of 2007 grants data and Kneebone and Garr (2010).

by calculating the rate of grant making to service providers in the suburbs based on the number of poor people living in the suburbs in each region. We use Knee-bone and Garr's totals for the number of poor living in the suburbs in each region in 2008 (table 7-1) and the total amount of grant dollars to suburban service providers in workforce training, housing, and human services in 2007 (table 7-2). The results are reported in table 7-3.[63] Denver has the highest rate, and Atlanta the lowest, of suburban grant making per poor person. While Denver philanthropies gave more funding to suburban service providers than philanthropies in the other three regions, Denver also has the lowest level of suburban poverty among the four regions. On the other hand, Atlanta philanthropies gave the fewest grant dollars to suburban service providers among the three regions, but Atlanta has the highest rate of suburban poverty among the regions.

These disparities in grant-making rates could be related to the grant-making capacity of suburban community foundations. We also calculated the assets of suburban community foundations per poor person in the suburbs (table 7-3). Atlanta's suburban community foundations have the fewest assets per poor person in the suburbs, while Denver's have the most. Chicago also has a relatively high level of assets per poor person for suburban areas. We do not expect that suburban service providers would primarily rely on the limited assets of suburban foundations for their funding. However, these numbers provide an additional indicator of the limited capacity of the philanthropic sector in suburban areas—particularly in places with growing need for services, such as suburban Atlanta. These results provide a broad perspective on grant making to service providers in suburban areas, but they do not show whether the grantees are based in communities where the need for services is greatest. To address this question, we must look at areas of high poverty within each region and examine the specific locations of service providers that received foundation grants.

63. Number of suburban poor drawn from Kneebone and Garr (2010). Kneebone and Garr use metropolitan statistical areas in their analysis, which do not include Boulder County, so for the Denver region we have included grant, asset, and poverty data for Boulder County in these calculations.

Greater Need, Fewer Grants

Prior research has shown that nonprofit service providers are often not located in the areas of greatest need.[64] Is this also the case with foundation grants? Or, are foundations countering this trend by providing additional funding to organizations in the neediest suburban areas? We address this question by mapping 2003 and 2007 foundation grants to human services organizations along with 2005 and 2008 poverty rates in the four regions.[65] We selected the human services grants because human services organizations are often smaller entities that serve residents in the surrounding neighborhood. Housing and workforce training providers often serve a larger area.

The maps are displayed in figures 7-2, 7-3, 7-4, and 7-5. Each map shows the proportion of people at or below 150 percent of the poverty level, an income level at which residents are likely to seek and qualify for services.[66] The data are presented at the PUMA (public use micro area) level, as designated by the U.S. Census. The population contained within PUMAs is large enough to generate single-year estimates based on the American Community Survey (ACS). We assume that grants awarded in a given year are used by organizations to fund future activities. Thus, we sought to pair our grant data with poverty data from the subsequent year. The 2003 grant data are paired with 2005 poverty data, because ACS data at the PUMA level are not available prior to 2005. The 2007 grant data are paired with 2008 poverty data. Layered on top of the PUMAs are the locations of human services grantees, based on matching zip codes within each PUMA. The size of the circles represents the amount of dollars for grantees within each area.

In both 2003 and 2007, human services grants were relatively concentrated in the central city areas of Atlanta, Chicago, and Denver, matching the higher rates of poverty in these central cities (figures 7-2, 7-3, and 7-4). In Detroit, human services grants are largely divided between the city of Detroit and Oakland County; there are few grants in other parts of the region (figure 7-5). Given the short period of time—three years—between our two measures of poverty, we did not expect substantial changes in the geography of poverty in these regions. Nonetheless, the maps do indicate areas of growing suburban poverty in

64. Allard (2009); Joassart-Marcelli and Wolch (2003).

65. With the exception of the Detroit MSA, we have focused on the core of our metropolitan areas for the maps. The density of grant making is relatively thin in many outlying counties of the larger metropolitan areas. Thus, we focus on the core areas of our metropolitan areas in order to highlight variation in grant-making between urban areas and more densely populated suburbs.

66. However, the recession of 2007 expanded the range of new clients to include those who had been earning higher incomes.

Figure 7-2a. *Atlanta Region*

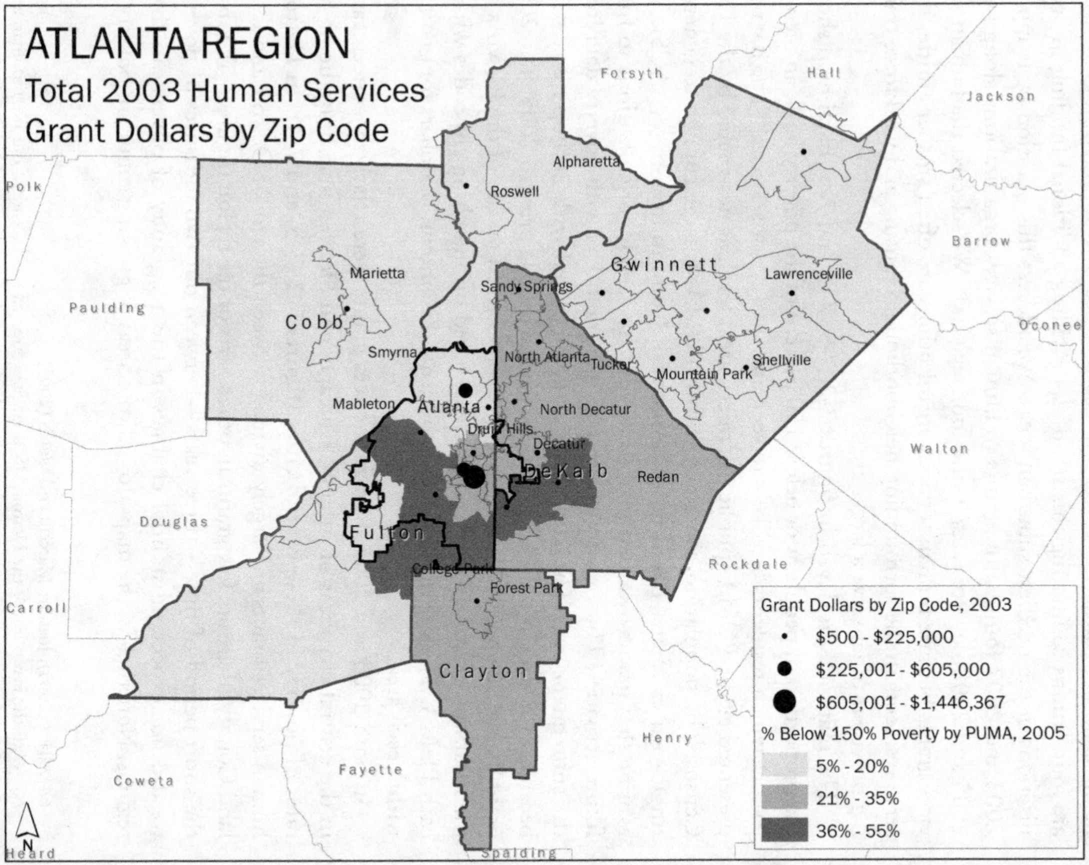

ATLANTA REGION
Total 2003 Human Services
Grant Dollars by Zip Code

Grant Dollars by Zip Code, 2003
· $500 - $225,000
● $225,001 - $605,000
⬤ $605,001 - $1,446,367

% Below 150% Poverty by PUMA, 2005
5% - 20%
21% - 35%
36% - 55%

Figure 7-2b. *Atlanta Region*

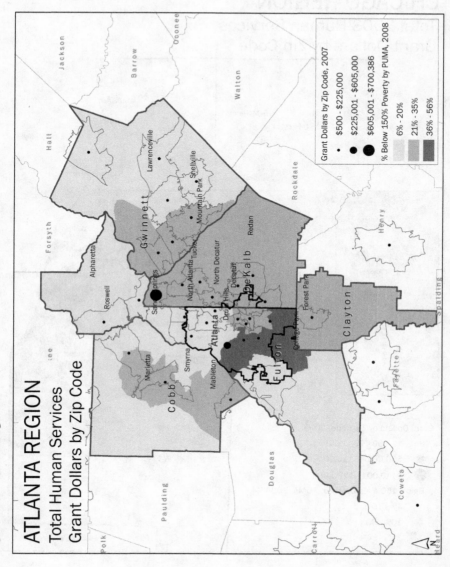

ATLANTA REGION
Total Human Services
Grant Dollars by Zip Code

Grant Dollars by Zip Code, 2007
· $500 - $225,000
● $225,001 - $605,000
⬤ $605,001 - $700,386

% Below 150% Poverty by PUMA, 2008
6% - 20%
21% - 35%
36% - 56%

Figure 7-3a. *Chicago Region*

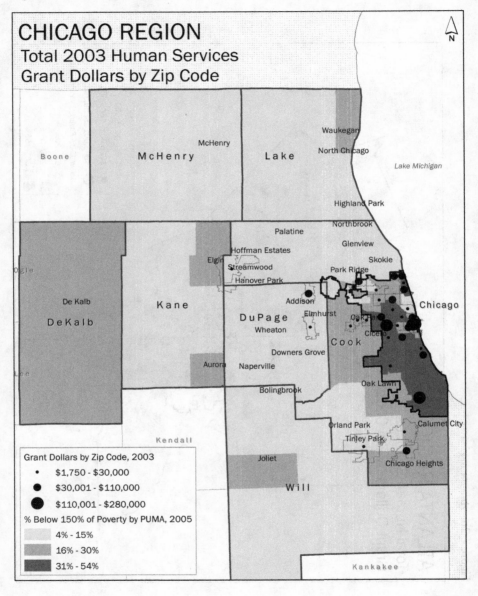

Figure 7-3b. *Chicago Region*

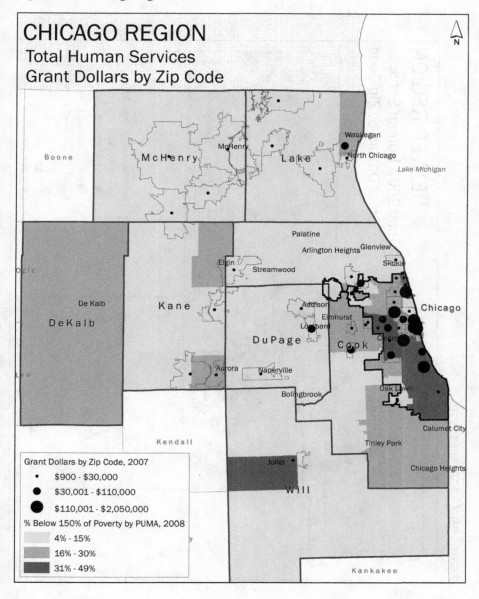

Figure 7-4a. *Denver Region*

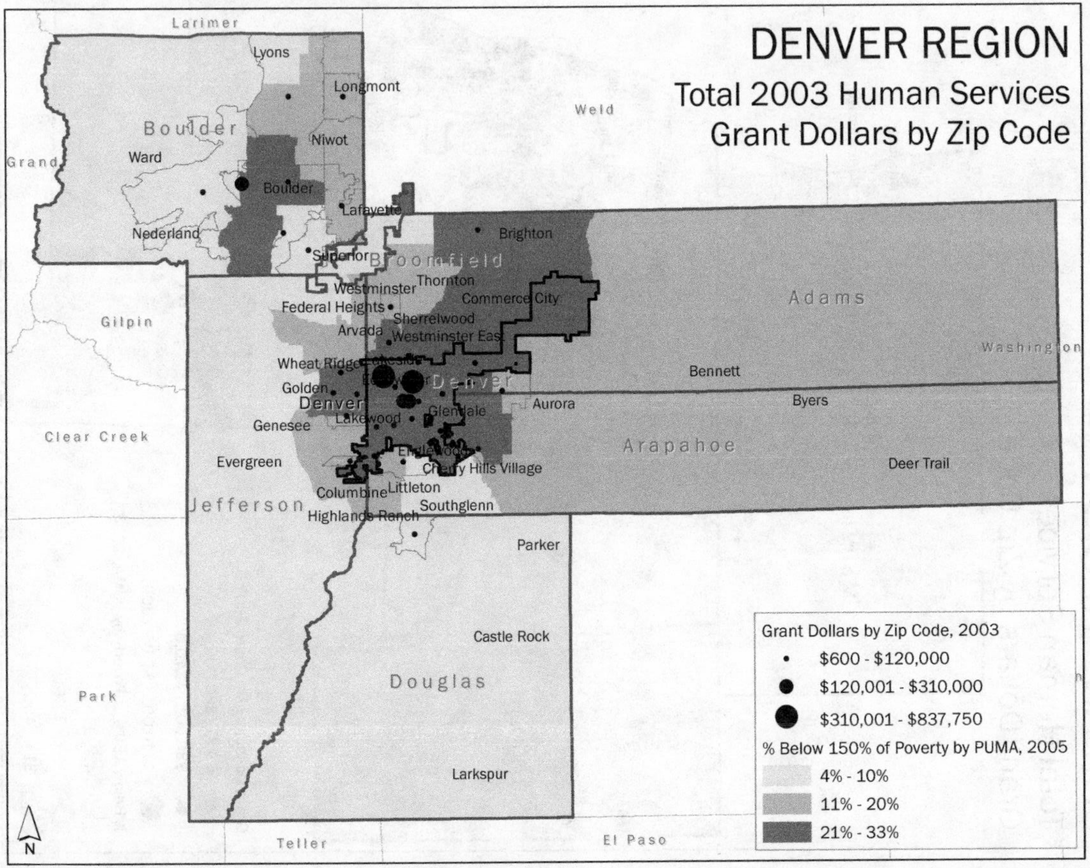

DENVER REGION
Total 2003 Human Services
Grant Dollars by Zip Code

Grant Dollars by Zip Code, 2003

- • $600 - $120,000
- • $120,001 - $310,000
- ● $310,001 - $837,750

% Below 150% of Poverty by PUMA, 2005

- 4% - 10%
- 11% - 20%
- 21% - 33%

Figure 7-4b. *Denver Region*

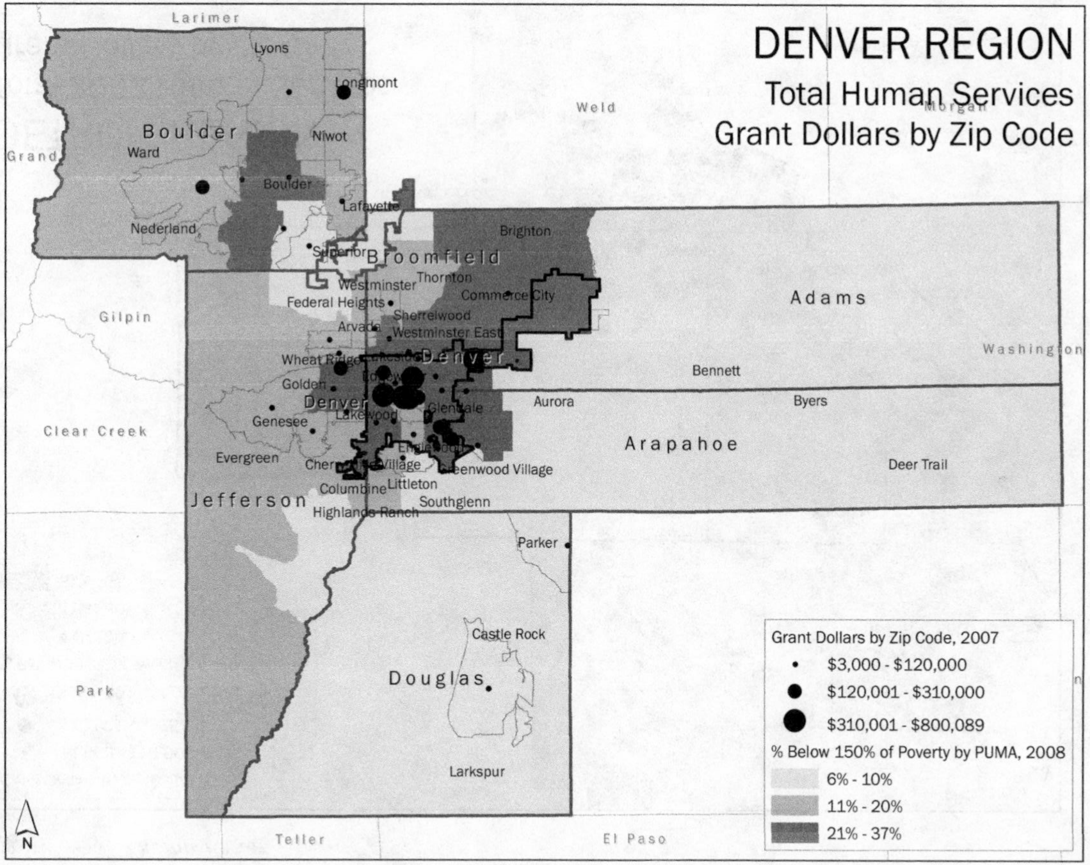

DENVER REGION
Total Human Services
Grant Dollars by Zip Code

Grant Dollars by Zip Code, 2007
· $3,000 - $120,000
● $120,001 - $310,000
⬤ $310,001 - $800,089

% Below 150% of Poverty by PUMA, 2008
6% - 10%
11% - 20%
21% - 37%

Figure 7-5a. *Detroit Region*

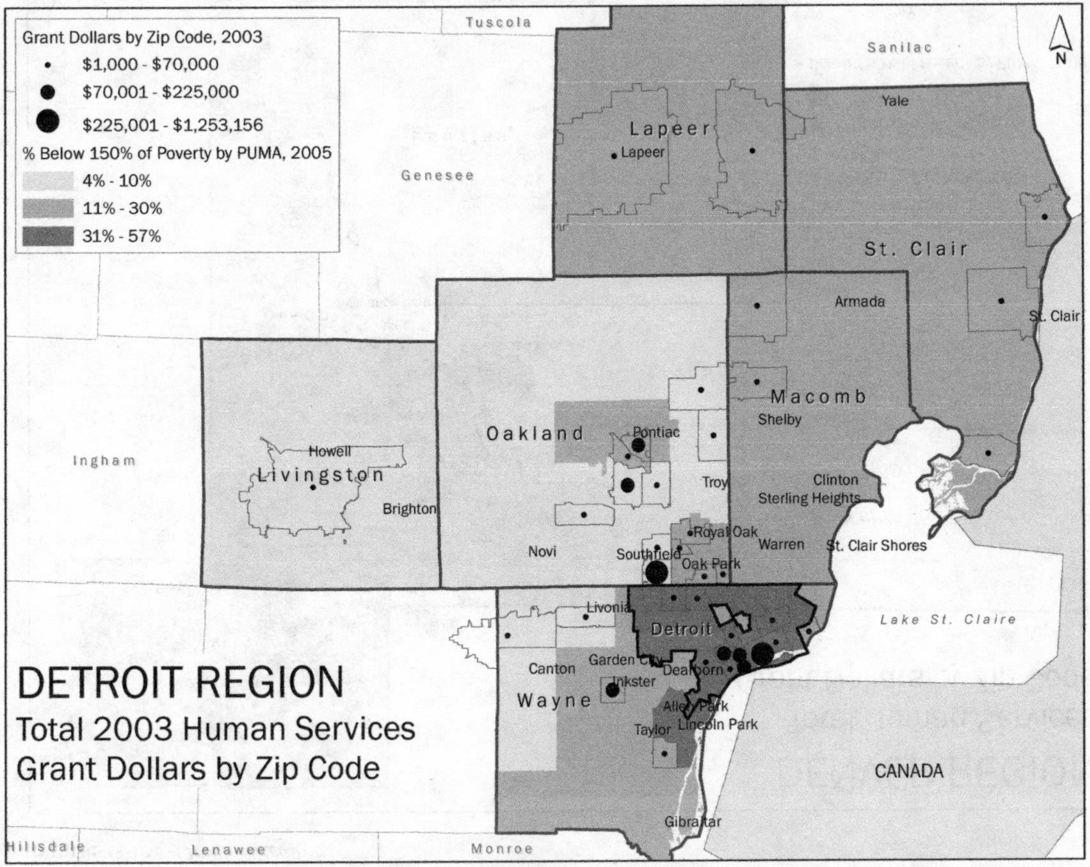

DETROIT REGION
Total 2003 Human Services
Grant Dollars by Zip Code

Figure 7-5b. *Detroit Region*

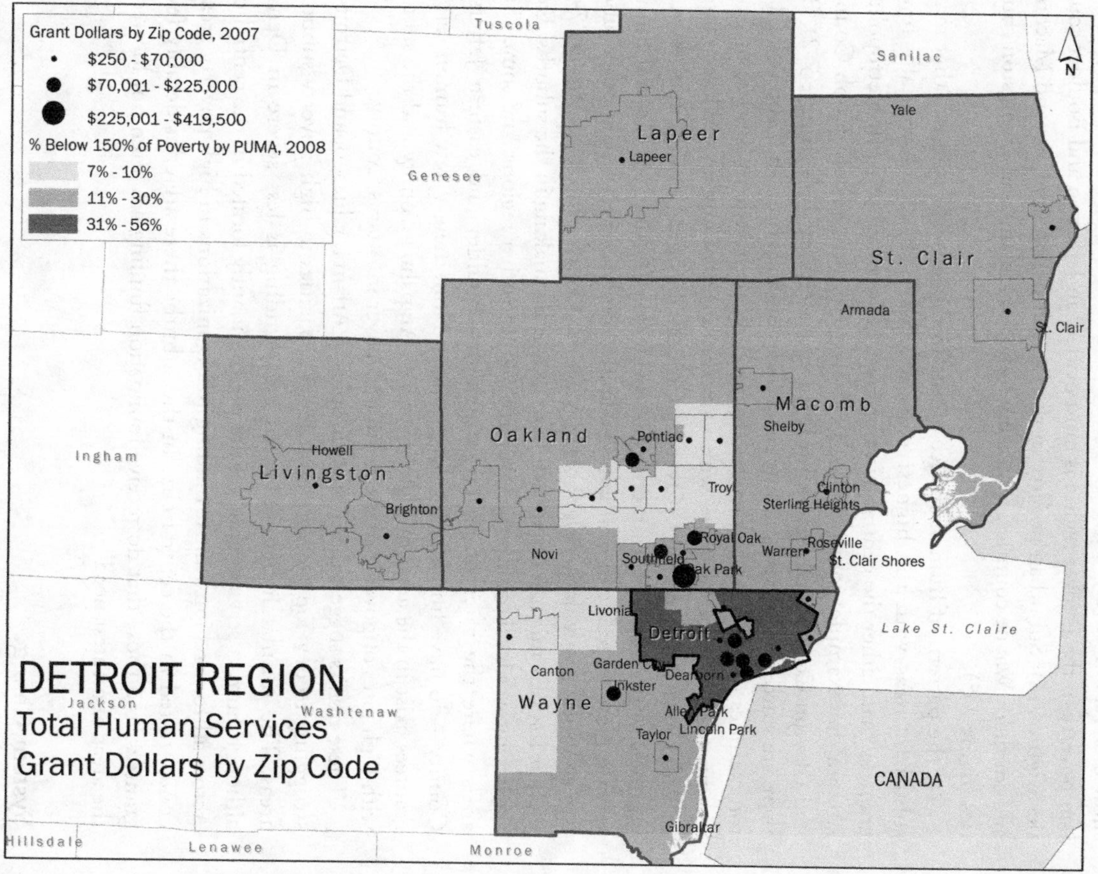

DETROIT REGION
Total Human Services
Grant Dollars by Zip Code

Grant Dollars by Zip Code, 2007
· $250 - $70,000
● $70,001 - $225,000
● $225,001 - $419,500

% Below 150% of Poverty by PUMA, 2008
7% - 10%
11% - 30%
31% - 56%

each of the four metropolitan areas. In the Atlanta region, poverty grew in parts of Cobb and Gwinnett counties between 2005 and 2008 (figure 7-2). In the Chicago region, Will County (particularly Joliet) and southern Cook County show increases in poverty rates from 2005 to 2008 (figure 7-3). Growing suburban poverty in the Denver region is most evident in Jefferson and Boulder counties (figure 7-4). Suburban poverty in the Detroit region grew beyond Macomb and southern Wayne counties, increasing in both Oakland and Livingston counties (figure 7-5).

Yet the pattern of human service grants in the suburbs suggests that many suburban areas with the highest rates of poverty have substantially fewer grantees than either the central cities or lower poverty suburbs. In metropolitan Atlanta, for example, southwestern Gwinnett County, western Cobb County, and Clayton County had significant levels of poverty by 2008 (figure 7-2). But there are scarcely any grants to human services organizations in Cobb and Clayton counties. In the Chicago region (figure 7-3), the southern suburbs of Cook County are a high poverty area with a small number of human services grantees in 2003 and none in 2007. Overall, Chicago has very few human services grantees in the suburbs. In metropolitan Detroit (figure 7-5), several human services grantees reside in southern Oakland County, but few are in other suburban counties, particularly neighboring Macomb County. In Denver (figure 7-4), there is less of a mismatch between need and grant making in the suburbs. Denver has a lower level of suburban poverty than the other regions, and some of the areas where the rates of poverty are high—Boulder and eastern Jefferson County—do have human services grantees. Nonetheless, few human service grantees exist in the areas of high poverty in Arapahoe County and the suburbs with high rates of poverty to the north of Denver in Adams County.

These results suggest that philanthropies in Atlanta, Chicago, and Detroit are struggling to develop new organizational capacities in high-poverty suburban areas. The mismatch between need and funding is less severe in Denver, although human services grantees are predominantly located in the central city. Across all four regions, most funding to organizations in high poverty areas is concentrated in the central city. In the suburbs there are considerably fewer grantees, and those that do receive foundation funding are often not located in the areas of greatest need.

System Change

Although community foundations continue to fill the more "traditional" role of providing charitable donations to local organizations, many are beginning to make larger and more strategic grants to help promote system change and reform

Table 7-4. *System Change Grants and Organizations, 2007*

Type of grant	Atlanta	Chicago	Denver	Detroit
Housing, human services, and workforce grant (million$)	7.3	39.9	8.5	3.2
System change grant (million$)	2.5	29.3	1.7	1.3
System change grants (percent)	34.3	73.0	20.0	41.3
System change organizations	4	29	7	6

the social safety net. Furthermore, the private foundations in each region typically make large grants focused on specific initiatives. These grants may help forge new partnerships among service providers or address challenges at a regional level. When coding the grant data, we identified the large grants (above $50,000) that were intended to support system change and those that supported organizations that work toward system change (see appendix B).

In table 7-4, we report the total amount of workforce training, housing, and human services grant dollars from 2007, and the amount of grant dollars in each region that were coded as supporting system change. Among the four regions, Chicago had the most grant dollars devoted to system change in 2007, more than $29 million. This total includes the $26 million LISC grant for housing, as well as smaller grants, such as a $50,000 grant to the Alliance to End Homelessness in suburban Cook County. Chicago also has the largest amount of grant dollars devoted to system change as a share of total giving in these areas, 73 percent. In the other three regions, foundations support system change at much lower levels, although Atlanta foundations give more grant dollars for system change than Denver and Detroit. Yet these overall grant totals may miss an important underlying indicator of system change—the number of organizations in the region receiving grants to work toward system change. Based on this indicator, Chicago also has substantially more support for system change organizations than the other three regions. Twenty-nine separate organizations in the Chicago region received grants supporting system change. In Atlanta, four organizations received grants for system change.

Although the $26 million LISC grant is focused on neighborhoods in the city of Chicago, many of the system change grantees in Chicago work at a regional scale. For example, the human services system change grants include several regional human service agencies, such as Catholic Charities of the Archdiocese of Chicago (serving Cook and Lake counties), Metropolitan Family Services (serving Cook, Lake, and DuPage counties), and the Greater Chicago Food Depository (serving Cook County). Furthermore, some organizations focus entirely on suburban areas, such as the DuPage Federation on Human Services Reform, which received a $55,000 grant to create a primary portal homepage for social service providers.

Atlanta had the next highest amount of grant dollars for system reform, about $2.5 million, although these grants supported only four organizations. Three of these are regional organizations—the Atlanta Community Food Bank, Pathways Community Network, and the United Way of Metropolitan Atlanta. Another system change grantee in the Atlanta region is the Center for Family Resources, based in Marietta. Much like those in Atlanta, the system change grants in Denver and Detroit include funding for the regional United Ways as well as regional food banks. Denver's other system change grantee organizations included Energy Outreach Colorado and Colorado Coalition for the Homeless. In Detroit, system change grantees included one major suburban human services organization, Lighthouse of Oakland County, and one major city-based human services and housing organization, Southwest Solutions. Thus, although Atlanta's system change grant making largely focuses on a few key regional organizations, Denver and Detroit have a slightly broader base of organizations receiving system change grants. Still, it is clear that none of the other regions come close to the funding levels and organizational infrastructure supporting system change in Chicago.

Challenges in Building a Regional Safety Net

As the traditionally city-centered philanthropic sector has begun to extend its efforts to the regional level, some kinds of initiatives have proven easier to launch than others. The function of supporting and connecting existing organizations has been the most prominent activity. Foundations have encountered much more difficulty in creating new philanthropic capacities in the suburbs and in establishing new suburban or regional organizations. A closer look at the activities that foundations have successfully launched and the obstacles they have confronted raises questions about what kind of contributions we can expect the local philanthropic sector to make toward building a regional safety net.

Much of the significant regional philanthropic activity has supported existing organizations that define their activity regionally. These include regionally focused food banks in all four of our regions and affordable housing organizations, such as the Atlanta Neighborhood Development Partnership, and Denver's Habitat for Humanity. Foundations have also promoted connections among existing organizations through network building. Chicago's Grand Victoria Foundation, which works outside the city of Chicago, sees network building as central to creating more capacity in regions.

Atlanta's Civic League, with help from the Community Foundation for Greater Atlanta among others, has convened an annual regional neighborhood summit for the past two years.[67] Foundations have also supported the activities of United Ways in each region. Over the past two decades United Ways have worked, with varying success, to consolidate their operations at the regional level. The United Ways in all four of our regions now define their service area to extend beyond the main city, although in the Atlanta and Chicago regions several independent organizations continue to exist.

The one case in which foundation support did help create a new regional agency occurred in Chicago. The MacArthur Foundation's regional program was critical to the long campaign to create a new unified regional planning agency, the Chicago Metropolitan Agency for Planning (CMAP).[68] Unlike most metropolitan planning organizations (which are authorized by federal transportation law), CMAP—at the insistence of its board—included human services as one of its six working committees. This decision ensures that information about the extent and availability of human services is incorporated into the long-range regional plans required by federal transportation legislation. The Chicago Community Trust has worked closely with CMAP in producing the plans related to human relations, education, health, and social services. Inclusion of these issues creates a regularized process for assessing some of the problems related to poverty at the regional scale and engages regional leaders in developing a long-range vision for how to address them.

The human services element of its work allowed CMAP to play a role in creating a regional 211 system, which provides callers with information about a variety of social services with a single telephone number. Pioneered by Atlanta's United Way, the 211 network is a national initiative of the United Way now operating in forty-seven states.[69] As one CMAP staffer put it, "We never would have been involved with that before. We would have never had those connections; 99 percent of the people here probably don't know what 211 is. I didn't know what it was until they came to talk to me. Different human services approached us to do a planning effort to get the state to listen."[70]

The hope is that CMAP's information about need and gaps in human services can eventually influence decisions about how and where to allocate resources for new services, such as preschool centers. Despite the potential benefits of building a human services component into regional planning, planning has no impact on spending decisions. These decisions are currently made

67. See www.neighborhoodsummit.org/index.html, 2010.
68. Sevin (2000); Weir, Rongerude, and Ansell (2009).
69. For more information on how the 211 system works, see www.211us.org/status.htm.
70. Interview with authors, Chicago, June 22, 2009.

according to a state funding formula or on the basis of the political clout of those lobbying for a new service. Both approaches have their drawbacks. Formulas are not flexible and lag behind the changing contours of need. Basing services on political clout may be especially harmful to areas of new immigrant concentration, since a significant proportion of new immigrants are unlikely to be voters. The disconnect between planning and spending also occurs in local and regional decisionmaking. Townships have some formal responsibility for social services and taxing authority to support them. But these officials have shown little interest in participating in CMAP's regional planning. As one CMAP official put it, "A lot of these people [the township officials] are only part-time people, [there is] not enough staff, they don't see the value, they are a bastion of local politics, provide services in their area and they don't coordinate with others."[71]

In Detroit, foundations have had some success promoting new collaborations among existing organizations at a regional scale. In 2007 the Detroit-based Skillman Foundation brought together local organizations to explore the Center for Working Families concept, a national project of the Annie E. Casey Foundation designed to support financial stability for low-income families. This led to a new collaboration between the United Way for Southeastern Michigan and LISC Detroit to develop a regional network of Centers for Working Families, with United Way and LISC providing technical assistance, resources, data collection, and ongoing training.[72] Although LISC focuses on the city of Detroit for its programming, both LISC and United Way will offer technical support for the entire regional network. United Way will provide additional financial support on a regional scale. Currently, five centers have been established in the region—four in Detroit and one in Oakland County—and twelve are planned. Future expansion will also be funded by a federal grant to LISC through the Social Innovation Fund.[73]

The philanthropic sector has not experienced much success in creating new community foundations in suburban areas. In each of our regions, established community foundations in the city sought to jump-start new community foundations in the suburbs. Most of these organizations are very new. But, as figure 7-1 shows, they have not grown substantially since their inception. The obstacles to their growth are varied but several stand out. In the Chicago region, some wealthy suburban areas have a tradition of philanthropy but they define themselves as part of the city, not the broader suburban area. As one Chicago interviewee put it, "The wealthy communities along the lakeshore identify with

71. Interview with authors, Chicago, June 22, 2009.
72. Interview with authors, Detroit, November 17, 2010.
73. See Corporation for National and Community Service, "Social Innovation Fund" (www.nationalservice.gov/about/programs/innovation.asp).

Chicago, and that is where the money is going; they don't identify with the communities to the west. Their challenge is to convince those people in Lake Forest [a wealthy suburb] that Waukegan [a deindustrialized community that has attracted a significant low-income immigrant population] is part of their community."[74] In Atlanta, by contrast, the Greater Atlanta Foundation established local funds to promote philanthropy in areas that did not want to join a broader regional organization centered in Atlanta. Yet, these local funds remain very small even in relatively wealthy counties. In other areas, such as the south suburbs of Chicago or the southern part of Wayne County in Detroit's suburbs or Clayton County, Georgia, there are few concentrations of wealth and only weak capacity to support community-based philanthropy.

Even the larger city-based community foundations are likely to remain restricted in their ability to foster new regional capacities. These foundations are already supporting substantial programs directed at low-income communities in the city. Moreover, donor-advised funds still constitute a majority of the resources for many of these foundations. Such funds, which allow donors to advise how grants are allocated, are much less likely to promote system change. Moreover, city donors are less likely to support grants for suburban capacity building. Donor-advised funds have grown in recent years, a reflection both of growing wealth among higher-income Americans and of the increasing competition with private sector donor-advised funds.[75] A 2000 survey conducted by the Columbus Foundation showed that nearly one-fourth of community foundation assets were in donor-advised funds.[76] In our metropolitan areas the percentages were considerably higher. For example, two-thirds of the Chicago Community Trust's assets consist of donor-advised funds, as are the great majority of the Greater Atlanta Foundation's funds.

Foundations have encountered substantial difficulties in building new organizations and new networks in the suburbs. The challenges are especially acute in lower-income suburban areas. For example, the foundations working in the racially diverse high-poverty southern suburbs of Chicago report difficulties in building robust organizational networks. The Grand Victoria Foundation has sponsored several networks in this area as has the Chicago Community Trust. The latter, for example, launched the South Suburban Coordinating Council, whose aim is to build connections among fifteen human service organizations and to promote "an intentional conversation about the region."[77] These initial attempts at network building confronted significant obstacles. The combination

74. Interview with authors, Chicago, June 19, 2009.
75. Ostrander (2007).
76. Luck and Feurt (2002).
77. Interview with authors, Chicago, June 17, 2009.

of deep political fragmentation, restricted resources, and mistrust across racial lines posed significant barriers to cooperation.[78]

Yet, this groundwork and ongoing foundation support proved essential in preparing the southern suburbs to take advantage of new federal funding. In 2009, twenty-eight small jurisdictions in these suburbs, part of a larger South Suburban Mayors and Managers Association, formed a collaborative to receive funds from the Neighborhood Stabilization Program, the federal grant program designed to help localities address the problem of foreclosures.[79] Built on the base of the earlier foundation-supported efforts at fostering cooperation, the new collaborative relied on regional organizations such as CMAP, the Metropolitan Mayors Caucus, and the Metropolitan Planning Council as it formulated its plans. Philanthropic organizations also played a key role in keeping the collaboration going throughout the granting process. As a study by the Federal Reserve Bank of Chicago noted, the federal granting process was not well matched to support the collaborative's multijurisdictional strategy and "third-party funding (from foundations) was instrumental in allowing the collaborative to move forward while they waited for formal approvals and signed contracts."[80] Although the collaborative and its partners did not win the stiff national competition for the second round of funding, the collaboration has led to other successes in winning grants including a Sustainable Communities Challenge grant from HUD to the South Suburban Mayors and Managers Association.

Clayton County, south of Atlanta, has had little comparable regional support for building local capacities. An area that had attracted a black middle-class population seeking affordable housing over the past decade, Clayton County has also become home to many poor black Atlantans. The county has been plagued by political scandals, which caused its public schools to lose accreditation from 2008 to 2010. Residents took a further blow in 2010, when the county eliminated its bus system due to fiscal pressures. The pressure of new needs and insufficient services meant that many poor Clayton residents continue to rely on services in Atlanta. The elimination of the bus system has amplified the difficulty of accessing services. Since the recession hit in 2007, the low level of service provision in Clayton County combined with restricted resources has made it difficult for funders or other service agencies to provide effective assistance. As one informant put it, there is "just not enough energy and resources in Clayton to meet both the philanthropists and service providers in that middle ground."[81]

---

78. Hendrick and Mossberger (2009).

79. Kari Lydersen, "Emerging from Chicago's Shadow," *Shelterforce*, Fall/Winter (February 12, 2009) (www.shelterforce.org/article/1857/emerging_from_chicagos_shadow/P0/).

80. Newberger (2010, pp. 5-6).

81. Interview with Ryan Hunter, Atlanta, July 21, 2010.

These areas of growing suburban poverty are, in some respects, similar to the high-poverty suburbs south of Los Angeles, where Joassart-Marcelli and Wolch found relatively few nonprofit organizations.[82] Allard and Roth, in a 2010 study of nonprofits, likewise, found that the ratio of poor persons to nonprofits was significantly less favorable in high-poverty suburbs than in lower-poverty suburbs.[83] The barriers to building organizations and connections may be particularly high in such politically fragmented, resource-poor suburban settings. Our data certainly suggest that there is less foundation investment in these areas, which in our cases include Chicago's southern suburbs, western Gwinnett and north Clayton counties in the Atlanta region, and southern Wayne and southern Macomb counties in the Detroit area. The recent forward movement in Chicago's southern suburbs suggests that the philanthropic community may be able to influence capacity in these areas. However, experience shows that the process is likely to be slow and that the lure of now diminishing federal funds may be critical to promoting coordination.

In wealthier suburban areas, it may be possible to launch and connect new organizations addressing poverty. In the relatively affluent Chicago suburb of DuPage County, the DuPage Federation on Human Services Reform emerged in 1995 with state funding and support from the Annie E. Casey Foundation, a national foundation.[84] With local philanthropic support and a link to a local university, the DuPage Federation has since grown into a significant resource providing information about demographic changes and need in the county. Among its activities are providing data for nonprofits to use in their grant writing; identifying gaps in service; and navigating the human service system's complex web of agencies and funding to ensure that the area receives state and federal funds for which it is eligible. The countywide approach of the organization may be significant. In an area where poverty has grown as low-income residents from Chicago have relocated and new immigrants, including refugees, have settled, county-level organization has allowed the federation to bypass the parochial and often NIMBY (not–in–my–back–yard) politics of municipal governments.[85] The organization has found county government a responsive partner, while municipal governments have been largely indifferent to its efforts.

---

82. Joassart-Marcelli and Wolch (2003).

83. Allard and Roth (2010).

84. The initiative was an effort to build capacity to address the new needs of low-income residents in the post-welfare-reform era. After three years, the state decided it did not need to connect with local actors. Of the local organizations supported, theirs was the only county-level federation and the only organization to survive.

85. Interview with authors, June 29, 2009. It is also worth noting that the sizable refugee population is eligible for significant federal resources not available to other low income residents.

The Atlanta suburb of Gwinnett County displays a similar pattern. Until very recently an overwhelmingly white and middle-class community, Gwinnett has experienced rapid, large-scale immigration and a significant rise in poverty over the past two decades.[86] More recently, it has become the county with the highest number of foreclosures in the region. As in DuPage County, an outside organization, in this case the United Way, launched the Gwinnett Coalition for Health and Human Services, a nonprofit organization that serves as an umbrella planning organization for services in the county. Even so, suburban resistance limits some of the services available. For example, Gwinnett County lacks a general emergency shelter for individuals without children who need temporary housing; as a result it sends people needing this service to Atlanta. Likewise, the county has resisted creating the transportation systems that would help low-income people access services more easily. Fear of attracting low-income people from Atlanta, intertwined with the deep racial divisions in the Atlanta region, affects the willingness of suburban areas to offer some services.[87]

A decade ago, the community philanthropic sector sought to spark new organizations and connections that could serve as initial steps in creating a regional safety net. Recognizing that the bulk of funds for the nonprofit service sector came from public sources, leaders in the philanthropic sector urged community foundations to carve out a role in promoting system change, including building regional networks. Their efforts varied considerably across regions. In Chicago, which benefited from earlier philanthropic efforts to promote regional connections, our data suggest that foundations have played a stronger regional and system change role than in the other regions. However, the experiences of foundations, even in Chicago, offer a sobering assessment of the contributions that the philanthropic sector is likely to make in building and sustaining system reform at the regional level. The difficulty in creating an independent suburban philanthropic sector, the challenges in sustaining regional or suburban organizational networks, and the obstacles to creating new organizations in suburbs—especially low-income suburbs—will not be easily overcome.

Conclusion: Strategies for Building a Resilient Regional Safety Net

The philanthropic experience to date offers some guidance for what state and federal governments might do to foster a more resilient regional safety net. The

---

86. Alan Ehrenhalt, "Immigrants and the Suburban Influx," *Governing*, November 30, 2009 (www.governing.com/topics/economic-dev/sustainable-communities/Immigrants-and-the-Suburban.html).

87. Interview with authors, Gwinnett County, Georgia, July 23, 2010.

initiatives here focus on building an organizational structure to match the new geography of need as well as the new demands placed on services in the post-welfare reform era.[88] Three types of initiatives stand out. The first is to strengthen the role of regional intermediaries and coalitions. The second would support the inclusion of human services as a component of regional planning. The third is to rethink the relationship between state human services departments and the myriad nonprofits in metropolitan regions by building permanent regional networks of social service providers connected to state bureaucracies.

Initiative One: Support Regional Intermediaries

In the absence of regional government, nonprofit intermediaries can play critical roles in promoting the growth and capacity of nonprofit organizations across metropolitan regions. Foundations in Chicago provided crucial support to the Illinois Facilities Fund, which offers capital and technical assistance to nonprofits seeking to purchase real estate and construct or renovate buildings. They have been especially proactive in identifying needs for child care facilities in the post-welfare reform era.[89] This organization offers a model that could be supported by states, with a specific mandate to assess regional needs and supply capital and training to provide the needed social service facilities.

The other kind of intermediary that could benefit from public support to enhance its regional role is the United Way. Over a decade ago, United Ways across the country launched a process of regional consolidation. The success of these endeavors varied, but it did give many United Ways some regional basis for action. Nonetheless, United Ways still face some constraints to expanding their regional capacity. For example, they mainly fund established organizations, rather than foster new organizations. Also, changes in workplace giving cast increasing doubt on how robust the United Way model will remain in the future.[90]

As these organizations work to recast themselves regionally, there is room for ongoing philanthropic support to help them define their regional role. They could also eventually serve as linkages for state and federal funds aimed at building capacity in new places. This role may be particularly important in low-resource suburbs. In the Detroit region, the United Way for Southeastern Michigan (UWSEM) is developing a new approach to building capacity for the region's

---

88. For an analysis of the challenges of financing the state and local safety net, see Gais, Dadayan, and Kwan (2009); Allard (2009).

89. Interview with authors, Chicago, June 19, 2009.

90. Rick Cohen and Ruth McCambridge, "United Ways 2009: A Confusing Mix of Missed and Missing Goals," *The Nonprofit Quarterly*, 2009 (www.nonprofitquarterly.org/index.php?option=com_content&view=article&id=1466%3Aunited-ways-2009-a-confusing-mix&catid=168%3Atrend-alert&Itemid=137).

safety net. In 2010 UWSEM launched a Rethinking the Safety Net study for the region. Currently under way, the study is identifying existing funding streams, providers, and services throughout the region, with the goal of finding new leverage points in the system and ways to help the system operate more effectively.[91] The research has been paired with an ongoing engagement process, involving hundreds of service providers in the region, both as contributors of data for the study and as potential consumers of the findings. As a regional actor, United Way organizations are well situated to gather this type of data and engage service providers throughout the region.

In addition to funding intermediaries, foundations can play a critical role in supporting networks and coalitions among existing organizations. Such networks allow small organizations to expand the scope of their professional knowledge, acquainting them with new practices and sources of support. Building coalitions of nonprofit organizations provides essential support for the advocacy role of nonprofits. With limited time and resources, nonprofits may be unable to build broader cooperative ties with other organizations. Yet, advocacy coalitions are essential to providing nonprofits with a strong voice in the state venues where key funding decisions are made. Foundation resources can provide the impetus and the glue to hold coalitions together.

Initiative Two: Federal Incentives for Regional Human Services Planning

The second initiative would provide federal incentives to include human services in regional planning, modeled on what CMAP has begun to do in Chicago. Bringing human services into metropolitan planning venues would highlight emerging trends in connections and disconnections among demographics, access, need, and services. Transportation plays a big role in ensuring access to human services in the suburbs, where needy people and services are much more dispersed than in cities. Incorporating concerns about human services into plans for future public transit and transit-oriented development is especially relevant. States could enhance the utility of such planning by mandating that local taxing and spending entities, including townships and counties, participate in these regional planning venues.

Initiative Three: Statewide Human Services Networks

Finally, state departments of human services can play a role in creating stronger regional organization among social service providers and in using that network to generate political pressure for social services. Human service providers and advocates for the poor have largely operated defensively, working to protect

---

91. Interview with authors, Detroit, November 17, 2010.

existing programs and prevent further retrenchment. The defensive approach has been particularly prevalent recently in the face of severe state budget deficits and funding cuts to providers.

Despite these fiscal challenges, policy entrepreneurs in several states have gone on the offense. These governors, state legislators, bureaucratic agency heads, and advocacy organizations have adopted a shared political frame—poverty reduction and economic opportunity—and a shared set of policy tools, including poverty reduction targets, state-level anti-poverty commissions, and state poverty summits.[92] The poverty reduction strategy has taken root in several states; eleven states have set targets for reducing poverty by 2020, and since 2008 nine states have held poverty summits. In most states, the poverty reduction agenda was promoted through fairly typical state-level political channels—new state legislation, an executive order from the governor, or the formation of a new state-level council or commission.

Although it is too early to gauge the effectiveness of these strategies, the more traditional political levers seem disconnected from the extreme variation at the local level in the availability of service providers. But building strong relationships between state bureaucrats and local service providers could furnish the state with a base for experimenting with new policies and forging a supportive coalition. Recent efforts in Michigan provide elements of the new approach. Following Michigan's statewide poverty summit in November 2008, the state's Department of Human Services (DHS) has supported ongoing poverty reduction planning in eight regional networks. Each region is charged with creating a poverty reduction initiative linked to every county in the region and developing a network for sharing best practices in poverty reduction and community engagement. By building bottom-up organizations and ongoing ties with a state bureaucracy, these regional networks could ultimately help state departments of human services to function as effective organizers of regional welfare systems. Although this initiative began during Governor Jennifer Granholm's administration, all eight regional networks have continued operating since Governor Rick Snyder took office in 2011.[93]

These three initiatives highlight ways that state and federal governments can build on strategies that the philanthropic community has promoted. But the federal government could also do more to promote transparency in the complex web of funding streams and organizations, public and nonprofit, which now make up the social safety net. One way to do so would be to resurrect the federal Advisory Commission on Intergovernmental Relations to provide ongoing

---

92 Levin-Epstein and Gorzelany (2008).
93. Correspondence with authors, May 9, 2011.

analyses and cross-state comparisons of the metropolitan (and rural) safety net. Such information will promote learning across states and may also help build support for reducing the organizational and funding complexity that has come to characterize the social safety net.

Behind this set of ideas is the recognition that building and maintaining regional systems requires public leadership. The philanthropic sector has long led the way in sparking innovation among nonprofits; it has likewise sponsored significant system-building initiatives, especially in the area of housing. But innovation alone does not ensure a strong regional safety net. Especially as demographic changes have increased the need for services outside cities, strong and consistent public engagement, in partnership with a regionally focused philanthropic sector, is needed to build a responsive and effective social safety net.

Appendix A. Foundations Analyzed

Atlanta

Coweta Community Foundation
Community Foundation for Greater
  Atlanta
Community Foundation of West
  Georgia
Cobb Community Foundation
Community Foundation for
  Northeast Georgia
Community Foundation of
  Northwest Georgia

Chicago

John D. and Catherine T. MacArthur
  Foundation
Barrington Area Community
  Foundation
Chicago Community Trust
Community Foundation of the Fox
  River Valley
DeKalb County Community
  Foundation
DuPage Community Foundation
Evanston Community Foundation
Grand Victoria Foundation
Highland Park Community
  Foundation
Lake County Community Foundation
McHenry County Community
  Foundation
Oak Park/River Forest Community
  Foundation
Will County Community Foundation

Denver

Broomfield Community Foundation
Rose Community Foundation
Denver Foundation
The Community Foundation—
  Boulder County
Daniels Fund

Detroit

Kresge Foundation
Anchor Bay Community Foundation
Canton Community Foundation
Community Foundation for
  Livingston County
Community Foundation for
  Southeast Michigan
Community Foundation of Greater
  Rochester[94]
Community Foundation of St. Clair
  County
Community Foundation of Troy
Four County Community
  Foundation
Lapeer County Community
  Foundation
Livonia Community Foundation
Northville Community Foundation[95]
Shelby Community Foundation
Southfield Community Foundation
Sterling Heights Community
  Foundation

94. 2004 data.
95. 2002 data.

Appendix B. Coding Guidelines

Coding for the Low-Income Category

We developed a coding scheme to designate grants as targeting low-income populations drawing on data from the Foundation Grant Database in the Foundation Directory Online. First, we counted grants as low-income if they were previously coded (in the Foundation Directory database) in certain subject categories that typically target low-income populations. These subject areas included "economically disadvantaged," "minorities/immigrants," or "human services." If none of those categories applied, we scrutinized the grant more closely by examining either its description or the grantee's website. We counted the grants as low income if they pertained to a second list of subject areas we developed (including Boys and Girls Clubs, early childhood education, adult literacy, and community organizing). A smaller group of grants were counted only if their services were provided at free or reduced rates (including employment services and disability services).

We made a decision to cast the net widely rather than narrowly, that is, to count grants as low-income when there was some ambiguity. That said, we did not count grants as low income if we could gather little or no information on the grant at all.

Coding for System Change

Using data from the Foundation Grant Database in the Foundation Directory Online, we analyzed grants of $50,000 or more for system change, relying on information from an organization's website regarding its work, collaborations, and geographical scope. Grants were coded as contributing to system change if the organization that received the grant had one or more of the following characteristics: (a) engaged in networking or capacity-building activities, (b) served as an intermediary for other organizations, supporting them or convening groups of them, (c) engaged in data gathering or research. These organizations included coalitions and broad-purposed foundations. In addition, we coded organizations as positive for system change if they provided an array of services to a large regional area, for example, to a metropolitan area that included a city, suburb(s), and/or the county. Otherwise, organizations were coded as negative (0) for direct service if they did not meet these guidelines. Types of organizations generally coded as not engaged in system change included most churches and places of worship, most arts organizations, single-purpose foundations (for example, the Atlanta Police Foundation), grants given to direct-service organizations for capital improvements (for example, a new hospital wing), grants given to expand or provide new services at direct service organizations, organizations for which no information exists online, primary and secondary schools, charter schools, and hospitals.

References

Allard, Scott W. 2009. *Out of Reach*. New Haven: Yale University Press.

Allard, Scott W., and Benjamin Roth. 2010. "Strained Suburbs: The Social Service Challenges of Rising Suburban Poverty." Metropolitan Opportunity Series. Metropolitan Policy Program, Brookings.

Bernholz, Lucy, Katherine Fulton, and Gabriel Kasper. 2005. *On the Brink of New Promise: The Future of U.S. Community Foundations*. San Francisco: Blueprint Research & Design and the Monitor Institute (September).

Berry, Jeffrey M., and David F. Arons. 2003. *A Voice for Nonprofits*. Brookings.

Berry, Jeffrey M., and others. 2006. "Power and Interest Groups in City Politics." Report for the Rappaport Institute for Greater Boston, Kennedy School of Government, Harvard University (December).

Corbin, John J. 1999. "A Study of the Factors Influencing the Growth of Nonprofits in Social Services." *Nonprofit and Voluntary Sector Quarterly* 28, no. 3: 296–314.

Dreier, Peter, John Mollenkopf, and Todd Swanstrom. 2001. *Place Matters*. University Press of Kansas.

Gais, Thomas, Lucy Dadayan, and Sun Kyun Kwan. 2009. "Retrenchment Continued: State and Local Social Welfare Spending, 1977–2007." Paper presented at Reducing Poverty: Assessing Recent State Policy Innovations and Strategies, Emory University, November 19–20.

Graddy, Elizabeth A., and Donald L. Morgan. 2006. "Community Foundations, Organizational Strategy, and Public Policy." *Nonprofit and Voluntary Sector Quarterly* 35, no. 4: 605–30.

Grønbjerg, Kirsten A., and Laurie Paarlberg. 2001. "Community Variations in the Size and Scope of the Nonprofit Sector: Theory and Preliminary Findings." *Nonprofit and Voluntary Sector Quarterly* 30, no. 4: 684–706.

Gupta, Sapna. 2004. "Immigrants in the Chicago Suburbs: A Policy Paper." Chicago Metropolis 2020 (February).

Hamilton, David K. 2002. "Regimes and Regional Governance: The Case of Chicago." *Journal of Urban Affairs* 24, no. 4: 403–23.

Hamilton, Ralph, Julia Parzen, and Prue Brown. 2004. "Community Change Makers: The Leadership Roles of Community Foundations." Discussion paper. Chapin Hall Center for Children at the University of Chicago.

Henderson, Jason. 2006. "Secessionist Automobility: Racism, Anti-Urbanism, and the Politics of Automobility in Georgia." *International Journal of Urban and Regional Research* 3, no. 2 (June): 293–307.

Hendrick, Rebecca, and Karen Mossberger. 2009. "Uneven Capacity and Delivery of Human Services in the Chicago Suburbs: The Role of Townships and Municipalities." Report submitted to the Chicago Community Trust. University of Illinois, Chicago.

Hula, Richard C., and Cynthia Jackson-Elmoore. 2001. "Governing Nonprofits and Local Political Processes." *Urban Affairs Review* 36, no. 3: 324–58.

Joassart-Marcelli, Pascale, and Jennifer R. Wolch. 2003. "The Intrametropolitan Geography of Poverty and the Nonprofit Sector in Southern California." *Nonprofit and Voluntary Sector Quarterly* 32, no. 1 (March): 70–96.

Joassart-Marcelli, Pascale, and Alberto Giordano. 2006. "Does Local Access to Employment Services Reduce Unemployment? A GIS Analysis of One-Stop Career Centers." *Policy Sciences* 39, no. 4 (December): 335–59.

Johnson, Elmer W. 1999. *Chicago Metropolis 2020: Preparing Metropolitan Chicago for the 21st Century.* Chicago and Cambridge, Mass.: Commercial Club of Chicago and the American Academy of Arts and Sciences.

Kenworthy, Lane. 2011. *Progress for the Poor.* Oxford University Press.

Kneebone, Elizabeth, and Emily Garr. 2010. "The Suburbanization of Poverty: Trends in Metropolitan America, 2000–2008." Metropolitan Opportunity Series. Metropolitan Policy Program, Brookings.

Kruse, Kevin M. 2007. *White Flight: Atlanta and the Making of Modern Conservatism.* Princeton University Press.

Levin-Epstein, Jodie, and Kristen M. Gorzelany. 2008. *Seizing the Moment: State Governments and the New Commitment to Reduce Poverty in America.* Washington: Center for Law and Social Policy.

Luck, James I., and Suzanne L. Feurt. 2002. "A Flexible and Growing Service to Donors: Donor-Advised Funds in Community Foundations." Columbus, Ohio: Columbus Foundation (September) (www.cof.org/files/Documents/Community_Foundations/CF_Columbus_DAF.pdf).

Marwell, Nicole P. 2007. *Bargaining for Brooklyn.* University of Chicago Press.

Murphy, Alexandra K., and Danielle Wallace. 2010. "Opportunities for Making Ends Meet and Upward Mobility: Differences in Organizational Deprivation across Urban and Suburban Poor Neighborhoods." *Social Science Quarterly* 91, no. 5 (December): 1164–86.

Newberger, Robin. 2010. "Pre-Implementation Findings from the Neighborhood Stabilization Program: Milwaukee, Wisconsin, Lafayette, Indiana, and Cook County Suburbs." *Profitwise: News and Views Spotlight* (Chicago: Federal Reserve Bank of Chicago, November).

Nicolaides, Becky. 2002. *My Blue Heaven: Life and Politics in the Working-Class Suburbs of Los Angeles, 1920–1965.* University of Chicago Press.

Ostrander, Susan A. 2007. "The Growth of Donor Control: Revisiting the Social Relations of Philanthropy." *Nonprofit and Voluntary Sector Quarterly* 36, no. 2: 356–72.

Pastor, Manuel, Jr., Chris Benner, and Martha Matsuoka. 2009. *This Could Be the Start of Something Big.* Cornell University Press.

Pendall, Rolf, Kathryn A. Foster, and Margaret Cowell. 2010. "Resilience and Regions: Building Understanding of the Metaphor." *Cambridge Journal of Regions, Economy and Society* 3, no. 1: 71–84.

Puentes, Robert, and Myron Orfield. 2002. "Valuing America's First Suburbs: A Policy Agenda for Older Suburbs in the Midwest." Report, Metropolitan Policy Program, Brookings.

Rusch, Lara C. 2008. *Accountability through Diversity: Challenges for Congregation-Based Community Organizing in Detroit.* Ph.D. dissertation, University of Michigan.

Safford, Sean. 2010. *Why the Garden Club Couldn't Save Youngstown.* Harvard University Press.

Sevin, Joshua S. 2000. *The Role of Catalyst Organizations in the Formation of Metropolitan Coalitions: Metropolitics in Baltimore and Chicago.* Unpublished master's thesis, Department of Urban Studies and Planning, Massachusetts Institute of Technology.

Singer, Audrey, Susan W. Hardwick, and Caroline B. Brettell, eds. 2008. *Twenty-First Century Gateways.* Brookings.

Sink, Todd, and Brian Ceh. 2011 "Relocation of the Urban Poor in Chicago: HOPE VI Policy Outcomes," *GeoForum* 2: 71–82.

Small, Mario Luis. 2010. *Unanticipated Gains: Origins of Network Inequality in Everyday Life.* Oxford University Press.

Smith, Steven Rathgeb, and Michael Lipsky. 1995. *Nonprofits for Hire*. Harvard University Press.

Smith, Steven Rathgeb, and Kirsten A. Grønbjerg. 2006. "Scope and Theory of Government-Nonprofit Relations." In *The Non-Profit Sector: A Research Handbook*, 2nd ed., edited by Walter W. Powell and Richard Steinberg. Yale University Press.

Sugrue, Thomas. 2005. *The Origins of the Urban Crisis*. Rev. ed. Princeton University Press.

Twombly, Eric. C. 2003. "What Factors Affect the Entry and Exit of Nonprofit Human Service Organizations in Metropolitan Areas?" *Nonprofit and Voluntary Sector Quarterly* 32, no. 2 (June): 211–35.

Wallis, Alan. 2008. "Developing Regional Capacity to Plan Land Use and Infrastructure." In *Urban and Regional Policies for Metropolitan Livability*, edited by David K. Hamilton and Patricia S. Atkins, pp. 92–125. Armonk N.Y. and London: M. E. Sharpe.

Weir, Margaret. 1996. "Central Cities' Loss of Power in State Politics." *Cityscape: A Journal of Policy Development and Research* 2, no. 2 (May): 23–40.

Weir, Margaret, Jane Rongerude, and Christopher Ansell. 2009. "Collaboration Is Not Enough: Virtuous Cycles of Reform in Transportation Policy." *Urban Affairs Review* 44, no. 4: 455–89.

Wial, Howard, and Alec Friedhoff. 2010. "MetroMonitor: Tracking Economic Recession and Recovery in America's 100 Largest Metropolitan Areas." Metropolitan Policy Program, Brookings.

Wilson, William Julius. 1990. *The Truly Disadvantaged*. University of Chicago Press.

Index

AARP, 153
ACM. *See* Aerospace Components Manufacturers
ACS. *See* American Community Survey
Adams County (Colo.), 306
Advantage Carolina project, 228, 250
Advisory Commission on Intergovernmental Relations (U.S.), 317–18
Aerospace Components Manufacturers cluster (ACM; Conn.), 246
"Aerotropolis" (Detroit), 215
Aetna, 242
African Americans: in Boston area, 175, 176; in Charlotte (N.C.), 134; city planning and, 149; incomes of, 115; in Los Angeles, 122; in Miami, 18–19, 168, 170, 172; sustainable cities and, 149
Akron (Ohio), 221
Alameda Corridor (Calif.), 140
Allard, Scott, 280, 282, 283, 313
Allentown (Pa.), 20, 286
Alliance to End Homelessness (Cook County, Ill.), 307
Amazon, 236, 238
American Association of Retired Persons. *See* AARP
American Community Survey (ACS), 47, 297
American Defense, 234
Ames (Iowa), 47–48
Analyses: cluster analysis, 86–87; regression analysis, 199n29, 203, 258–59, 260, 265–67; descriptive analysis, 10; equilibrium analysis, 193; quantitative analysis, 10, 209–10, 211, 238. *See also* Case studies; Hypotheses, calculations and equations; Research
Anchor tenants, 19
Ann Arbor Spark (Mich.), 215
Arapahoe County (Colo.), 306
Arizona: boycotts of, 123; foreclosures in, 84; housing prices in, 84; immigration to, 105–06, 114, 136–37, 142; immigration law of (Senate Bill *1070*), 100, 123, 127, 136–37, 140–41;
political issues in, 136–37. *See also* Arpaio, Joe; Maricopa County; Phoenix
Arons, David F., 280
Arpaio, Joe, 101. *See also* Arizona
Arvada (Colo.), 159
Asian immigrants and immigration, 6, 105, 115
Asian immigrants and immigration—specific cities: in Charlotte (N.C.), 134; in Los Angeles, 113; in New York, 126–27; in San Jose (Calif.), 109, 113, 132–33, 138–39
Atkins, Patricia, 193–274
Atlanta, 12, 286–314, 319
Atlanta—case study of resilient social safety nets: challenges in building regional safety nets, 308–14; distribution of anti-poverty investments, 292–96; grant distribution in, 297, 306; grants supporting system change, 307–08; maps of human services, 298–99; poverty and philanthropic response, 285–89; regional philanthropic resources, 289–92; system change and, 306–08
Atlanta Community Food Bank, 308
Atlanta Neighborhood Development Partnership, 308
Augusta, 54, 55
Aurora (Colo.), 159
Aurora Housing Authority (Colo.), 161, 185
Automobiles and automobile industry: Big Three auto makers, 213, 215, 217, 250; land development and, 150; national economic downturns and, 213, 214, 279; revival of, 215. *See also* Detroit; Industry; Manufacturing

Baca, Lee, 123
Baltimore, 54, 55
Bangladesh, 126–27
Bank of America, 133, 225, 229
Bankruptcy, 83
Banks and banking: bank-owned properties (REOs), 75, 84–85, 87, 88, 90; branch banking, 226, 227; in Charlotte (N.C.), 224, 225,

226–27; economic downturn and, 225; inter-state banking, 226–27; service to communities, 186; targeted transparency and, 89–90

Banks and banking—individual banks: Bank of America, 133, 225, 229; First Union Bank, 227, 229; GMAC Financial, 229; Golden West Financial, 225; Merrill Lynch, 225; North Carolina National Bank, 226, 227; Wachovia, 225, 229; Washington Mutual, 238; Wells Fargo, 225, 229

Beacon Alliance, 247

Belk, John, 228

Berry, Jeffrey M., 280

Big Dig mitigation plan (Boston), 176

Bing, Dave, 216

BioEnterprise (BioE; Ohio), 221, 222

Blacks. *See* African Americans

Blanchard, Olivier, 196

Bloemraad, Irene, 138

Bloomberg, Michael, 123, 127, 139

Blumenthal, Pamela, 193–274

Boeing Company, 236–40, 241

Boise (Idaho), 54, 55

Boston: case study of transit-oriented development in, 174–80; dot-com recession and, 54; housing in, 174–75, 177, 178, 179, 185, 186; increasing benefits and decreasing costs of rail stations, 177–78; obstacles to development, 178–80; Route *128* development in, 20; transit-oriented development in, 8, 9, 152, 156, 183, 187, 188; urban living in, 179. *See also* Fairmount Corridor; Fairmount/Indigo Corridor; Massachusetts

Boston Redevelopment Authority, 178, 179–80

Boulder (Colo.), 161

Boulder County (Colo.), 306

Bridgeport (Conn.), 126

Bridging Borders in Silicon Valley: Summit on Immigrant Needs and Contributions (IRIS; *2000*), 132

Briguglio, Lino, 198

Brookings Institution, 1, 36, 39, 62

Brown, Mike, 234

BRR Network. *See* Building Resilient Regions Network and project

Bruneau, Michael, 38–39

Buffalo (N.Y.), 84

Building Resilient Regions (BRR) Network and project, 1, 28, 42–43, 62, 108

Bureau of Labor Statistics (U.S.), 225

Burlington-South Burlington (Vt.), 47–48

Business First, 228

Business issues: advance planning, 253; immigration, 7, 133, 139; resilience, 27–28, 249

Business Leaders for Michigan, 215

Bus Riders' Union, 152, 189

Calculations. *See* Analyses; Hypotheses, calculations and equations; Research

California: foreclosures in, 84; housing prices in, 84; immigration to, 105–06, 136; regional economic resilience capacity and, 49. *See also individual California cities*

Cambridge (Mass.), 18. *See also* Massachusetts

CAMP. *See* Cleveland Advanced Manufacturing Program

Campbell, Scott, 188

Capacity: building resilience and, 15; for coping with stress, 32; cycle of resilience capacity and performance, 29–30; definitions and conceptions of, 3, 31–34; dimensions of, 50; local foundations and organizational capacity building, 283–84; measurement and assessment of, 34, 44–52; natural disasters and, 32; preparation and, 29–30; resilience and, 14–15, 26, 28, 29, 33; resilience capacity score, 47, 51; variables of, 44–47. *See also* Resilience

Capacity—types of: administrative capacity, 92, 94; buffering capacity, 14–15; collaborative capacity, 92, 93–94; community competence capacity, 32; community connection capacity, 3; economic development capacity, 32; information and communications capacity, 32; local capacity, 92; regional economic capacity, 3, 45–46; regional resilience capacity, 3, 33; socio-demographic capacity, 3; social capital capacity, 32; strategic collaborative capacity, 92, 93–94

Capital: human capital, 27, 197–98, 206, 216, 248; investment capital, 183; financial capital, 65, 69, 93, 197; mass transit capital, 9, 182; mortgage capital, 64; "patient" capital, 178; physical capital, 69; social capital, 32, 66, 69, 76, 93, 214; supply capital, 311. *See also* Education issues

Case studies, 6, 7, 8, 10, 11, 12, 13. *See also* Analyses; Research

Case studies—immigration: Charlotte (N.C.), 133–35; Chicago, 129–31; Los Angeles, 122–25; New York, 125–29; Phoenix, 135–37; San Jose (Calif.), 131–33

Case studies—regional resilience and nonresilience: Charlotte (N.C.), 224–30; Cleveland, 218–24; Detroit, 213–17; Grand Forks (N.D.), 230–36; Hartford (Conn.), 241–48; Seattle, 236–41

Case studies—resilient social safety nets: Atlanta, 285–314; Chicago, 285–314; Denver, 285–314; Detroit, 285–314

Case studies—transit-oriented development: Boston, 174–80; Charlotte (N.C.), 162–68; Denver, 156–62; Miami, 168–74

Case Western Reserve University, 88, 221, 223

Catholic Charities of the Archdiocese of Chicago, 307

CATS. *See* Charlotte Area Transit System
CBSA. *See* Core Based Statistical Area
CDGBs (community development block grants).
   See Grants
CDC Collaborative (Boston), 177
CDCs. *See* Community development corporations
Center for Advanced Manufacturing Puget
   Sound, 240–41
Center for Family Resources (Marietta, Ga.), 308
Center for Neighborhood Technology, 153
Center for Immigration Studies, 137
Center for Responsible Lending (CRL), 65–66
Center for Transit-Oriented Development
   (CTOD), 21–22, 153, 154
Center for Venture Development (Cleveland), 220
Center of Excellence in Life Sciences and
   Advanced Technologies (University of North
   Dakota), 235
"Centers, Corridors, Wedges Growth Framework"
   (study; N.C.), 163
Centers for Working Families (United Way-LISC,
   Detroit), 310
Central America, 110
Chandler (Ariz.), 135–36
Chapel Hill (N.C.), 164
Chappel, Karen, 196
Charlotte (N.C.): banking in, 224–27, 229; case
   study of immigration to, 133–35; case study of
   transit-oriented development in, 162–68; economic downturns in, 11, 224; economic
   upturns in, 133–34, 224; energy sector in, 229;
   housing in, 162, 166–68, 185, 186; immigration to, 6, 7, 101–02, 109–22, 133–35, 138,
   139, 142; institutional service responses in,
   134; political issues in, 126, 134, 135, 139,
   164–65, 181; resilience of, 11; section *287*(g)
   program in, 135; transit-oriented development
   in, 8, 9, 21, 156, 183, 184, 188. *See also* North
   Carolina
Charlotte—case study of resilience and nonresilience: advance planning by, 254; economic
   downturns in, 225–26, 227–28, 249; employment in, 224, 225, 226, 228, 229; explaining
   resilience and nonresilience, 226–27, 249;
   regional economic resilience/nonresilience,
   225–26; responses to shocks, 227–29, 250;
   results, 229–30; shocks in, 211, 212, 224–25
Charlotte Area Transit System (CATS), 163
Charlotte Chamber of Commerce, 228, 229, 250
Charlotte Housing Authority, 166
Charlotte-Mecklenburg Planning Commission
   (N.C.), 163
Charlotte-Mecklenburg Police Department
   (N.C.), 67
Charlotte metropolitan regions, 133–35
Charlotte Motor Speedway, 228

Charlotte Quality of Life Study, 166
Charlotte Regional Partnership, 228
Chicago: Boeing relocation to, 239, 241; case
   study of immigration to, 129–31; foreclosure
   prevention in, 77, 78; foreclosures in, 66, 67,
   85; foundations and grant funding in, 13, 319;
   immigration to, 101, 106, 107, 109–22, 126,
   133, 138, 139, 142, 286; political issues in,
   126, 129, 130, 131, 135, 139; poverty and
   antipoverty resources in, 12, 286–314; regulation of predatory lending by, 73; response to
   immigration to, 6, 7, 138; section *287*(g)
   agreements, 123–24, 131. *See also* Illinois
Chicago—case study of resilient social safety nets:
   challenges in building regional safety nets,
   308–14; distribution of anti-poverty investments, 292–96; grant distribution in, 297,
   306; grants supporting system change, 307–08;
   maps of human services, 300–01; poverty and
   philanthropic response, 285–89; regional phil-
   anthropic resources, 289–92; system change
   and, 306–08
Chicago Community Trust, 78, 309
Chicago Machine (political), 130
Chicago Metropolis *2020*, 131, 287
Chicago Metropolitan Agency for Planning
   (CMAP), 287, 309–10, 312
Chicago metropolitan region, 129, 131, 132–33
ChildServ (Chicago), 295
China, 113, 126–27, 131–32
CHIRLA. *See* Coalition for Humane Immigrant
   Rights in Los Angeles
Chronicle of Philanthropy, 294
Cicero (Ill.), 131
CIGNA, 242
Cities. *See* Urban areas
Clayton County (Ga.), 306, 311, 312, 313
Cleveland: data collection system of, 88–89; eco-
   nomic downturns in, 11, 218; foreclosures in,
   75; Strategic Investment Initiative of, 93–94.
   See also Cuyahoga County
Cleveland—case study of resilience and nonre-
   silience: economic downturns in, 218, 249,
   250; employment in, 218, 219; explaining
   resilience and nonresilience, 218–19; regional
   economic resilience/nonresilience, 218, 254;
   responses to shocks, 219–23; results, 223–24;
   shocks in, 211, 212
Cleveland Advanced Manufacturing Program
   (CAMP), 220
Cleveland Clinic, 223
Cleveland State University, 221
Cleveland Tomorrow, 220–21, 222
Cleveland Tomorrow Committee, *1980*, 221
CMAP. *See* Chicago Metropolitan Agency for
   Planning

Coalition for Humane Immigrant Rights in Los Angeles (CHIRLA), 125
Cobb Habitat for Humanity (Atlanta), 295
Codman Square Neighborhood Development Corporation (Boston), 177
Collaboration. *See* Networks and collaboration
Colleges. *See* Universities and colleges
Colombia, 126–27
Colorado, 159, 160. *See also* Denver
Colorado Coalition for the Homeless, 308
Colorado Housing Finance Authority, 160
Commerce Department (Wash.), 239
Community development block grants (CDBGs). *See* Grants
Community development corporations (CDCs), 69, 78, 93. *See also* Foundations
Community development corporations—specific cities: Boston, 174–75, 176, 177, 178–79, 183, 186; Miami, 172, 173
Community development corporations—specific organizations: Codman Square Neighborhood Development Corporation (Boston), 177; Dorchester Bay Economic Development Corporation (Boston), 177
Community issues: community connections and stability, 46–47; community lending agreements, 89–90; foreclosures and neighborhood decline, 68; resilience, 46–47, 49; social cohesion and income, 46
Community Reinvestment Act (CRA; *1977*), 70, 90, 186
Connecticut, 245–46. *See also* Hartford
Connecticut Business and Industry Association, 246
Connecticut Center for Advanced Technology, 247
Connecticut Technology Council, 247
ConnStep, 246
Consejo de Federaciones Mexicanas en Norteamérica, 125
Conservation Law Foundation, 176
Cook County (Ill.), 73, 291, 306, 307. *See also* Chicago; Illinois
Core Based Statistical Area (CBSA), 125–26
Corelogic (previously McDash Analytics), 87
Corporation for Public Broadcasting, 77
Costco, 236, 238
Cowell, Margaret, 16, 193
CRA. *See* Community Reinvestment Act
Crime: in Detroit, 217; foreclosures and, 4, 17, 65, 66–67, 68f; immigration and, 127, 128, 136; low-income populations and, 166
CRL. *See* Center for Responsible Lending
Crutchfield, Edward, 227, 228
CTOD. *See* Center for Transit-Oriented Development
Cultural issues. *See* Sociocultural issues

Cupertino (Calif.), 132
Current Population Survey (*2009*), 108
Cutter, Susan, 32, 55
Cuyahoga Community College (Ohio), 221
Cuyahoga County (Ohio), 77. *See also* Cleveland

Daley, Richard M., 123, 130, 131
Deaton, Joyce, 135
Defense Base Realignment and Closure Commission, 231
De Graauw, Els, 138
Deloitte, 250
Denver: case study of transit-oriented development in, 156–62; foundations and grant funding in, 13 , 319; housing in, 158–61, 185–86; inclusionary zoning in, 161; low-income populations in, 181; political issues in, 164, 168, 181; poverty and antipoverty resources in, 12, 286–314; transit-oriented development in, 8, 9, 183, 184, 188. *See also* Colorado
Denver—case study of resilient social safety nets: distribution of anti-poverty investments, 292–96; grants in, 297, 306, 307–08; maps of human services, 302–03; poverty and philanthropic response, 285–89; regional philanthropic resources, 289–92; system change and, 306–08
Denver Business Network, 287
Denver Housing Authority (DHA), 157, 185
Denver Regional Council of Governments, 157
Department of Housing and Urban Development-Department of Transportation-Environmental Protection Agency Interagency Partnership for Sustainable Communities (HUD-DOT-EPA Interagency Partnership), 177, 182, 185
Detroit: auto industry in, 11, 16, 213, 215, 217, 250, 251, 253, 279; economic downturns in, 11, 213; employment in, 213; foundations and grant funding in, 13, 319; poverty and antipoverty resources in, 12, 286–314; school system in, 217; vulnerabilities of, 252, 294
Detroit—case study of regional resilience and nonresilience: economic downturns, 213–14, 216, 249, 250; employment in, 213; explaining resilience and nonresilience, 214–15, 250, 252; political issues, 214; regional economic resilience/nonresilience, 213–14; responses to shocks, 215–16, 250; results, 216; shocks in, 211, 212, 213, 252
Detroit—case study of resilient social safety nets: challenges in building regional safety nets, 308–14; distribution of anti-poverty investments, 292–96; grant distribution in, 297, 306; grants supporting system change, 307–08; maps of human services, 304–05; poverty and

philanthropic response, 285–89; regional philanthropic resources, 289–92; system change and, 306–08
Detroit Economic Growth Corporation, 215
Detroit News, 292
Detroit Regional Chamber of Commerce, 215
Detroit Regional Economic Partnership, 215
Detroit Renaissance, 215
Development, Relief and Education for Alien Minors Act (DREAM Act), 140
DHA. *See* Denver Housing Authority
DHS. *See* Human Services, Department of
Diamond, Jared, 28
Dickson, Stuart, 228
Disasters: capacity indicators and, 32; resilience and, 14, 27–28, 39, 40; shock and, 16, 34. *See also* Shocks
Dominican Republic, 113, 126–27
Dorchester (Mass.), 175, 176
Dorchester Bay Economic Development Corporation (Boston), 177
Dot-com recession, 53–57
Downs, Anthony, 92
DREAM Act. *See* Development, Relief and Education for Alien Minors Act
Duke Power (N.C.), 229
DuPage County (Ill.), 129–30, 307, 313
DuPage Federation of Human Services Reform (Ill.), 308, 313
Durham (N.C.), 164
Duval, Romain, 198

East St. Louis (Mo.), 152
Ecology and ecologists, 27, 63, 70
Economic and Community Development, Department of (Conn.), 246
Economic Development Administration (EDA), 232
Economic Development Commission (Wash.), 239
Economic issues: behavioral economics, 68; city planning, 149; diversification, 46; earnings per worker, 196; economic models, 10; income, 10, 46, 115, 117f, 185–87, 197–98, 205, 207–08, 249, 252; increasing benefits and decreasing costs of rail stations, 177–78; industry structure, 205; international economic development, 198; "lock-in," 18; national economic downturns, 213; norms and economic development, 198; option-based theory, 70; recessions, 53; regional economic growth, 197–98; regional economic structure, 10; regional rail systems, 148–49; resilience to economic shocks, 9–10, 40; scarcity of capital, 178; sunk costs, 19; transit-oriented development, 152–54, 165. *See also*

Capital; Employment issues; Great Recession; Markets; Recovery; Resilience—economic; Shocks—economic
EDA. *See* Economic Development Administration
Ecuador, 126–27
Education issues: economic downturns, 205; educational attainment of immigrants, 118, 120f; employment, 10; recovery, 10; regional resilience, 197, 207, 209, 248–49; resilience capacity, 49; response to stress, 46; shock resistance and, 206
Elgin School District (Ill.), 131
Elmeskov, Jorgen, 198
El Paso (Texas), 105
Eminent domain issues, 154
Employment issues: dot-com recession, 53–55; economic downturns, 205; education, 10, 206; employment diversity, 45–46; employment downturns, 207; employment growth rate, 201; export industries, 205, 206, 209; foreclosures and, 70; healthcare and social assistance employment, 208; income and wage disparities, 10, 205, 207; labor market flexibility, 10; recovery, 10; resilience, 10, 56, 207–08, 249; shocks, 10, 195–96; tradeoffs in performance, 41. *See also* Manufacturing; Union and labor issues; Shocks
Energy and Environment Research Center (University of North Dakota), 235
Energy Outreach Colorado, 308
Enterprise Seattle, 239, 250
Environmental issues, 28, 188, 189, 190
Environmental Protection Agency (EPA), 176
E Pluribus Unum Prize (Migration Policy Institute), 130
Equations. *See* Hypotheses, calculations, and equations
Europe, 6, 109, 113, 130, 138
Experimentation and innovation, 17–18
Export industries. *See* Industry—export industries

Fairmount Corridor (Boston), 152, 175–76, 178–79, 183, 186, 188
Fairmount/Indigo Coalition (Boston), 176, 178
Fairmount/Indigo Corridor (Boston), 174–80
Families First (Atlanta), 295
FasTracks (Denver), 157n23, 158, 181, 182
FDO. *See* Foundation Directory Online
Federal Emergency Management Administration (FEMA), 232
Federal Reserve Bank of Chicago, 78, 312
Federal Reserve Board, 90
Federal Transit Administration (FTA), 163, 176–77, 185. *See also* New Starts program
Federation for American Immigration Reforms, 124

FEMA. *See* Federal Emergency Management Administration

Feyrer, James, 196

Ficenec, Sarah, 193–274

First Union Bank, 227, 229

Flexibility: adaptive governance and, 19–22; building resilience and, 15; business resilience and, 27–28; challenges of, 16; shock resistance and, 15. *See also* Resilience

Florida, 84, 186. *See also* Miami

Folklife District. *See* Overtown

Food banks, 295, 308

Foreclosure mills, 81

Foreclosures: causes of, 70–74; collapse of housing bubble and, 4; costs of, 78; counseling and, 5, 78–79, 88; data and local empowerment, 86–90; effects and spillovers of, 4, 17, 20, 61, 63, 65–69, 74–76, 83, 91; feedback and, 17, 83; financial collapse of *2007–08* and, 60, 70; Home Affordable Modification Program and, 5; housing bubble and, 4, 70; information about, 20; interventions in, 86; investor losses and, 75; length of the foreclosure process, 61; local government stress and deteriorating services, 67–69; market responses to, 4–5, 84; mortgages and lending and, 4–5, 69; nature of the challenge for places, 63–69; Neighborhood Stabilization Program and, 91; numbers and rates of, 78, 84–85; predatory lending and, 4, 17, 70–74; prevention of, 70, 71–83; process of, 87; property and housing values and, 65–66, 69, 87; resilience and, 61, 63, 83–84; social disorder and crime and, 66–67; strategic collaborative capacity and, 93, 94; stress and, 63; system dynamics and, 64; vicious cycle of, 64–65. *See also* Government; Housing; Loans and lending; Mortgages; Neighborhood stabilization

Foster, Kathryn, 2, 14–15, 16, 24–59, 62, 102, 193

Foundation Directory Online (FDO), 293

Foundations: assets of, 289–90, 291, 296; associations of foundations, 284; challenges of building regional safety nets and, 308–18; community foundations, 289, 290–91, 296, 306–07, 311, 314; foundation grants, 292–93, 306–08; local foundations and organizational capacity building, 283–84; national foundations, 284, 289–90; private foundations, 289–90, 307; regional data clearing houses and, 90. *See also* Community development corporations; Grants; Living Cities; Nonprofit organizations; Philanthropic organizations; Poverty and the poor; Social service organizations

Foundations—specific, 319; Annie E. Casey Foundation, 310, 313; Barr Foundation, 177; Boston Foundation, 177; Carnegie Foundation, 228; Chicago Community Foundation, 291; Chicago Community Trust, 290, 291, 311; Cleveland Foundation, 219, 220, 221–22, 223; Columbus Foundation, 311; Community Foundation for Greater Atlanta, 290, 291, 309; Community Foundation for Southeast Michigan, 290, 292; Community Foundation of Detroit, 215; Daniels Fund, 289–90; Enterprise Foundation, 185; Ewing Marion Kauffman Foundation, 216; Ford Foundation, 215–16, 283; GAR Foundation, 222; Grand Victoria Foundation, 291, 308, 311; Greater Atlanta Foundation, 311; Gund Foundation, 219, 220, 221, 222; Haas Foundation, 141; Hyams Foundation, 177; Irvine Foundation, 140; John D. and Catherine T. MacArthur Foundation, 1, 13, 62, 162, 289–90, 295, 309; Kresge Foundation, 215–16, 289–90, 292; Skillman Foundation, 310; Surdna Foundation, 177; University of North Dakota Research Foundation, 235; Woodruff Foundation, 290

Foundations—support: support for Atlanta, 291, 293–94, 295, 297, 298; support for Charlotte (N.C.), 228; support for Chicago, 21, 291–92, 293–94, 295, 297, 299; support for Cleveland, 219, 220, 221–22; support for Denver, 293–94, 295, 297, 300; support for Detroit, 215, 250, 292, 293–94, 297, 301; support for social services for the poor, 13, 276; support for suburban areas, 295–96, 297

Four Corners Action Coalition, 175

Frey, William, 117–18

Friedhoff, Alec, 193–274

Frostbelt (U.S.), 285. *See also* Chicago; Detroit

FTA. *See* Federal Transit Administration

Fund for Our Economic Future (Ohio), 222, 223

Furseth, Owen J., 135

Gainsborough, Juliet, 7–9, 148–92

Gantt, Harvey, 163

Garr, Emily, 278, 288, 296

Gary (Ind.), 129

Gates, Bill, 238, 249–50. *See also* Microsoft

Gates, Bill, Sr., 240

Gateways. *See* Immigration

GCP. *See* Greater Cleveland Partnership

GDP. *See* Gross Domestic Product

Gentrification, 148, 153, 161, 167–68, 179, 186, 278, 279

George Washington University Institute of Public Policy, 1

Georgia, 105–06. *See also* Atlanta
Georgia Regional Transportation Authority, 287
Gilbert (Ariz.), 135–36
Gleaners Community Food Bank (Detroit), 295
Gleeson, Shannon, 138
Glendale (Ariz.), 135–36
GMAC Financial, 229
GMP. *See* Gross Metropolitan Product
Golden (Colo.), 159
Golden West Financial, 225
Gordon, Phil, 136
Government, 89, 94
Government—federal: anti-poverty efforts of, 12; causes of the Great Recession and, 4; foreclosures and, 17, 95; immigration and, 6, 100–101, 141; innovation and experimentation and, 18, 21; neighborhood stabilization and, 6, 95; recommendations for antipoverty resources, 13, 316, 317–18; regional resilience and, 16; regulation of mortgages and, 89, 94; regulation of predatory lending and, 4, 71–73, 94–95; stressors and, 16; transportation system development and, 9, 182–83, 185, 187. *See also* Home Affordable Modification Program; *individual legislative acts, agencies and departments*
Government—local: immigration and, 100, 141; local boundaries, 19; local resilience, 94; market recovery strategies and, 93; neighborhood stabilization and, 5–6; poverty and, 284; regulation of mortgages, 95; regulation of predatory lending and, 71, 73; spillover costs of foreclosures and, 4, 67–69
Government—regional, 19
Government—state: immigration and, 100, 140, 141; innovation and experimentation and, 18, 21; recommendations for antipoverty resources, 13, 316–17; regional networks and, 21; regional resilience and, 16; regulation of mortgages and, 95; regulation of predatory lending and, 4, 71, 72–73; stressors and, 16
Gramlich, Ned, 71
Grand Forks (N.D., Minn.): agricultural economy in, 230; as a destination city, 234; employment in, 11, 230; resilience and recovery in, 11; university in, 230, 233, 234–35
Grand Forks—case study of resilience and nonresilience: economic development in, 234; economic downturns in, 230, 249, 250; employment in, 230–32, 235–36, 252; explaining resilience and nonresilience, 232; flood and flood protection system in, 231, 233–34, 235; political issues, 232–33; regional economic resilience/nonresilience, 230, 231–32, 252; responses to shocks, 232–35, 250, 251; results,

235–36; shocks in, 211, 212, 230, 231, 250, 252
Grand Forks Air Force Base, 230, 235
Grand Forks Growth Fund, 234
Grand Forks Herald, 233
Granholm, Jennifer, 317
Grants: coding of, 320; geographic pattern of grant making, 292; location of grantees, 292; suburban service providers and, 295–96; system change and, 306–08
Grants—specific: community development block grants, 232, 233; donor-advised funds, 311; formula grants (NSP*1*, NSP*2*), 91, 94; foundation grants, 292–93, 306–08; HOPE VI grants, 157, 161, 166; Sustainable Communities Planning grants, 94; sustainable community challenge grants, 182, 312; TIGER II planning grants, 182
Greater Chicago Food Depository (Cook County, Ill.), 307
Greater Cleveland Growth Association, 220, 221
Greater Cleveland Partnership (GCP), 221, 222
Greater Cleveland Roundtable, 221
Greater Hartford Chamber of Commerce, 250
Great Recession: causes of, 4; effects of, 277, 279, 281, 286, 312
Great Recession—specific cities: Charlotte (N.C.), 229–30; Grand Forks (N.D.), 232; Hartford (Conn.), 243, 248; Seattle, 236, 237–38, 241
Grønbjerg, Kristen A., 281
Gross Domestic Product (GDP), 53, 200
Gross Metropolitan Product (GMP), 53
Gwinnet Coalition for Health and Human Services (Ga.), 314
Gwinnett County (Ga.), 306, 313, 314

Haas Foundation, 141
Habitat for Humanity (Denver), 308
Hahn, James, 122, 123
Haiti, 126–27
Hamilton Sundstrand, 242
HAMP. *See* Home Affordable Modification Program
Hart-Celler Act of *1965*, 104–05
Hartford (Conn.): 11, 55, 241–42, 243. *See also* Connecticut
Hartford—case study of resilience and nonresilience: advance planning by, 254; economic downturns in, 242, 243, 247–48, 249; employment in, 242–44, 252; explaining resilience and nonresilience, 244; political issues in, 245; regional economic resilience/nonresilience, 243–44; responses to shocks, 244–47, 250; results, 247–48; shocks in, 211, 242, 243, 244, 245, 247–48

Hartford Financial Services Group, 242
Hazelton (Pa.), 101
Hialeah (Fla.), 168–69, 170
Hill, Edward, 9–11, 14, 16, 32, 53, 60–61, 193–274
Hispanics. *See* Latinos
HMDA. *See* Home Mortgage Disclosure Act
HOEPA. *See* Home Ownership and Equity Protection Act
Home Affordable Modification Program (HAMP; *2009*), 5, 79–81, 82–83
Home Affordable Refinance Program (HARP), 79
Home Mortgage Disclosure Act (HMDA; *1975*), 87, 89, 90
Homeownership, 76, 78, 87, 150. *See also* Housing
Homeownership Preservation Initiative (HOPI; Chicago), 77, 78
Home Ownership and Equity Protection Act (HOEPA; *1994*), 72
Honda, Mike, 132
HOPI. *See* Homeownership Preservation Initiative
Housing: abandonment of, 84; affordable or mixed-income housing, 9, 158–59, 187, 308; community stability and, 47; declining property values, 65–66, 67–68; fair share housing, 19; household cost of, 85; housing bubble and crisis, 70, 279; housing policy, 85; incentives for affordability of, 9; local administration of housing policies, 61; prices of, 64–65, 68, 70, 71; subsidized housing, 153–54; supply of and demand for, 63–65, 68, 84, 85. *See also* Foreclosures; Loans and lending; Markets; Mortgages; Real estate issues; Transit-oriented development
Housing and Urban Development, Department of (HUD; U.S.), 70, 90, 92, 94, 187, 312
Housing Initiative of North Fulton (Atlanta), 295
Howland, Marie, 197
HUD. *See* Housing and Urban Development, Department of
HUD-DOT-EPA Interagency Partnership. *See* Department of Housing and Urban Development-Department of Transportation-Environmental Protection Agency Interagency Partnership for Sustainable Communities
Human Services, Department of (DHS; Mich.), 317
Hurricane Andrew, 244
Hurricane Katrina, 39. *See also* New Orleans
Hypotheses, calculations and equations: exports and resilience inhibition, 198; immigration, receptivity, and resilience, 103; performance analysis, 54n37; resilience performance, 29; resilience performance score, 54; resilience

score, 54; tension between efficiency and resilience, 60–61. *See also* Analyses; Research

ICE. *See* Immigration and Customs Enforcement
Ideal Aerosmith, 234
IFS. *See* Insurance and Financial Services
Illegal Immigration Reform and Immigrant Responsibility Act (*1996*), 124, 127
Illinois, 105–06, 291. *See also* Chicago; Cook County
Illinois Facilities Fund, 315
Illinois Immigrant Rights Coalition, 130–31
Immergluck, Dan, 66, 88
Immigrant Relations and Integration Services (IRIS), 132
Immigrants and immigration: birthright citizenship and, 140–41; border controls and, 105; business issues and, 7, 133, 139; demographic divergence of, 117–17, 119f; destinations of, 105–07; educational attainment of, 118, 120f; English acquisition by, 115, 118f; federal legislation and, 6, 104–05; "freeriding" and, 138, 142; gateways of, 105, 106, 107, 108, 109–10, 112, 126, 129, 131, 286; human services and, 310; incomes of immigrants, 115; management of the impact of, 102; national debate over, 100–01, 108; nonprofit capacities and, 282–83; poverty and, 277, 278, 281–82; "racialization" and "deracialization" of, 113, 119, 130, 133, 137, 138, 139; receptivity and resilience, 49, 102, 104–08, 120–42; responses to, 6–7, 18; section *287*(g) agreements, 123–24, 131; shock and stress of, 6, 101, 137; sources of immigrants, 113; in suburban and urban areas, 278, 282–83; voting by, 118–19, 121t. *See also* Case studies—immigration; Development, Relief and Education for Alien Minors Act; Mexican immigrants and immigration; Political issues; Suburban areas; Urban areas; *individual cities and states*
Immigrants and immigration—undocumented immigrants: amnesty for, 105; estimates of 113–14; in the Charlotte (N.C.) area, 135; in the Los Angeles area, 124–25; in the New Haven (Conn.) area, 126; in the New York City area, 127, 138; in the Phoenix area, 136–37, 139; in the San Jose (Calif.) area, 133; political issues of, 139, 140; racialization and, 113, 119; receptivity or resilience and, 103, 107, 115, 119; state and local approaches to, 101
Immigration and Customs Enforcement (ICE; U.S.), 123–24
Immigration and Nationality Act (*1965*), 124
Immigration Reform and Control Act (IRCA; *1986*), 105, 110, 140

Inclusionary zoning (IZ). *See* Zoning
Income. *See* Economic issues; Poverty and the poor
Index of Silicon Valley (Joint Venture), 133
India, 113, 126–27, 131–32
Indiana, 281
Indexes, 3, 41, 55, 198
Indexes—regional resilience index: capacity factor interactions and, 33; development and use of, 3, 25, 38, 42, 55; relative resilience and, 36; subdimensions of, 3. *See also* Resilience
Indexes—resilience capacity index: indicators and variables of, 45–52; utility and versatility of, 49
Indigo Line (Boston), 175–77
Industry: diversification of, 46n29, 197, 206, 216, 238, 251; downturns and, 248; regional resilience and, 254. *See also* Detroit; Manufacturing; Seattle
Industry–export industries: cyclical patterns of, 206; diversity of, 209; economic downturns and, 205, 248, 249; in Grand Forks (N.D.), 236; in Hartford (Conn.), 246; industry shocks and, 199, 206, 248; major export industries, 203; in Seattle, 236, 237, 238
Initiative for Affordable Housing DeKalb (Atlanta), 295
Inland Empire (Calif.), 122, 125, 132–33. *See also* Los Angeles
Innovation. *See* Experimentation and innovation
Innovation Center (University of North Dakota), 235
Institutional "lock-in," 18
Insurance and Financial Services cluster (IFS; Conn.), 246
Investors and investing: foreclosure-related losses and, 75; housing investment, 86; mortgage-backed securities and, 74, 81; predatory lending and, 71; tranche warfare and, 82n75
IRCA. *See* Immigration Reform and Control Act
IRIS. *See* Immigrant Relations and Integration Services
Irvine Foundation, 140
IZ (inclusionary zoning). *See* Zoning

Jacksonville (Fla.), 85
Jefferson County (Colo.), 306
J. M. Kaplan Fund, 141
Joassart-Marcelli, Pascale, 281, 313
John D. and Catherine T. MacArthur Foundation. *See* Foundations—specific
Joint Venture: Silicon Valley Network, 133, 139–40
JumpStart (Ohio), 222–23
Justice for Immigrants Coalition, 125

Katz, Lawrence F., 196

Kelly, Tom, 130
Kendall (Fla.), 168–69
Kenworthy, Lane, 281
KETC (TV station, St. Louis, Mo.), 78
Keynes, John Maynard, 69
King County Economic Development Council. *See* Enterprise Seattle
Kingsley, Tom, 63
Kneebone, Elizabeth, 278, 288, 296
Koch (Edward; "Ed") administration, 127
Kolko, Jed, 196
Koreatown Immigrant Workers Association (Los Angeles), 125

Labor. *See* Employment issues; Union and labor issues
Lake County (Ill.), 129–30, 307
Lakewood (Colo.), 158
Lakewood Housing Authority, 161
Land development, 150, 162
Latin America, 6, 105, 113
Latinos: city planning and, 149; immigration of, 6, 7, 105, 126, 130, 132, 133, 135, 137; income of, 115; population of, 110–11
Leaders and leadership, 18, 28
Lee, Bill, 227, 228, 229
Lester, T. William, 196
Levy, Steve, 128
Liberty City (Fla.), 168–69
Lighthouse of Oakland County (Mich.), 308
LIIA. *See* Long Island Immigrant Alliance
LISC. *See* Local Initiatives Support Corporation
Littleton (Colo.), 159
Living Cities, 62, 90, 93–94. *See also* Foundations
Livingston County (Mich.), 306
LM Wind Power, 234
Loans and lending: community lending agreements, 89–90; data and local empowerment, 86–90; defaults, 70, 76; definitions, 71n39; foreclosure prevention and loan modification, 74–83; pooling and servicing agreements of, 81–82; predatory and subprime lending, 4, 17, 64, 69, 70–74; resets of, 87; risky behaviors and, 76; robo-signing scandal and, 81. *See also* Banks and banking; Foreclosures; Housing; Mortgage lending industry; Mortgages; Real estate issues
Local Initiatives Support Corporation (LISC; Chicago), 177, 295, 307
Local Initiatives Support Corporation Detroit, 310
Locke, Gary, 239–40
Lofgren, Zoe, 132
Long Island (N.Y.), 114, 125–26, 128. *See also* Nassau County; New York State; Suffolk County

Long Island Immigrant Alliance (LIIA), 128–29
Longmont (Colo.), 161
Los Angeles: case study of immigration to,
122–25; city council of, 122; immigration to,
101, 106, 107, 108–22, 126, 127, 138, 140,
142; political issues in, 126, 129, 135, 140;
poverty in, 279, 281, 313; rail struggles in,
188, 189; response to immigration in, 6, 7,
122–24, 138; Special Order *40* and, 123, 124
Los Angeles County Metropolitan Transportation
Authority, 152
Los Angeles County Sheriff's Department, 123–24
Los Angeles metropolitan area. *See* Los Angeles
Lowe, Kate, 7–9, 148–92
Low-income people. *See* Poverty and the poor
Lucero, Marcelo, 128
Lucy, William, 85
LYNX light-rail system (Charlotte, N.C.),
162–64, 165

MacArthur Foundation. *See* Foundations—
specific
MacArthur Foundation Research Network on
Building Resilient Regions, 25
Macomb County (Mich.), 306, 313
Madison (Wisc.), 47–48
MAGNET. *See* Manufacturing Advocacy and
Growth Network
Maidenburg, Mike, 233
Making Home Affordable program (*2009*), 79, 83
Management, 27–28
Manufacturing: decline of, 278; downturns and,
205–10, 212, 248; poverty and, 278, 286;
resilience and, 9, 10, 11, 16, 32, 196, 207–09,
248, 253. *See also* Automobiles and automobile
industry; Industry
Manufacturing—specific cities: Charlotte (N.C.),
224–30; Cleveland (Ohio), 217–24; Detroit,
213–17; Grand Forks (N.D.), 230–36, 251;
Hartford (Conn.), 241–48; Seattle, 236–41
Manufacturing Advocacy and Growth Network
(MAGNET; Ohio), 220, 221, 222, 223
Manufacturing Extension Partnership, 220, 246
Margaret (Sister; North Fork Hispanic Apostolate), 128
Maricopa County (Ariz.), 135–36. *See also* Arizona; Phoenix
Markets: housing markets, 87; market conditions,
84; market confidence, 86; market failures, 65;
market fundamentals, 68–69; market recovery,
88; market recovery strategies, 84, 85–86,
92–93, 95; market theory, 64, 67. *See also* Eco-
nomic issues
Martinez, Raul, 169
Massachusetts, 174, 176, 178, 180. *See also*
Boston; *other Massachusetts cities*

Massachusetts Bay Transportation Authority
(MBTA), 174, 175, 176. *See also* Boston;
Massachusetts
Massachusetts Affordable Housing Trust Fund,
178
Massachusetts Department of Transportation, 176
Massey, Douglas S., 106
Mattapan (Mass.), 175, 176
Maywood (Calif.), 122, 124, 125. *See also* Los
Angeles
MBTA. *See* Massachusetts Bay Transportation
Authority
McAllen-Edinburg-Allen (Texas), 48, 49
McColl, Hugh, 227, 228, 229
McCrory, Pat, 134, 135
McDash Analytics. *See* CoreLogic
McHenry County (Ill.), 129–30
McKinsey and Company, 219, 220, 221, 223,
250
Measurement and assessment. *See* Analyses;
Capacity; Case studies; Hypotheses, calcula-
tions and equations; Outcomes; Performance;
Recovery; Research; Resilience; Stress
Mecklenburg County (N.C.), 134, 163, 228. *See
also* Charlotte
Mecklenberg County Sheriff's Department, 135
Melrose Park (Ill.), 131
Mercy Housing (Denver), 185
Merrill Lynch, 225
Mesa (Ariz.), 135–36
MetLife, 242
MetroHartford Alliance (Conn.), 246
Metro Mayors Caucus (MMC; Denver), 8, 156,
157, 160, 181, 185
MetroMonitor (Brookings), 36
Metromover (Miami), 169
Metropolitan areas: capacity for resilience, 47–52;
definition of, 288; distribution of foreclosures
in, 69; economic growth in, 102; feedback
processes and, 17; foreclosure rates in, 84–85;
fragmented areas, 156, 181, 182; immigration
to, 101–44; immigration reform and, 140;
jurisdictional boundaries in, 19; land use and
transportation in, 150; opportunity space
within, 61; poverty in, 277–79, 285–89;
regional economic resilience capacity of, 49;
regional resilience of, 102, 103; regional rigidity of, 103; resilience and, 16, 149; resilience
capacity scores, 51. *See also* Suburban areas;
Transit-oriented development; Urban areas; *specific areas by city name*
Metropolitan Family Services (Ill.), 307
Metropolitan Mayors' Caucus (Chicago), 287,
312
Metropolitan Organizing Strategy Enabling
Strength (MOSES; Detroit), 287–88

Metropolitan Planning Council (Chicago), 312
Metrorail (Miami-Dade County, Fla.), 168–70, 171–73
MetroWest Housing (Denver), 185
Mexican American Legal Defense and Education Fund, 125
Mexican immigrants and immigration: amnesty for, 105; in Charlotte (N.C.), 7, 113; in Chicago, 7, 109, 113, 126, 129–30, 139; in Phoenix, 113, 136, 137, 139; in Los Angeles, 113, 126, 127, 138; in New York City, 113; in San Jose (Calif.), 109, 113, 126, 132. *See also* Immigrants and immigration
Mexico, 35, 42
Miami: case study of transit oriented development in, 168–74; economic issues in, 172–73, 174; housing in, 168, 171–72, 174, 185, 186–87; immigration to, 101, 107; political issues in, 168, 174, 181; poverty in, 181; transit-oriented development in, 8–9, 18–19, 156, 183–84, 188
Miami-Dade County (Fla.), 168–71, 173–74, 181
Miami-Dade County Commission, 170
Miami-Dade Transit, 170
Miami-Fort Lauderdale-Pompany Beach (Fla.), 49
Miami-Fort Lauderdale-West Palm Beach metropolitan area (Fla.), 169
Miami Intermodal Center, 170
Miami International Airport, 170
Michigan, 292. *See also* Detroit
Michigan State University, 216
Microsoft, 236, 238, 239, 241, 249–50
Midwest (U.S.), 278
Migration Policy Institute, 130
Minneapolis-St. Paul-Bloomington (MN-WI), 47–48
Minutemen, 124, 125
MMC. *See* Metro Mayors Caucus
Models. *See* Research
Molina, Gloria, 123
Mollenkopf, John, 6–7, 16, 18, 19, 49, 100–147
Moral hazard, 76
Moreno-Zavala, Orlan Enrique, 128
Mortgage Bankers Association, 88
Mortgage lending industry: disintegration of the mortgage financing market, 74; foreclosure and, 82–83; loan modification and, 74–75, 82–83; net present value (NPV) calculations and, 82–83; regulation of predatory lending and, 71–72; robo-signing scandal and, 81; servicer incentives and fees, 82, 83; venue shopping by, 17, 71–72
Mortgages: data and local empowerment, 86–90; "drive 'til you qualify" mortgages, 84–85; greenlining and redlining, 72, 89, 90; leveraging of bad mortgages, 65; modification of, 4–5;

pooling and securitization of, 5, 81; subprime mortgages, 64; usury limits on, 72. *See also* Foreclosures; Housing; Loans and lending
MOSES. *See* Metropolitan Organizing Strategy Enabling Strength
Mt. Zion Community Development Corporation, 173
Myers, Dowell, 115
Myrick, Sue, 163

NASCAR Hall of Fame, 228
Nassau County (N.Y.), 128. *See also* Long Island; New York State
National Association of Latino Elected Officials, 125
National Community Reinvestment Coalition, 90
National Foreclosure Mitigation Counseling (NFMC) program, 77, 78, 79
National Housing Conference, 62
National League of Cities, 62, 141
National Neighborhood Indicators Project, 90
National Vacant Property Campaign, 90
NationsBank, 133
Neighborhood Housing Services (NHS; Chicago), 77, 78
Neighborhood Progress, Inc. (NPI; Cleveland), 93–94
Neighborhood stabilization: administrative capacity and, 92; federal policies and, 91–94, 95; identification of transitional neighborhoods, 86–87; interventions and strategies for, 83–84, 95; needs for and goals of, 5; neighborhood resilience and, 85; strategic collaborative capacity and, 92; targeting of, 5–6; in the wake of foreclosures, 83–86. *See also* Foreclosures
Neighborhood Stabilization Program (NSP), 91–92, 312
NeighborWorks America, 77
NEO-CANDO. *See* Northeast Ohio Community and Neighborhood Data for Organizing
Networks and collaboration: building collaborations, 20–21; business redundancy and resilience and, 28; cross-functional collaboration, 92; cross-governmental collaboration, 93; cross-sectoral collaboration, 92–93; immigration and, 102; regional resilience and, 20; strategic collaborative capacity, 92
Neumark, David, 196
Nevada, 105–06
New Americans' Initiative, 131
Newark (N.J.), 126
New Communities program (Chicago), 295
New Economy Initiative for Southeast Michigan, 215, 216, 250, 292
New England, 197. *See also* Boston; Connecticut; Hartford; Massachusetts

New Haven (Conn.), 101, 125–26
New Orleans, 27, 57. *See also* Hurricane Katrina
New Orleans Index (Brookings), 39
New Starts program (Federal Transit Administration), 9, 163–64, 185
New York City: accessibility-improvement plans of, 127–28; case study of immigration to, 125–29; Executive Orders (*34, 41, 124*) of, 127; immigration to, 101, 106, 107, 108–22, 125–29, 138, 142; New York metropolitan area and, 125–26; political and policy issues in, 126, 127, 129, 135; poverty in, 279; recovery from *9/11* of, 35, 42; resilience of, 57; response to immigration to, 6, 7, 127, 138. *See also* New York State
New York City Police Department, 127
New York metropolitan area, 125–26, 129, 139–40
New York-Northern New Jersey-Long Island (NY-NJ-PA), 49, 125–26
New York State, 49. *See also* Long Island; Nassau County; New York City; Suffolk County
NFMC. *See* National Foreclosure Mitigation Counseling program
Nguyen, Mai, 7–9, 148–92
NHS. *See* Neighborhood Housing Services
Nonprofit organizations (NPOs): anti-poverty nonprofits, 281–83; challenges to the nonprofit safety net, 277; effectiveness of, 280–81; experimentation by, 18, 19; foreclosures and loan modification and, 74; foundations and, 13, 283–84; funding for, 276, 279–80, 282, 283, 284; market recovery strategies and, 93; poverty and, 275–76, 279–81; resilience of, 77; in the suburbs, 282; super nonprofits,280; welfare reform and, 280–81. *See also* Foundations; Philanthropic organizations; Poverty and the poor; Social policies; Social service organizations
Norris, Fran H., 32, 42
NorTech (Ohio), 220, 221, 222
North Carolina, 72–73, 105–06, 162. *See also* Charlotte
North Carolina National Bank, 226, 227
Northeast (U.S.), 202, 205, 278. *See also* Boston; Connecticut; Hartford; Massachusetts; New York
Northeast Ohio Community and Neighborhood Data for Organizing (NEO-CANDO), 88, 90
Northeast Ohio Council, 220
North Fork Hispanic Apostolate, 128
Northglenn (Colo.), 159
NPI. *See* Neighborhood Progress, Inc.
NPOs. *See* Nonprofit organizations

NPV (net present value). *See* Mortgage lending industry
NSP. *See* Neighborhood Stabilization Program
Nuclear Cluster Group (N.C., S.C.), 229

Oakland (Calif.), 73
Oakland County (Mich.), 306, 308, 310
Oaxaca (Mexico), 129
OCC. *See* Office of the Comptroller of the Currency
Odegard School of Aerospace Sciences (University of North Dakota), 235
Office of Economic Opportunity (U.S.), 275
Office of Immigrant Affairs (Los Angeles), 123
Office of Management and Budget (OMB; U.S.), 47
Office of the Comptroller of the Currency (OCC; U.S.), 74
Office of Thrift Supervision (OTS; U.S.), 74
Ohio, 88. *See also* Cleveland
Ohio Polymer Strategy Council, 222
Ohio Technology Partnership, 222
OMB. *See* Office of Management and Budget
One North Carolina Fund, 228
Opportunity space, 61–62
Orange County (Calif.), 140
OTS. *See* Office of Thrift Supervision
Outcomes, 14, 26
Overtown (Miami),168–69, 172–74, 183–84, 186

Paarlberg, Laurie, 281
Pacific Northwest Aerospace Alliance (Seattle), 240
Pakistan, 126–27
Panarchy. *See* Resilience–theories
Partnership for a New American Economy, 139
Pastor, Manuel, 6–7, 16, 18, 19, 49, 100–147
Pathways Community Network (Atlanta), 308
Pendall, Rolf, 7–9, 16, 18–19, 21–22, 33, 148–92, 193
Penelas, Alex, 169
People's Transportation Plan (PTP; Miami), 169–70, 174, 180, 181–82, 188
Performance: capacities and, 28; conceptions of performance, 35–44; indicators of, 53; individual factor performance, 41–42; measurement and assessment of, 34, 36–44, 52–57; performance analysis, 54n37; resilience and, 28, 38–42; resilience performance ratio, 54–55; tradeoffs in, 41; variables and indicators of, 38–42, 52
Peru, 126–27
Pew Research Center Survey, 94
Philanthropic organizations: anti-poverty nonprofit sector and, 283; collaboration among housing nonprofits and, 21; distribution of philanthropic anti-poverty investments, 292;

regional philanthropic resources, 289–92; research questions, data, and methods, 285–86, 292–93, 297; in the suburbs, 296, 297–301, 306. *See also* Foundations; Nonprofit organizations

Phoenix: case study of immigration to, 135–37; crime and violence in, 136; economic issues in, 136; immigration to, 6, 7, 101–02, 109–22, 133, 138, 139, 140, 142; political issues in, 126, 129, 135–37, 140; size and population of, 135. *See also* Arizona

Phoenix Companies, Inc., 242

Phoenix metropolitan region, 135

Pindus, Nancy, 1–22

Political issues: adaptation to stress, 16, 17; experimentation and innovation, 18; in fragmented metropolitan areas, 156; funding of nonprofit organizations and, 282–83; human services, 309–10; immigration, 7, 18, 102, 107, 108, 124–25, 126, 139, 140–41, 142; immigration reform, 140–44; jurisdictional boundaries, 19; noncoercive policy tools, 83; nonprofit organizations, 13; opposition to rail, 164–65; redistribution, 19; regional resilience, 149; transit-oriented development, 149, 152, 168. *See also individual cities*

PolicyLink (Oakland, Calif.), 153, 154

Pooling and servicing agreements (PSAs), 81, 82n75. *See also* Mortgages

Population issues: age distribution, 117; foreign-born population, 110–13, 116; population size and resilience capacity, 49; resilience, 196. *See also* Immigrants and immigration

Port of Seattle, 240. *See also* Seattle

Post-traumatic stress disorder (PTSD), 42

Poverty and the poor: anti-poverty nonprofits and, 281–83; changes of last *15* years in, 275; growing significance of the nonprofit service sector for, 279–81; infrastructure for federal anti-poverty efforts, 12; institutional rigidity and, 19; low-income housing, 161, 172; new geography of, 12, 277–79, 281–83; recommendations for antipoverty resources, 13; social policies for, 275; transit-oriented development and, 152, 154. *See also* Foundations; Nonprofit organizations; Social safety nets; Suburban areas; Urban areas; *individual cities*

Powell, Walter W., 18, 19

Pratt & Whitney, 242, 248

Private sector, 284

Prosperity Partnership (Seattle), 240

PSAs. *See* Pooling and servicing agreements

Psychology, 26–27

PTP. *See* People's Transportation Plan

PTSD. *See* Post-traumatic stress disorder

Puerto Rico and Puerto Ricans, 130, 138

Putnam, Robert, 49, 93

Raleigh (N.C.), 164

RAND Corporation, 219, 220, 221–22, 250

Ratings agencies, 64

Reagan, Ronald, 140

Real estate issues: real estate markets, 68–69; real-estate owned properties (REOs), 75, 84–85, 87, 88, 90. *See also* Community issues; Foreclosures; Housing; Loans and lending; Mortgages

RealtyTrac, 87

Reckhow, Sarah, 12–13, 15, 19, 21, 275–323

Reconnecting America, 153

Recovery: ease and difficulties of, 10; length of time to, 10; measures of, 3; resilience and, 39–40; timeframe of, 42–44, 52. *See also* Resilience; Shocks

Redlining. *See* Mortgages

Redundancy, 28

Reform Immigration for America (RIFA), 125

Regional Homeownership Preservation Initiative (RHOPI; Chicago), 78

Regional issues: capacity, 3; complexity of regions, 33; definition of regions, 194; economic growth, 197–98; exports from, 194n6; regional performance and regional performance score, 3; resilience and nonresilience of regions, 33, 194, 196. *See also* Capacity; Indexes; Resilience

Regional Transportation District (RTD; Denver), 157, 158, 159, 160

Re-Imagining Detroit *2020* (Kresge Foundation), 216–17

Reinvestment Fund (Philadelphia), 86

REOs (real-estate owned properties). *See* Banks and banking; Real estate issues

"Report to Congress on the Root Causes of the Foreclosure Crisis" (HUD; *2010*), 70, 82

Research: design and concepts, 199–201, 202–10; model *1*: explaining downturns, 255, 258–60; model *2*: explaining shock resistance, 260, 261–62; model *3*: explaining regional responses to economic shocks, 260, 263–64; model *4*: explaining length of time to resilience, 260, 265–67; summary statistics, 268–71. *See also* Analyses; Case studies; Hypotheses; calculations and equations; Philanthropic organizations; Resilience—economic; Social safety nets; Transit-oriented development

Research Enterprise and Commercialization Center (Grand Forks, N.D./Minn.), 234

Research Enterprise and Commercialization Park (University of North Dakota Research Foundation), 235

Resilience: absolute or relative resilience, 36–38; building resilience, 14–22, 28; business factors of, 27–28, 249; categories of, 32; concepts of, 29–31, 36–38, 193, 248–49; cycle of resilience capacity and performance, 29–30; decision-making and, 11; definitions of, 1, 2–3, 14, 24, 26–29, 32, 33n19, 60, 77, 149; diversity and, 60–61; ecological resilience, 27; federal regulations and, 17; feedback and, 15, 16–17; fiscal resilience, 40; GMP resilience, 207–08; immigration and, 7; income disparities and, 10, 249; indicators, 53, 55; local resilience, 61; low resilience, 15; measurement and assessment of, 3, 6, 24–25, 33–35, 36–38, 40–41, 44–57; neighborhood resilience, 85; as an outcome, 14; place-based resilience, 63, 83–84; preemptive resilience, 70; resilience capacity score, 47; resilience pathways, 29–31; resistance to, 15; rigidities, 16–18; shocks and, 10; strategic collaborative capacity and, 93–94; stress and, 26, 29; studies of, 14; trajectories of, 42–44, 260, 262, 265–71; undermining of, 16. *See also* Capacities; Flexibility; Indexes—regional resilience index; Performance; Recovery; Shocks; Stress

Resilience—community, 33, 198

Resilience—economic: definitions and concepts of, 10, 14, 32, 193–95, 199; employment shocks and, 195–96, 201; explaining shock resistance and resilience, 206–10; industry shocks and, 201; length of time to resilience, 208; literature review of, 195–99; research designs and concept operationalization, 199–201, 202–10, 255–71

Resilience—regional: advance planning and, 251, 253–54; age of the area and, 197; definitions and concepts of, 28–29, 102, 194–95, 200–01, 276; economic factors of, 197; economic shocks and, 201–02; explaining shock resistance and resilience, 206–10; foundations and, 284; immigration and, 102; industrial factors of, 197; literature review of, 195–99; political issues of, 149; pre-stress capacities and, 31–32; regional receptivity to immigrants and, 137–40; regional resilience trajectories, 30–31, 201–02; resilient regional safety nets, 285; responses to shocks and, 250–51; shock resistance and resilience and, 196, 201–02; subjective component of, 252; trajectory of, 208; transit-oriented development and, 187–90; urban infrastructure and, 149

Resilience—theories: experimentation and, 17; panarchy (cross-scale relations), 16; resilience performance, 29; tension between efficiency and resilience, 60–61, 81

Rethinking the Safety Net (study; UWSEM), 316

RHOPI. *See* Regional Homeownership Preservation Initiative

Riegle-Neal Interstate Banking and Branching Efficiency Act of *1994*, 226–27

RIFA. *See* Reform Immigration for America

Right-to-work laws. *See* Union and labor issues

Rigidity, 16–18

Rochester (Minn.), 47–48

Rock Hill (S.C.), 163

Roth, Benjamin, 313

Route *128*. *See* Boston

Rowland, John, 245, 246, 247

Roxbury (Mass.), 176

RTD. *See* Regional Transportation District

Sachem Quality of Life, 128

Sacerdote, Bruce, 196

Safford, Sean, 20, 286

St. Clair, Travis, 193–274

St. Louis (Mo.), 77–78

St. Louis County (Mo.), 66, 91

Salamon, Lester, 83

San Bernardino Catholic Diocese, 125

San Bernardino Valley (Calif.), 122, 124, 125. *See also* Los Angeles

San Diego, 18

San Fernando Valley (Calif.), 140

San Francisco, 18, 85, 101

San Jose (Calif.): case study of immigration to, 131–33; immigration to, 6, 7, 109–22, 126, 130, 138, 139, 140; political issues in, 126, 129, 132, 140. *See also* Silicon Valley

San Jose City College, 132–33

Santa Clara County (Calif.), 132. *See also* California; San Jose

Saxenian, AnnaLee, 20

SCAT. *See* Sensible Charlotte Area Transportation

Scottsdale (Ariz.), 135–36

Seattle, 11, 236

Seattle—case study of resilience and nonresilience: economic downturns in, 236–37, 249; employment in, 236–37; explaining resilience and nonresilience, 238–39, 249–50; regional economic resilience/nonresilience, 237–38; responses to shocks, 239–41, 250; results, 241; shocks in, 211, 212, 236

Seattle Chamber of Commerce, 239, 240

Section *287*(g), 123–24

SEMCOG. *See* Southeast Michigan Council of Governments

Senate Bill *1070* (Ariz.), 100, 123, 127, 136–37, 140–41

Sensible Charlotte Area Transportation (SCAT; Charlotte, N.C.), 165

September *11, 2001*. *See* New York City

Service Employees International Union *1199*, 128

Sheffi, Yossi, 27–28

Shocks: advance precautionary planning and, 11–12; effects of, 10, 201–02; explaining shock resistance and resilience, 202–10; feedback and, 16–17; information about, 20; recovery and, 14; resilience and, 10, 11, 248, 260, 262, 265–71; responses to, 11, 16, 200, 260, 263–64; selective buffering and, 19; shock resistance, 14, 260, 261–62; transit-oriented development and, 187. *See also* Disasters; Economic issues; Stress

Shocks—economic: data and analysis of, 202–04; definitions and concepts of, 199, 201, 202; economic downturns, 10, 194–95, 200–01, 202–03, 207, 213, 255, 258–60; economic resources and, 198; employment issues, 195–96, 198, 201; explaining shock resistance and resilience, 206–10. *See also* Resilience—economic

Shocks—specific types: acute shocks, 16, 34; chronic shocks, 16, 34; economic downturns and shocks, 194, 199, 201, 202, 204–06, 207, 260, 263–64; employment downturns and shocks, 201, 206, 207, 256; external shocks (disasters), 10, 18, 194; gross metropolitan product (GMP) downturns and shocks, 200, 201, 205, 207, 257; industrial downturns, 10; industry shocks, 194, 199–200, 201, 202, 205, 206, 207; non-economic shocks, 200; slow burn shocks, 16, 34

SII (Strategic Investment Initiative). *See* Cleveland

Sikorsky Aircraft, 242

Silicon Valley (Calif.), 20, 131–32. *See also* San Jose

Six Pillars initiative (Hartford, Conn.), 247

Simpson, Dick, 130

Singer, Audrey, 107, 115

Smith, Geoff, 66

Smith, Heather A., 135

Snyder, Rick, 317

Social equity, 155, 159

Social failure, 28

Social Innovation Fund, 310

Social policies, 275, 279–80

Social safety nets: anti-poverty nonprofits, 281–83; building a resilient safety net, 285; case studies, 285–306; challenges in building regional safety nets, 308–14; defining the challenge, 288–89; grants, 297–306; local foundations and capacity building, 283–85; nonprofit service sector and the poor, 279–81; philanthropic anti-poverty investments, 292–96; poverty and, 275–79, 281–83; regional philanthropic resources, 289–92; research data and methods, 320; strategies for building resilient regional safety nets, 314–18; system change

and, 306–08. *See also* Atlanta; Chicago; Denver; Detroit

Social services and social service organizations, 12. *See also* Foundations; Poverty and the poor

Sociocultural issues, 117–18

South (U.S.), 205, 226–27, 278, 279. *See also* Charlotte; North Carolina

South Carolina, 240, 241

Southeast Michigan Council of Governments (SEMCOG), 287

South Florida Regional Transportation Authority, 169

South Suburban Coordinating Council (Chicago), 311

South Suburban Mayors and Managers Association (Chicago), 312

Southwest Solutions (Detroit), 308

Soviet Union, 126–27

Speed Channel, 228

Stapleton Airport (Denver), 158–59

Starbucks, 236, 238

Stern, Ariel Dora, 196

Stewart, Potter, 57

Stoecker, Randy, 178

Stone Park (Ill.), 131

Strategic Economics, 153

Strategic Investment Initiative (SII). *See* Cleveland

Stress: buffered and unbuffered stress, 16, 17; capacities for coping with, 17, 32; commonality of, 35; conceptions of stress, 34–35; definitions of, 3; foreclosures and, 4, 65–69; of immigration, 6; indicators for, 53; measures of, 3, 34–35, 54; preparation for, 29–30; resilient systems and, 15; stress resistance, 41–42; time and, 42–43; types of, 34. *See also* Economic issues; Resilience; Shocks

Summa Health System, 223

Sunbelt (U.S.), 285–86. *See also* Atlanta; Denver

Surface transportation program, 182

Suburban areas: CDCs in, 78; challenges in building safety nets, 310–14; city-suburban antagonisms, 287; city-suburban support, 295; development of, 150; foundations and grant funding in, 13, 290–91; immigration to, 101–02, 107, 114–15, 138, 141–42; market recovery strategies and, 93; nonprofit capacities in, 282; problems of living in, 150–51; services to immigrants in, 19; transit-oriented development in, 184. *See also* Metropolitan areas

Suburban areas—poverty and antipoverty resources: anti-poverty nonprofits, 281–82, 286; geography of poverty, 277–79; grants, 297–306; growth of poverty, 275–76, 279, 281–82, 288–89, 313; providers of social services, 276, 295. *See also individual cities*

Surdna Foundation, 177
Suffolk County (N.Y.): civic activism in, 132–33; immigration to, 128; political issues of, 128; population of, 128. *See also* Long Island; New York City; New York State
Swanstrom, Todd, 4–6, 14, 15, 16, 17, 18, 20, 21, 60–99
System change, 306–08, 320

211 system and network, 309
2025 Integrated Transit/Land Use Plan (Mecklenburg County, N.C.), 163
TANF. *See* Temporary Assistance to Needy Families
Targeted transparency policies, 89
Taxation issues: Boeing tax incentives, 241; foreclosures, 67; low-income housing tax credit programs, 161, 168, 172, 186, 187; transportation funding, 157, 163, 165, 169, 170
TeamNeo (Ohio), 222, 223
Teaneck (N.J.), 126
Technology Alliance (Wash.), 240
Technology Leadership Council (Ohio), 220
TechTown (Detroit), 216
Temporary Assistance to Needy Families (TANF), 77
Texas, 105–06, 136
Thornton (Colo.), 159
Tijuana—San Diego (immigration gateway), 105
Time and timeframes: foreclosure process, 61; recovery and, 10, 42–44, 52; regional resilience trajectories, 30–31, 201–02; stress, 42–43; trajectories of resilience, 42–44, 260, 262, 265–71
TOD. *See* Transit-oriented development
Trachtenberg School of Public Policy and Public Administration, 1
Trade Development Alliance (Seattle), 240
Transit Alliance (Denver), 157
Transit-oriented development (TOD): case studies, 148–49, 156–80; challenges of, 180–83; creation of, 151; effects of, 149, 165; equity considerations in, 8, 9, 151–54, 187, 188, 189; federal funding for, 148; future needs and development, 8; housing and, 187, 189; incentives for, 180, 182, 185; income mixing in the TOD agenda, 185–87; low-income people and, 148–49, 180; mixed-income development and housing in, 9, 149, 152–54; obstacles to development of, 183–85; political issues of, 149, 152, 180–81, 187, 188–89; private investment and, 179, 183, 184, 187; public participation process in, 184; questions and issues of, 8, 151; regional rail systems, 148; research questions, data, and methods, 154–56, 180–87; resilience and, 151, 187–90; in

resilient regions, 8. *See also* Boston; Charlotte; Denver; Miami; Political issues
Transit systems, 34–35
Transparency, 89–90, 317
Transportation: household cost of, 85; infrastructure of, 8; innovation and experimentation and, 21; regional transportation agencies, 287; significance of transportation policies, 7–9; transportation planning, 286
Transportation Equity Network, 22
Transportation Expansion Project (T-REX project; Denver), 157
Travelers Insurance, 242
Trenton (N.J.), 125–26
T-REX project. *See* Transportation Expansion Project
Tri-Rail (commuter rail system, Fla.), 169
Truly Disadvantaged, The (Wilson), 279
Turner, Joe, 124

ULC. *See* Urban Land Conservancy
Union and labor issues: immigration and, 125, 133; right-to-work laws, 10, 205, 207, 209, 249. *See also* Employment issues
United States (U.S.): ethnic and racial character of immigrants in, 6, 105, 106f; location of new immigrants in, 6; median household income in, 115, 117f; percent of population foreign-born, 104, 105f. *See also* Immigrants and immigration; Population; *headings under U.S.*; *individual cities, states and regions*
United States Postal Service (USPS), 88
United Technologies Corporation, 242
United Way, 308, 309, 314, 315–16
United Way of Metropolitan Atlanta, 308
United Way for Southeastern Michigan (UWSEM), 310, 315–16
Universities and colleges: Piedmont Community College, 228; University at Buffalo Regional Institute, 25; University of Michigan, 216; University of North Carolina-Charlotte, 228; University of North Dakota, 230, 233, 234–35
University Hospitals Health System, 223
"Urban and Regional Policy and Its Effects" (conference; *2010*), 1, 4
Urban areas: challenges in building regional safety nets, 311; city-suburban antagonisms, 287; city-suburban support, 295; definition of primary cities, 288; depopulation and renewal, 85n90; development of, 150; foreclosure rates in, 84; foundations and grant funding in, 13, 289–92; immigration to, 101–02, 114–15, 141–42; philanthropic resources in, 289; planning for, 149; poverty and antipoverty resources in, 275–76, 277–79, 281, 284, 288–89; problems of living in, 150; sanctuary

cities, 124; services to immigrants in suburbs and, 19; transit-oriented development in, 149, 151, 184. *See also* Case studies; Metropolitan areas; Transit-oriented development; *specific cities*
Urban Institute, 1, 78
Urban Land Conservancy (ULC), 162
U.S. Census and American Community Survey, 288
USCIS. *See* U.S. Citizenship and Immigration Services
U.S. Citizenship and Immigration Services (USCIS), 141
UWSEM. *See* United Way for Southeastern Michigan

Varaiya, Pravin, 197
VDARE.com, 124
Vietnam, 113, 126–27, 132
Villaraigosa, Antonio, 122, 123, 130
Vogel, Lukas, 198
Voinovich, George, 219

Wachovia, 225
Wall Street. *See* Investors and investing
War on Poverty (*1964*), 275, 279, 283
Washington-Arlington-Alexandria (DC-MD-VA-WV), 49
Washington Mutual, 238
Washington Technology Industry Association, 240

Waukegan City Council (Ill.), 131
Wayne County (Mich.), 306, 311, 313
Wayne State University, 216
Weir, Margaret, 1–22, 275–323
Weis, Judy, 131
Welcoming America, 141
Welfare legislation (*1996*), 275–76, 277, 280
Wells Fargo, 225, 229
West (U.S.), 205, 208, 278–79. *See also* Colorado; Denver; Seattle; Washington
West Africa, 126–27
West Indies, 113, 126–27
West Virginia, 49
Wial, Howard, 1–22, 193–274
Will County (Ill.), 129–30, 306
Wilson, William Julius, 279
Wiseman, Michael, 197
Wolch, Jennifer R., 281, 313
Wolman, Harold, 1–22, 193–274
Working Partnerships USA, 133
World Association of Nuclear Operators, 229

Yonkers (N.Y.), 126
Ypsilanti (Mich.), 215
Youngstown (Ohio), 20, 221, 286

Z-score, 47, 49, 54, 55
Zoning: in Boston, 178; inclusionary zoning (IZ), 153, 161, 186; point system in, 167; rapid transit zones, 171